Subject & Place for
Watercolour Landscapes

Subject & Place for Watercolour Landscapes

James Fletcher-Watson
R.I., R.B.A.

B.T. BATSFORD LTD., LONDON

First published 1985

ISBN 0 7134 3748 0 (cased)

Typeset by Keyspools Ltd, Golborne, Lancs
and printed in Great Britain by
Anchor-Brendon Ltd
Tiptree, Essex
for the publishers
B. T. Batsford Ltd.
4 Fitzhardinge Street
London W1H 0AH

Contents

List of colour plates 6

Preface 7

1 Painting in Norfolk 8

2 Painting in the Lake District 28

3 Painting in the Cotswolds 55

4 Painting in France 78

5 Painting in Scotland 91

6 Painting in Venice 110

7 Painting in Wiltshire 122

8 Painting in London 133

9 Painting in other places 138

Index 143

List of colour plates

Between pages 120 and 121
1 Fishermen's cottages, Salthouse
2 Flood tide at Morston Quay
3 Ullswater
4 Windrush Mill
5 Snow Scene, Windrush
6 Northleach Church, from the south
7 Uzes, Provence
8 Pont du Garde, Provence
9 Loch Torridon
10 Bridge near Kishorn
11 Kishorn Estuary
12 Kerrysdale
13 Rio di Bragadin, Venice
14 Wylye
15 River Avon, Middle Woodford
16 New End Square, Hampstead

Preface

Since writing my first book on watercolour painting I have had talks with many students and painting friends, and they have nearly all said if you write another one please give us more ideas about *how to choose a subject*. This is such an important matter, and now that my publishers have asked me to write another book I felt that I could not do better than make the main theme of the book 'choosing a subject'. I have therefore divided this book into chapters on different *places* to paint: Norfolk, Scotland, Venice and so on. All these places have very different characteristics and call for different methods of handling a landscape picture, and, by giving you this wide range of subjects, I cover the use of many colour mixes and techniques.

Some people have asked for more on how to paint *skies*, others say they find *foregrounds* difficult, and many painters seem to find *buildings* hard to portray. I hope to give you all a hand with these and many other items which, when put together, make for the perfect landscape picture. The perfect picture! What a goal to aim for and how far short of it we all fall. But we must keep trying and keep painting out-of-doors from nature itself; that I am sure is the secret of success. Paint in the studio some of the time, but paint *mostly* in the open air.

This book is addressed mainly to those who have already made a little progress with watercolours but also to the beginner. We are all of us students in the painting game however long we have been at it. I am personally always learning something new from painter friends of mine, by looking at their work or watching them paint. My advice to you all is do not be down-hearted if you don't always pull off a winner, just keep on trying and learn to simplify the subject and you will win through. I shall have something to say about simplification in the following chapters.

1 Painting in Norfolk

Before getting on to the actual creating of pictures let me say a brief word about painting materials. I gave full details in a whole chapter on materials in *Water-Colour Painting: Landscapes and Townscapes* (Batsford 1982) so I am only going to touch on the subject now.

Colours

The watercolours which I have used for all the pictures illustrated in this book and which I always use are as follows:

1 Cadmium Lemon.
2 Cadmium Yellow.
3 Raw Sienna.
4 Burnt Sienna.
5 Burnt Umber.
6 Light Red.
7 Indian Red.
8 Rose Madder.
9 Cobalt Blue.
10 French Ultramarine.
11 Winsor Blue (similar to Prussian Blue).
12 Payne's Gray.

One does not want to have too many colours in one's box and twelve is a very ample number. I often paint pictures with only four colours, and I do many only using eight. I shall have a lot to say about mixing colours as we go through the book.

Brushes

I always use best Sable brushes for the important part of a painting, but I have been trying out the much less expensive synthetic brushes which have recently come on to the market. I find they are quite good, especially the ones which are a mixture of sable and synthetic; these are only a quarter of the price of pure sable and I always have some of them in use.

The size of brushes I use are Nos. 0, 1, 3, 5, 7, 9, 12 and 16. You can manage with far less, say Nos. 1,5,9 and 12, especially if you are a beginner and want to go carefully on expenditure. But do not buy very cheap brushes as these will lead to doing bad work.

I also have a large squirrel hair brush which is floppy and useful for skies etc. It is inexpensive. I like to have a hog hair oil painter's brush, about a quarter inch (6mm) wide, for 'lifting' colour off the paper. One more brush that can be useful is a *flat* brush about half inch (12mm) wide, of sable or synthetic. This is useful for foregrounds and thin blades of grass etc.

Paper

There are a number of papers available from art shops for watercolour work and one well-known make called Whatman has recently returned after a lapse of some twenty years. This used to be considered by most watercolour painters as the leading paper, and it is now gaining popularity again. I use it quite a lot, and it has a whiteness which gives a very brilliant result. It is made up to a weight of 200lb which I find a little on the thin side. I prefer the 300lb Arches French paper which is slightly cream in colour and the 'NOT' surface has a very attractive texture to work on. There are many other papers; Bockinford is a good inexpensive one and I highly recommend this for beginners. Barcham Green is an excellent paper which I like using, but it is fairly expensive.

Paper has a variety of thicknesses and textures. Everyone has to find his or her own favourite paper after experimenting with various types. The lighter weight papers have to be stretched on a board before using, otherwise they will cockle when wet and become difficult to work on.

Painting

Now we will start to discuss what this book is all about, namely how to paint watercolour landscape pictures.

Norfolk is an unusual and beautiful county of England, having large areas of flattish land which causes any slight rise in the ground to stand out with considerable prominence and produce attractive focal points in the landscape.

Let us start with figure **1, Salthouse Church** (30cm × 46cm (12in. × 18in.)) as seen from the south, looking out to sea in the distance on the right-hand side of the picture. The village of Salthouse is close to the sea along the north coast of Norfolk, and the ground inland rises quickly one or two hundred feet to where the church stands as a proud sentinal overlooking the village clustered below.

I said earlier, we are going to put emphasis on *how to choose a subject* and here is a case in point where the subject was crying out to be painted. As I passed through the village the church could be seen on its hill and I turned into a very narrow uphill lane in the hope of getting an exciting high-level view, and what a reward it was suddenly to see this marvellous view through a gateway in the hedge. The field had been ploughed and rolled and it was a rich dark brown, and the large fifteenth-century church with its lovely gray

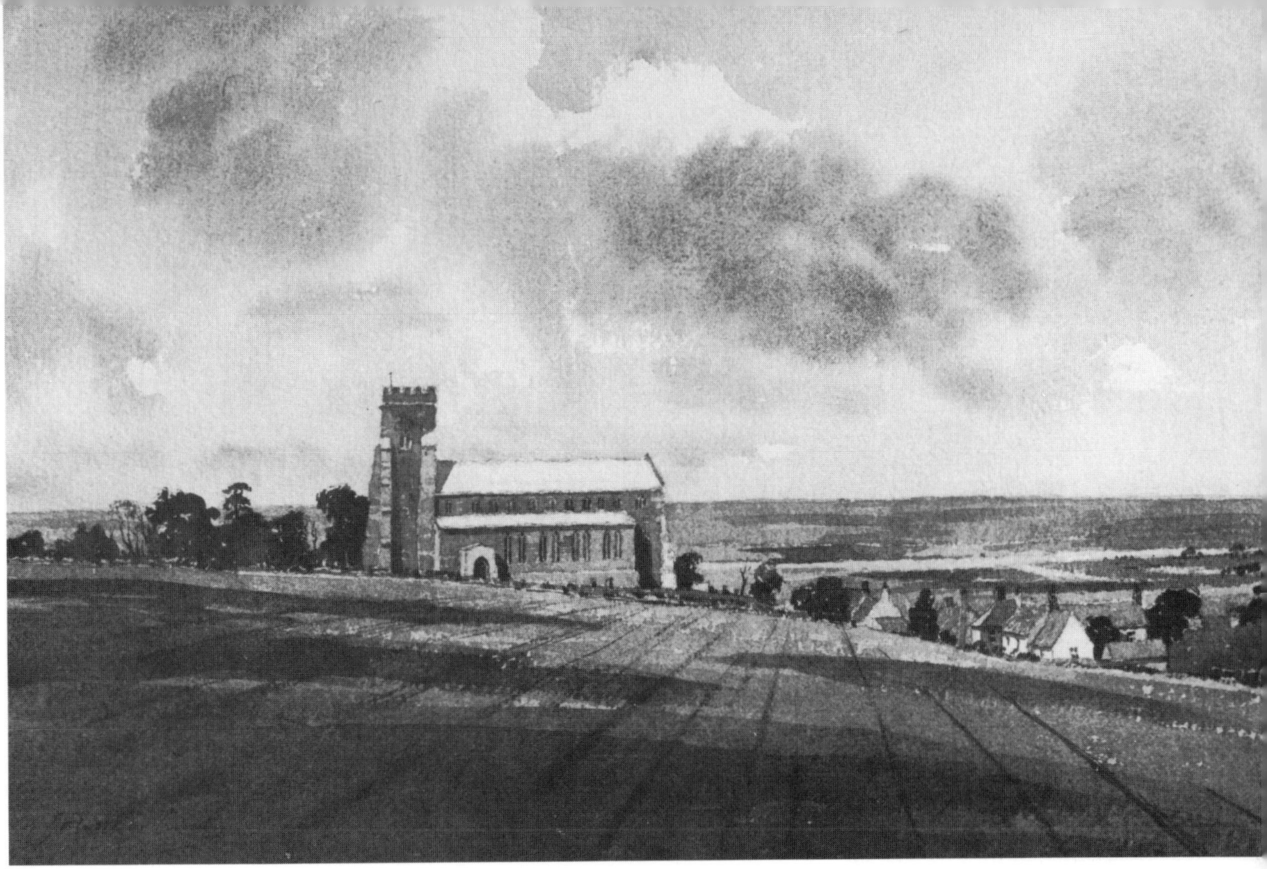

1 Salthouse Church.

walls of Norfolk flint-work stood out magnificently. Here was a subject that could be treated in a *simple* way.

Composition

1 The church obviously had to be *left* of centre so as to allow space for the village roof tops on the right.

2 The field wanted to be about one-third the height of the picture, leaving two-thirds for the sky – a typical Norfolk proportion, where the sky is often an important feature. There were a few furrow marks in the field which gave distance from foreground to middle distance and led the eye into the picture nicely.

3 The dark trees on the left were a useful foil to the gray church and it was worth emphasizing the strength of these brown-green trees; the time was early April and there was still winter colouring to the trees.

There were some red and brown colours in the pantile roofs of the cottages and some trees amongst them, and this gave a nice feeling of pattern to this side of the picture.

4 The distant marshes and gray-green sea were treated with simple washes which gave the far-away look.

5 Finally the sky, which was actually painted first, was a windy, cloudy one and cast cloud shadows on the distant sea and the foreground which were particularly helpful to give interest to the latter rather wide expanse.

Composition plays such an important part in choosing a subject, that I have dwelt on it at some length here. It is how you arrange the features of your subject *on the paper* that matters. Painters often choose too difficult a subject, one with too many features, and they give equal emphasis to everything thereby making a disturbed and restless picture.

I will now look at a more simple subject, figure **2, The road to Stiffkey Marsh** (31.5cm × 48cm (12½in. × 19in.)). Stiffkey village is about six miles further west from Salthouse, along the north Norfolk coast road, and a little side road leads down from the village to the large area of Marshland, a great place for bird watchers.

This picture is indeed a simple one; all we have is sky, a tree and a road. It was painted on a gray, cloudy, wet day from the shelter of the car. There were glimpses of sun occasionally, hence the tree shadow and the foreground shadow on the road.

The distant sea was a gray-blue merging with the sky with no horizon line, and the marsh was a pinkish blue owing to the remains of mauve sea lavender, the time of year being September.

The emphasis of this picture is on the big sycamore tree with its heavy foliage and leaves partly blown away, exposing bare branches. The colour scheme is greens and grays. The tree itself was a mixture of Raw Sienna and Winsor Blue for the less dark green areas and Burnt Umber and Winsor Blue for the very dark foliage. This latter mixture gives an excellent dark green.

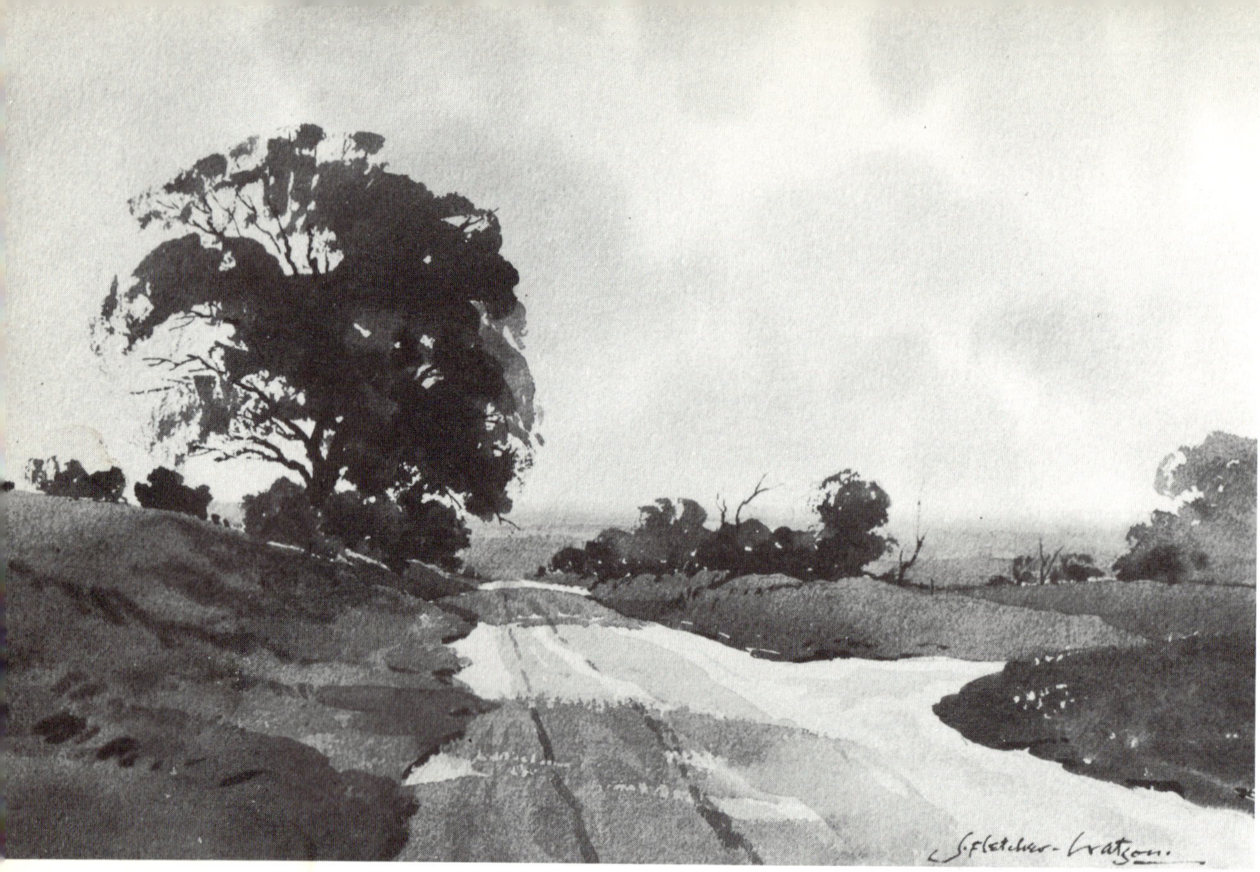

2 The road to Stiffkey Marsh.

This is the sort of subject that can be painted by almost anybody, especially beginners, and that is why I recommend Norfolk as a sketching ground as it abounds in beautiful trees and simple subjects – if you know how to look for them. To find them, you have got to be thinking in your mind of that rectangle of paper you are going to cover and how you are going to *place* the objects. If it is a complicated subject, don't attempt it unless you already have a bit of experience.

Having said that let us take a more complicated subject by way of contrast. Look at figure **3, Salthouse village**, from the marshes (30cm × 46cm (12in. × 18in.)). We don't seem to be able to get away from Salthouse, but quite honestly there is so much to paint within these few miles along the north Norfolk coast one can spend weeks here, and it is one of my favourite sketching grounds.

This picture was painted in the autumn, facing into the sun so that the *tone* of the colour of church and cottages was dark and strong. I found this view by turning off the main road which runs past the village, on to a little narrow track leading to the sea. After a few hundred yards I looked back and there was this superb little view, with an intriguing irregular sky-line. The church was again the dominant feature as in figure 1. I walked up and down the track to adjust to a good composition. I wanted to include some water and reeds in the foreground and I wanted the church off centre to the right, and the dark clumps of trees must be included too. The narrow track up towards the church on the right was in a way a disturbing influence, but the sunlight falling on it and the cottage walls at this point was counter-balanced by the bright light on the foreground water.

This is not a subject for the beginner as there is a lot of drawing and perspective required, but don't let me stop a beginner from having a try as there is a lot to learn from this type of subject. A picture with many buildings like this can easily fall apart and look 'bitty', but it was held together by the judicious use of cloud shadows falling across groups of several cottages together, notably those on the left side.

FISHERMEN'S COTTAGES, SALTHOUSE

(colour plate 1, between pages 120 and 121)

31.5cm × 47.5cm ($12\frac{1}{2}$in. × $18\frac{3}{4}$in.)

I would now like to go through the detailed stages of painting a Norfolk subject and I will take some fishermen's cottages in Salthouse. These cottages are at the west end of the village and jut out near the main road, which is seen on the left of the picture. They form a delightful group, and you do not have to be an advanced painter to tackle a subject like this. It is in fact an easy subject and because of its simplicity it makes a very good picture.

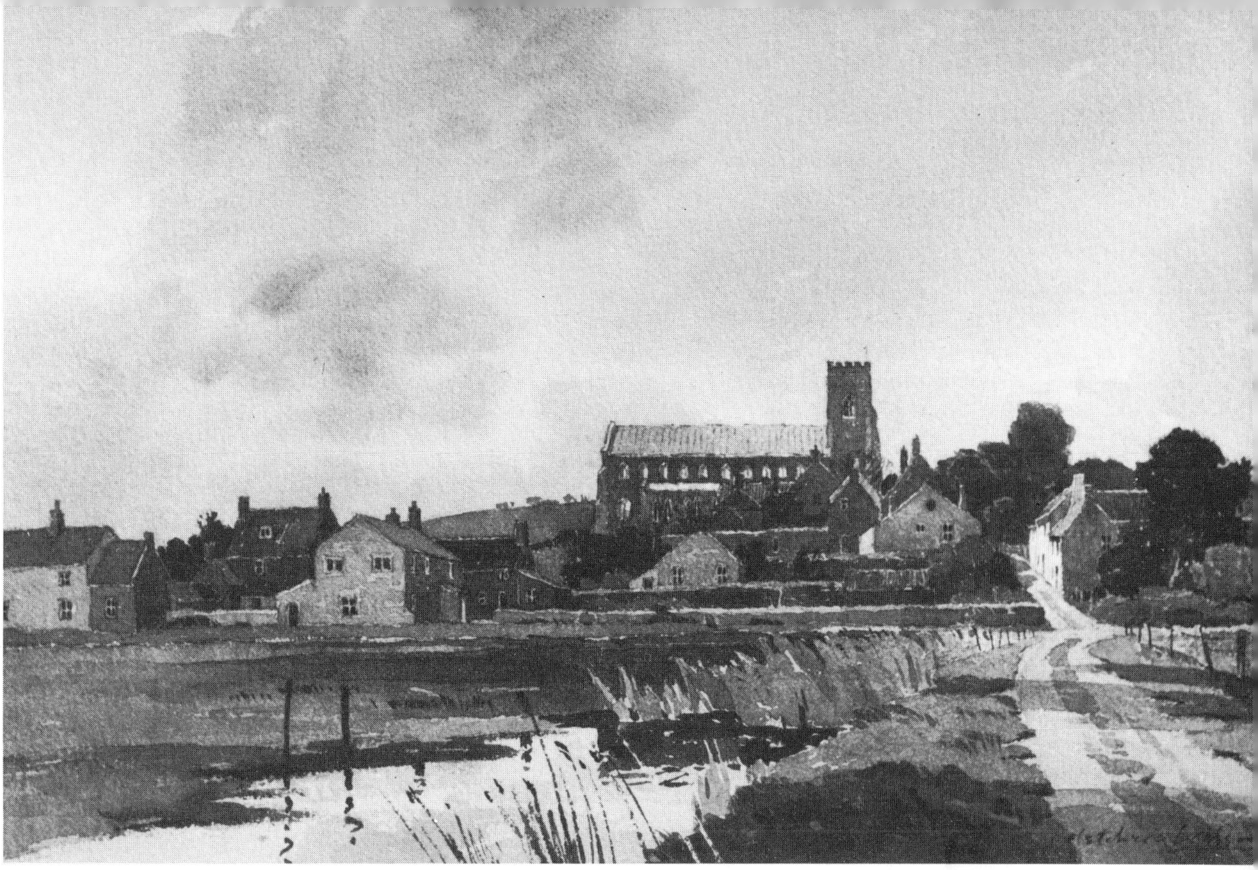

3 Salthouse village from the marshes.

Composition

Composition was the first consideration and this was easily decided. I wanted the buildings to be on the right so that there would be a nice bit of distance of marshland and slightly rising ground on the left. I found a spot to sit where the balance seemed just right.

This was on a brilliant sunny day in April and I decided to use a piece of Whatman paper. With its dead white colour I could be helped in capturing the brilliance of the day.

Drawing

I first drew in with my forefinger the main features; this is an old trick and saves you making a mistake with a pencil. You are able to see if you are getting things the right size, the buildings, the tree on the right, the road pattern etc. Then you can start with pencil with the confidence that it is all going to fit in properly.

I used a B pencil and drew in the cottages fairly firmly, noting the shadows with a light line in case these changed by the time I came to painting. The roads were carefully drawn as it was important to get the grass areas right. The distance received only the faintest line so as not to interfere with a light wash that would be required. The trees were sketched in lightly.

Painting

I used *nine* colours to paint this picture – Raw Sienna, Burnt Sienna, Burnt Umber, Light Red, Indian Red, Cobalt Blue, French Ultramarine, Winsor Blue and Paynes Gray. That is to say, one yellow, one brown, three reds and four blues.

I was sitting down as I prefer this to standing, and I have a very low deck-chair type of seat which enables me to have my painting board on my knees and also to reach my paint-box on the ground beside me. This means one can have plenty of room to have paints, water pot and brushes spread out ready for quick action. I usually have an old rug which can be spread out to level out any unevenness in the ground. I like to be able to tilt the picture this way and that as washes go on and the sitting position makes this easy. One can always stand up and look at the picture from a distance now and then to see how it is going.

It is very seldom that one does not paint the sky first because it is nearly always the lightest thing in a landscape and one wants to be able to paint the darker objects against it.

Damp the paper first

With clear water and a large No. 16 brush (a No. 10 or 12 would do) I wetted the sky area *only*, down to the horizon leaving the rest dry. I did not flood it with water, in fact I left one or two places in the sky quite dry and these places would be where I wanted a crisp edge to a white cloud. The sky was full of moving clouds from the slight breeze and large patches of blue.

I next ran a light wash of Raw Sienna well diluted into the damp sky not all over but in various areas. Then I mixed a light gray with Burnt Umber and French Ultramarine and washed in gray areas of cloud with the paper still damp.

Blue sky areas
Next I added the all-important blue patches using French Ultramarine a little diluted, being careful where I put these blue patches; a strong patch on the right, a weaker patch on the left, adding a little more clear water to the paper to make sure the blue ran nicely giving a soft cloud effect. Some of the blue was on a dry paper place and gave the desired sharp cloud edge. I added a touch of Light Red to some of the blue to tone it down a trifle.

It is very important to place one's Blue in the right spot as this can make or mar a whole picture with the wrong sort of blue treatment.

Darker gray clouds
Finally, the darkish gray cloud to the lower left was painted on the still damp paper. This is important as a gray cloud usually has soft edges. I used the same two colours, Burnt Umber and Ultramarine, for the gray but a darker mix. I sometimes add a little Indian Red to this mixture if I want a darker cloud; it gives a slightly purple touch which can be very effective, but I did not do it in this particular case as it was not a stormy sky.

Gray wash
I finally mixed a little more light gray with the same two colours but slightly more Burnt Umber and carried a wash down over the whole of the bottom half of the picture excluding the right-hand cottage and windows of the centre cottage which were left dead white. This gray-brown colour would be the final colour of the road.

Allow to dry out
The whole picture area was now allowed to dry completely before any more painting was done.

I have dealt with this sky painting at some length as so many people have asked me for more detail about skies.

Distance
I next painted the distant rising ground of Weybourne far away to the east. This was nothing more than a gray smudge and I used French Ultramarine and Light Red; these two colours mixed give an excellent gray for distances. I used a No. 5 brush.

Grass areas
I then mixed Raw Sienna and Winsor Blue, not too much of the latter, to give a yellow-green and painted in the grass areas from background to foreground. As this was drying I added a little Burnt Sienna to the distant grass on the marshes. I varied the green by adding more Winsor Blue and floated this in on the foreground triangle of grass. I was using a No. 9 brush.

The cottages
The order in which one paints features of a landscape is largely dictated by tone values. The lighter tones should be painted in first, gradually working towards the darkest passages. We have completed most of the lighter tones now and it is time to tackle the cottages.

With a No. 7 brush I started on the central roof using Burnt Sienna for the most part and one or two touches of Raw Sienna and Burnt Umber dabbed in, as the pantile roof had several variations of colour in it. The right-hand roof, partly behind a tree, was a little browner and I added a little Cobalt Blue to the Burnt Sienna for this one.

I next gave the walls of the central cottage a light wash of gray using Light Red and Cobalt Blue. While this was drying I painted in the right-hand cottage, behind the large tree, an all over darkish gray, again using Light Red and Cobalt but a stronger mix. This cottage was often in cloud shadow and I felt that this helped to set it in the background and improved the composition. When dry, I added the red roofs to it and the low outbuildings.

Now I took a No. 3 brush and mixed a dark blue-brown using Ultramarine and Burnt Umber, mostly the latter, and painted the windows. By making rectangular panes you can suggest the shape of the white glazing bars and window frames and windowsill. It is worth studying the type of window, whether it is a casement or sash window, because this gives the character of the house. In this case they are all casement windows, i.e. opening sideways on hinges.

I then touched in, with the same brush, the brick-work round the windows of the central cottage with Burnt Sienna. This cottage had flint walls, and flint-work always needs brickwork to form window and door openings. The right-hand cottage was plastered and was all white in colour.

Now the chimney pots and the brick chimney stack were painted in red using the same brush.

Shadows
When everything was dry, I painted in the shadows on the cottages; this was a most important item as it would give the necessary feeling of sunlight.

A No. 7 brush was about right for this and I used the same gray mix again, Light Red and Cobalt Blue: first the left-hand gable walls and chimneys and then the shadows under the roof eaves and the sloping shadows cast on the walls. I was careful to leave out the light gray windows in the shadow walls. The red roof that faces left was painted over with a darker red of similar mix.

Next I used the same shadow gray as for the cottage walls for the boundary wall running along the road, making it a little darker at the far end as it started to bend round. I saw that the gable wall facing me was darker flintwork than the others so I gave this a further light wash of gray.

Darker toned items

We were now working towards the darker passages and, still using a No. 7 brush, I mixed a yellow-green for the shrub at the left-hand end of the centre cottage, mixing Raw Sienna and Winsor Blue, the former predominating. The wind was off the sea blowing the shrub to the right, and I used quick brush strokes with the side of the brush to give the broken edges to the foliage. Care was taken to paint round the notice board and post. While this was still damp I quickly mixed a darker green with Raw Sienna and Payne's Gray and, using a smaller No. 3 brush, painted in the low bushes each side of the shrub. The dark tone items helped to set off the garden wall and the cottage. I also put in some vertical dark green lines to indicate the little white gate with a No. 1 brush.

Now the dark little trees against the dark gray cottage wall and white cottage to the right were painted. A No. 3 brush was first used to paint the trunks and branches with a dark brown, mixing Burnt Umber and a little Payne's Gray. Then the foliage of this evergreen shrub came in with a No. 7 brush using Burnt Umber and Winsor Blue. Quick downward strokes of the brush with a stiff mix of paint, i.e. not much water, meeting the branches at appropriate places, gave the necessary shape to this little collection of small trees. As one of the darkest things in the picture, this valuable item had the effect of setting back the cottages from the road.

At the same time I used the same dark green for the small group of bushes overlooking the low wall.

And now the bigger tree on the right was dealt with. A No. 7 brush was used for the main trunk and No. 3 for the thin branches, with Burnt Umber and Payne's Gray as before. It was too early in the year for this tree to be in leaf and the mass of small twigs was indicated by sketchily applied strokes of a No. 7 brush using Burnt Umber and a touch of Payne's Gray in varying strengths. The small branch areas could have been indicated by drawing with a very small brush dozens of individual branches. They are all there to be seen if you look closely, but the effect of this treatment is niggly and fussy, and when you close your eyes you do not see individual twigs but only the brown mass and general tree shape. This is all part of the simplification process which I want you to adopt in painting watercolours. Too much detail distracts the eye from the general overall impression we are trying to produce. We are trying to convey a breezy bright day on the Norfolk coast, and we don't want to get bogged down with too much detail.

I will be giving you more ideas about painting trees in later chapters.

Final touches

The cows on the left had been left the white of the paper when placing the various early washes, and now all they required was some dark patches to give them form. This was done with Burnt Umber and Payne's Gray and a No. 3 brush.

Cloud shadows were falling on grass and road in various places and it was a matter of choosing *which* places would suit the balance of the picture best to have them. A foreground shadow is often a nice one to have as it has the effect of sending the landscape into perspective. Sometimes such a shadow comes from a building or tree outside the picture. The advantage of cloud shadows is that they can be varied in intensity according to the thickness of the cloud and the sun penetration.

Here, I swept in a foreground cloud shadow and used a gray mixture of Cobalt Blue and Light Red washed over road and grass, and while still damp a little Indian Red on the road area to give it a touch of purple. Then when dry I added some dark green, a strong mix of Raw Sienna and Winsor Blue, to the shadow on the grass adding plain water to taper off the dark green. I added darker green to a clump of grass in the foreground and the dark brown post and another post further away.

Then the other cloud shadows were brushed in across the left-hand road and grass, and across distant marshland getting into thin lines to give perspective. Wood posts were indicated across the marsh with a small brush.

A few tufts of grass of darkish green along the bottom of the boundary wall and in various other places were required to give texture to these grass areas. I used a No. 7 brush for this work like a chisel, flattening it on the palette in a stiff mix of colours so that it stayed the flat shape to give a very thin line or a thick one as desired. The alternative is to have a square-ended sable brush as used in oil painting; you can of course get various sizes. You want to be careful not to overdo these grass tufts; you *don't* want to have them dotted evenly all over the place, even if they may be in reality, as this makes a painting look fussy and overpainted.

I now touched in some light gray-brown wheel marks or ruts in the right-hand side road and some indication of grass growing in the centre of the main road on the left. This is perhaps my only dishonest bit of painting as this was not actually there. It gives the rather nice effect of an *old* country road which I sometimes can't resist! Of course one can still find plenty of old, not much used, roads with grass down the middle, especially in places like Scotland and the Lake District.

Finally, I added touches of dark brown to the grass

edges of the roads; these are muddy edges which most secondary roads have. This completed the picture.

During the painting of this picture I had stood up and away from the picture once or twice to see how the general tone values were going. When you are close up to a picture you sometimes miss getting the accent and emphasis in the right place. But this comes with experience and you learn to give strength to a painting where it is needed as you go along. I still find it is extremely useful to put a picture under a mount when I get home, and one can then assess its quality much better than on the spot out of doors.

4 CLEY MILL

31.5cm × 47.5cm ($12\frac{1}{2}$in. × $18\frac{3}{4}$in.)

Now let us move west along the coast road to the village of Cley, only a mile or two away. Cley (which is pronounced Cly) is a village full of paintable groups of old houses, and I am particularly fond of a view of its famous windmill seen from the east as you approach the village from Salthouse. If you turn down a track leading to the sea you get this charming view which includes Blakeney church in the distance. The mill was built in 1713 of dark red brick and is kept in an excellent state of preservation including its sails and fantail gear, an automatic device to keep the sails facing the wind. I have often painted this view and it is a comparatively easy one to do, but I never get tired of it because you can vary the viewpoint.

In this case I manoeuvred myself so as to get some of the village houses and trees on the left of the picture and the mill near to the centre, and then the distant church tower away to the right giving a good counter-balance.

The dark line of trees behind the mill is a big asset, and when the cloud shadows are on it, the trees become very dark and effective. One always wants to look out for really dark areas in a landscape. Constable was masterly with his dark green and almost black tree groups giving contrast to the sunlit fields.

The foreground was marshy land and note the tufts of grass and cloud shadows breaking up the green expanse and giving the necessary perspective and distance. The reeds are a help as well in the immediate foreground.

4 Cley Mill.

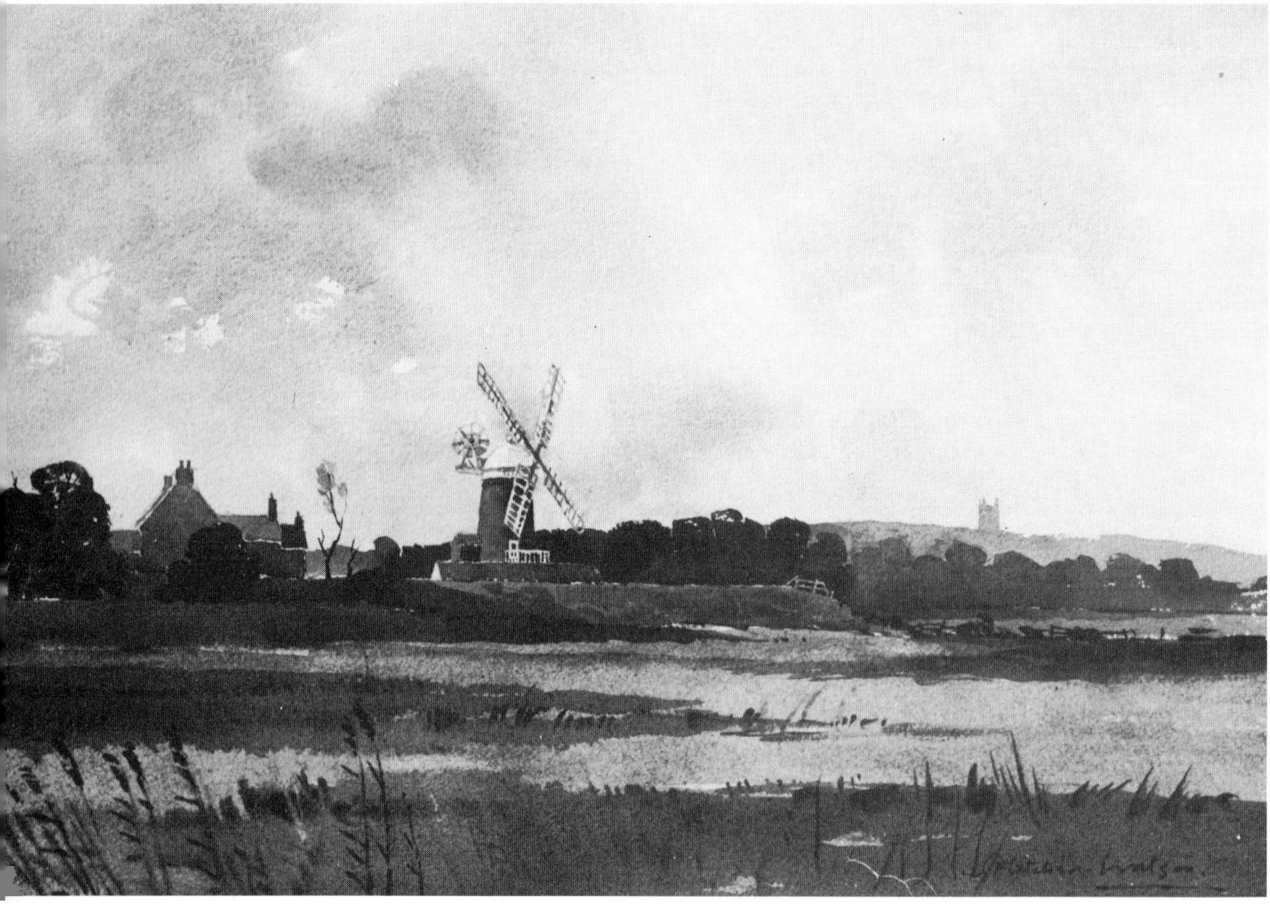

Care had to be taken with the mill itself so that the white sails and wood cap and white painted gallery would stand out. Figure 5 'detail' shows how this was done.

When painting the sky which was all gray clouds I left a few bits of white paper showing on the sails and painted carefully round the cap or dome of the mill and the circular fantail. I was using the Whatman very white paper so these white features would show up well. When it came to painting the brick tower of the mill it was not difficult, with a small brush, to paint round the shape of the bottom sail and paint small rectangles indicating the framework of the sail by leaving the white pieces of wood. The same treatment was given to the white wood gallery. When the dark trees behind the mill were painted, the gallery woodwork was also painted round and left the white of the paper.

Although this work is rather laborious I always think one gets a much nicer effect by using the white of the paper rather than using white paint which is the alternative. There are rare occasions when white paint can successfully be used but I don't think this is one of them.

5 Cley Mill, detail.

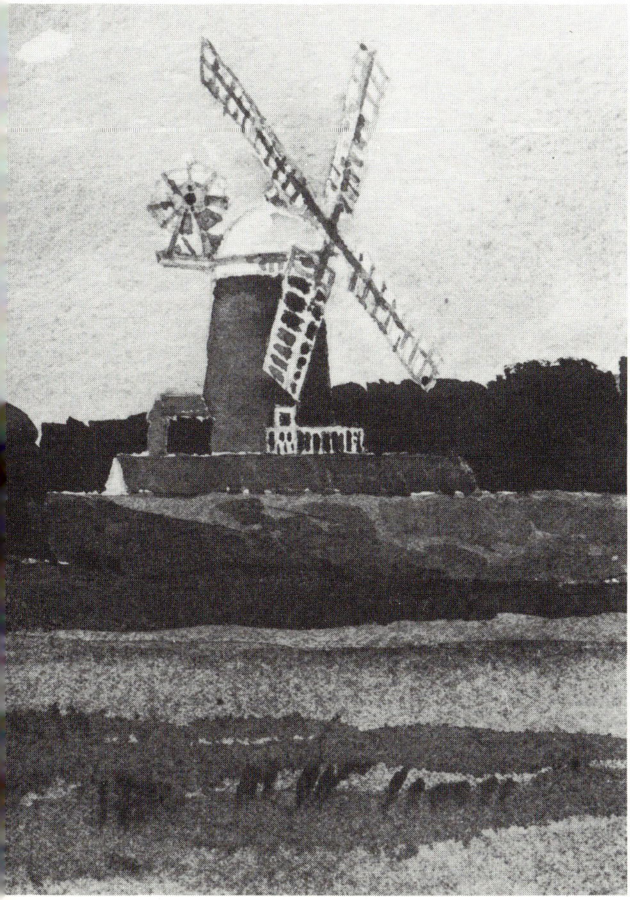

6 STUBBLE FIELD NEAR MORSTON

31.5cm × 47.5cm ($12\frac{1}{2}$in. × $18\frac{3}{4}$in.)

I was exploring this part of Norfolk inland a short distance from Morston in September and I came across the perfect simple subject, a stubble field and a small wood.

Figure 6 shows this subject in black and white and you must imagine the colours which were very lovely and very simple. The stubble field itself was a beautiful golden yellow-brown, the sky had quite a lot of yellow with the gray and there were one or two patches of blue. I caught a boy and a man and a dog walking across the field which added interest.

The big tree on the right was on the edge of a road which was hidden by a small grass bank. This was in September when the tree foliage was heavy and very dark green and I used Burnt Umber and Winsor Blue for most of this tree and the background wood. But there were beginning to be signs of Autumn with yellow colouring in some of the trees and I ran in some strong Raw Sienna to mix with the dark greens in one or two places. I love painting at this time of year because the trees are such a rich dark colour and it is fun slopping on the colour with a full brush, using a No. 9 and No. 12 for much of it in this case, but a No. 5 for the small trees at the left end of the wood where the leaves were beginning to come off the branches.

The paper I was using was Arches 300lb 'Not' surface made in France (but available in English art shops). This weightly thick paper is lovely to work on, does not cockle when wet and does not require stretching which is a very big advantage.

The stubble field was a mixture of Raw Sienna and Burnt Umber well diluted for the first wash, and as it dried off I painted on the same mix but stronger, giving the perspective lines which had been caused by the machine doing the cutting of the crop. Then while this was still damp I marked in the stubble sticking up vertically with a still stronger mixture with Burnt Umber predominating. And then when it was all dry I painted the tree shadows and cloud shadows across horizontally, using a larger brush and a mixture of Burnt Sienna and Cobalt Blue.

Going back to the big tree on the right, I started with the trunk working it upwards with a No. 9 brush and Burnt Sienna and Ultramarine to give it a dark brown, and then worked in some green Raw Sienna and Winsor Blue for the ivy creeper that was on part of the trunk. Then while the trunk was still wet I used a larger brush for the foliage of dark green and painted a lot of this and kept changing back to paint the dark brown branches using a smaller (No. 3) brush. The idea is to

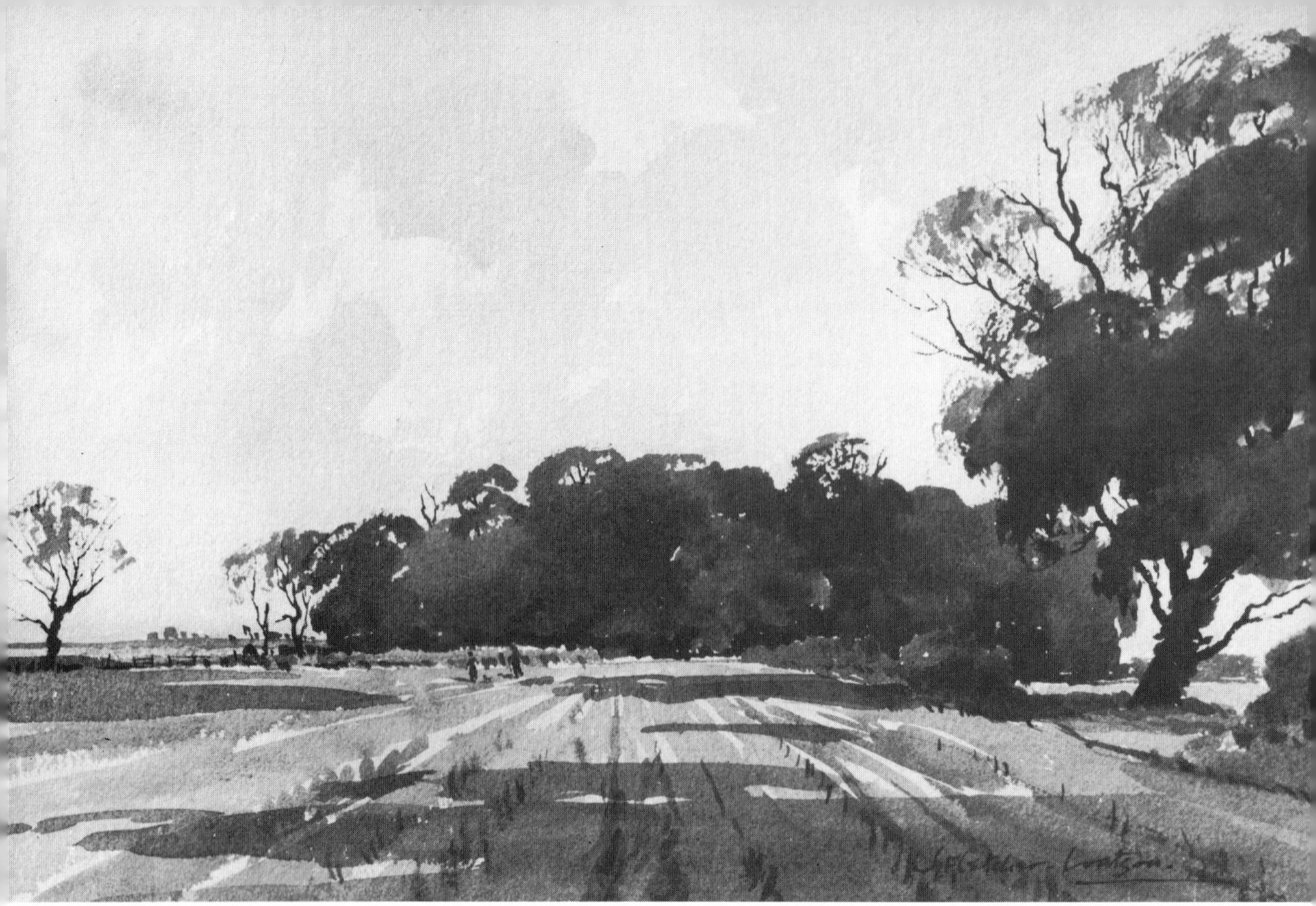

6 Stubble field near Morston.

keep branches and foliage wet so that one runs into the other slightly and this gives a good homogeneous effect.

I painted this picture very quickly because there was limited time. It didn't do any harm to paint it under pressure, in fact it made it very much better as I avoided any unnecessary detail and stuck to essentials. I think this picture took about one and three-quarter hours.

It is much better to paint watercolours fairly quickly so that they are fresh and spontaneous. If you are too long at it the work tends to become laboured and too careful, and we want to avoid this.

7 TOWARDS LANGHAM

31.5cm × 47.5cm ($12\frac{1}{2}$in. × $18\frac{3}{4}$in.)

When you are finding it difficult to find a subject, remember that a small country road is often a good one.

I came across this view looking towards Langham village with the church tower showing above the trees. The time was again September, and the sky was a good one and the general colouring superb.

I got to work quickly before the sky changed too much. I did very little pencil work so as to get on with the painting as soon as possible. Working against the clock, as I have just said, is a good thing. The road had to be carefully drawn; I was using a B pencil and working on Arches paper 'Not' surface again. You must always be careful to get a curved road drawn correctly so that the grass verges go round the corner properly. This did not take long, and the church tower and trees were lightly sketched in with very few lines quite rapidly.

The windy cloudy sky was painted using plenty of water; there were some dark gray clouds in places and a strong patch of blue just above the large tree on the right. I ran the light gray sky wash right down over the rest of the picture leaving out the white house in the distance to right of church. This gave a useful tone to the paper and a suitable colour for the road.

I then painted the green grass verges and field on the left and the tall hedge with the sapling sticking out on extreme left. This hedge was a useful balancing feature in the composition.

The big trees were varying shades of green and were painted in by the same method as described for the previous picture No. 6.

Many of the churches in Norfolk have extremely tall towers, perhaps in order to show up over the flat countryside. A church tower is always a nice focal point. You will be able to find many subjects like this without any difficulty in Norfolk.

8 TREES AT SHARRINGTON

31.5cm × 47.5cm ($12\frac{1}{2}$in. × $18\frac{3}{4}$in.)

One early April when I was in north Norfolk I was driving back to my hotel in the afternoon after a day's painting and I spotted this group of old trees half covered with ivy (8), and, although it was getting late, I could not resist stopping and having a go at it. There is something about winter trees with ivy clad trunks that has a romantic appeal. Perhaps it goes back to childhood – fairy stories and mysterious woods. This seemed a perfect subject; do try just a simple tree group some time and you will be delighted to find what an attractive picture it can make.

I kept the paper damp while I was painting the main big trees so that the ivy would run a little bit and give a blurred effect; you don't want to have too hard an outline. The twig masses at the top of the trees were painted in with a No. 7 brush and a dryish mix of Burnt Umber and Payne's Gray, using the brush sideways and dragging it quickly downards across the paper.

FLOOD TIDE AT MORSTON QUAY

(colour plate 2, between pages 120 and 121)

31.5cm × 47.5cm ($12\frac{1}{2}$in. × $18\frac{3}{4}$in.)

Let me now run through a detailed description of painting Morston Quay, looking across the salt marshes with Blakeney Church in the distance.

This was painted in April when the colour of the marshes was light brown rather than green, and it was a morning sketch when the light was particularly attractive and the colouring delicate. I decided to use the slightly cream coloured Arches paper 'Not' surface.

It was flood tide with quite a big expanse of water and all the sailing boats had gone out to sea. At very low tide there is only a narrow trickle of water and the rest is all mud, so one has to choose one's moment for painting rather carefully. I had about an hour and a half before the waterline started dropping very much.

Stage 1

I started drawing with a 2B pencil and kept the horizon line about one-third the height of the picture with a nice big two-thirds sky. I did not need to draw very much, in fact the less the better with this type of subject as one wants to put the washes on clear and fresh with no pencil at all when possible. I did not pencil in the distant church and gray line of trees as I wanted this to be a delicate wash, so I drew just the horizon of the marshes and the indents of mud and grass bank to indicate the shape of the water area, and virtually nothing else.

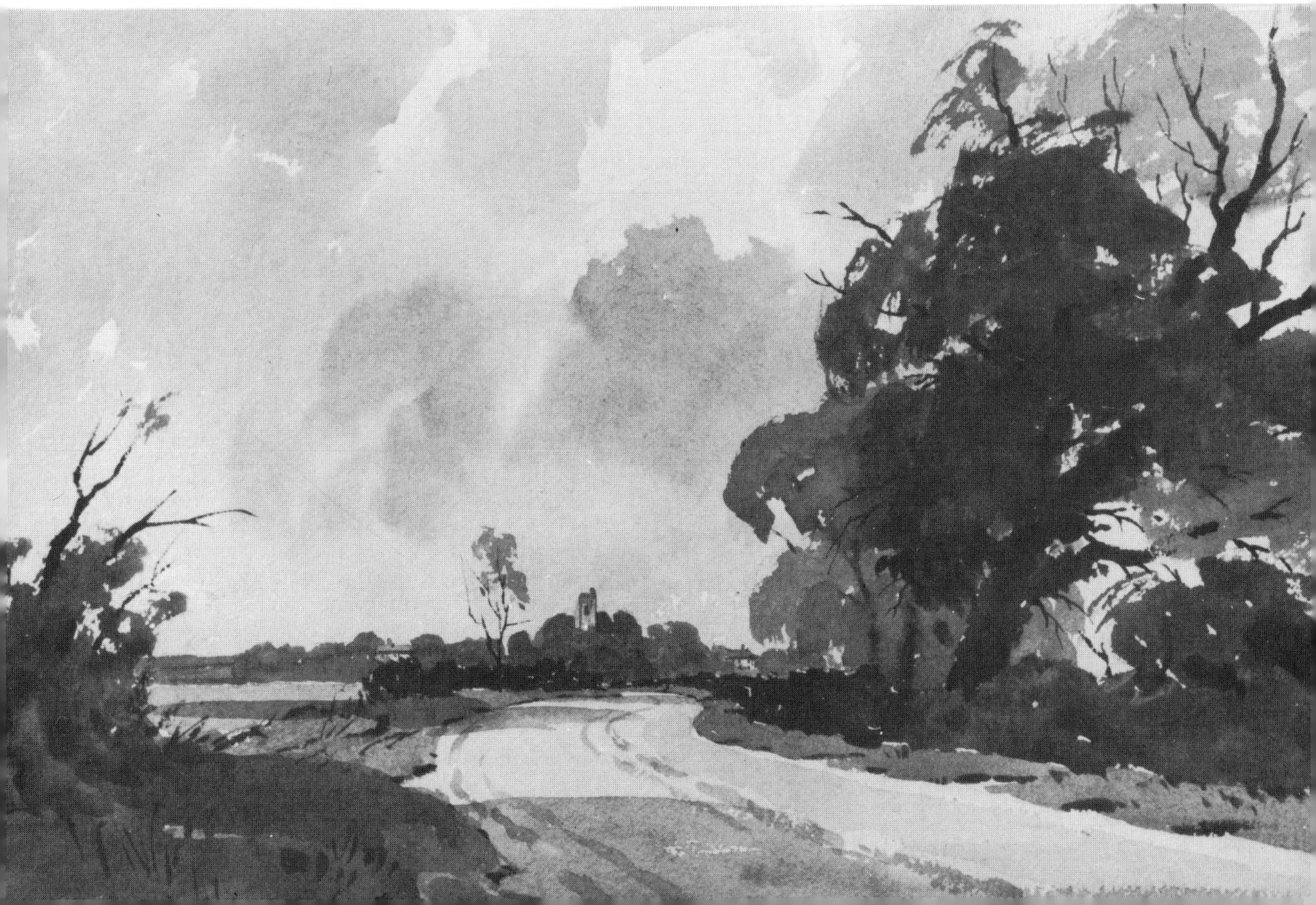

7 Towards Langham.

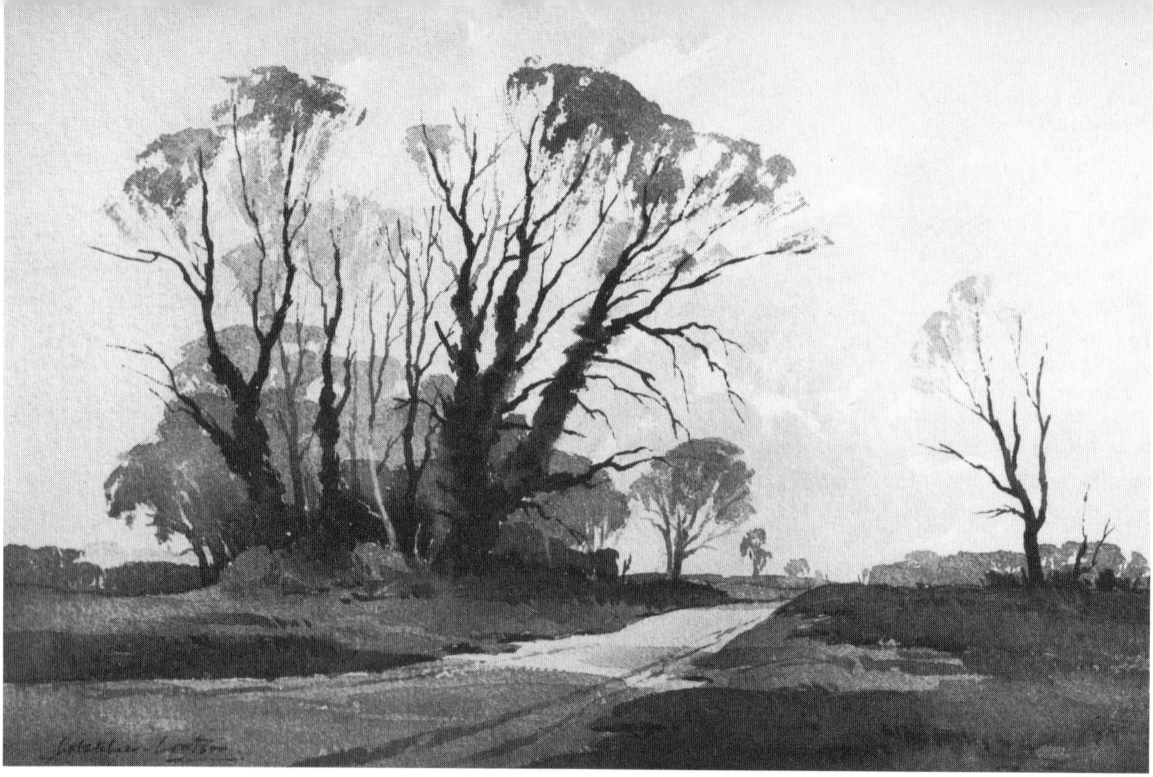

8 Trees at Sharrington.

I was now ready to start painting, using the same *nine* colours as for colour plate no. 1 of the Fishermen's Cottages, with one exception: instead of Burnt Sienna I used an extra yellow, Cadmium Yellow. First, I covered the sky with a clear wash of water. The gray clouds were a rather blue-gray and I used Burnt Umber and French Ultramarine, the latter predominating. I ran this mixture into the wet paper, giving it a light gray tone in most areas but leaving a large central white area uncoloured. Then I used a well diluted Winsor Blue for the blue sky just above the white cloud; this blue ran into the gray quite happily. I then mixed a stronger gray of the same two colours and washed in the darker clouds to the left and right. I had been using a No. 12 brush. The sky was still a little damp and I quickly floated in a touch of Indian Red mixed with the light gray on the skyline near the horizon. One often gets a pink colour near the horizon.

The sky was now completed and again I used Burnt Umber and Ultramarine, but this time I made it a light *brown* and washed this over the whole of the lower part of the picture *excluding* the water area. Everything was now allowed to completely dry off.

Stage 2

Mixing a warm gray, Cobalt and Light Red, I used a No. 5 brush and painted the far-away line of trees, fading this at the left-hand end as the trees went further into the distance, and strengthening them to the right. I used a No. 3 brush to paint in the church and you will notice it has two towers, one a very thin one.

Now I wanted a light brown for the land on the far side of the water and Burnt Umber and Payne's Gray well diluted gave the right tone and colour. I applied this with a No. 7 brush and as it dried I painted a band of pure Burnt Umber to mark the top portion of the mud bank. The bottom part of the mud bank was then painted in a gray-brown colour by adding in some Payne's Gray.

On the horizon of this land was a very dark line of marsh growth, a dark green colour, and I used Burnt Umber and Winsor Blue and with a No. 3 brush I drew in the irregular line indicating tufts of growth and the odd vertical post.

With the same No. 3 brush I touched in the same dark green for crevices in the mud at the water's edge at various places along the bank. This far side of the water was now finished and I turned my attention to the near side.

First I ran a wash all over the foreground and background area of gray-brown using Burnt Umber again with Payne's Gray. This was a slightly darker tone than the land on the far side. I used a No. 12 brush for this wash.

While drying out I painted the green bank on the right (just below the distant dark trees) using Raw Sienna and Winsor Blue with a No. 5 brush. I then painted some darker gray-brown horizontal marks which are visible over the foreground areas of mud with a No. 7 brush, and then a darker still tone of reddish-brown just below the green bank with the same brush and a mixture of Burnt Umber and Indian Red.

These various markings on the mud were partly changes in colour as the ground became clay or gravel but partly cloud shadows. I finally washed a mixture of Burnt Umber and Payne's Gray in the immediate foreground and this definitely was a cloud shadow.

To finish this land area two more things had to be done; first the green turf in the foreground with the gorse bush and post. I used a strong mixture of Cadmium Yellow and Winsor Blue to give a light green; it had to be fairly strong to show up on the gray wash below. The bush consisted of Raw Sienna and Winsor Blue for the main green, and Burnt Umber added to give the very dark green at the left-hand end of the bush. Both turf and bush were put in with a No. 7 brush. A No. 5 brush, chisel shaped as previously described, with a stiff mixture of paint was used for the tufts of spikey grass. The post was dark brown painted with a No. 3 brush. I used the same brush and again dark brown to give the little narrow earthy edges to the green turf.

Now the second item; the dark range of shrubs and low trees in the middle distance on the right, along the top of the green bank and the higher ground beyond. These were a very dark colour of evergreen growth, in fact they were the darkest thing in the picture and gave a crispness to the scene. I used Burnt Umber and Winsor Blue which gave the perfect colour, and painted in the bushes with a No. 5 brush. As the bushes thinned out at the right-hand end the strength of the colour was reduced a little. This feature had the desired effect of setting the distant trees and church well into the background.

Stage 3

All that now remained was the water, the boat and a few posts etc. At the moment the water had been left the white of the paper. Reflections are usually a slight tone darker than what is being reflected, but in this case the sky reflection seemed to be as light and bright as the sky itself, probably because I was sitting low down at water level.

I first damped the water area with clear painting water. I then mixed a gray the same as for the sky itself and floated in a wash leaving a few gaps of white to echo the white clouds above. I touched in a few darker areas with some vertical strokes and the water was done. I used a No. 7 brush for this work.

Now with a No. 5 brush I carefully painted the rowing boat with a dark brown, mixing Burnt Umber and Ultramine. I also put in the small amount of boat reflection in the same colour.

Then the timber jetty and tall vertical wood posts were painted in the same dark brown with a No. 1 brush. The post reflections were painted with a slightly diluted brown.

Finally the two large posts and the third little one on the far bank were put in with their reflections in the same way. Reflections of posts usually have a kink in them indicating a movement in the water. The picture was now completed.

This picture did not take very long to paint, about two hours, as it mainly consisted of simple washes. The great thing was to keep watching the tone values by half closing your eyes as you looked at the view and then to get the washes down on paper without wasting a minute. The painting of fishermen's cottages in colour plate 1 took a little longer, about two and three quarter hours, because there was detail in the buildings and trees and these can take a little more time.

It was time for lunch but I didn't waste much time. The tide had been going down steadily for the past half hour and when I turned to face the opposite direction there was a marvellous second view of the estuary, mud coming into prominence and a very simple view which I felt I must do.

9 MORSTON QUAY, LOOKING WEST

31.5cm × 47.5cm ($12\frac{1}{2}$in. × $18\frac{3}{4}$in.)

Figure 9 shows this view. It is a beautifully simple subject, with the low tide and the mud banks, it is just a little creek, a peaceful little bit of Norfolk.

I felt that this could be a pure watercolour with no pencil guidelines at all so I started straight in with the sky mostly gray clouds facing in this direction with a small touch of light blue near the top.

Directly the sky was dry I painted a thin brown line indicating the horizon with a no. 3 brush and I followed this up quickly with a brown-gray wash, using similar colours to the previous picture. I used a No. 12 brush for these big washes with clean sweeps on the virgin white paper, the Whatman 200lb paper.

When it was nearly dry I painted in with a No. 5 brush the dark skyline grasses and low bushes and a rather faint smudge of a line in the distance, right of centre. The colour was Burnt Umber and Winsor Blue mixed to give dark green.

The same mixture was used on the right-hand grass areas which came to the top edge of the bank. And a little of the same grass was painted in the left foreground. I then painted the horizontal timbers forming the jetty and the various vertical posts using a dark brown mixture of Burnt Umber and Ultramarine.

When everything was dry I washed in gray cloud reflections over the water area and the post reflections.

The foreground mud banks needed a darker wash of brown-gray and this had then pretty well completed the picture. It had taken about one hour and a quarter.

Anyone, from the complete beginner to the experienced painter, can try a subject like this and I

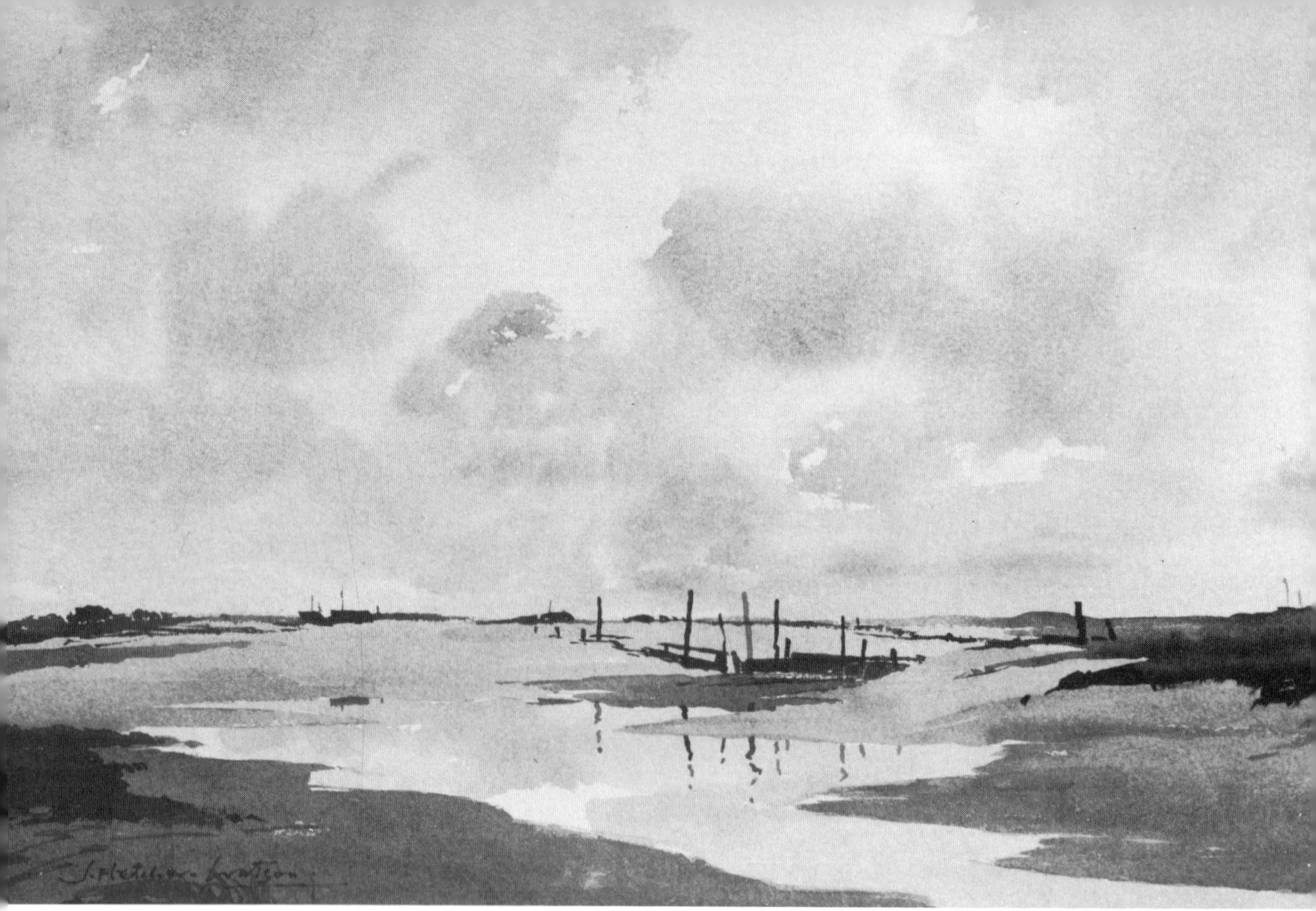

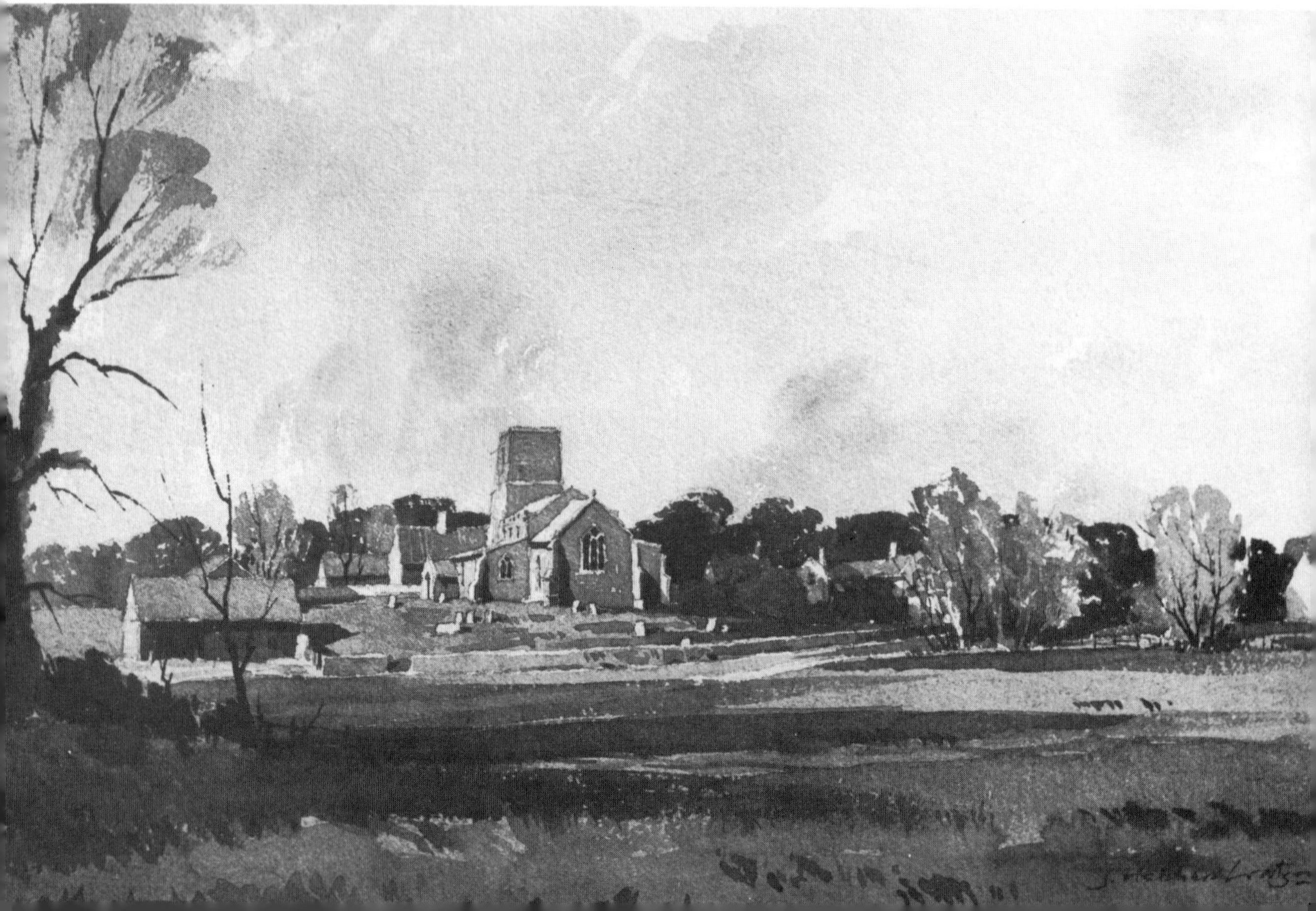

hope many of you who have never been to Norfolk will be able to pay a visit soon and find the enjoyment of these simple subjects.

10. MORSTON CHURCH, FROM SOUTH-EAST

31.5cm × 47.5cm ($12\frac{1}{2}$in. × $18\frac{3}{4}$in.)

While we are still thinking about Morston let us look at the church, which can be painted from various directions. Figure 10 shows a nice view taken from the south-east. It makes a good composition with trees on the right and small barn on the left and a big tree on a bank in the foreground. The church itself is on an attractive little hill and you can see it from several miles away as you approach along the coast road. As I said at the beginning of this chapter, little rises in ground take on much more significance in Norfolk than they do in many other counties.

Having painted this view I wanted to try another one, so I moved closer and over to the north-east.

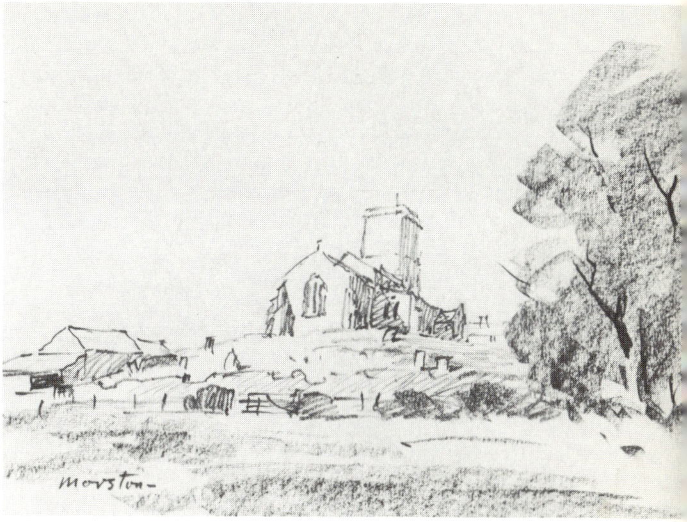

11 MORSTON CHURCH, FROM NORTH-EAST,

preliminary sketch. 18cm × 25.5cm (7in. × 10in.)

I occasionally try out a view with a preliminary sketch in a sketch book of cartridge paper. Here is one at figure 11. I like using a soft pencil about 5B for these quick sketches, combined with a stick of Conte crayon. These are available in $\frac{1}{4}$in. square $2\frac{1}{2}$in. long sticks, and you

9 Morston Quay, looking west.

10 Morston Church, from south-east.

11 Morston Church, from north-east, preliminary sketch.

12 Morston Church, from north-east, finished picture.

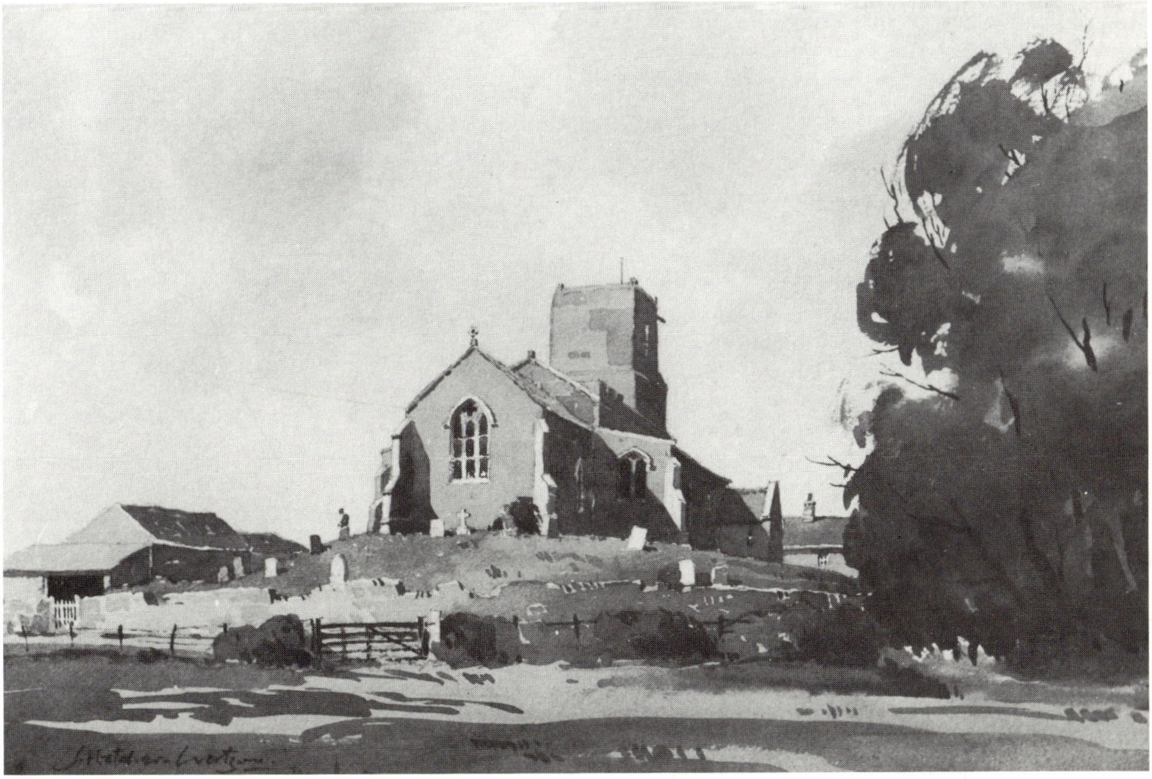

can break them easily to about ½in. length and use them sideways getting a lovely broad sweep of gray tone. I used it on the right-hand trees and the foreground in this sketch, and it saves time shading with a pencil and is really more effective. This sketch took about eight minutes and told me that I had got a good view-point and composition. I sometimes do two or three rough sketches to try out different view-points for a subject, and I strongly recommend this idea when you are not quite certain about your subject.

12 MORSTON CHURCH, FROM NORTH-EAST,
finished picture. 31.5cm × 47.5cm (12½in. × 18¾in.)
There was not a very wide range of colours to this subject – gray church, light green-gray grass, dark green-gray trees and gray-blue sky. So I decided to do the picture with three colours only! Raw Sienna, Burnt Sienna, Payne's Gray. With these three one can get a very good variety of colours with careful mixing. I strongly recommend trying a limited palette like this as it teaches you to get your tone values right, which is *such* an important part of landscape painting.

Drawing

This subject required some careful drawing to start with. I decided on a piece of Whatman 200lb paper and I used a well sharpened B pencil. I started by drawing the ground line of the hump on which the church was sitting. The position of the church was roughly the centre of the paper and I followed my rough sketch for this.

It was necessary to get the proportion of the east gable wall with the big window correct to begin with, and to get the corner buttresses right. Having drawn that, the rest followed on and came easily. Care was taken to get the perspective right with the roof eaves slanting downwards and the little porch sticking out nicely. The shadow on this porch was delightful and vital. It was important to get the tower proportion correct, and you could gauge its width by the position of its sides in relation to the body of the church.

The other features of the picture were lightly sketched in; the barns on the left, the trees on the right and the flint wall round the churchyard. A road ran along this side of the wall and then came the fence and field gate this side of the road.

Painting

Now I could start painting the sky and, having wetted the paper, I ran in a little Raw Sienna and then a diluted Payne's Gray to form the clouds. I would mention here that the Winsor and Newton Payne's Gray is a blue-gray whereas the Rowney Payne's Gray is a black-gray and therefore I find the Winsor and Newton a more useful colour especially for skies.

I mixed Payne's Gray a little stronger for the darker clouds and the first diluted wash then looked like a pale blue sky. I let the light Payne's Gray wash run right over the church but carefully avoiding the buttresses and big window which was left white. I carried this light gray wash down over everything but avoided some of the tombstones as I wanted them to stand out white.

I am not going to go into too much detail of painting, but I will deal briefly with the colour mixing as I would like you to try painting a picture yourself with these three colours.

The gray church was a mixture of Payne's Gray and Burnt Sienna and the shadow side of the walls was the same thing only a darker mix. But there was a variation in these shadows which I saw as I looked carefully, and it was a warmer colour so I added some Raw Sienna in certain places which gave a pleasing tone.

If you look at figure 13, which is an enlarged detail of the church, showing buttresses, shadows, windows etc., you will see how the shadow tones were varied. Also note the windows painted dark with a stiff mix of Burnt Sienna and Payne's Gray and put in with a small brush. The stone tracery shows up well because the windows were left pale with the initial gray wash.

The roof of the chancel and the porch was pure Payne's Gray. The barn walls were the same, put on diluted on the sunny side and strong on the shadow side. The churchyard wall was again the same colour.

The roofs of the barns and the cottage to the right of the church were fairly strong Burnt Sienna and these gave a nice touch of bright colour to the picture.

The grass of the mound or churchyard was Raw Sienna and Payne's Gray mixed but mostly Sienna, and the foreground field grass was the same again but mostly Payne's Gray. The foreground shadows on the grass were the same mixture but stronger.

The hedges in the fence along the road were again Raw Sienna and Payne's Gray mixed fairly strong.

Now for the big trees on the right. I used all three colours with plenty of water and strong colour and a large brush, varying the mixture so that near the top it was lightish blue-gray and yellow. In the middle it was a strong green and at the bottom I graded it to very dark green by using more Burnt Sienna with the Payne's Gray.

The branches and the gate and the fence posts were Sienna and Payne's Gray mixed very thick to give a brown-black colour. This went for the dark opening in the barn also.

I do hope you will try out these three colours for a painting some time and you could add one more, Burnt Umber, which will allow for slightly more variety.

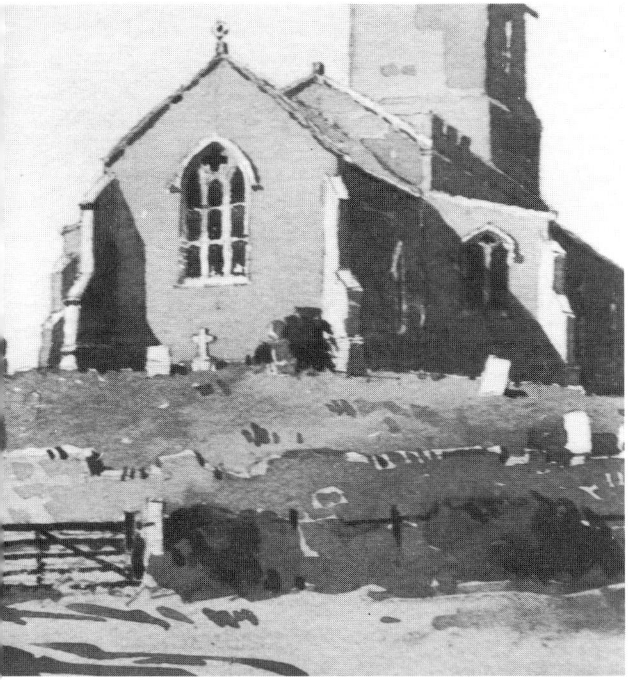

14 WIVETON CHURCH
31cm × 47cm ($12\frac{1}{4}$in. × $18\frac{1}{2}$in.)
Another attractive little church is Wiveton standing, like Morston Church, on a little rise in the ground. The block of trees behind the church was a most valuable feature and I adjusted my position this way and that until I had it to my satisfaction.

Note the flat field in front; some of you, I know, have difficulty with foregrounds especially when there isn't much there. There was a broken down fence on the left and various slight unevennesses in the ground with tufts of grass which could be made the most of, and a few cattle were grazing in the middle distance. The cloud shadows probably helped more than anything to break up the monotony and give distance.

13 Morston Church, detail.

14 Wiveton Church.

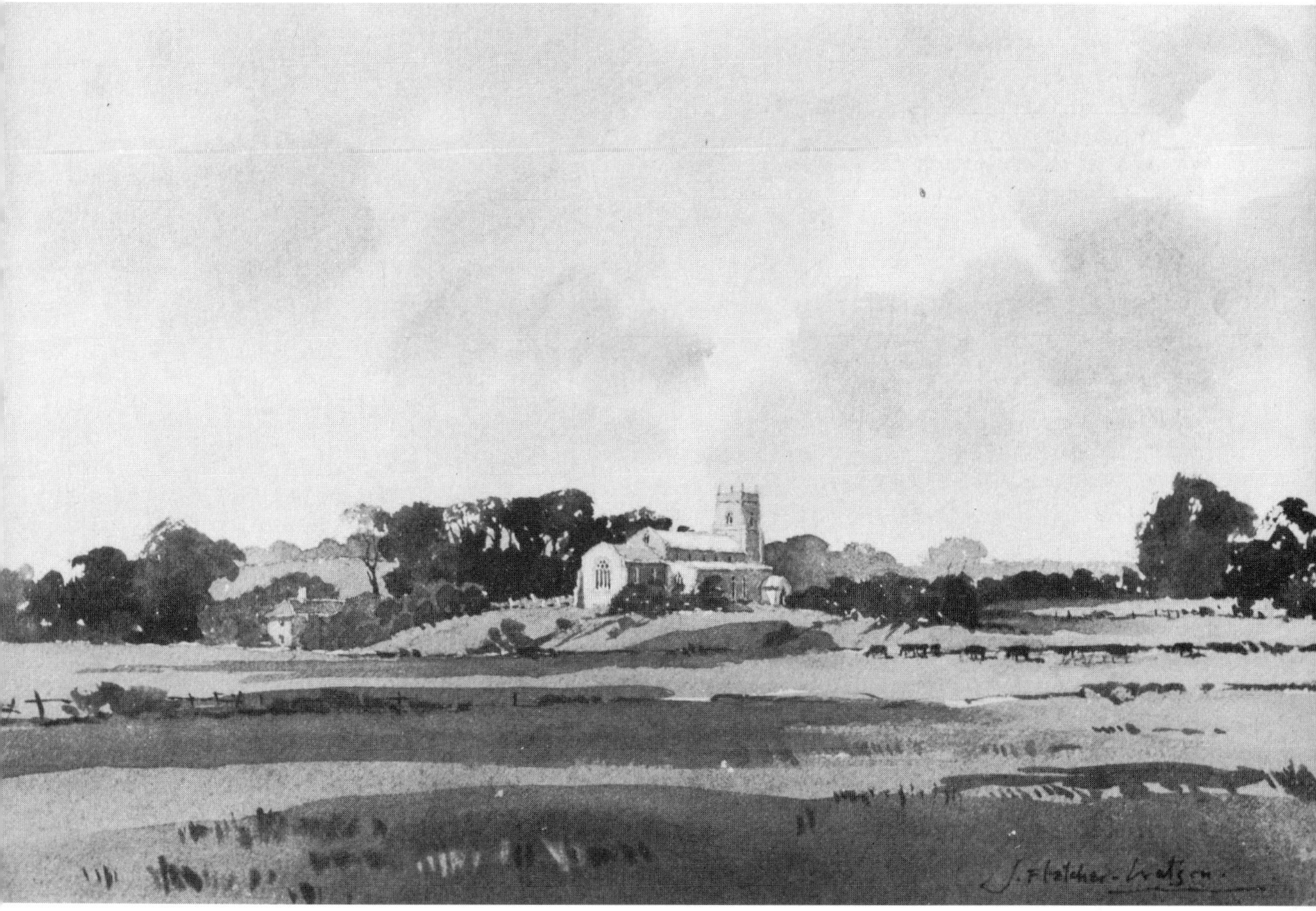

15 LANGHAM

25.5cm × 39cm (10in. × $15\frac{1}{2}$in.)

A pleasing village subject is Langham two miles inland from the sea, and figure 15 shows a view looking down the road with the sea in the distance. It is a good subject and very colourful with the gray flint cottage walls and their steep roofs of pink pantiles. The group of dark trees on the left is a helpful feature in the composition. There are many villages along this part of the Norfolk coast and a large choice of subject awaits the visiting painter.

16 FARM AT SHARRINGTON

24cm × 35.5cm ($9\frac{1}{2}$in. × 14in.)

Another subject with buildings is seen at figure 16. Here we have a red brick farmhouse and brick barns round it, and a glimpse on the right of the village church. What more charming subject could one want.

17 SHERINGHAM HALL

24cm × 35.5cm ($9\frac{1}{2}$in. × 14in.)

This picture was a commission by a cousin of the owner of Sheringham Hall, Thomas Upcher. The house is delightfully sited against a tree covered hill, mostly oak trees, and this gives a lovely background to the house as well as good protection from cold north-east winds.

The walls are of mellow gray brick and the roof is a green-gray slate often used in some of the larger houses of Norfolk. It is late Georgian and very interesting architecturally as it was designed for Abbot Upcher by the great landscape architect, Humphrey Repton. The building was started in 1812.

Careful drawing was necessary for the house itself, and for this type of picture one has to study the time of day so as to have the shadows in an interesting position to show off the building.

18 MALTHOUSE BROAD

26.5cm × 37cm ($10\frac{1}{2}$in. × $14\frac{1}{2}$in.)

I hired a rowing boat to paint this picture as I wanted to get to the other side of this broad and look back at the church.

It was a beautiful cloudy day with areas of blue and a lovely light that one so often gets in Norfolk. This was a typical Norfolk broad surrounded by trees, but of course there are some big broads like Hickling which have very few trees and are surrounded by reeds, giving lovely wide open spaces.

16 Farm at Sharrington.

17 Sheringham Hall.

15 Langham.

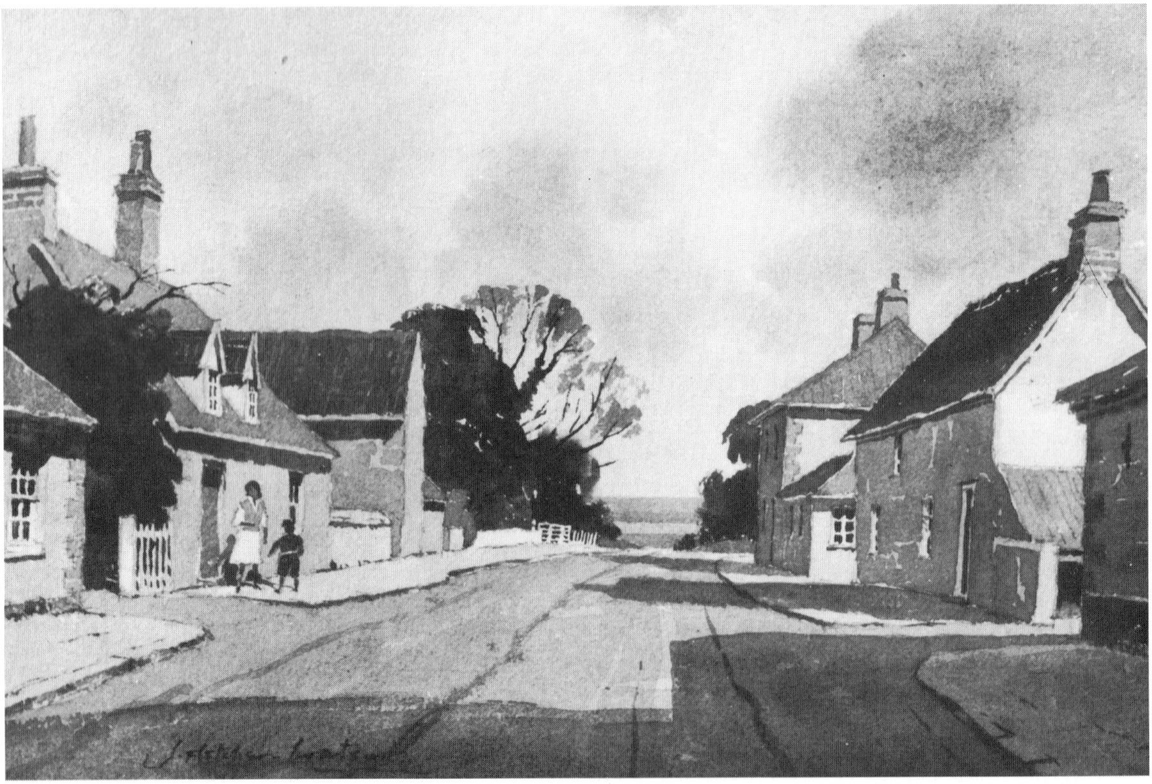

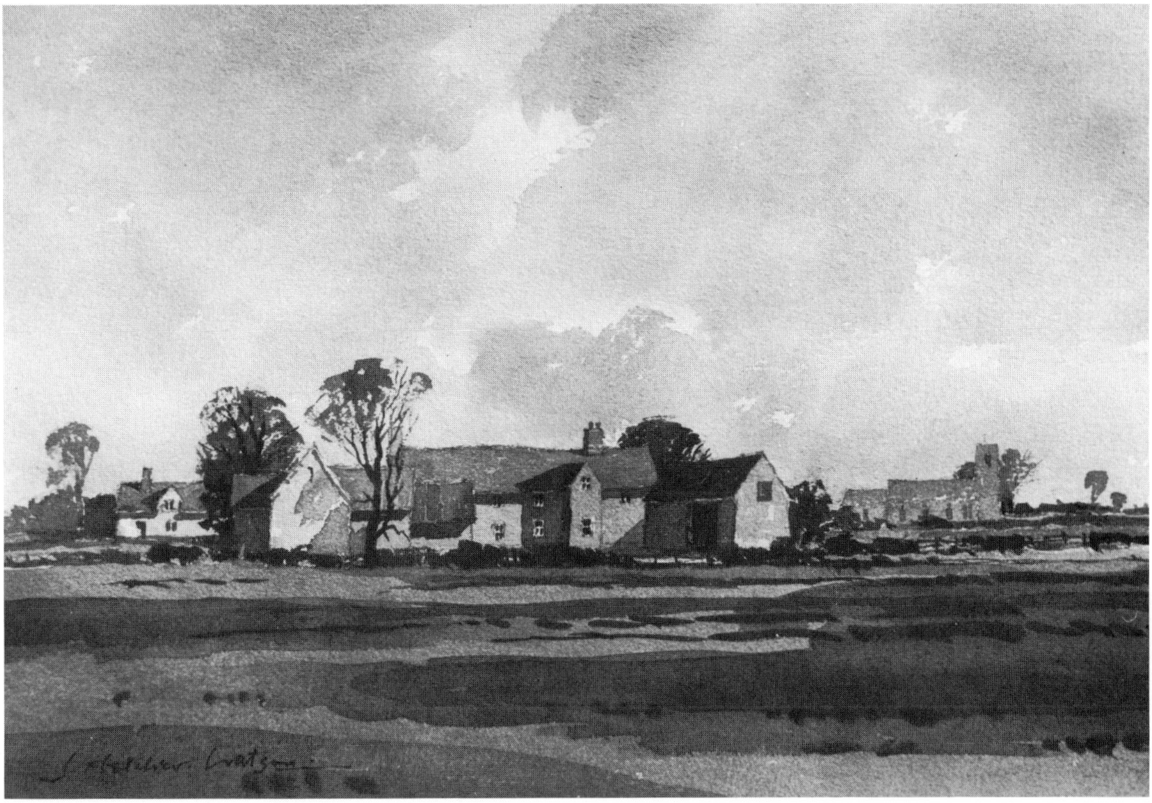
J. Fletcher-Watson

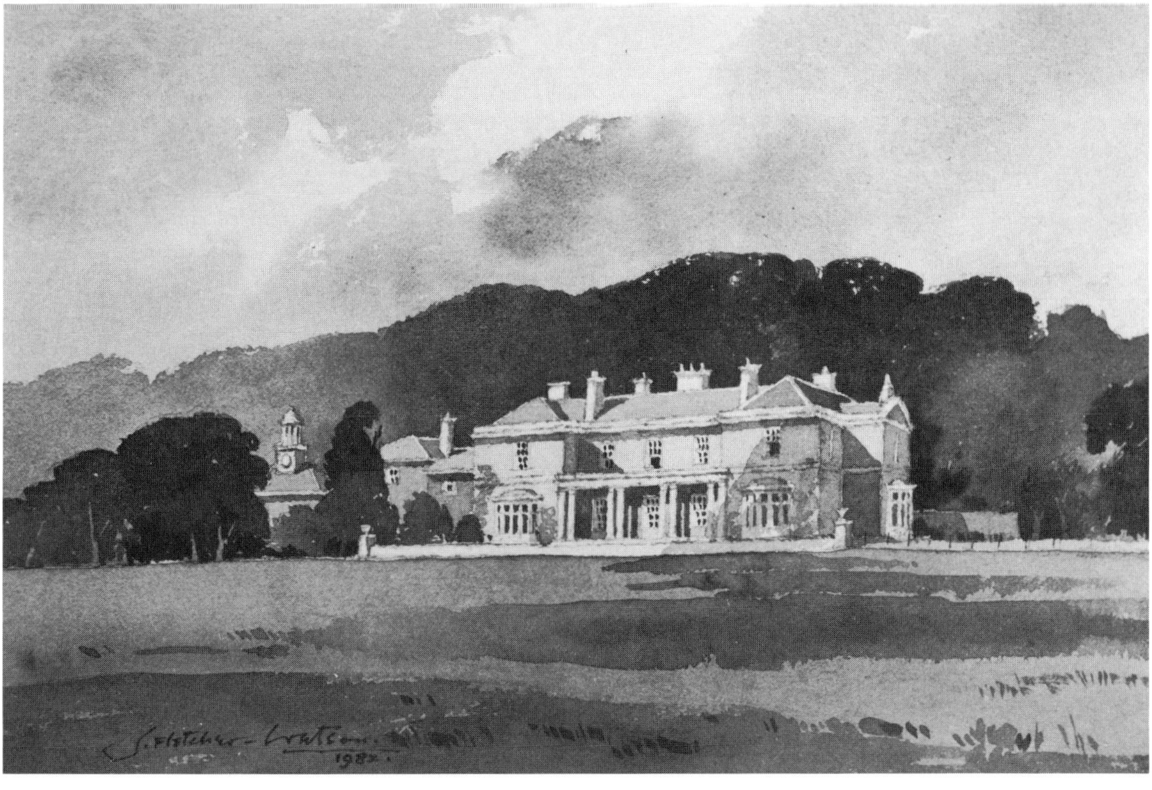
J. Fletcher-Watson

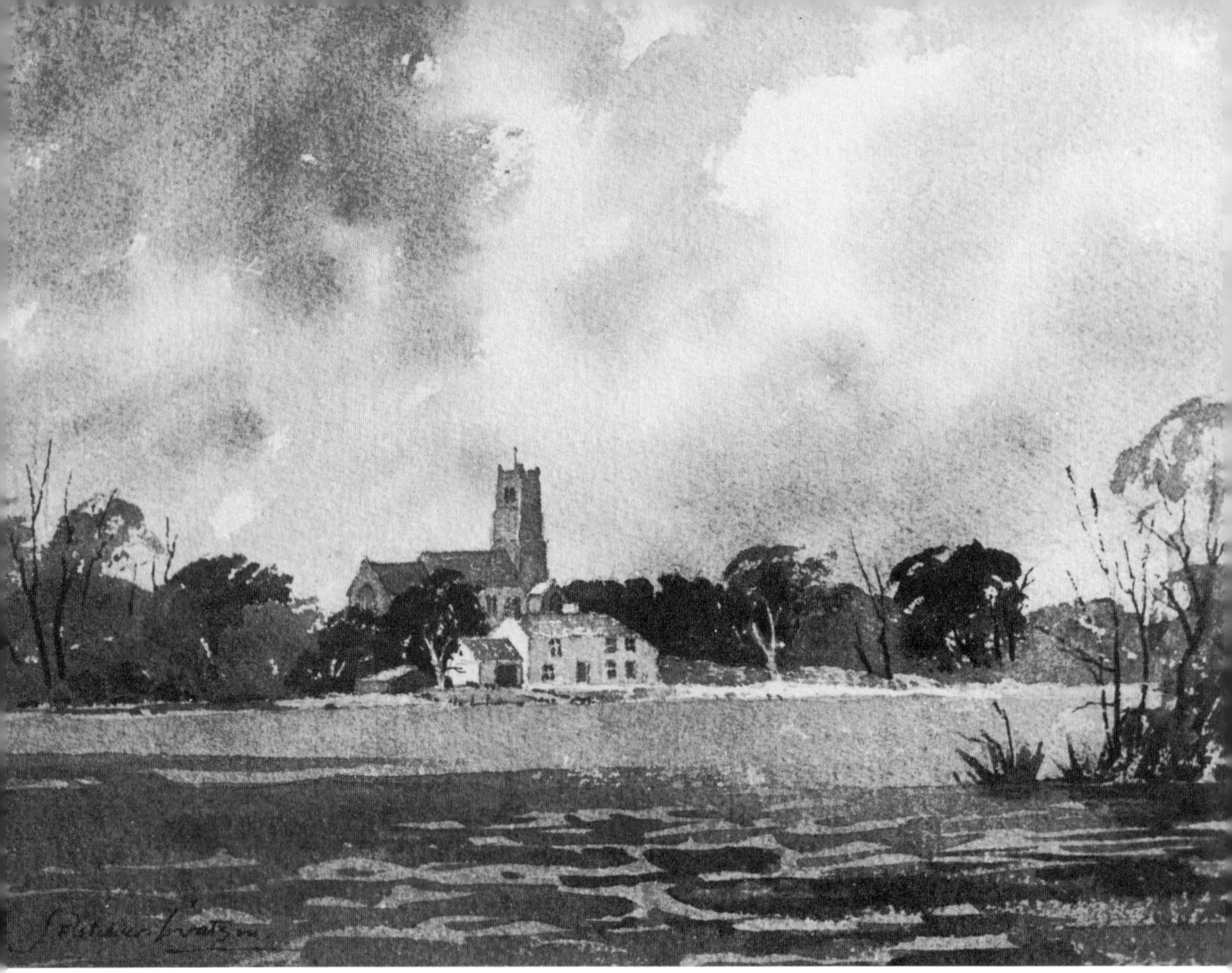

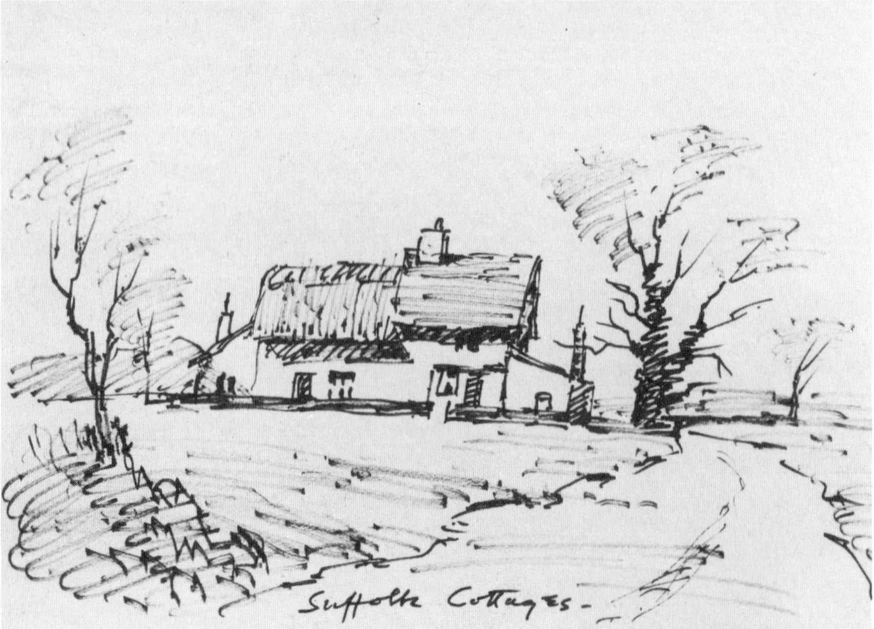

18 Malthouse Broad.

19 Suffolk cottages, preliminary sketch.

20 Suffolk cottages, finished picture.

In this view the church dominated the picture as it was on a little hill as is so often the case. This is Ranworth church and it is famous for its very fine painted wood screen of about the fifteenth century. The Broads district of east Norfolk is a place where one could easily spend a couple of weeks painting and find an abundance of subjects of river, broad, old windmills and bridges.

If you want to paint buildings, Norwich is a lovely city, full of old streets and churches, and the cathedral itself is very paintable. I have spent many sketching days in Norwich.

19 SUFFOLK COTTAGES,
preliminary sketch. 18cm × 25.5cm (7in. × 10in.)
For my last picture in this chapter I have gone just over the Norfolk border near Diss into Suffolk. I felt the need to do a rough felt-pen sketch first (19), in order to get the hang of the grouping of road, cottages and trees. Just a quick sketch in about five minutes is all one wanted, and I immediately felt a watercolour was worth while.

20 SUFFOLK COTTAGES,
finished picture. 31cm × 47cm ($12\frac{1}{4}$in. × $18\frac{1}{2}$in.)
Houses and cottages in Suffolk, and in south Norfolk for that matter, often have plastered walls painted white or very pale pink. A lot of the early cottages were built with clay-lump walls which had to be thickly plastered to keep out the wet. They were surprisingly strong and many of them have lasted for hundreds of years.

This pair of farm cottages was painted white which glistened in the sun; the left-hand one had a steep thatched roof and the right-hand one had dark red mellow plain tiles. It was a stunningly attractive pair with the lean-to wash-houses and tall, thin chimneys at each end.

The sun's position was just right for shadows and a lovely big shadow was cast from the deeply overhanging eaves of the thatched cottage. The big tree on the right with ivy creepers was a nice feature with its bare branches, the time of year being early April.

I am including this picture to help those who are looking for places to go painting and to whet their appetites, I hope, for visiting Suffolk. A tour of the county, which is full of the most attractive paintable villages, is to be highly recommended.

When I am painting Norfolk my mind is never far from the Norwich School of painters, 1803 to 1840, and John Sell Cotman who was the leading water-colourist of the school. At the Norwich Castle Museum a wonderful collection of the works of Cotman, Crome, Thirtle, Bright and Middleton and many others can be seen. When I visit Norfolk I try and find time to look in at the Museum and receive a great wave of inspiration.

Norfolk is a unique area of England where the land, the sea and the sky come together in a perfect unity, and always one is conscious of the great sky above. It is certainly a place where one can learn to paint skies if nothing else.

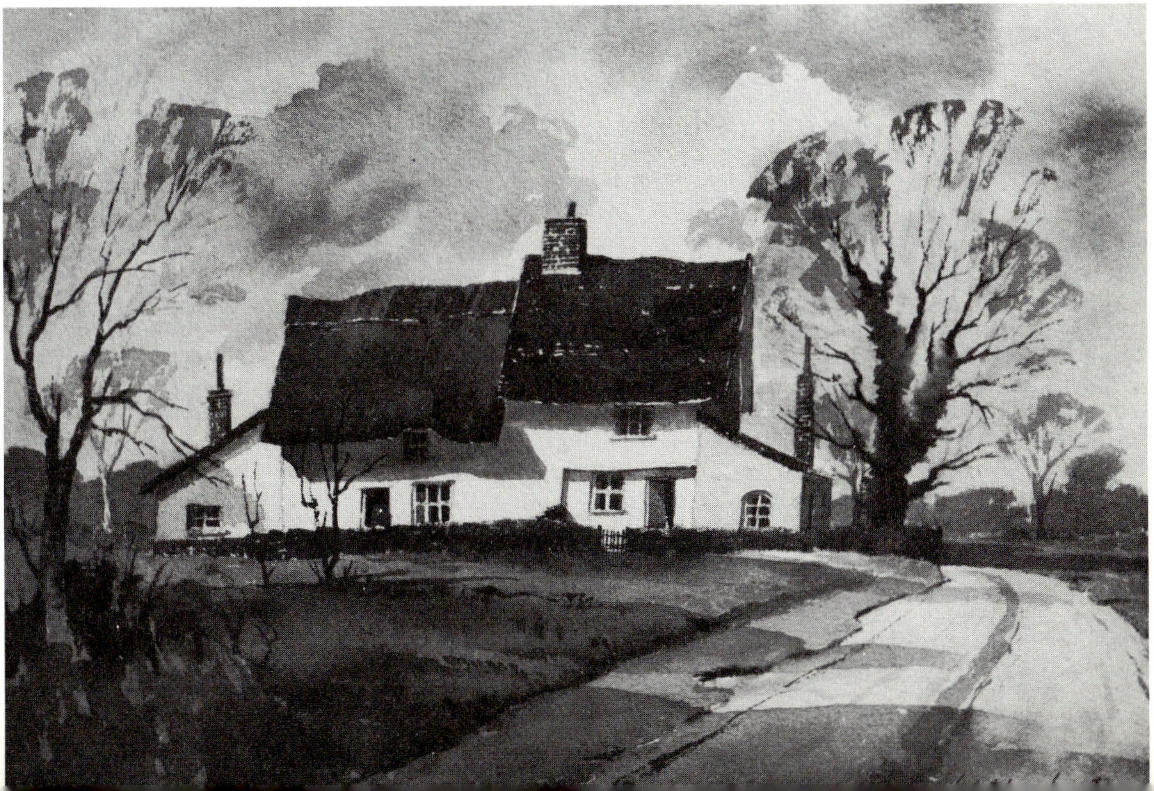

2 Painting in the Lake District

Sometimes artist friends ask me which is my favourite part of the British Isles to paint. This is always a difficult question because I have so many favourites, but the Lake District is certainly very high on the list. Mountainous country makes a lovely contrast with flatter districts like Norfolk, and one has an entirely different choice of subject available, especially when in addition to mountains there is the attraction of water.

I will start with a *simple* subject, figure **21 Grange Bridge, Borrowdale** (31.5cm × 42.5cm ($12\frac{1}{2}$in. × $18\frac{3}{4}$in.). As a matter of fact a simple subject is not all that easy to find in Cumbria and that is where the real artist comes into it; we have to learn to *simplify* our subjects, leave out detail and reduce the picture to *essentials* only.

I was staying in Borrowdale in early November, a wonderful time of year for colour, and a wonderful part of the Lake District with a tremendous choice of subjects. The trees that year were still retaining their leaves with varied brown colours.

All we have here is a bridge, a distant mountain and a closer mountain on the right, a group of trees and the river with a shingle beach in the foreground. What could be simpler! Of course half the battle is putting things in their right place on the paper; in other words the *composition*.

It was a sunny day and not too cold for November. There is a second arch to this bridge crossing the River Derwent, just out of the picture to the right, and I was virtually sitting on an island with the river running each side of me.

I decided on a piece of Arches paper, 'Not' surface, and I drew in the scene very lightly with a 2B pencil. By keeping the bridge to the left I could get in a bit of the foot of the right-hand dark mountain; this helped the balance and was going to show up the gray wall too. One wants to think ahead about such things as *darks* showing up *light* objects. Similarly, the block of trees behind the bridge was a great help in showing up the bridge and was one of the first things I noticed as being the most important feature in the picture.

Having drawn the bridge I pencilled in the far bank of the river on the left and also where you could see it through the arch: it was important to get this far line correct. Then came the near side line of the river and this was important too, especially the bit of jutting out beach.

Then I marked lightly the outline of the tree group beyond the bridge and the right-hand steep slope of the mountain which was covered with dark trees. I did *not* attempt to pencil in the background mountain as I wanted this to be washed in with pure watercolour.

I now decided that a little penwork would be a good idea and I mixed up a dark brown with Burnt Umber and Payne's Gray giving a sepia tone. With a fairly thick nib to my pen, I drew in the outline of the brige, the small grass bank at the right side of the bridge and also the edges of the river on both sides. I put in a touch of penwork on the foreground shingle and the arch stones of the bridge.

This penwork was done in quick strokes of the pen, not too carefully but in a sketchy manner, varying the thickness of the line with different pressure. One doesn't want to make a picture too 'careful' or it will become photographic and loose the feeling of being a spontaneous work of art.

Now I could get on with the painting. I will not describe this in detail but just mention the colouring briefly. It was a very nice cloudy blue sky and this was dealt with first, and I continued a gray wash down from the sky area over everything including the shingle beach, which was a light gray.

When this had dried I painted in the background mountain; the right-hand half of the range was light blue-gray but the left end was quite dark and I used strong Payne's Gray for this. I let the ends of this mountain run into clear water so as to avoid a hard edge where I should later be painting brown trees.

Next I painted the grass banks to the left of the bridge and seen *through* the bridge and the bank to the right of the arch, in a light yellow-green colour.

Now came the exciting part, the painting of the tree group behind the bridge. With a No. 7 brush and various mixtures of Burnt Sienna, Burnt Umber and touches of Payne's Gray, the tree group was put in. I also used a No. 5 brush with dry colour to make quick downward strokes for the trees that had lost most of their leaves. Trunks and branches were drawn in with a very small brush later. At the same time I painted the

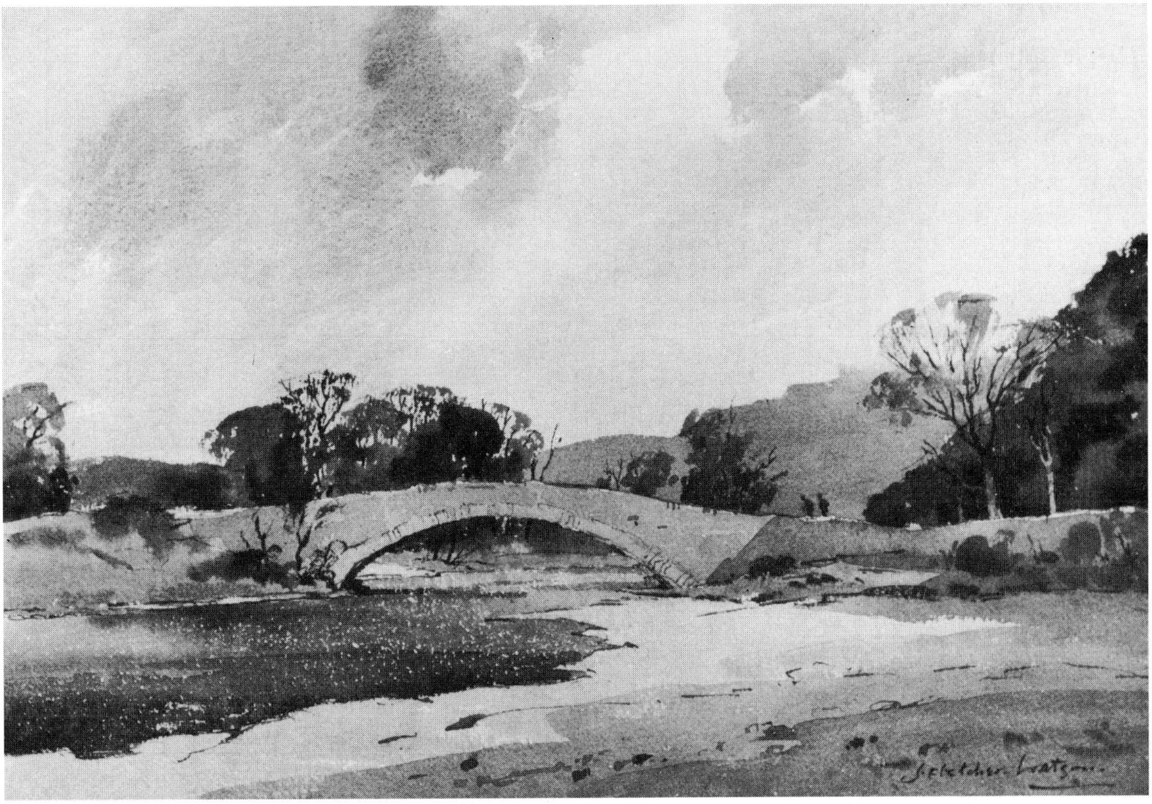

trees showing under the arch. Careful brush-work of course had to be used on the trees when marking out the shape of the bridge.

Next followed the other trees and shrubs along the bridge line and then the very dark trees on the slope of the right-hand mountain.

Now I could paint in the river with Payne's Gray. The light was playing funny tricks with cloud shadows. Sometimes the river was a very light tone and the shingle shore was very dark, and the next minute the water was extremely dark and the shingle almost white. I preferred the latter arrangement. The water had a sparkle owing to its movement and ripple and, by moving the brush quickly across the paper, little bits of paper texture showed up untouched by the dark colour; this is called 'dragged brush-work' and can be very useful.

Final items were dealt with, such as the bushes and grass clumps of the river banks and the foreground cloud shadows and a diagonal shadow on the wall of the bridge, and the picture was finished. You will note that all the washes are *flat* washes with very little small brush-work dabbing at trees or stonework, and only a few indications of stones in the foreground. This restraint is in the Cotman tradition where he used slabs of plain colour and only a very few small touches to indicate texture where necessary.

21 Grange Bridge, Borrowdale.

22 MUNGRISDALE

23.5cm × 35.5cm ($9\frac{1}{4}$in. × 14in.)

Moving now northwards out of Borrowdale to the area around Saddleback, we come to the village of Mungrisdale (22). This is a delightful lesser known corner of the Lake District and my wife and I were lent a cottage, which appears in this picture. We had a week in this place, and it isn't until you actually stay in a district that you manage to find all sorts of out of the way views up side roads and by walking instead of motoring. I will be showing you some other views found near this spot.

I have chosen this view next as it is another comparatively simple subject – a flat field, cottages, trees and a mountain or two. It is the cloudy days that give the Lake District its charm, and the clouds are so often coming down over a mountain which is why I want to give as much help in painting skies as I can. I will not describe the sky painting work in detail here as I want to do that for the picture reproduced in colour later in this chapter. Suffice it to say the clouds were good on this day in November and they never moved far away from the distant mountain in the centre. This had the effect of making the left-hand mountain very clearly defined as no cloud or mist was over it at all.

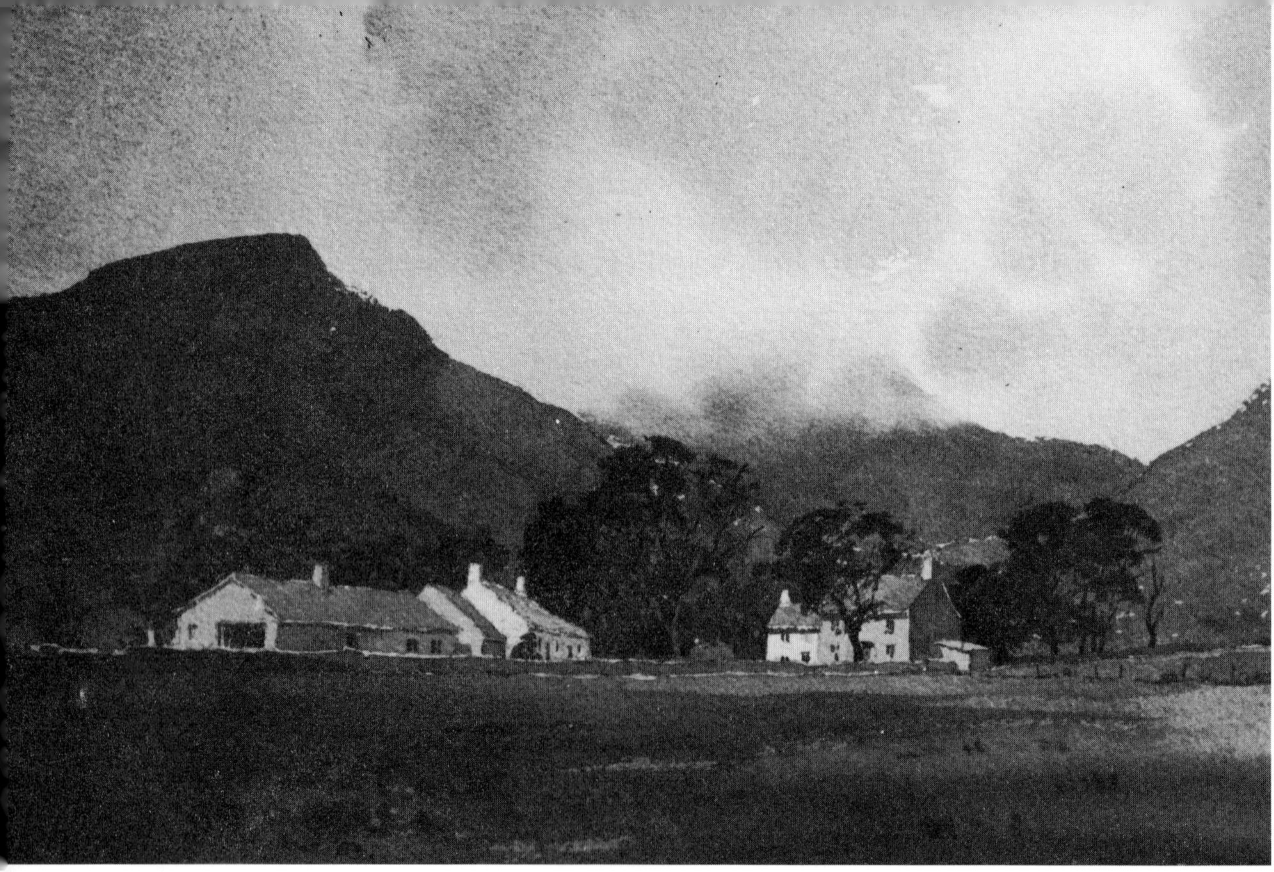

When starting on the picture I drew the cottages carefully and only touched in the left-hand mountain very lightly, and the other background mountains were not pencilled in at all. The less you draw mountains with a pencil, the more effectively you can handle them with the brush only.

The tree groups were perfect in this picture, lovely colours of browns and yellows, and most of the leaves were still on. While painting such a subject it is necessary to leave the buildings the dead white of the paper by painting carefully round them. Then you come back to them near the end of painting and put on light gray washes on walls and darker gray on roofs as required and finally paint in the windows and doors. The small cottage to the right of centre was very bright and was left completely white.

Before leaving this picture I must tell you the story about the bull which I noticed was grazing in the field every day with a few cows. I managed to find the farmer and I asked if I could sit in the field and whether the bull was quiet. He answered., 'He is quiet, but it is entirely at your own risk'. I had been hoping he would move the bull into another field for the morning, but no such luck.

So I took up my position, with the bull and the cows just out of the picture on the right. The farmer had at least given them some hay to eat at the far end. I was ready to do a quick dash over the stone wall of the Vicarage garden 20 yards to my right, if necessary.

22 Mungrisdale.

It is rather disturbing keeping one's eye on a bull when painting and I noticed him munching away quite happily. But suddenly he stopped eating and lifted his great head and stared right at me; he had only just noticed me sitting quietly with my painting things. At last, after some minutes he put his head down and started eating again. Then he looked up again and he did this three times and I thought he must be coming to investigate this strange intruder. But he suddenly quite slowly walked away after his cows who had just walked through an open gate into another field, and he went out of sight.

I felt better and got on with the painting but I never felt happy, and I am afraid I left the foreground and some of the work on the cottages to finish back at the cottage where we were staying.

23 PACK HORSE BRIDGE, MUNGRISDALE

23.5cm × 35.5cm ($9\frac{1}{4}$in. × 14in.)

In the middle of the village of Mungrisdale there was a perfect little stone bridge (23) over the stream, or *beck* as they are called in Cumbria. I had not got much time as we were shortly to leave for home, so I decided on a quick pencil sketch and a few washes of colour.

I used a light weight hand-made watercolour paper a friend had given me and I had not used this before. It turned out to be delightful to draw on and good for

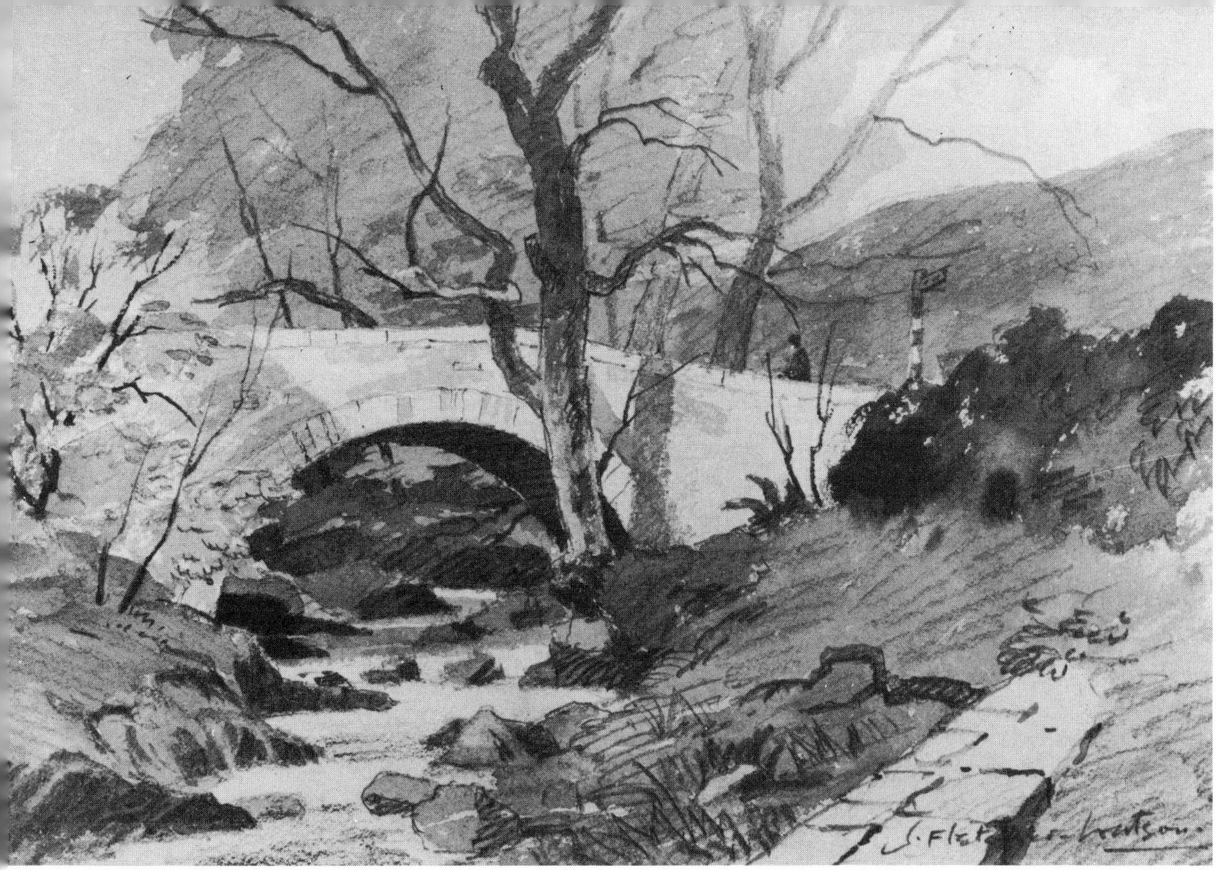

23 Pack horse bridge, Mungrisdale.

paint as well. I used a 4B pencil which 'bit' nicely into the soft paper.

The ash tree against the bridge had lost most of its leaves but the sycamores behind still had theirs in spite of it being November.

This type of subject can make a lovely composition. The beck was surrounded by trees and the broken sunlight filtered through most attractively. The drawing took about half an hour and the painting another twenty minutes.

24 COTTAGE AT MUNGRISDALE

31.5cm × 47.5cm ($12\frac{1}{2}$in. × $18\frac{3}{4}$in.)

Figure 24 is a study of a typical Lakeland cottage; it was just like a doll's house. Built of stone and painted white, the dressed stone round windows and door was painted gray. These stone surrounds are often left natural stone. The road was a dead end which became a track leading up over the fells. Altogether a lovely little corner to paint, this is the sort of subject any beginner can have a go at and learn a lot about painting Lakeland architecture. Note the gray slate roof with not a very big overhang to the eaves, but enough to cast a nice shadow when the sun is at an oblique angle. The eaves' shadow dips down into the window recesses which gives depth. Also note the door shadow and the chimney stack shadow on the roof.

The big shadow across the road is cast by a tree on the left, out of the picture, and is helpful in giving depth to the picture. Note how this shadow slopes downwards on the grass verge and then levels out on the road giving form to the grass area. I only mention these elementary items for beginners in watercolour painting.

25 SKELGILL FARM, NEAR DERWENT WATER

31.5cm × 47.5cm ($12\frac{1}{2}$in. × $18\frac{3}{4}$in.)

Back now a little way south near Derwent Water but still in November, I found a perfect gem of a subject: a lovely farmhouse and outbuildings on a steeply sloping hill. The National Trust do not allow farmers to build big modern barns for these farms, which would completely destroy the beautiful scale of the whole group. Many farms in other parts of the country have been so ruined, alas.

There were various view-points one could choose and I wanted to make a quick preliminary sketch to decide just where to sit.

Figure 26 (18cm × 25.5cm (7in. × 10in.)) shows the sketch made in black felt pen very quickly and roughly but enough to tell me what I wanted to know. The grouping was excellent and the far mountain perfect as a back-drop. This sketch took about ten minutes. In addition to felt pen I put in a few strokes with the Conte crayon on the foreground.

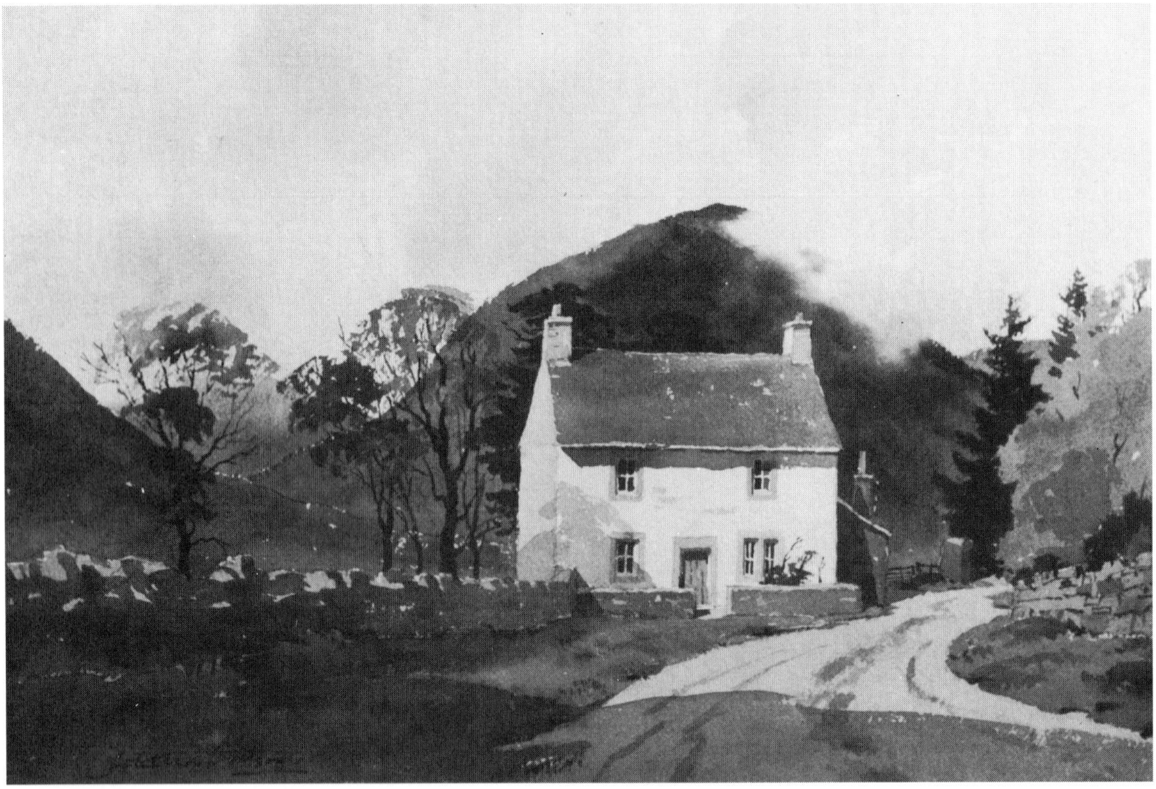

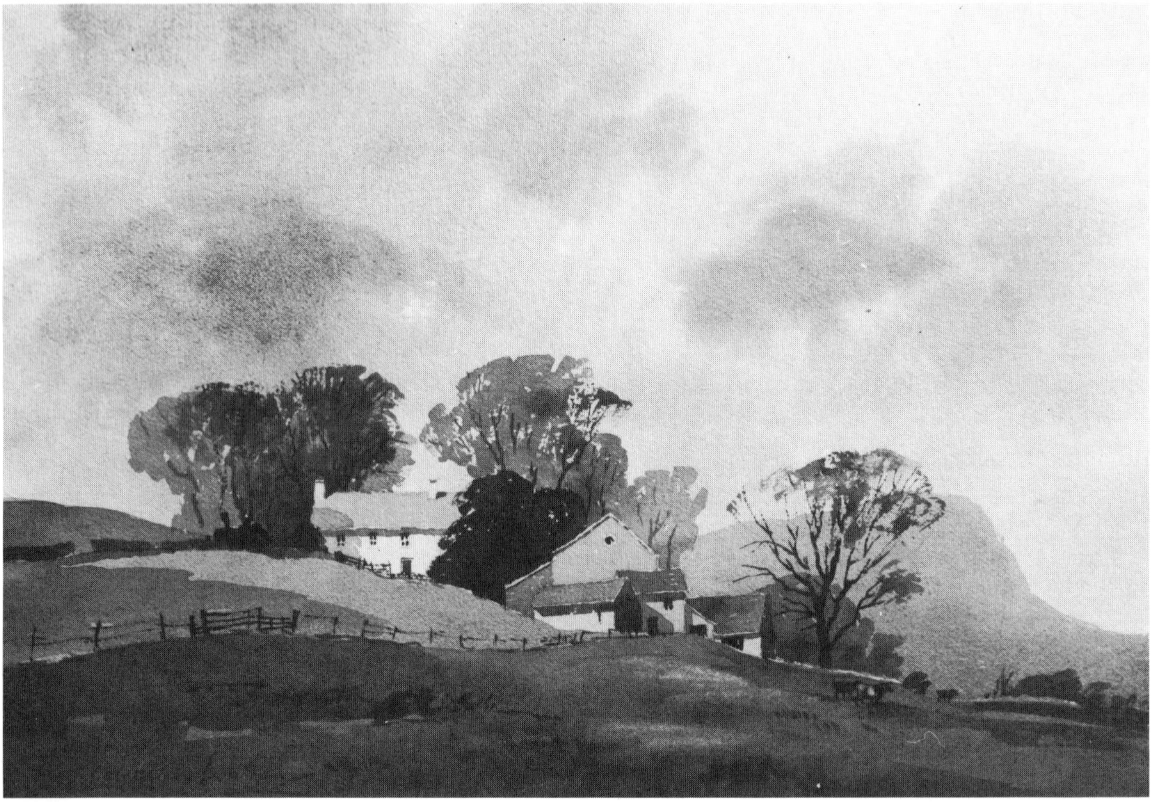

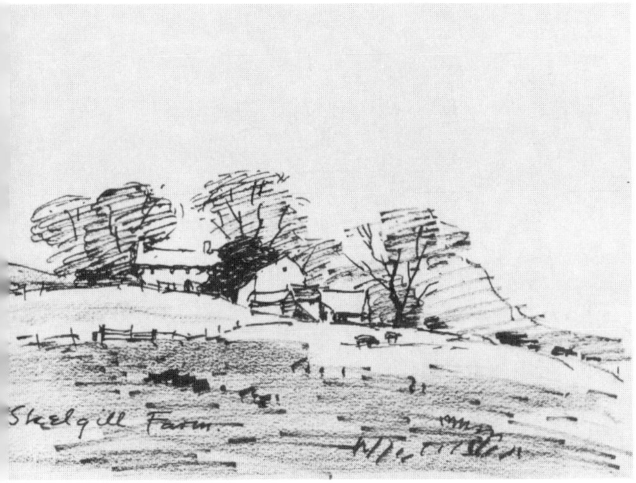

24 Cottage at Mungrisdale.

25 Skelgill farm, near Derwent Water.

26 Skelgill farm, preliminary sketch.

27 Skelgill farm, detail.

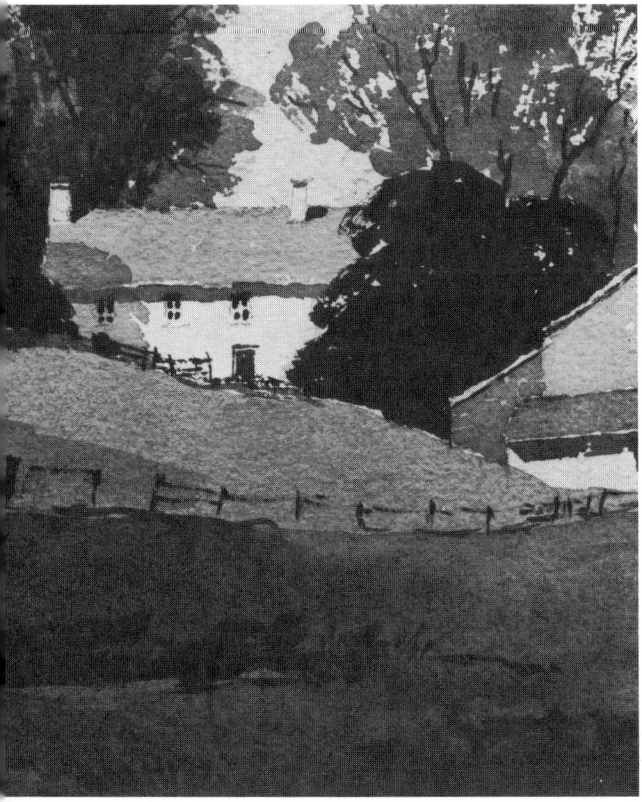

The sky on this day was a really strong one with dark gray moving clouds and bright glimpses of white and blue. The whole colouring of the scene was lit up brilliantly with bright incidents and dark mellow areas. I wish I could show you this illustration in colour but unfortunately these have to be limited.

The composition was about as perfect as you can get. The farmhouse was that long low proportion so prevalent in the Lakes, and it had been recently re-painted white so it stood out well. The post and wire fence led the eye into the picture and was a most valuable feature. The trees were still hanging onto their autumn leaves, and the one on the right was a nice mixture of leaves and bare branches where leaves had blown off.

The foreground field was a rich green mixture of Raw Sienna and Payne's Gray and the background mountain was French Ultramarine and Light Red.

Figure 27 shows a detail and you can see the treatment of the farmhouse with its strong eaves shadow and less strong shadow cast by the trees. The *very dark* evergreen yew tree group contrasting with the white house was painted with a strong mixture of Burnt Umber and Winsor Blue, which gives a very rich dark green. This dark tree area gave the tonal key to the whole picture.

28 FARM NEAR MUNGRISDALE
31.5cm × 47.5cm ($12\frac{1}{2}$in. × $18\frac{3}{4}$in.)
Here is another type of farm group, set on fairly level ground but with a lovely mountain back-drop. It is looking west towards Keswick with Saddleback beginning to rise up on the right. Note the ingredients for a good picture. **1** The rough track leading up to the farm which gives good perspective and recession. **2** The farmhouse and barns placed just to the right of centre. **3** The trees behind the farm giving a good *vertical* foil for **4** the horizontal treatment of woods to the left and the lower mountain ranges. **5** The change of direction with the steep mountain slope on the right suggesting giddy heights out of the picture. **6** The dark barn opening and shadows from buildings and the white gable of the farmhouse giving crispness and a focal point to the picture.

These are the sort of features to look for when painting in Cumbria. There is a magic about this part of England that cannot be found anywhere else. These lovely farms are unique and so also are the lakes themselves, which I am coming to later.

29 COUNTRY ROAD NEAR WATERMILLOCK
31.5cm × 47.5cm ($12\frac{1}{2}$in. × $18\frac{3}{4}$in.)
I would like to show you one or two pictures where roads play a part. The country road shown at figure 29 is about two miles north-west of Watermillock and there

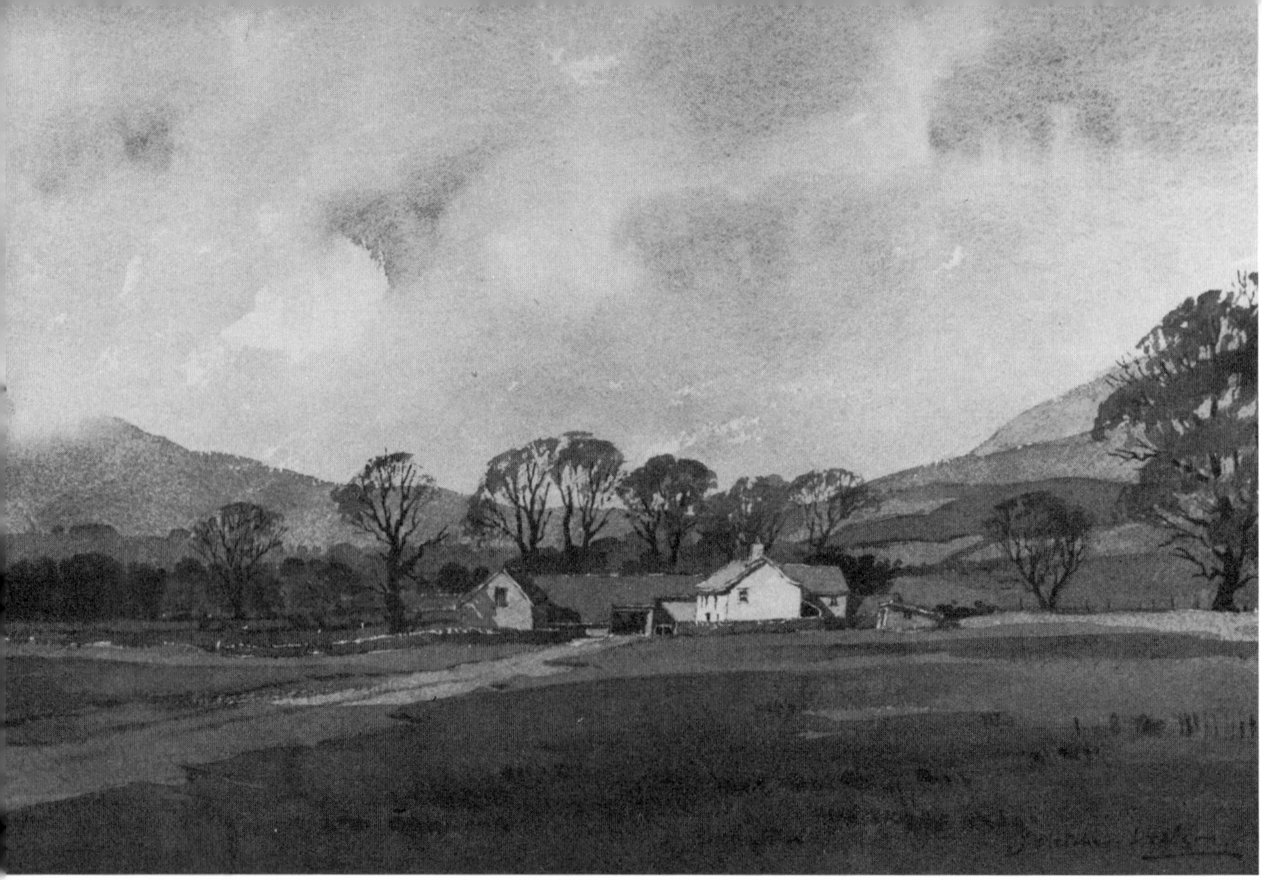

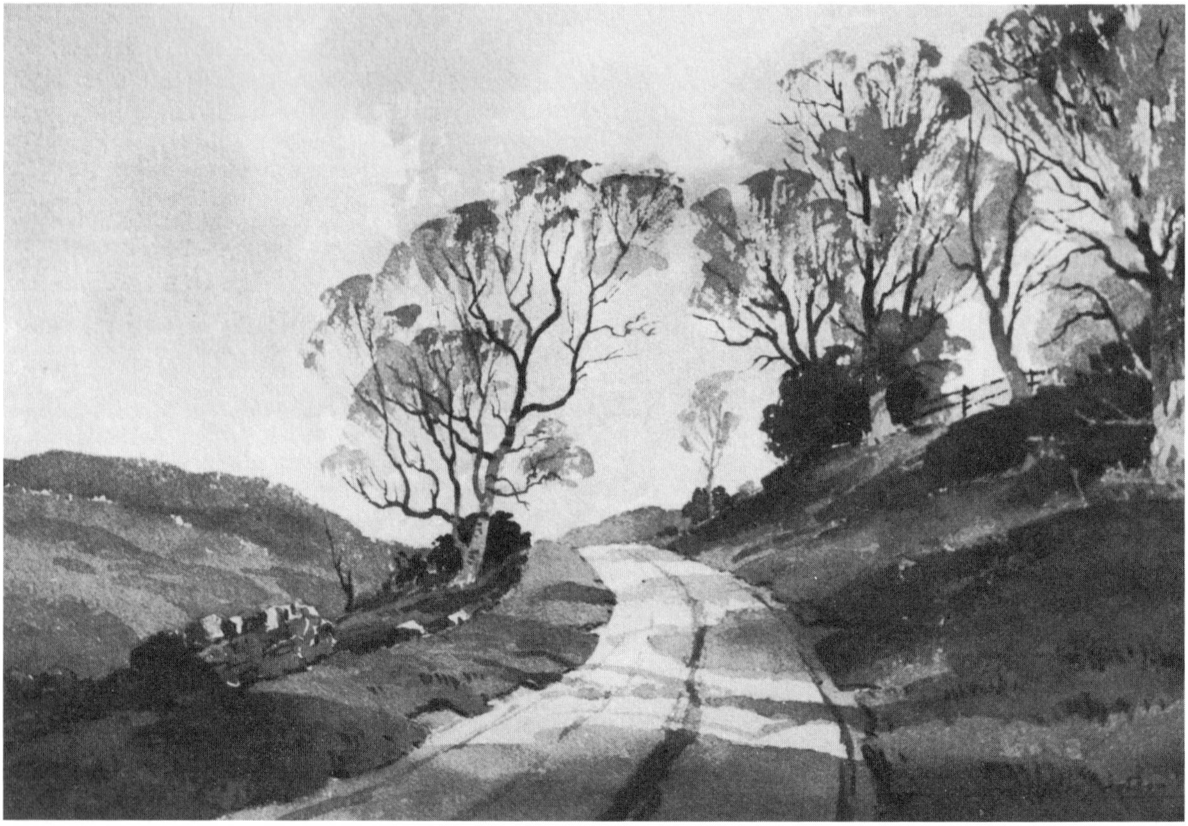

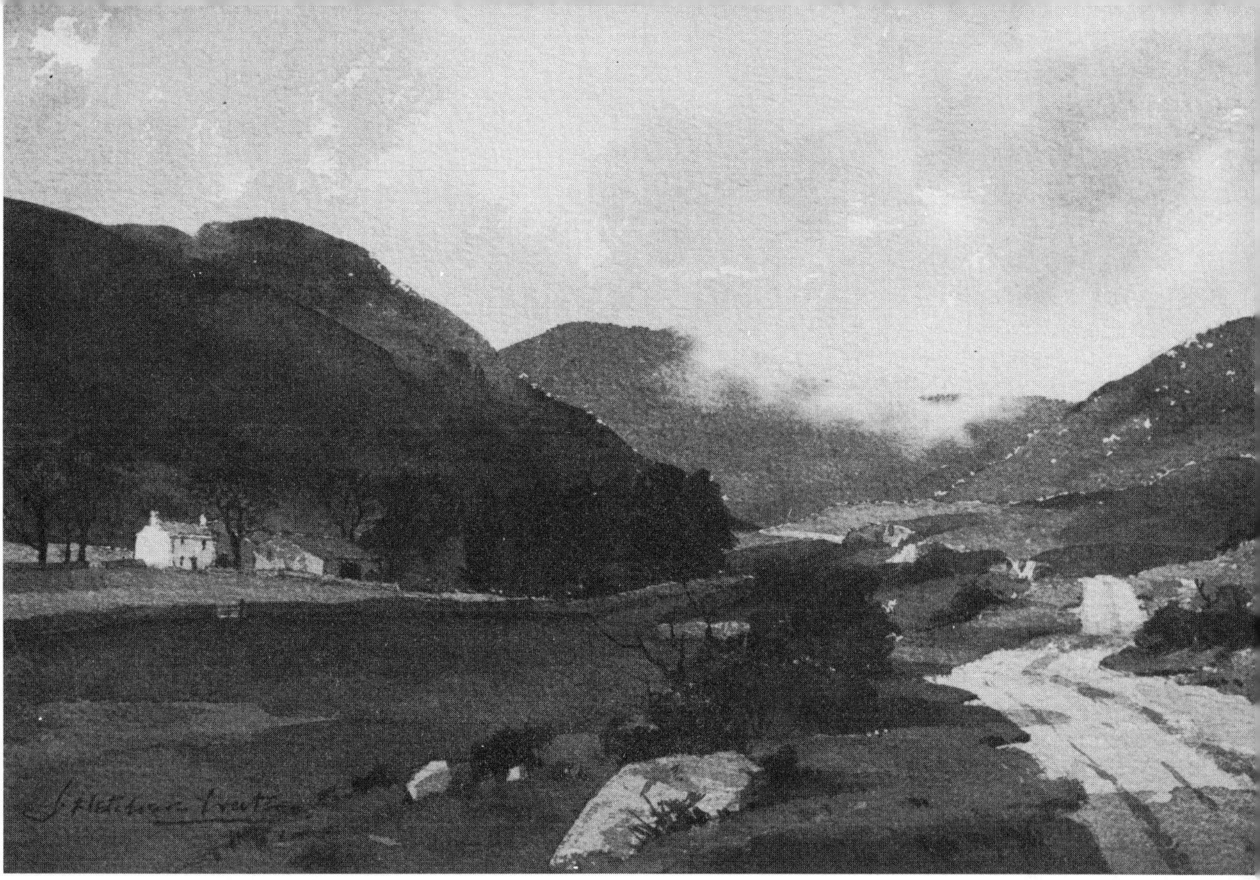

28 Farm near Mungrisdale.

29 Country road near Watermillock.

30 Mosedale, looking north.

are several little narrow roads around here which make you feel you are getting lost in an unfrequented part; it is rather fascinating and there are many subjects of a simple nature here. I was trundling along slowly in the car in April and this view caught my eye immediately, and I pulled up onto the grass verge and decided this was 'it' – a perfect little subject. It was extremely cold so I decided to paint from inside the car. I have fixed up an arrangement in my car whereby I can erect a wooden shelf between the two front seats. This will hold my paint-box and water jar and I sit in the passenger seat, which is pushed well back, and I have plenty of room for my painting board. My brushes are laid out on an old towel on the driver's seat beside me. I do like the feeling that I have a studio on wheels always available for cold weather so I can go on painting right through the winter if necessary.

The uphill road was an attractive feature making one wonder what was round the corner over the hill. The tree groups were good and one can always adjust tree positions a little if necessary to make the grouping just right. Note the dark bush behind the left-hand tree showing up the light colour of the trunk. This happened to some of the right-hand trees too; you always want to make the best of it when you find darks can show up lights.

I had had pleasant sunshine while doing this painting and when finished I went for a walk to warm up. To my amazement a sudden snow-storm and strong wind of some intensity developed; it only lasted about half and hour but everything was covered in white and the scene completely transformed. It was a good object lesson in striking while the iron is hot when you find a subject, and not messing about looking for a better view!

30 MOSEDALE, LOOKING NORTH

24cm × 35.5cm ($9\frac{1}{2}$in. × 14in.)

Here is another picture with a road which I painted one late November morning. The clouds were hanging over distant hills and it was an attractive little view with a dark tree group, a farmhouse and the delightful twisting old narrow road with grass down the middle in places. There is a wildness and loneliness about this northern part of Cumbria above Mungrisdale and never a car nor a person came in sight. One had got the country to oneself. I expect it is different in the height of the summer season when so many crowds come to the Lakes, but perhaps they don't explore this out of the way part. You will find it most satisfying to make a

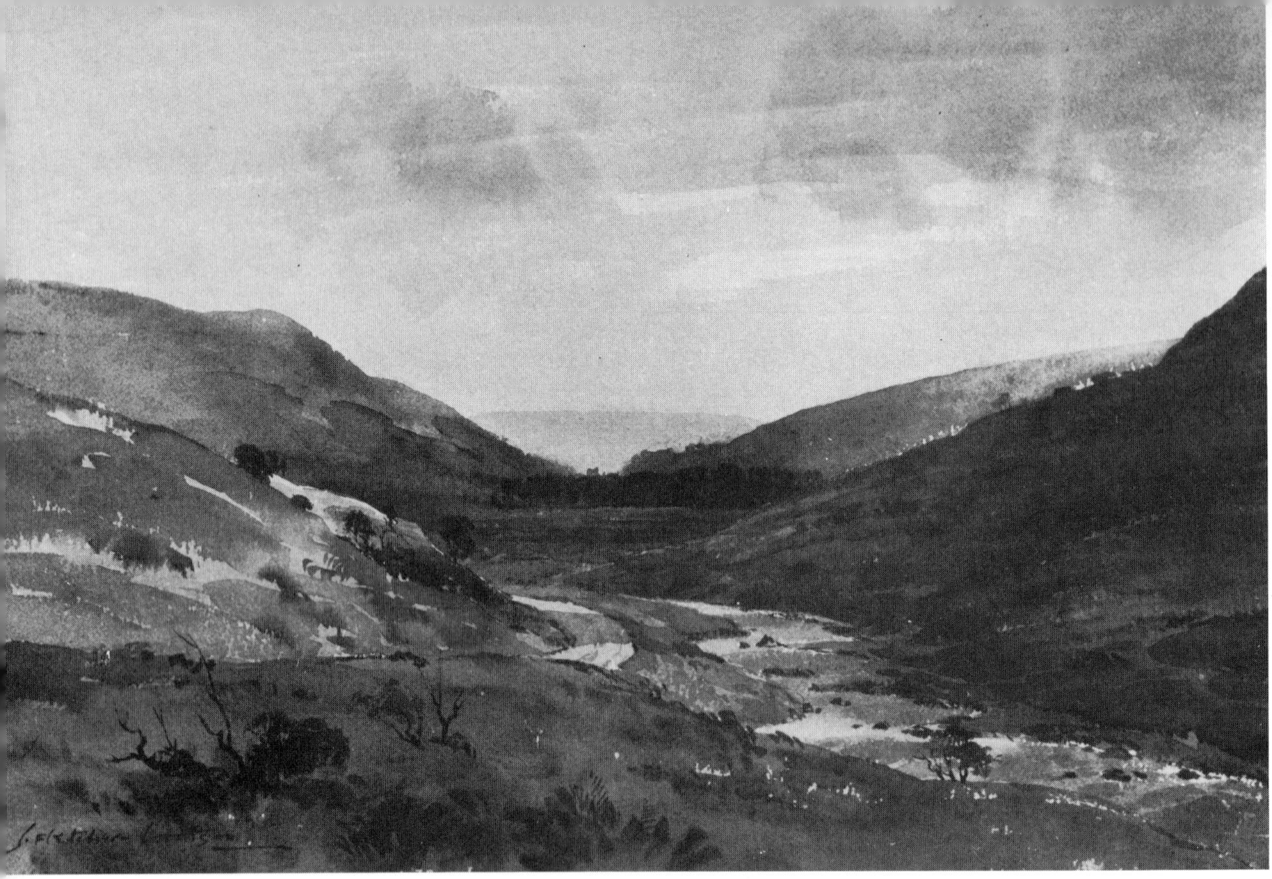

picture with a road disappearing into the distance: it adds a great feeling of depth.

By the time I had finished painting it was well into the afternoon and we took the dog for a walk up this lovely valley, one of the few occasions I had taken our dog with me on a painting trip. It was getting late as we turned the car to go home down the valley, and as we proceeded I was suddenly struck with the much better view looking back with the river and distant hills. The light was beginning to go but it was a glorious evening light and the sky had changed. I felt I must do a painting *immediately* so I set to work at full speed before the light completely went. The result was the next picture.

31 MOSEDALE, LOOKING SOUTH, AND CALDEW RIVER

There was not much road showing in the view I had chosen which was just as well as the river made the main feature. It was a lovely view and the colouring quite out of this world with the evening light. There was rich brown and red bracken in the foreground and brownish-green on the hills as they went away, with finally a dark brown wood in the distance. Beyond that a misty blue mountain far away. I was painting fast against the clock, and the picture had a rather rough look which didn't do it any harm as there was no time to fiddle with it or do unnecessary detail.

31 Mosedale, looking south, and Caldew River.

32 THE ROAD TO SEATHWAITE

31.5cm × 47.5cm ($12\frac{1}{2}$in. × $18\frac{3}{4}$in.)

Back to Borrowdale again and still in November and it rained gently all day! It was no good looking for distant views and I found the road to Seathwaite was full of fascinating close-up subjects where the rain did not obscure anything. One had of course to paint from the car but this is what I like about the Lake District, the weather need never stop you from painting.

On this gray day I decided to use De Wint paper, a buff coloured rough paper. It is not as thick as I would like and it cockles when wet. It really needs to be stretched but I had not done this. Some years ago they stopped making De Wint paper and then recently they re-started, and I regret to say the new is not *nearly* so good as the old paper. Of course the really good stuff was David Cox paper but they stopped making that a long time ago, very sadly, and I don't expect many people can remember it.

I quickly pencilled in the road and the top line of the banks each side of the road and a line or two indicating the trees on the right, but nothing else. One wanted to do this painting with the brush only.

Most of the sky was left the natural colour of the paper, but I damped it all with clear water and washed in the gray cloud formation in a light gray tone. I then painted the background mountain in a stronger blue-gray, letting it run into the sky in places where cloud was overhanging. I next washed in the banks of field and grass verges each side of the road. These were mostly green but had several areas of Burnt Umber and Burnt Sienna bracken. Then came the trees which were light blue-brown for the distant ones where they were getting lost in the misty rain, and stronger colours of brown, red, yellow and an occasional touch of green for the nearer trees on the right. It made a mellow tapestry-like picture which was well worth doing.

After the usual picnic lunch supplied by a very excellent guest-house at Seatoller, I turned the car round and drove back a few hundred yards and came to a bend in the road with a most inviting group of trees as shown in the next picture.

33 AUTUMN TREES, BORROWDALE

31.5cm × 47.5cm ($12\frac{1}{2}$in. × $18\frac{3}{4}$in.)

It was still raining but the colour of these great trees was a marvellously strong Burnt Umber with touches of Burnt Sienna in places.

I used Arches paper this time with 'Not' surface and after placing a gray sky I painted distant trees and hedges with the paper still damp. I had pencilled in the road line and I next painted the banks which were mainly yellow on the left, using Raw Sienna, and running into the top of the bank strong Burnt Sienna for the bracken. The right bank had green and brown mixed with the yellow.

The technique for the two big trees was to use two brushes and have lots of colour ready mixed in the paint palettes. A very dark brown for trunks and branches and the light brown for foliage. With a No. 7 brush I started with the big trunk at its base and changed to a No. 9 and sometimes a No. 12 for the foliage. With both colours always wet, one ran into the other a little giving a suitable soft edge. For the higher branches which were thinner I changed to a No. 3 brush.

This was a painting that did not require much in the way of finishing touches or strengthening up of certain features. One simply made the statement fairly boldly and left it without any fuss.

The final painting consisted of marking the dark edges of the road and some gray tones on the road surface and putting in the right-hand timber fence and small sapling.

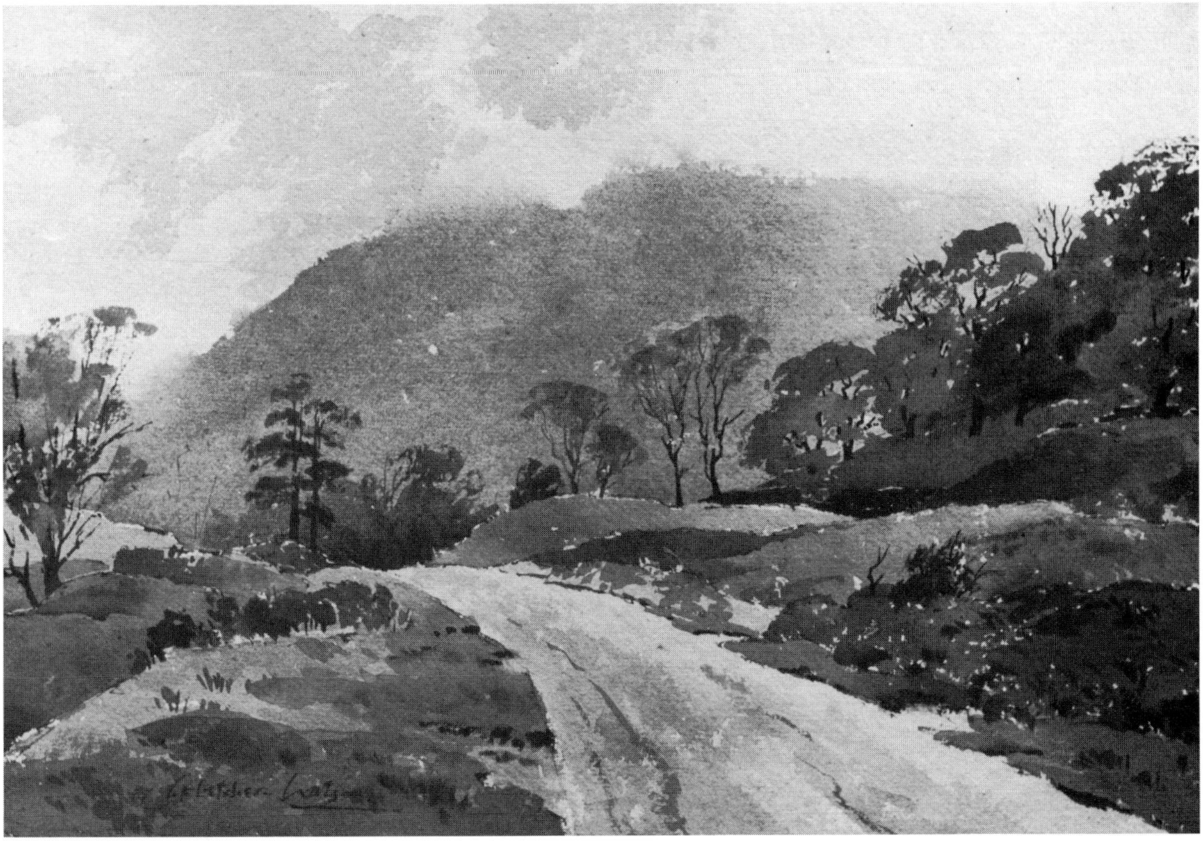

32 The road to Seathwaite.

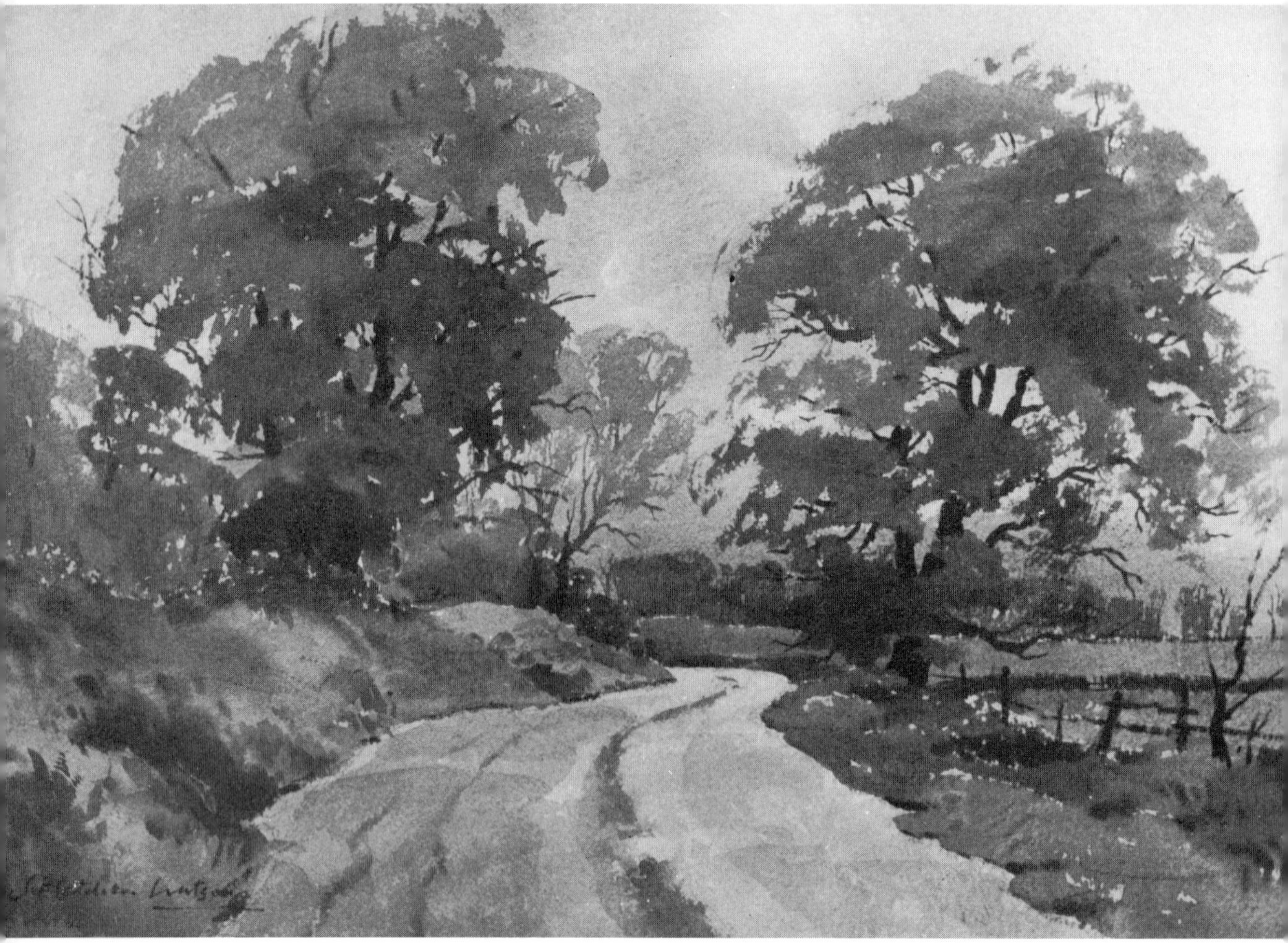

33 Autumn trees, Borrowdale.

It was nice to find one did not have to waste a painting day because it was wet, and to get two pictures done when some people were moaning about the weather.

ULLSWATER

(colour plate 3 between pages 120 and 121)
31.5cm × 48cm ($12\frac{1}{2}$in. × 19in.)
So far I have not touched on painting a *lake* in the Lake District, so I will describe the process in detail of painting Ullswater which is one of the larger lakes in length. It is not particularly wide and one can get many very attractive views of it with beautiful mountain backgrounds. I had arrived in Cumbria on 29 March and I painted this picture on 1 April, so it was still virtually winter and there was snow on the distant mountain.

One sometimes paints a mountain scene without any guide lines in pencil and I like doing this when possible, but with this subject with snow on the far range of mountains I would have to leave a little white paper and not use white paint. So I started by doing a little light drawing work with a B pencil. I was working on Arches 'Not' surface paper.

Composition

I used the trick of drawing with my forefinger an imaginary picture on the blank sheet of paper to decide where the different features were coming and to arrange the composition. This process is a great help as you can decide roughly the size of objects and the amount of foreground you want to have, in this case how much water to include, and what proportion of sky to allow. It really takes the place of doing a rough pencil sketch first.

The first thing I drew with my finger was the distant waterline and then the big mountain on the left going fairly high up the paper; the remaining mountains being further away would be lower and the picture balance would be right. I wanted a small amount of foreground shore on the right and the rather nice old winter tree.

All this was now decided in my mind's eye so I could proceed with pencil, but only the absolute minimum.

I drew the waterline first. It was more or less a level horizontal line, but was a very small bit lower for the left-hand closer mountain. Then I wanted the white capped mountain range carefully pencilled in as I would have to stop my sky wash along the mountain edge. (I rubbed out any pencil that showed after the painting was completed.) Having drawn this, I lightly drew an outline of left-hand and right-hand mountains and a line indicating the fore-shore. That was all that was required. I need not keep to these lines religiously when painting, and anyway they would not be seen when strong colour was put on.

Sky

The sky was a good one with plenty of variety, which was partly why I chose this subject. A mountain landscape with a lake is so much better with a good sky and this adds interest to the water reflections.

I wetted the sky area all over with clear water but stopped short of the snow-line on the far mountains. Then I floated in some Raw Sienna in the top central and left side. The great thing is to work *fast* with skies as one usually wants to keep everything fluid and get different washes on before it all dries. This is fairly easy in winter when the atmosphere is damp anyway. Now I wanted plenty of light gray, and Burnt Umber and French Ultramarine gave me this when mixed and well diluted. This light gray was washed over most of the sky including the left-hand top corner. I carefully painted the edge of the white snow mountain tops. Next I mixed Ultramarine blue with a *very* little Light Red to quieten the blue and I painted in the various blue sky areas. The blue *ran* into the gray and gave the desired effect of gray clouds drifting over a blue sky. The whole sky was still damp and I mixed up some darker gray with the same two colours and painted in the darker gray clouds; I used a No. 9 brush for this and the same brush was also used for the blue passages. For the earlier gray and yellow washes I had used a No. 12 brush.

I carried the light gray wash down over the left and right mountains but with the centre group of mountains I carefully painted the gray *below* the snow-line. I finished these gray washes at water-line level and left the water itself all white for the moment. I wanted to have some dead white on the water which was catching the sun.

Now I could afford to take a break and have some coffee. I was painting from inside the car as it was a very cold day but the road came close to the lake at this point and I was parked on a wide grass verge.

Mountains

Everything had now dried off well and I could start on the left-hand mountain using a No. 7 sable brush. I mixed a dark brown with Burnt Umber and Ultramarine but I wanted to get the cloud coming over the top of the mountain so I had to use a *special technique* for this. I damped the two areas where the clouds were coming over with a No. 5 brush and clear water, making sure not to damp the sky very much above the mountain line and *certainly not* on the sharp bit of mountain that had no low cloud. I then painted the brown mountain with strong colour and rather a stiff mix (i.e. not much water) and ran the colour against the damp areas and up into them from below. I made the formation of the low clouds irregular like floating smoke, and then continued on down the mountain to cover the whole area. I came back to the top of the mountain at one point with some *darker* brown, i.e. with more Ultramarine, while everything was still damp, as there were darker tones at the top. I worked in some dark colour with downward brush strokes on the right side of the mountain to give shadow and modelling to its shape. The sun was coming from the left and the *lighter* lower part down to water level brought the foot of the mountain forward. A little strong Burnt Sienna was stroked into the darker parts in places which gave it the rich colour that it had. On the right-hand edge there were some fir trees showing in silhouette and these were painted with a smaller brush while the mountain was still wet.

All this time the whole mountain area had remained damp and the different treatments merged in as one wash.

I let this mountain dry off and started on the centre group of far off mountains gradually painting them with varying mixes of Burnt Umber and Ultramarine. Some of this group was light brown with some strong blue passages up near the snow-line. The snow itself was left plain white for the moment. I now worked over to the large right-hand mountain, blocking in a big area of dark brown and then as it was drying I added some small areas of stronger *very* dark brown rock outcrop indications. Then high up on the extreme right I added some strong Ultramarine. Here I had more low cloud overhanging and went through the same process as for the left-hand mountain.

I had to be quick with the low group of reddish birch trees on the right-hand foreshore, and I had left a gap in the background mountain so that I could paint in the silver birches with Burnt Sienna and then I could bring down the dark background colour against the birches; the paint was dry enough not to run too much.

Now I could paint the foreshore areas using a No. 9 brush and washes of mossy green, yellow and brown, obtained with Raw Sienna, Winsor Blue and Burnt Sienna in different mixtures, and then grass textures using a smaller brush and darker mixes of these same colours.

I had left the lower part of the big tree trunk unpainted until all was dry, and I could now paint this tree in using a No. 5 brush to start with and No. 3 as the branches got thinner near the top. The lower part of the tree was light brown and the upper branches almost black using Ultramarine and Burnt Umber. The twig masses at the top were flicked in with the No. 5 brush and a gray-brown mix.

The tree trunk shadow on the ground was important and was painted a dark brown.

Water

The only important item remaining was the water. This was washed in with Payne's Gray and diluted to different tones. The distant wash was narrow and a light tone dragged across the paper from left to right with a steady hand, using a No. 7 brush.

Then came another wash a little darker, using a No. 9 brush, dragging it again in a sideways position fairly quickly and leaving white paper in suitable shapes to represent the sunlight on the water. This wash was brought right up to the near foreground, and then when half dry I ran in a darker wash with the big brush and a few thin dark marks with a small brush to indicate a few ripples. I did use a very small touch of Light Red to give a slight warmth to the wash furthest away.

Final items

Almost last, the small foreground bush was painted with a No. 5 brush with Raw Sienna and Winsor Blue mixed, and a No. 1 brush for the twigs. One more item was the very important treatment of the snow. The sun was catching it and shadows were painted with a No. 3 brush and Ultramarine and Light Red, not too much of the latter.

The trunks of the silver birches on the extreme right were formed by scratching out with a sharp pen-knife and that completed the picture. It had taken about three and a half hours.

The colours used were the following – Raw Sienna, Burnt Sienna, Burnt Umber, Light Red, French Ultramarine, Winsor Blue and Payne's Gray – only seven, which I think goes to show how few colours we really need for a watercolour landscape.

34 ULLSWATER, FROM THE DOCKRAY ROAD

31.5cm × 47.5cm ($12\frac{1}{2}$in. × $18\frac{3}{4}$in.)

If we look now at figure 34 we will see another view of Ullswater taken about half a mile from the lake up the Dockray road. It was done at the same time of year as

34 Ullswater, from the Dockray road.

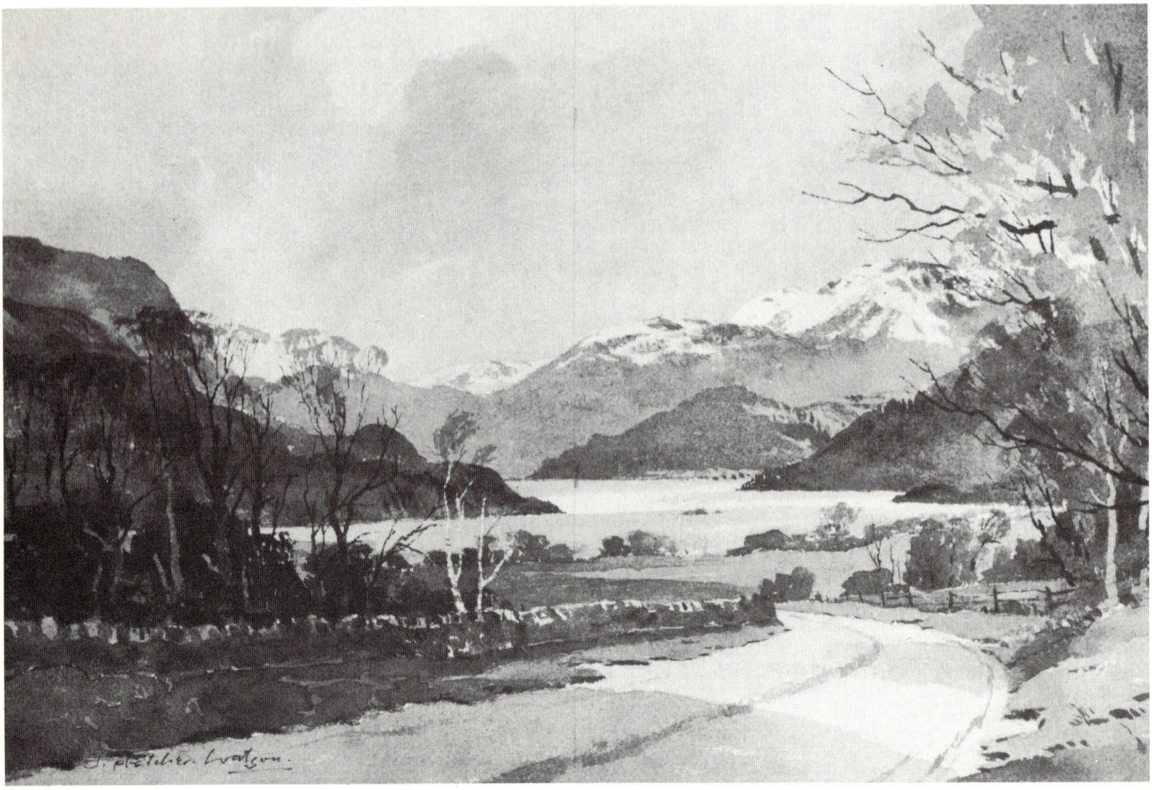

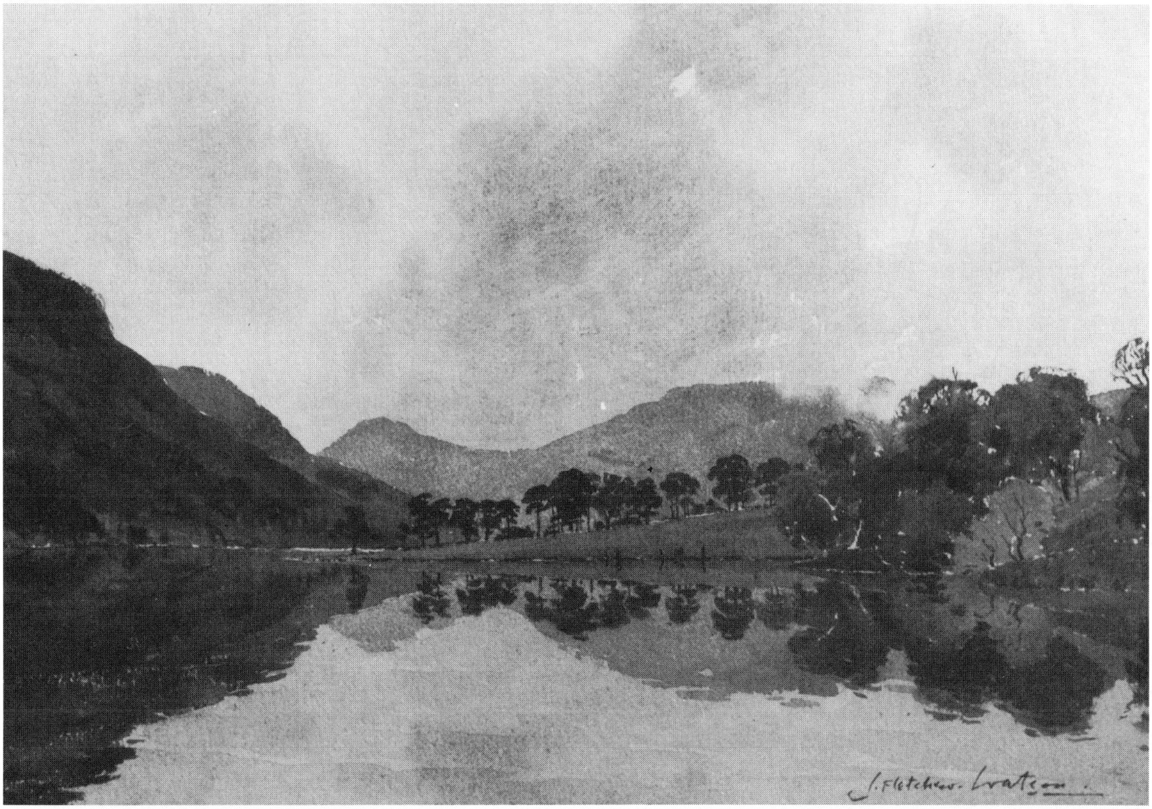

35 Buttermere reflections.

the last picture described and snow was still on the distant mountains and I was able to see a little further round the corner of the lake as it bent southwards. The dark trees on the left and the edge of the wood on the right gave the picture a nice composition. The small birch tree in the centre was dealt with by scratching out with a pen-knife but otherwise no special tricks were used. The painting proceeded in orderly fashion with sky first, then distant mountains, followed by light tone washes on foreground fields and verges to the road, and then darker mountains and trees and finally the water and shadows on the road and so on.

This picture was a little more difficult to paint than the last one of Ullswater as there were more features to sort out and bring together, such as the various trees, the stone wall and the road.

35 BUTTERMERE REFLECTIONS

31.5cm × 47.5cm ($12\frac{1}{2}$in. × $18\frac{3}{4}$in.)

Over to the west of Ullswater one enters a marvellous area of superb views and subjects for the artist and, having driven over the exciting Honister Pass, one comes to a chain of fascinating lakes, the first of which is Buttermere.

It was early November and a very still day with very little wind and the reflections were marvellous. So I decided at once to get painting before the weather changed and the wind got up and the reflections were lost; this can so quickly happen.

This picture is not as difficult as it looks. It is rather like painting two pictures and if you cover the bottom half with a sheet of paper up to the water-line you will see what I mean. The top half was really quite a *simple* landscape of a dark mountain on the left, a distant mountain and some trees. Incidentally, the autumn trees were a riot of colour with reds, browns and greens and this gave a lot of life to the painting.

So all you have to do is to paint the top half first leaving the water untouched until you have virtually finished the top view. A few pencil guide-lines were wanted and then I started off with sky, background mountain, right-hand sloping field, dark mountain to the left and finally the trees. The individual trees in the centre were on a sharp promontory sticking out into the lake. When this first part was completed, I pencilled in very lightly the individual tree reflections; then I started painting again. First, the distant mountain reflections went in with a blue-gray wash. Then the sky reflection of light grays and a touch of blue washed right over the water area up to the water-line.

As this was drying I painted the dark mountain

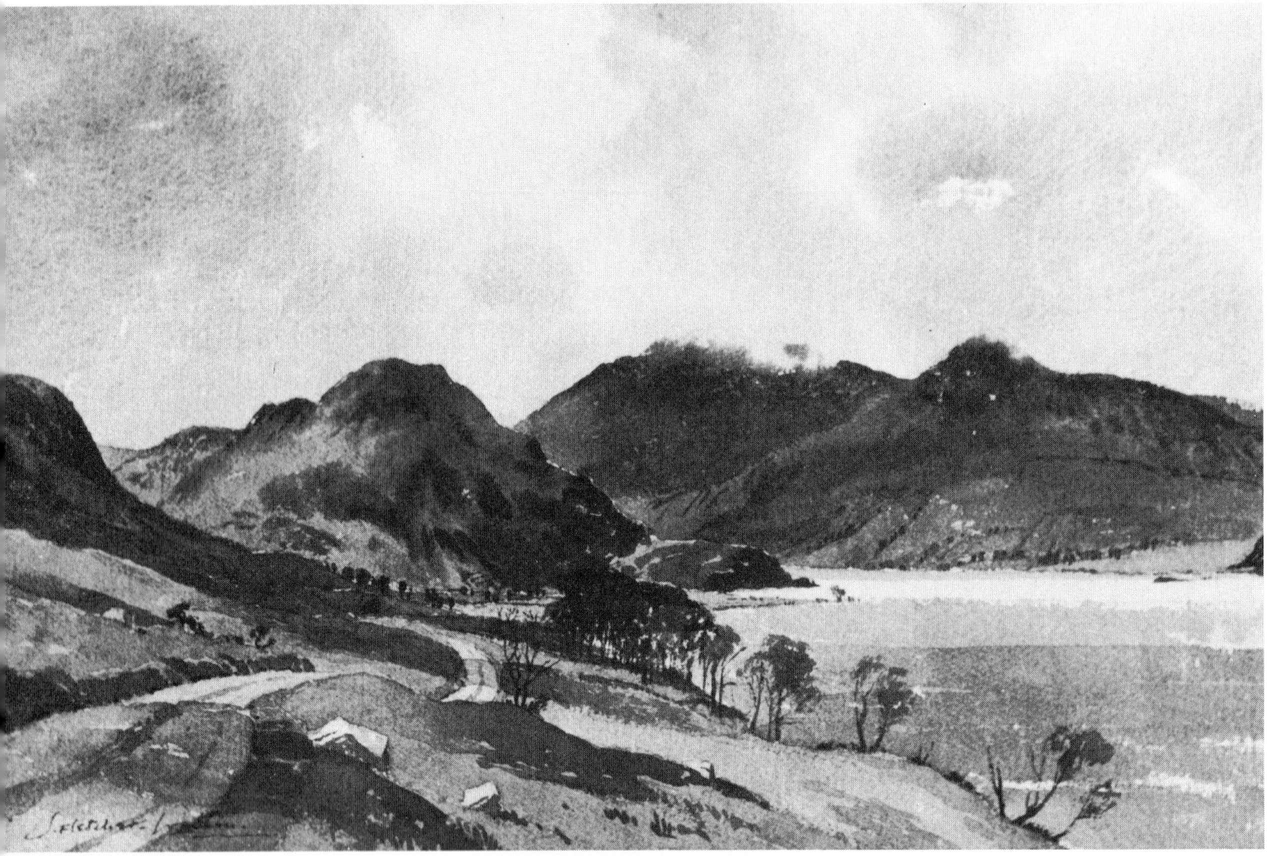

36 Crummock Water.

reflection to the left, giving it a broken edge as there was just a slight movement on the water. The paper was nearly dry and this suited me as I did not want too much of a blurred edge to the next reflections, namely the individual trees with their trunks showing quite clearly. I painted these in one by one giving the trunks a slight wiggle. I did of course first paint the sloping field reflections. As the field was sloping *away* from the water's edge, the reflection did not show very much of the field.

Then it was the turn of the reflection of the group of trees on the right; I painted the lighter toned trees at first and then the darker ones.

When all this was done and had dried out, the water needed a slightly darker tone all over it so I mixed a light gray with Payne's Gray and a touch of Light Red and washed it on, leaving a few horizontal lines near the bottom of the wash to indicate a few ripples.

The picture was completed; it had taken a good two and a half hours as there was quite a lot of work in it. But reflections are fun to do and I hope you will try this type of subject.

36 CRUMMOCK WATER

31cm × 47cm ($12\frac{1}{4}$in. × $18\frac{1}{2}$in.)

Further west along the valley we come to Crummock Water, surrounded by interesting inundations and promontories and attractive mountain shapes. Mountains vary so much; some have boring shapes with a simple rounded top and are not the least interesting to paint, where others have irregular shapes with jagged places and appealing slopes, and this type exist around Crummock.

I chose a view with the road close to the lake, undulating into the distance. It was the old theme of a road leading the eye into the picture. The position of the clump of trees in the centre made an excellent focal point. Cloud shadows were a help in the composition of this picture, tying the extreme left-hand mountain into the picture and preventing the eye wandering off from the centre. The darker stronger colours on the centre mountain held the attention to the middle and kept the picture together; with so many features such as trees, promontories and the road, it could easily fall apart and be restless.

The far mountain was given extra distance and height by the low cloud coming over the top, the mountain had some strong blue colouring which also sent it back.

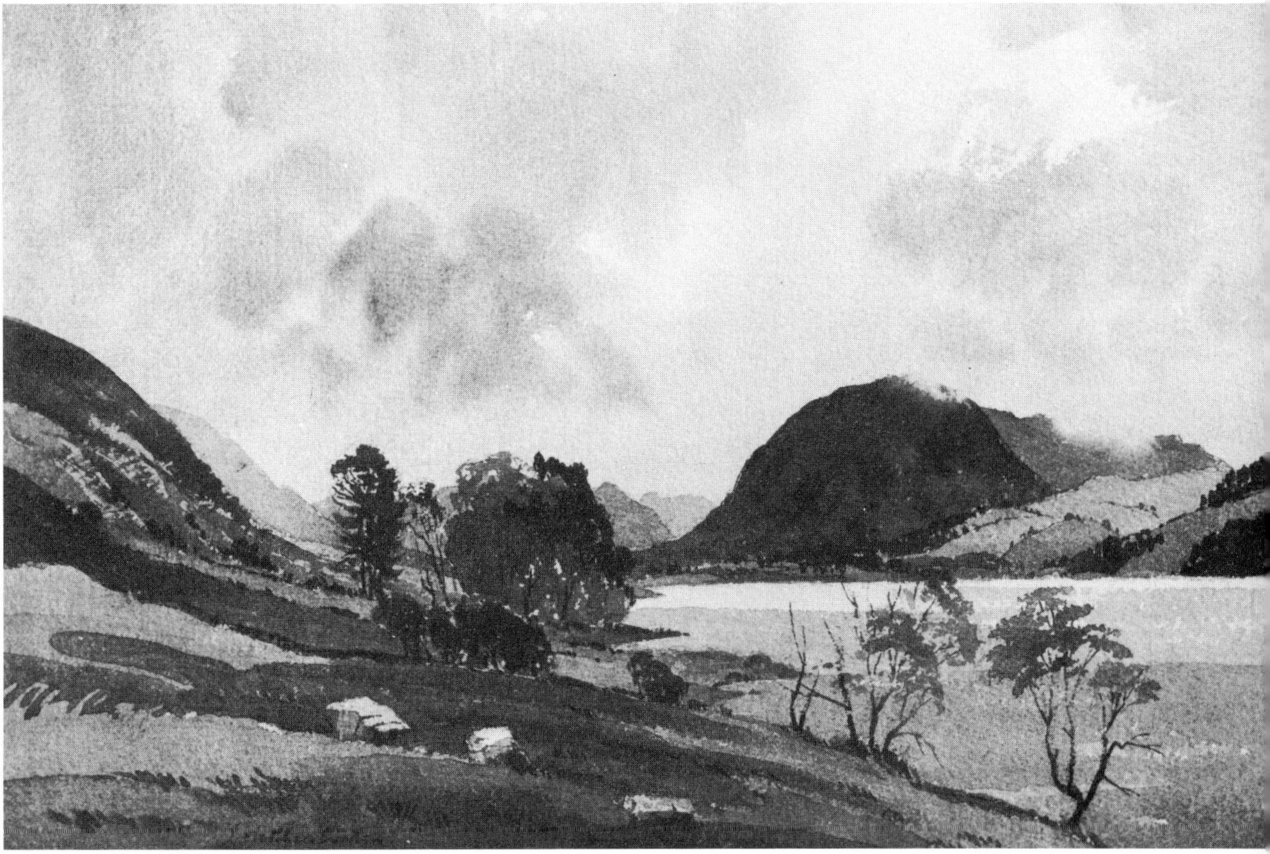

37 Lowes Water.

37 LOWES WATER

30cm × 47cm (12in. × 18½in.)

Moving again further along the valley, it divides into two. One valley goes northwards to Thackthwaite and the other goes west to Waterend; we take the western route and travel the road along the edge of Lowes Water lake. At the very end looking back there is a wonderful picture and in the far distance, six miles away, can just be seen the sharp point of Fleetwith Pike. The dark mountain the other side of the lake is Mellbreak, 1600 odd feet high. This view makes a wonderful composition. The sloping foreground is attractive and contrasts well with the level waterline of the lake. The tree group is perfect a little to the left of centre, and the dark mountain comes in the right place for balance. It would not be nearly so dark if it wasn't for the cloudy sky casting shadows on it.

Note the simple treatment of the water. There are no reflections when there is a little wind to ruffle the water, as on this occasion. The light coming from the left caught the water on the far side and gave it a gleam of brilliance; this was achieved by leaving the white paper un-coloured. The rest of the water was a series of light gray-blue washes.

This picture was a ready-made composition where you can't go wrong, and I advise you to have a go at it when you are next in Cumbria. I think you will be pleased with your results as long as you remember the great watch word, *simplify* what you see and leave out detail.

38 LAKELAND VISTA

31.5cm × 47cm (12½in. × 18½in.)

Re-tracing our steps along the narrow little road between Lowes Water and Crummock Water, we come to the *village* of Lowes Water, and looking south-east from here is one of the most spectacular views in the Lake District. It has to have the right day of course, plenty of exciting cloud and glimpses of sun. Some mountains will get lit up while others will be in dark shadow. Crummock Water is seen in the distance as a silver streak through the trees.

You will probably recognize the small dark mountain left of centre; it is the same one as shown in figure 36.

The mountains on the right are fascinating the way they recess one after the other, layer upon layer, and you have to observe the varying tones.

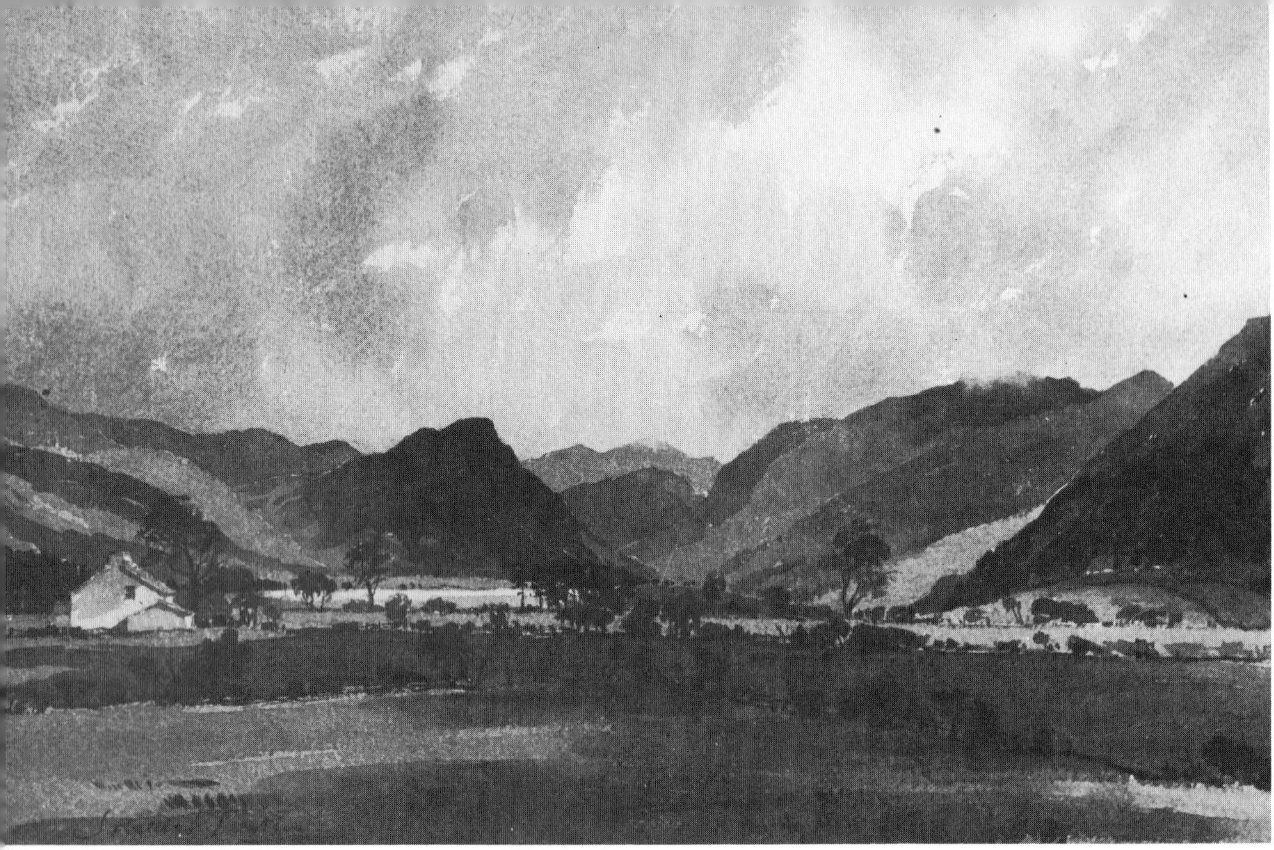

I was sorry to part with this picture when it was sold at one of my exhibitions. Every time I look at it, it beckons me to Cumbria.

This is a case where cloud shadows play the vital part and without them the picture would be nothing. I would like you all to pay a great deal of attention to the use of cloud shadows.

38 Lakeland vista.

39 Lanthwaite.

40 Fleetwith Pike.

39 LANTHWAITE

31.5cm × 47cm (12½in. × 18½in.)

Moving again eastwards back along our little valley road – what a wealth of subject matter there is along this road – we come to a spot beside Crummock Water at the north end. This view has a very nice gray stone farmhouse, big tree and road with good mountain background. It was April when tree branches could still be seen and the rough grass was a nice mixture of yellows, browns and a little green. Note how helpful the trees behind the house are in giving it sharp form. This is called 'counter change' and it happens all the time in nature: dark shapes are against light or light shapes against dark. You want to pick on these arrangements when you see them out painting and make the most of them.

There is always a pattern in nature and we want to bring this sense of pattern into our picture. It is part of composition and a good pattern can harmonize and unite a picture. In this picture the background mountain is part of the pattern but it is only a *flat wash* of blue-gray which sends it away back. The left-hand mountain going out of the picture is a strong part of the pattern but it does not distract because the road is even stronger with sun on it, pointing into the central distance.

40 FLEETWITH PIKE

31.5cm × 47cm (12½in. × 18½in.)

I am still on the same road and have passed along Buttermere, I stop near the east end of the lake and there looking up is the immensely powerful mountain called Fleetwith Pike, rather like some great prehistoric animal crouching. It is a favourite among mountain climbers and is quite a challenge to paint.

Mountains are ideal for watercolours as you can give them a soft rough edge against the sky by dragging the brush with a dryish mixture of paint quickly over the paper.

On this day there were small bits of cloud drifting low at times over parts of the mountain and then going away again. One had to choose one's moment depend-

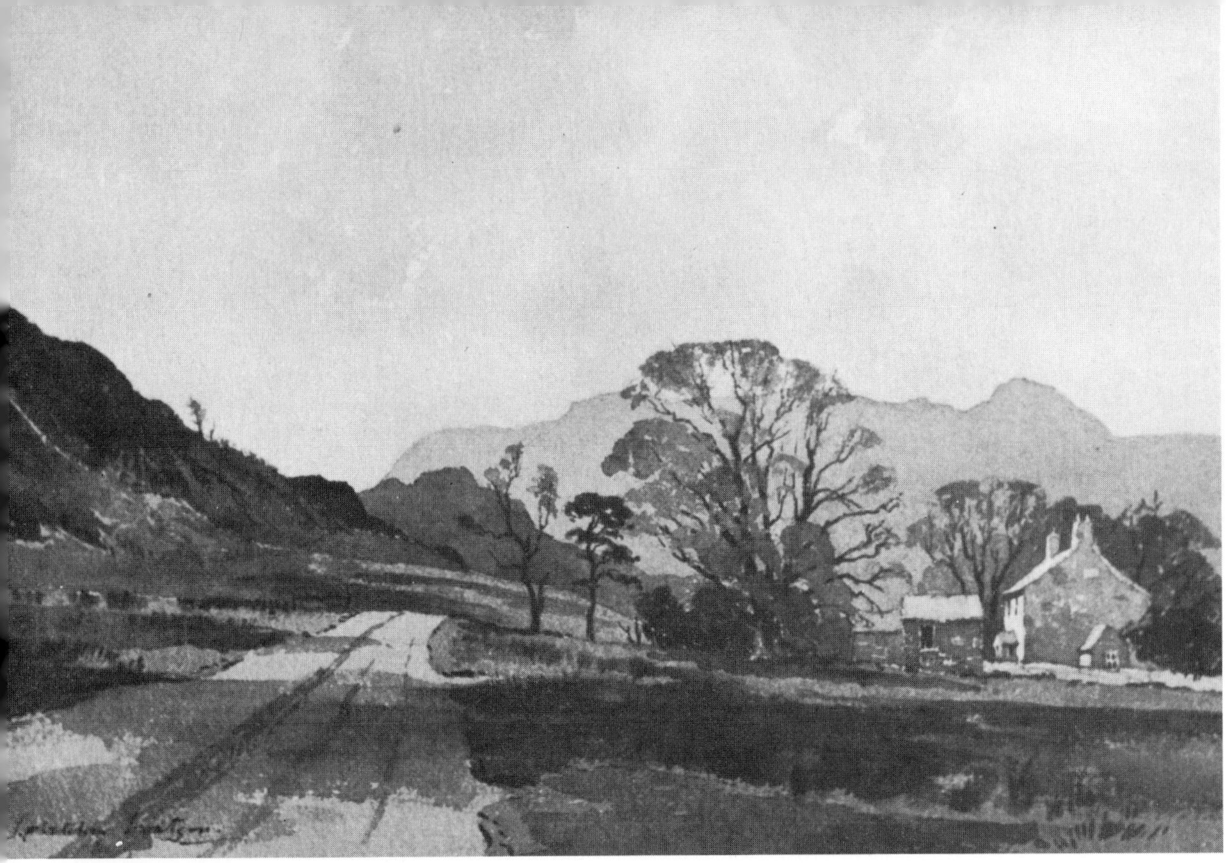

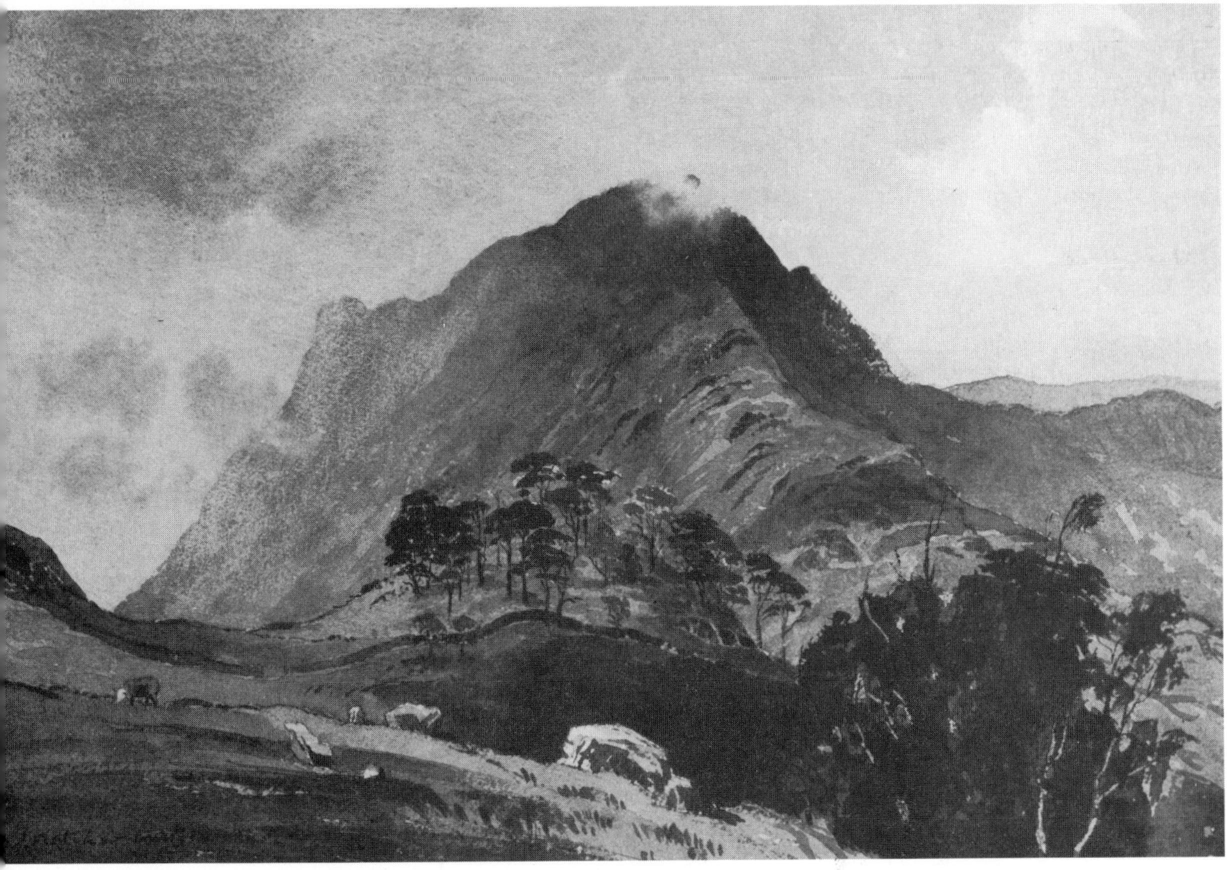

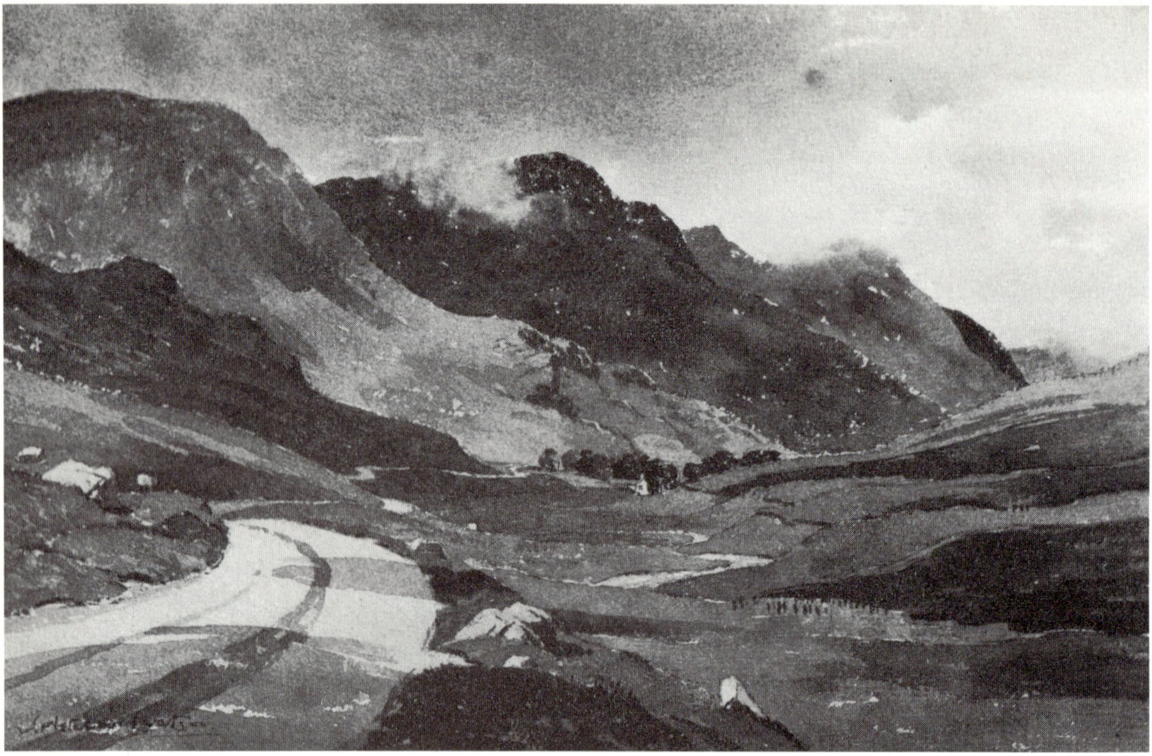

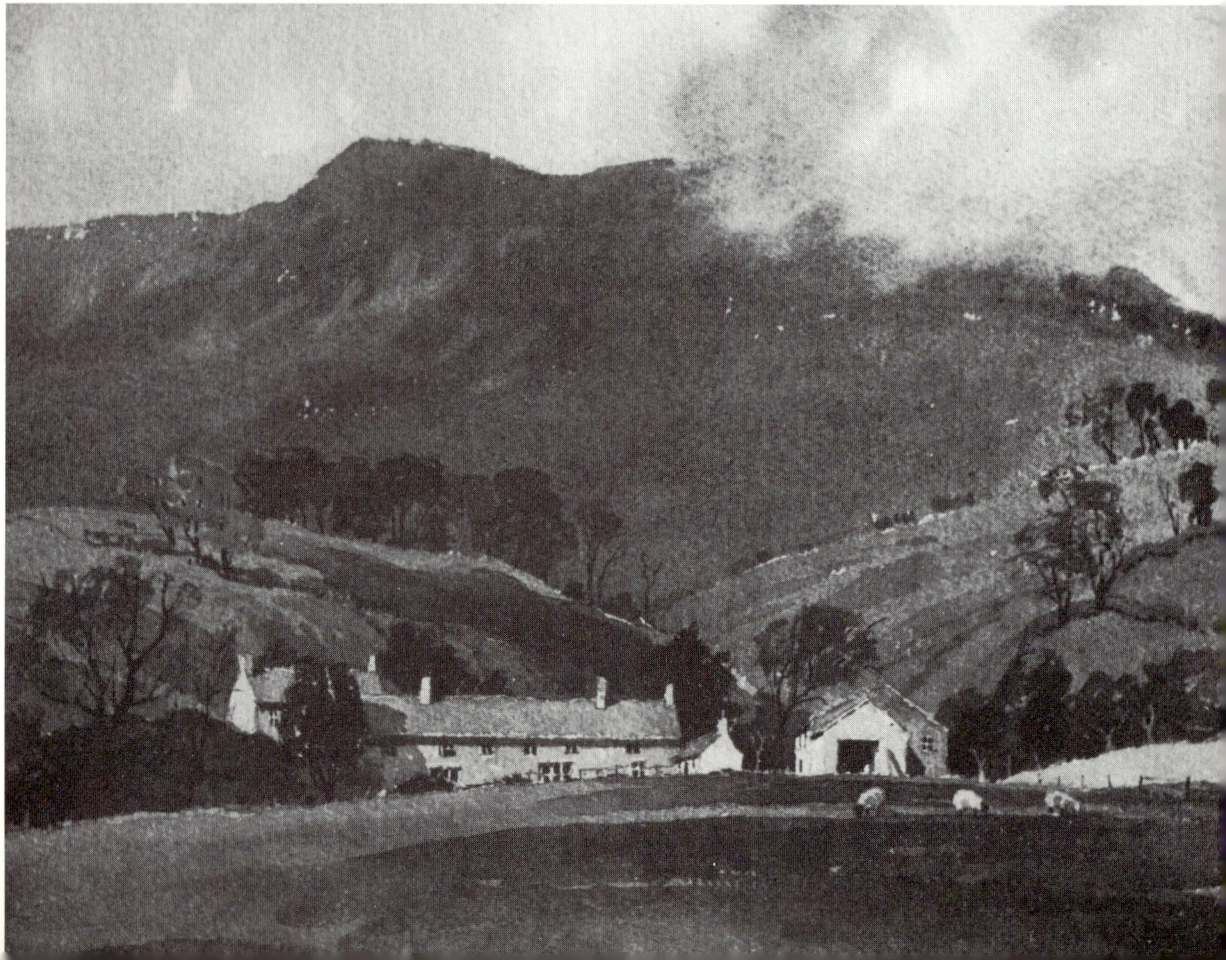

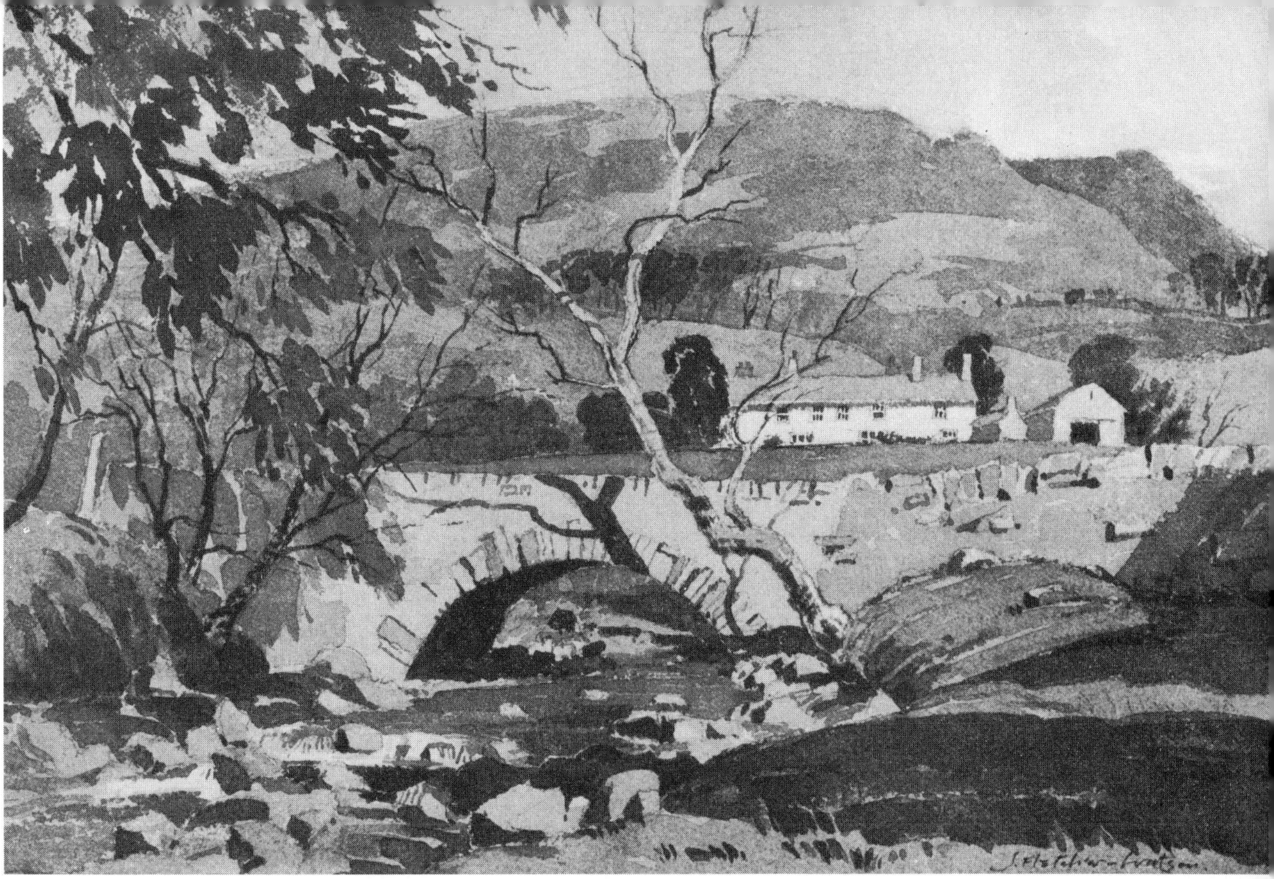

41 Honister Pass.

42 Seatoller and Honister Pass.

43 Mountain beck with bridge, Seatoller.

ing on where you liked these clouds to be and then paint them in quickly or memorize them. I say paint them in, but of course the technique I have described requires them to be *left out* by painting the dark mountain up to the damped part of the sky, letting the cloud shape run more or less as you want it to.

The central tree group of Scots firs was a nice feature on its little hill and the rocks and dark trees to the right gave strength and focus to the foreground. The big foreground rock was left white throughout the painting until the end when the sharp shadows were put in.

41 HONISTER PASS

31cm × 47cm ($12\frac{1}{4}$in. × $18\frac{1}{2}$in.)

Continuing along our road towards Borrowdale we have to go through the Honister Pass, which I have painted many times. This view is in the lower, less steep part of the Pass looking towards Buttermere. The thing that attracted me was the little group of trees and house at the bottom of the valley and the marvellous rich colours of the nearer foot-hills on the left. This was painted during May and the mossy green colour of these hills was quite magical. This picture eventually went to a collector in America so one day I shall do another spring picture of the view and keep it in the family.

It is an example of pure mountain landscape which should be painted with the brush only. I did use a small touch of the pencil for the road and house in the trees but nothing else.

42 SEATOLLER AND HONISTER PASS

28cm × 38cm (11in. × 15in.)

Travelling on now eastwards over the Honister Pass into Borrowdale we come to Seatoller, a little hamlet at the very foot of Honister.

This makes a very nice composition with the group of characteristic Cumbrian buildings, long and low in proportion, and the field with grazing sheep and High Scawdel mountain rising steeply up behind, nearly 2000 feet. The road to Honister Pass is in a steep valley just behind the row of trees on the sloping ground immediately above the long house.

I left the painting of all the buildings until last, as I usually do, carefully working the brush strokes round chimneys and roofs etc., leaving them the white of the paper. Then at the end of painting I put in the gray tones of roofs and walls and the dark windows and shadows. One can then gauge how much to leave almost white as the sun catches the walls.

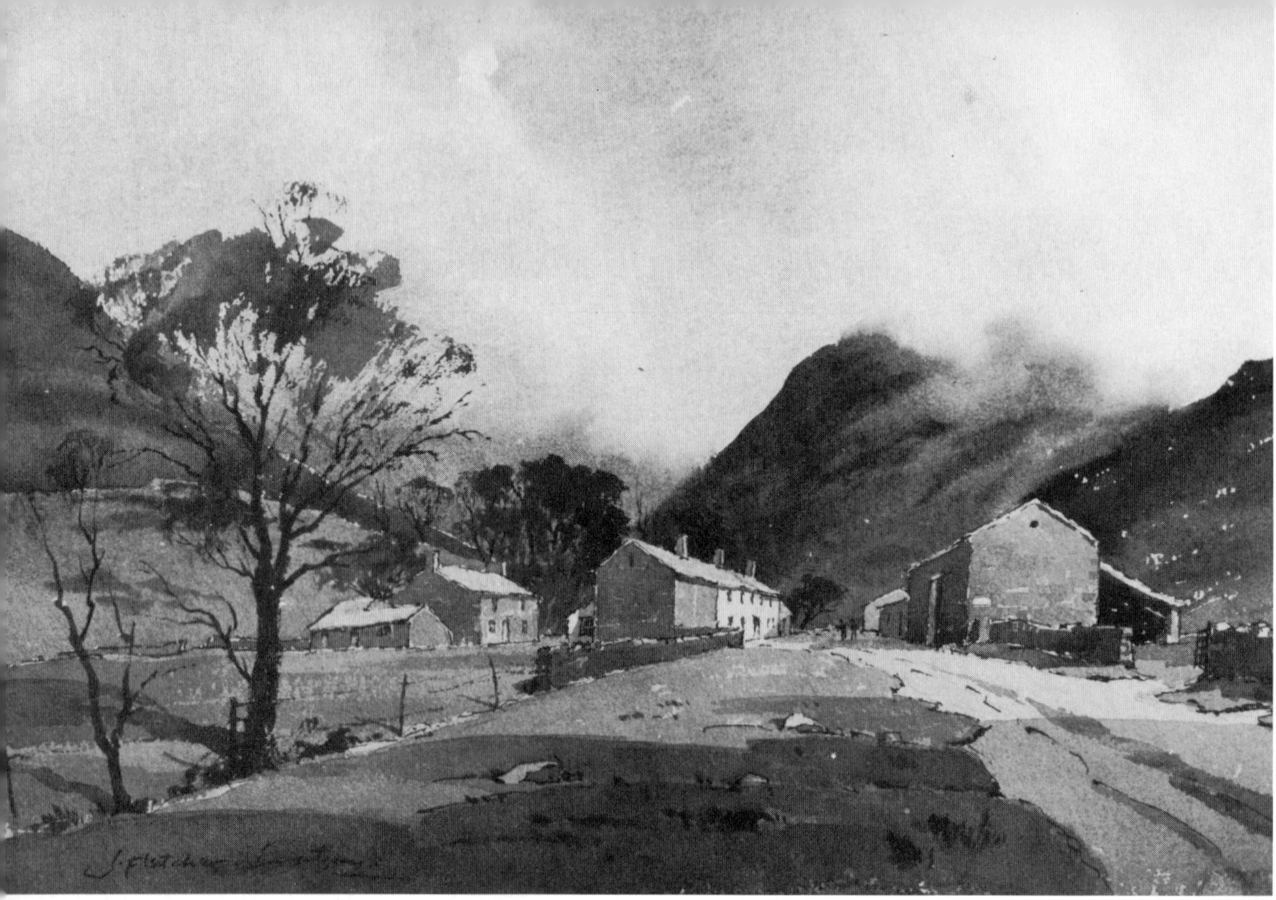

44 Seathwaite.

45 Stockley Bridge.

46 Stonethwaite, Borrowdale.

43 MOUNTAIN BECK WITH BRIDGE, SEATOLLER

30cm × 47cm (12in. × $18\frac{1}{2}$in.)

Just behind me as I painted the last picture, at the bottom of the field, was a bridge and a lane leading to Seathwaite.

This small stone bridge is so typical of the Lake District and it made a nice group with the house and High Scawdell up behind and the twisting old ash trees by the bridge. These little bridges can be found in many places and usually make good pictures; they are not difficult to paint.

44 SEATHWAITE

31.5cm × 47.5cm ($12\frac{1}{2}$in. × $18\frac{3}{4}$in.)

If we drive over the bridge just mentioned, the road comes to a dead end in a mile and a half at the little village of Seathwaite. It is from this village that many walkers and climbers start out for Great Gable and Scafell Pike and many other well-known peaks.

The view is attractive and has a splendid group of trees in just the right strategic place at the bottom of the steep foot-hills on either side. This arrangement is quite common and always so paintable.

I used pen work in this picture which is often a good idea with building groups in a landscape. The houses and road and walls were penned in first and you can see this if you look closely. I always use a mixture of dark brown watercolour rather than sepia ink because of the danger of the latter fading.

45 STOCKLEY BRIDGE

22cm × 32cm ($8\frac{3}{4}$in. × $12\frac{3}{4}$in.)

To reach this spot I had to leave my car and take to my feet and walk a mile or two along the climbers' track from Seathwaite towards Great Gable. Stockley Bridge is a lovely little spot and the beck water gushes through a miniature ravine into a deep green pool which is in the foreground of the picture.

I did quite a lot of pencil drawing before starting to paint as I wanted to get the exciting rock formations right.

One is always taking a risk with watercolours when you stray far from the car as rain storms in the Lake District can so quickly blow up but all was well on this occasion.

46 STONETHWAITE, BORROWDALE

31cm × 47cm ($12\frac{1}{4}$in. × $18\frac{1}{2}$in.)

This tiny village or hamlet is reached a littler further

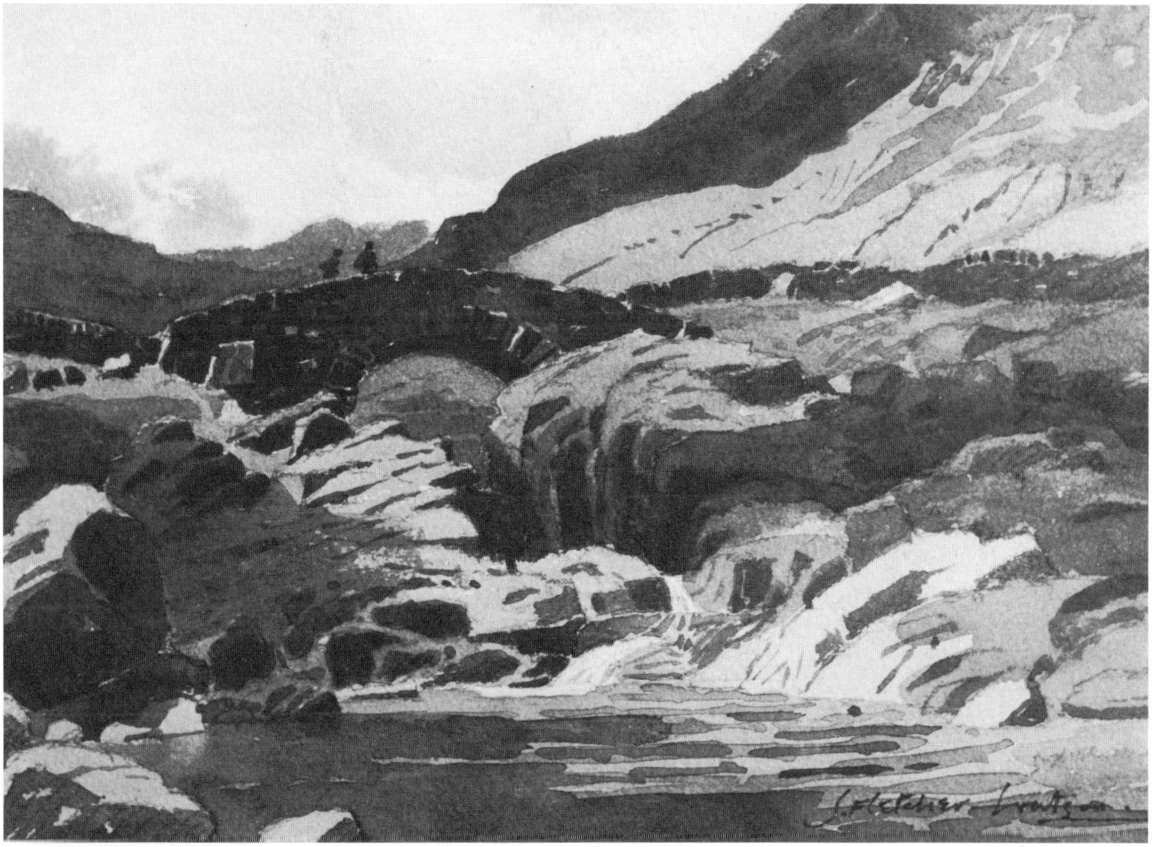

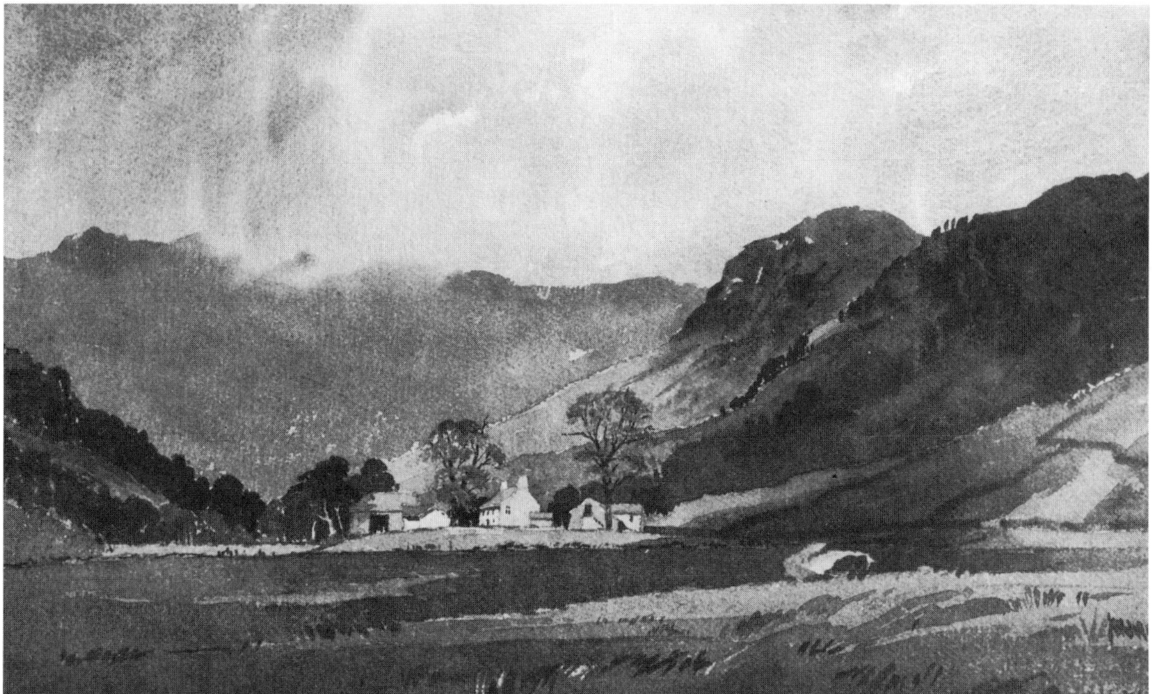

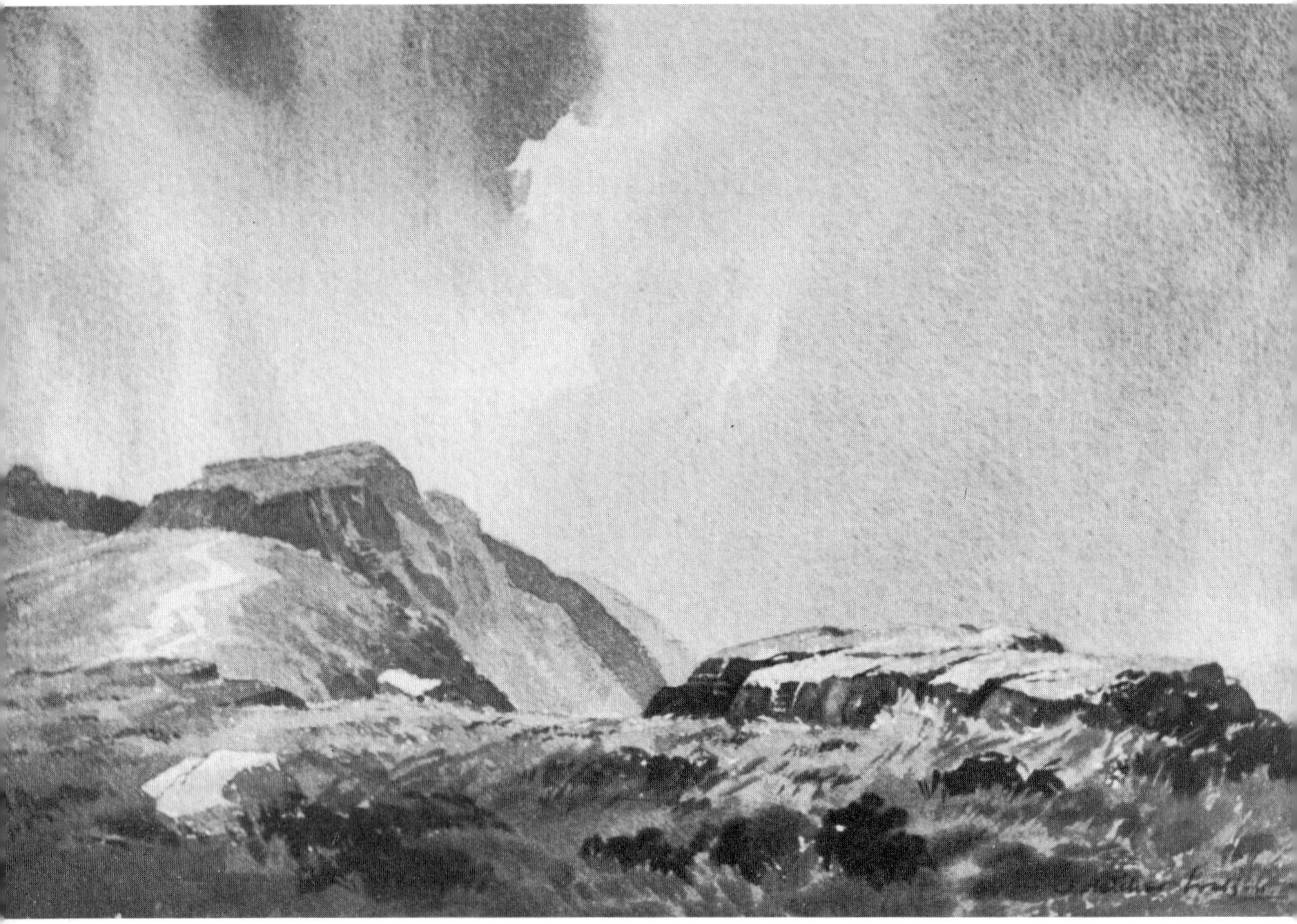

down the road from Seatoller and then turning right up a lane for a mile. It is a delightful subject, everything is just right for a picture. The mountains come steeply down to the valley and the groups of barns and cottages and trees make a perfect focal point. I have painted it several times on different visits and every time something is different: the clouds or the lighting or the colouring.

This time there was no blue sky ahead, and the gray clouds took on exciting shapes as they lifted up and down over the central mountain. But there were breaks in the clouds above and behind me and we had shafts of sun, lighting up the village and the fields. Great dark shadows moved over the mountain slopes giving life and excitement to the scene. It is the *atmosphere* that one seeks to capture in mountain country, and one has to concentrate on this and splash on the paint quickly and not worry too much about careful painting and detail. The essential shapes and patterns are what matter. This picture took about an hour and three quarters to do.

47 Sergent's Crag, from Eagle Crag.

47 SERGENT'S CRAG, FROM EAGLE CRAG

From Stonethwaite one day I was tempted by a friend to walk up onto the fells with my painting gear and be shown some exciting views. The weather was a little bit rough – it was October – but it did not actually rain. I managed this quick sketch from what seemed a very high spot on top of Eagle Crag. The wind was strong and there seemed to be an up-draught making the clouds and mist go in all directions. I think I have captured the feeling of loneliness and grandeur a little.

I used plenty of water in painting the sky, making the gray cloud colours run into each other. The foreground was finished off when I got home. It was too cold to stay long on the spot.

48 ROAD NEAR ENNERDALE

31cm × 47cm ($12\frac{1}{2}$in. × $18\frac{1}{2}$in.)

Returning now to the day in April when I painted Lowes Water, I wandered on westwards after this

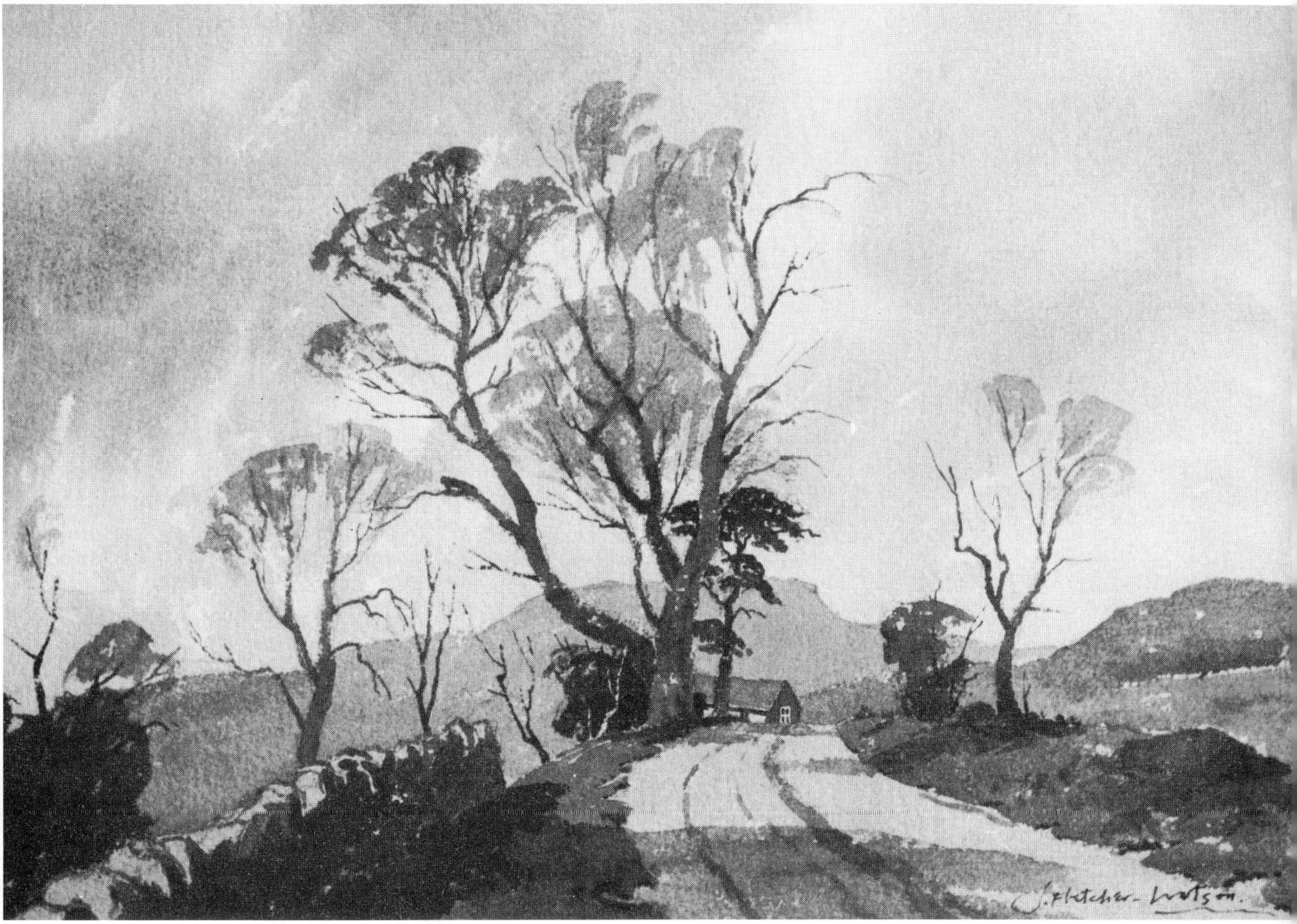

48 Road near Ennerdale.

painting was done, and then turned south to Ennerdale Water in search of a new subject. I was not so taken with Ennerdale but I came upon this charming tree subject along an old narrow road and I felt I had time left to do a quick painting of this simple scene.

It was a lovely old ash tree still in its winter state. The picture revolved round the tree, the bending road led up to it well and the far away mountains formed a good background, only a simple flat gray wash was required for them. The bush beside the tree was useful, giving a dark accent and the small dark fir tree behind helped show up the light colour of the tree trunk. This is a further example of how pleasant a 'road' picture can be.

49 PALACE HOW FARM, BRACKENTHWAITE
31cm × 47cm ($12\frac{1}{4}$in. × $18\frac{1}{2}$in.)
This lovely old farm with the superb mountains behind is one of my favourite pictures. These farm subjects do have the spirit of the Lake District, and there are always superb old trees, probably planted purposely hundreds of years ago, to give protection to the farmhouse. It was April and bare tree trunks and branches were still showing. It is such a good time of year for painting and it rivals the autumn, which I think perhaps is even better. What attracted me about the subject was the sloping foreground from right to left, and then the mountain behind steeply sloping from left to right in contrast. And finally the great mountain in the background looking dignified and remote. A few sheep grazing in the foreground gave the peaceful domestic touch, but through it all one can sense the severity of this part of the world knowing that the little farm has to stand up to gales and heavy snow in the winter, and the sheep farmer has to be tough and ready to battle with the elements to rescue his sheep.

I hope I am helping you with foregrounds in showing you these pictures; the cloud shadows, the groups of rough grass, the rocks and occasionally some sheep are all that is required to give the necessary recession and texture.

50 BRACKENTHWAITE AND WHITESIDE

31cm × 47cm ($12\frac{1}{4}$in. × $18\frac{1}{2}$in.)
Here is another farm subject; Whiteside is the name of the mountain behind it. There is the protective tree group again and the barn adjoining, with the barn doors open and the black opening which is always a helpful accent.

With practice you will develop the technique of leaving the buildings white and unpainted until the last thing or at least near the end. You can then give the necessary punch to the composition by making the white painted house stand out with a dark tree or hill up against it. The dark cloud shadows travelling across the lighter mountain gave a great feeling of movement and wind, and there were particularly outstanding shadows on hill and field on this day of bright sunlight.

51 FARM AT WATERMILLOCK

31.5cm × 48cm ($12\frac{1}{2}$in. × 19in.)
This farm near Ullswater was unusual in having so many barns and outbuildings, and the grouping was rather nice against the low hills. It was late March and the crows were already thinking about building their nests. There were many of them about and I put a few in which gave the right atmosphere. What a nice tradition it is in Cumbria for the stone houses to be painted white, and the interesting thing is that you very seldom see a dirty unpainted one. They are a great asset to the artist as a white building does sparkle up a picture which is full of browns and greens.

52 TROUTBECK

31.5cm × 17.5cm ($12\frac{1}{2}$in. × $18\frac{3}{4}$in.)
This picture was painted one late afternoon in November and the light was fading fast. The colouring was most attractive, all muted browns and grays. The distant mountain was disappearing into the low cloud, and the sky at the top was very pale blue. The foreground rough grass was brown with a touch of green, and the only darks were the trees near the house. It was a peaceful evening picture which I painted very quickly in about an hour, which was just as well as by

50 Brackenthwaite and Whiteside.

49 Palace How Farm, Brackenthwaite.

51 Farm at Watermillock.

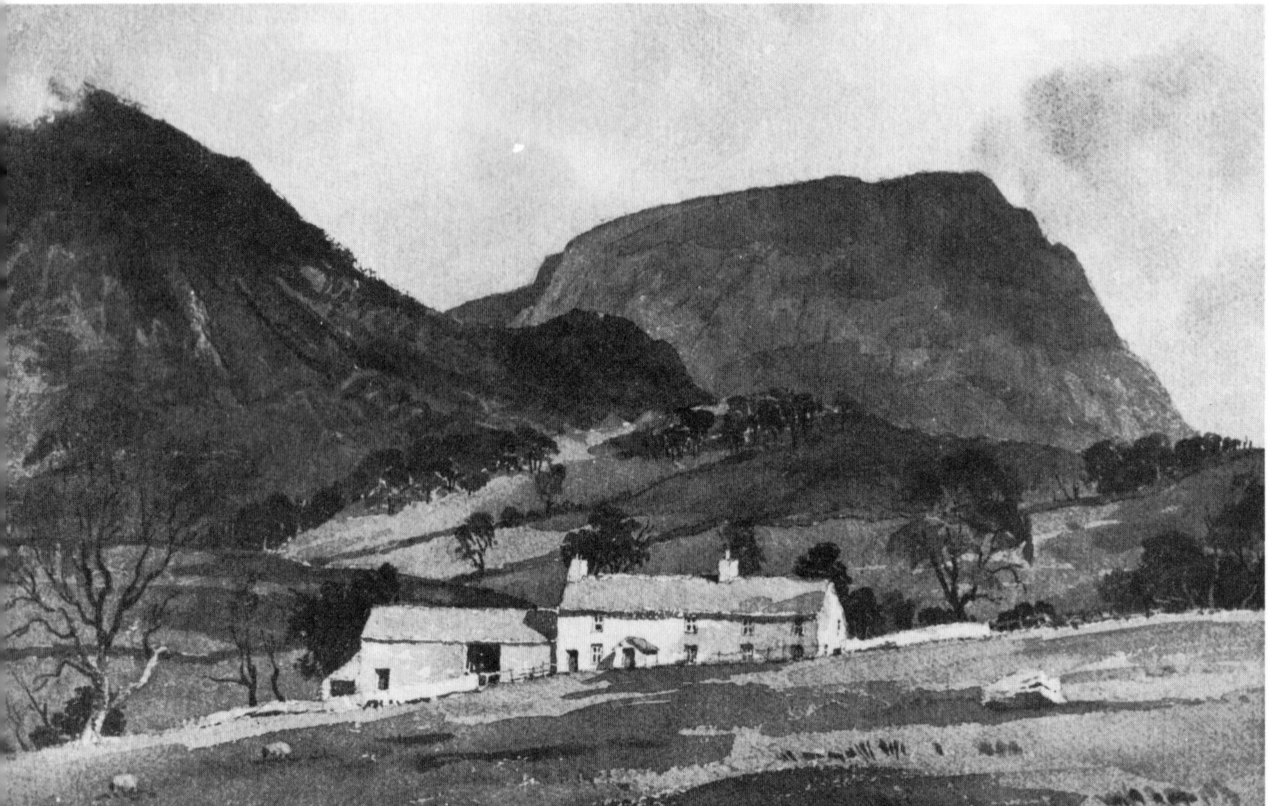

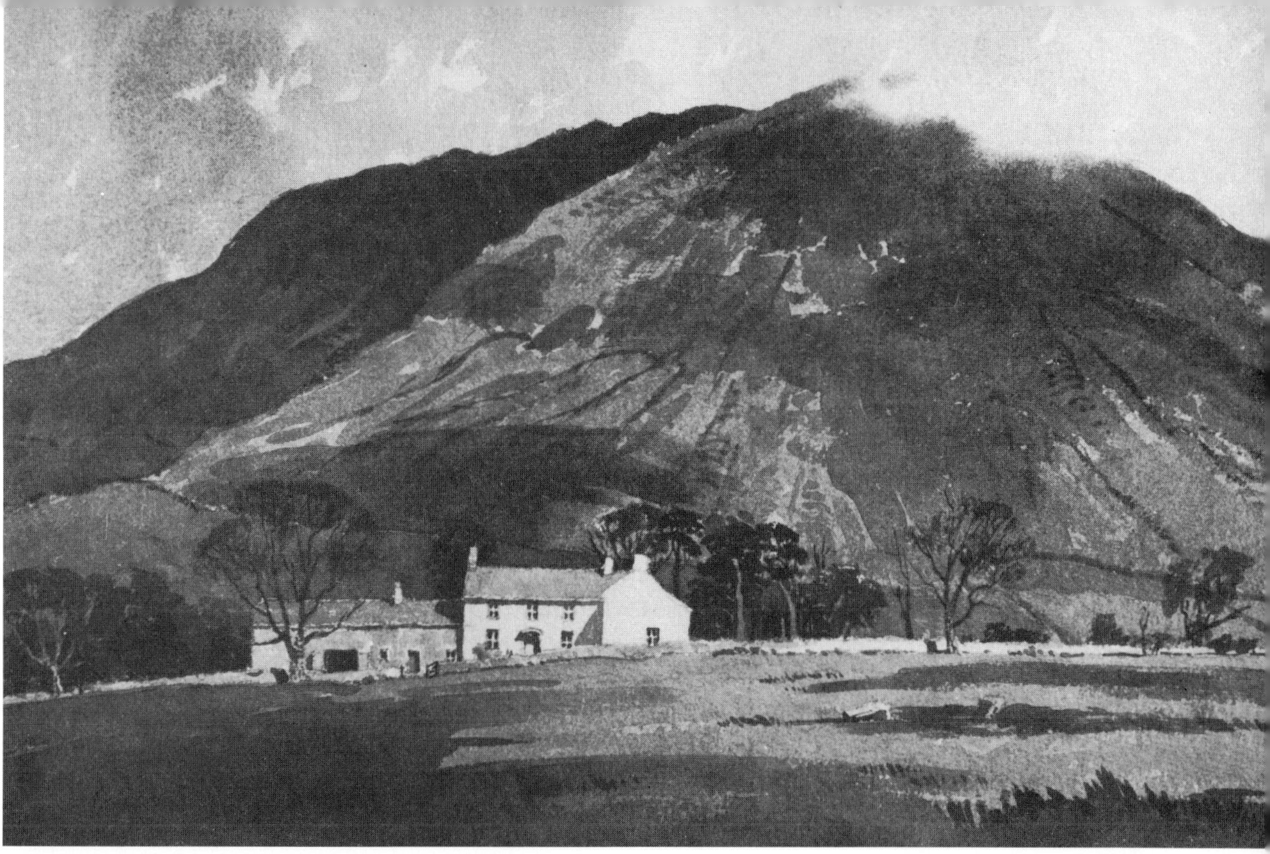

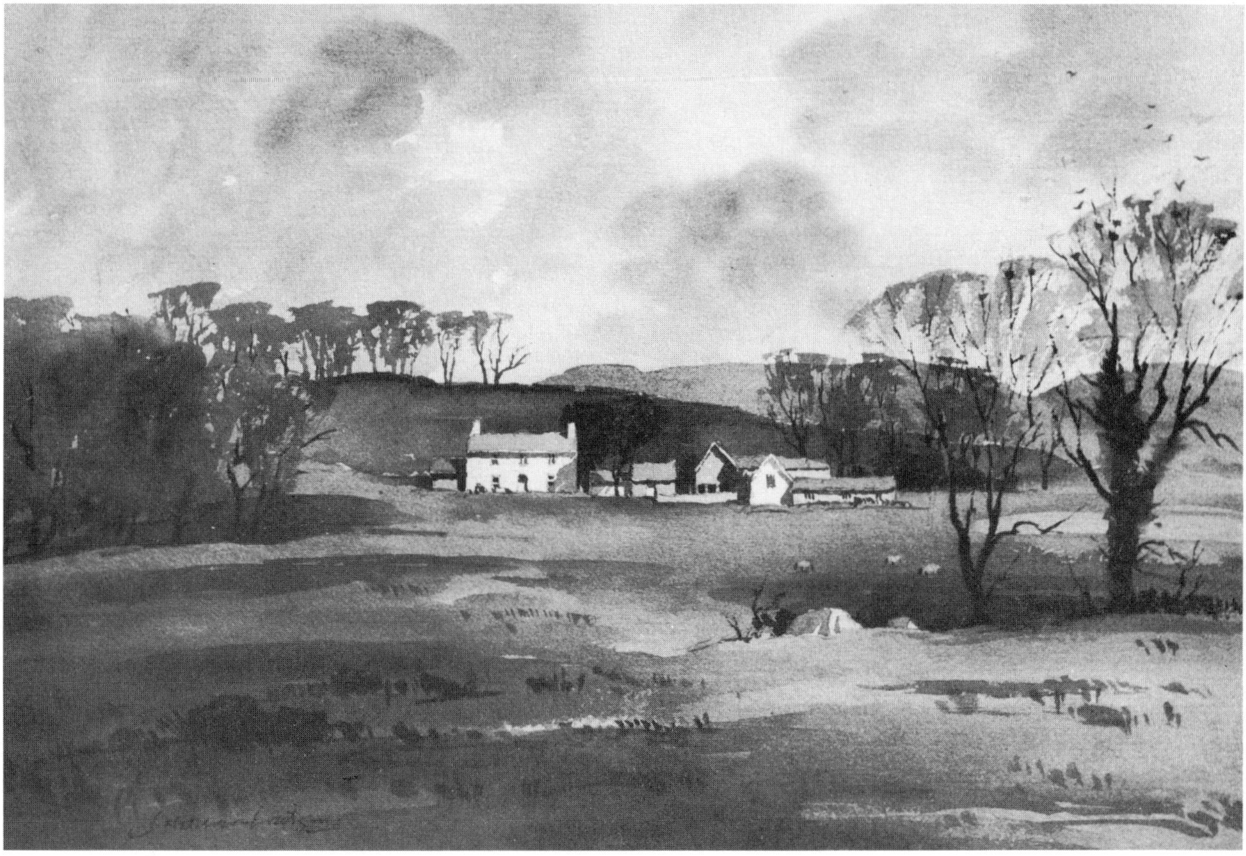

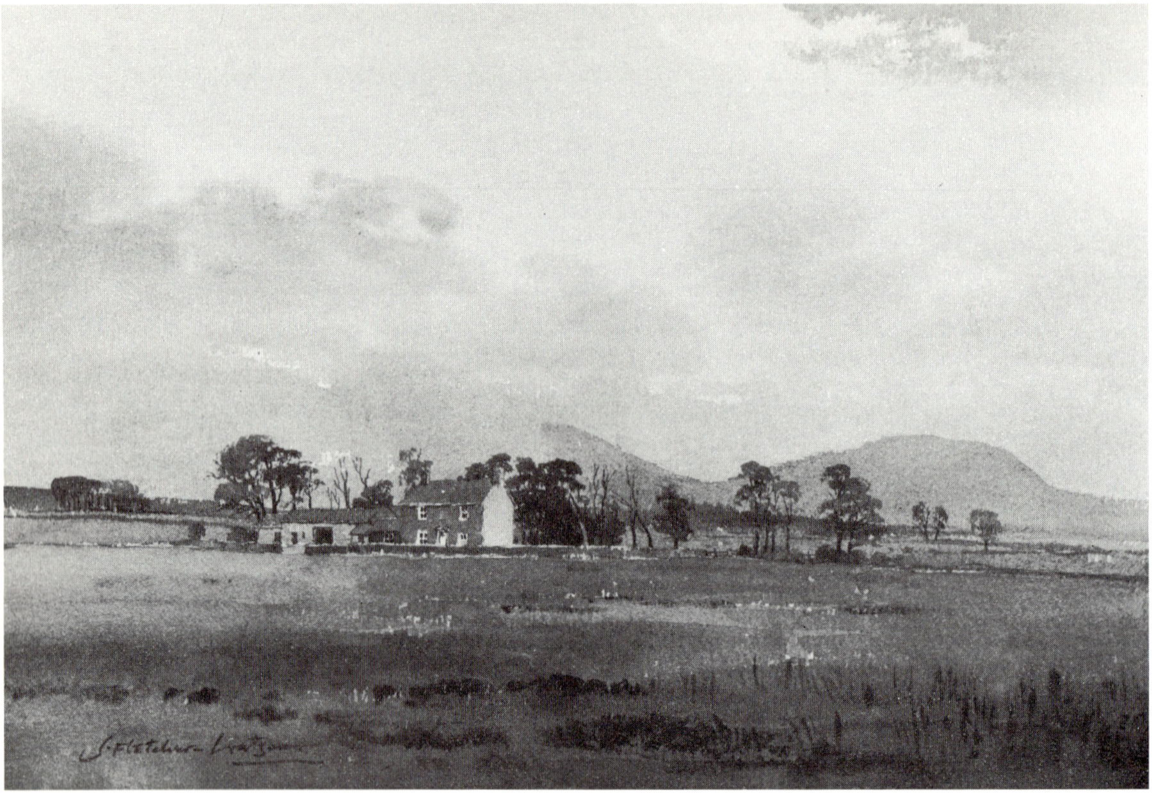

52 Troutbeck.

the time I had finished the final touches of foreground grass it was too dark to see.

Perhaps this is a suitable picture with which to end this chapter on the Lake District. My endeavour has been to give you a wide variety of mountain and lake subjects to help you in your *own* choice of subject to paint, and at the same time to enter into the techniques of painting which are required for this unique countryside – skies, clouds coming over mountain tops, snow on mountains, water, trees, roads, buildings and so forth.

In spite of all this beauty in Cumbria, there are other places we are going to visit and discuss which will have still further problems and delights for the painter.

3 Painting in the Cotswolds

When the name Cotswold is mentioned it immediately conjures up a picture in most people's imagination of old stone villages with gray stone roofs and walls, of steep gables with stone mullioned windows with leaded glazing, and rolling country with stone walls round the fields instead of hedges. All this is true of the Cotswolds and still exists, although farmers find it expensive to repair and rebuild stone walls and they sometimes use post and wire for their fences instead.

In spite of these difficulties there is a very strong desire in the Cotswolds to retain the predominance of stone, and all new buildings in the area have to be built in real stone or artificial stone as a matter of law insisted on by all local Councils. Because of this we have a countryside which is largely unspoilt and very attractive to the painter.

I will start with a view of Windrush village not seen from the street but looked at from behind the houses to the north, where many of the cottages look over a large sloping field to a distant view of the Windrush valley and the River Windrush twisting and winding through grazing lands and old willow trees.

If you look at figure **53 Windrush village**, from the north (31.5cm × 47.5cm (12½in. × 18¾in.)) you see a lovely collection of cottages with the church tower dominating and a useful group of lime trees which helps the composition. This was a September early morning, and the trees were a rich dark colour as they always are at the end of the summer – Burnt Umber and Winsor Blue gives just the colour for this. The morning light was coming from the left and the buildings were mostly in shadow which made them a strong stone gray. I find a good mixture for this Cotswold stone is Cobalt Blue and

53 Windrush Village, from the north.

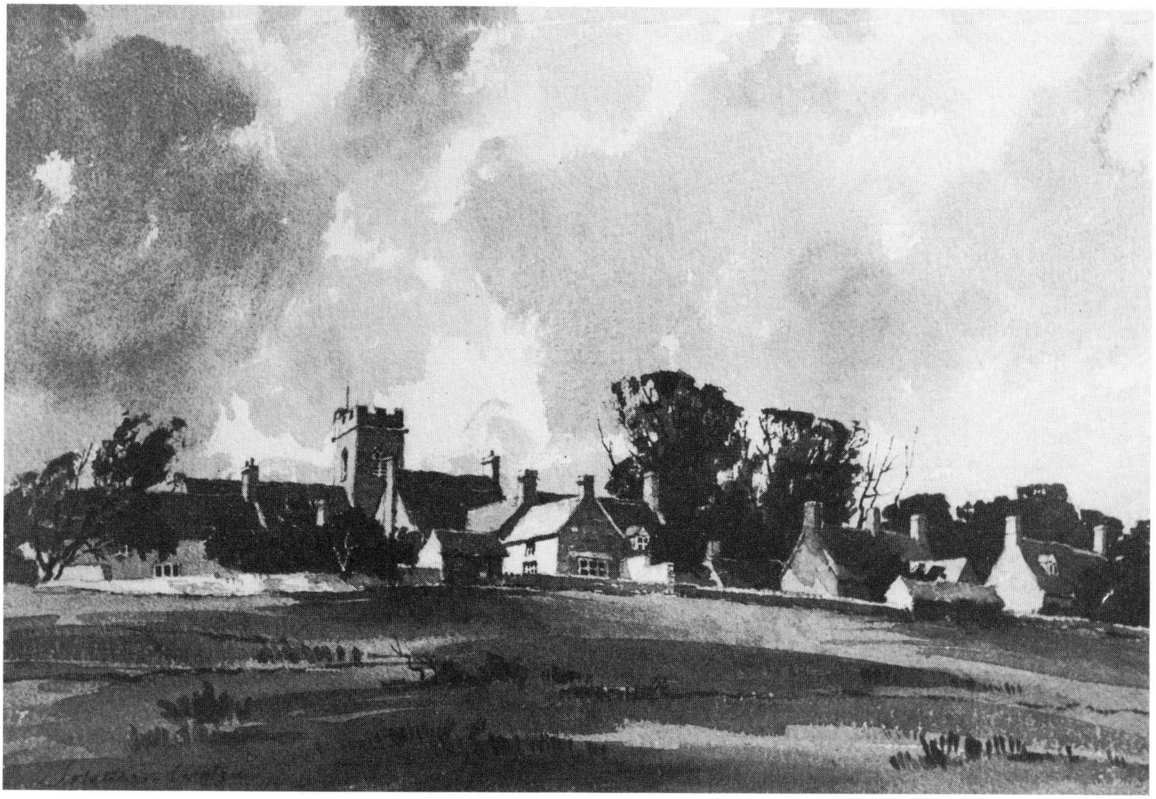

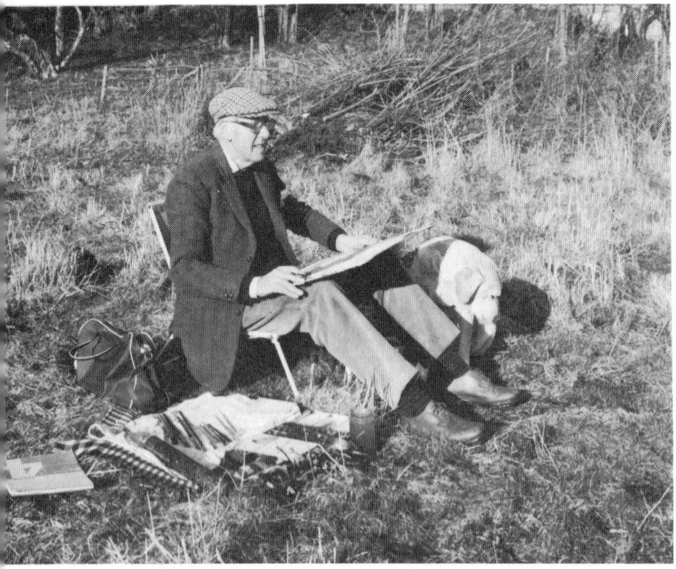

Light Red mixed strongly giving a gray, with a little Raw Sienna added to warm it up.

Before going too deeply into painting techniques I would like to say a further word about painting *materials* and add to what I said in Chapter 1.

I have already mentioned that I usually *sit* when painting, and if you look at figure 54 you will see a photograph of my sitting position. You will notice how *low* the seat of the chair is; I can quite easily reach my paints without having to bend. This is a tremendous advantage as I can use the ground as a table and therefore have plenty of room to spread everything out in a convenient way. My knee position is just right for the board to be slightly sloping towards me.

54 Fletcher-Watson sketching in Windrush.

55 Painting equipment.

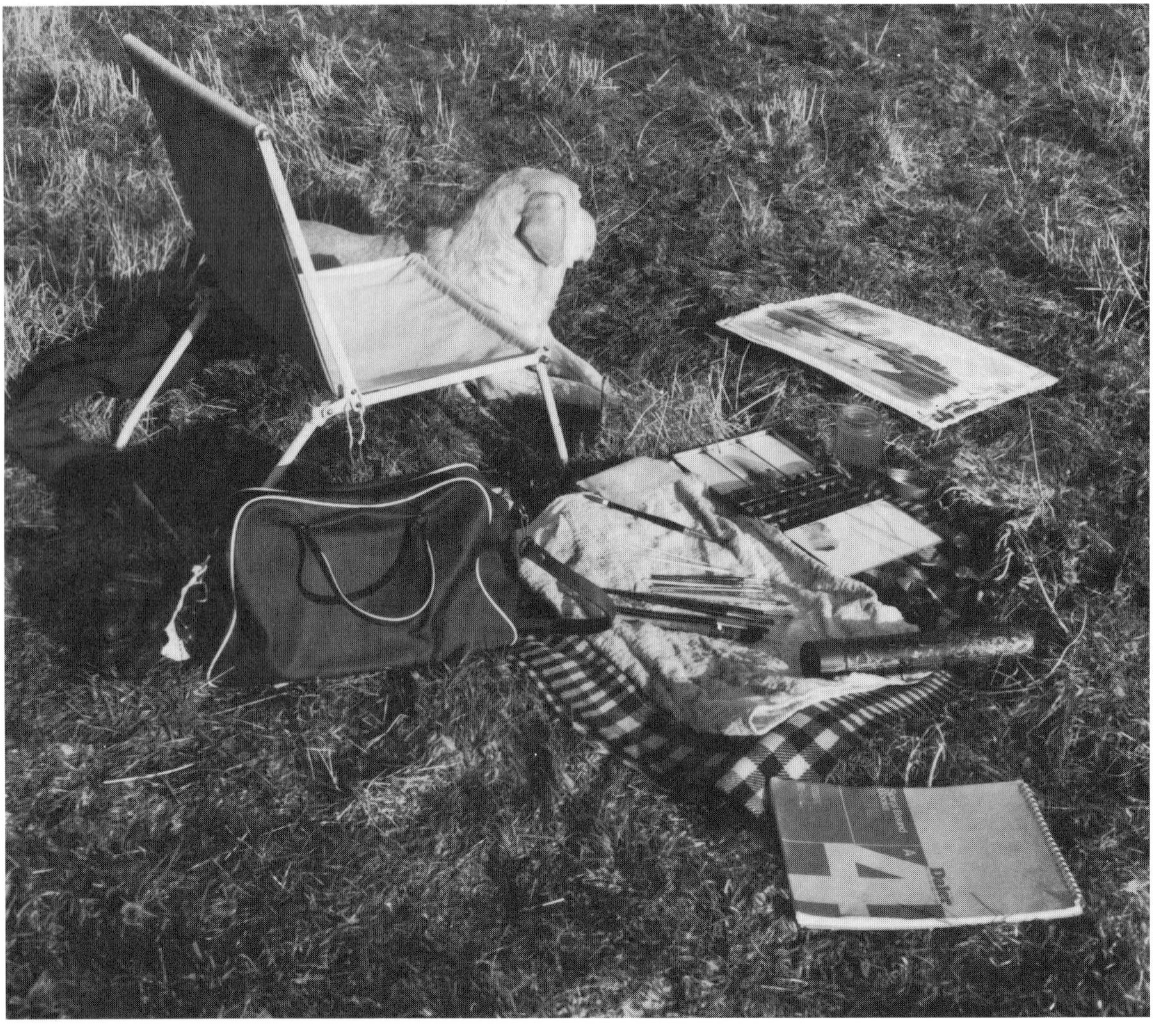

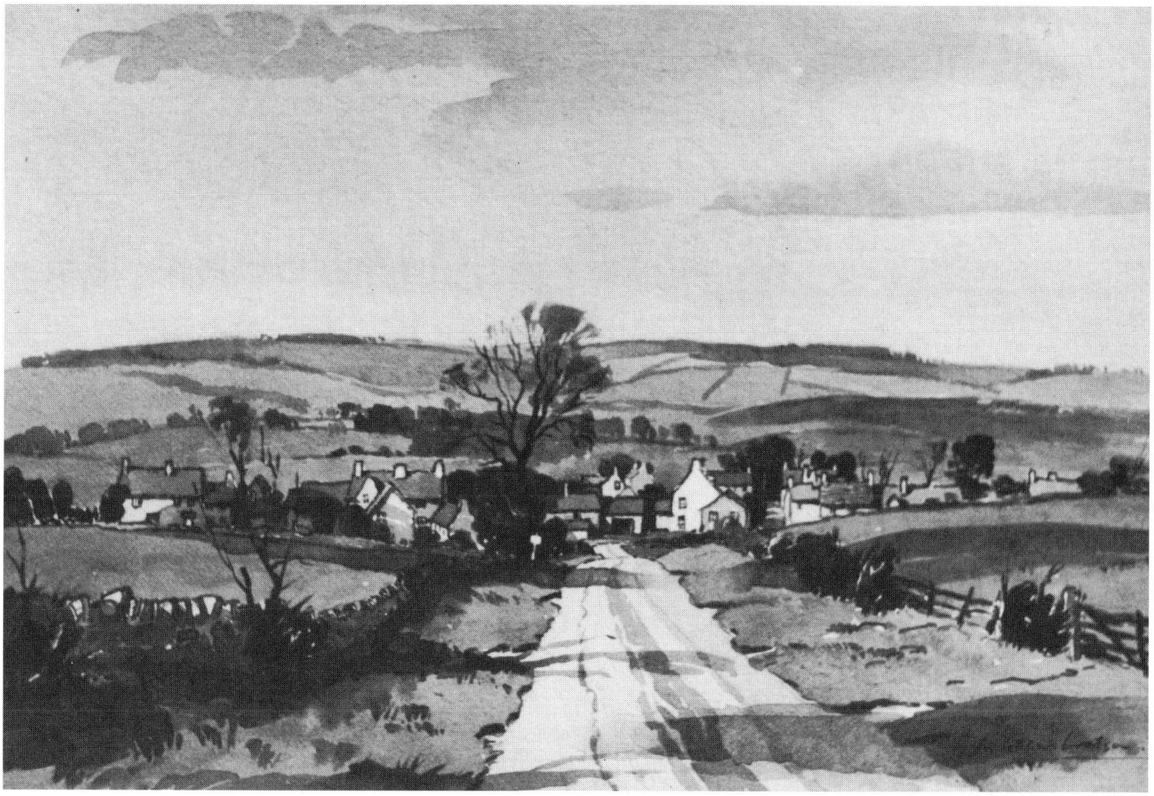

56 Chilson.

Figure 55 shows a closer view of the equipment. The chair has a back which is a great improvement on a stool with no back. Even when one is young one can get tired after two or three hours of sitting without a back to lean against.

You will see the old rug I use to level up the ground a little before placing the paint-box, and it is essential to have this level so that the mixing pans do not spill. I spread an old piece of towelling on the rug on which to place my brushes, arranged in rough order of size so I can grab the correct one quickly. And the water jar is just above the paint-box. A metal brush case can also be seen.

I carry all these items, except the rug, in an ordinary carrier bag which is beside the chair.

The board itself is simply a very stiff piece of cardboard 40.5cm × 56cm (16in. × 22in.) and to this I fix a sheet of watercolour paper with four very big paper clips – I think you can just see these in the photograph.

I have found after many years that this little lot of painting equipment is an easy load to carry quite a long way if necessary.

I need hardly say that my dog is not an essential part of the equipment although I like having him with me, and he often is when I am painting in the Cotswolds where I live. He does not often come on painting trips away from home; but he is an extraordinarily patient sitter!

Now back to the Windrush picture (53). One often finds that the *backs* of houses and cottages are more attractive than the fronts. They very often have not been altered since they were built two or three hundred years ago, whereas the fronts may have modern shop-fronts or alterations to doors and windows made in recent times and not always very suitably carried out.

In the case of Windrush there are small garden sheds seen at the back view, and 'privies' linked to the stone garden walls which all add character, and the numerous different roof levels and chimney stacks give a lot of interest to the grouping.

The Cotswolds abound in attractive stone villages, and I would say to beginners and experienced painters alike that you will find a visit to this part of England most rewarding and be able to find plenty of subjects.

Although I say this with great confidence I must add that there is considerable skill required in choosing the actual *view* of a Cotswold village.

Let us turn to figure **56** showing **Chilson in Oxfordshire** (31cm × 47cm ($12\frac{1}{4}$in. × $18\frac{1}{2}$in.)). This is an all stone Cotswold hamlet; there is no church, but it

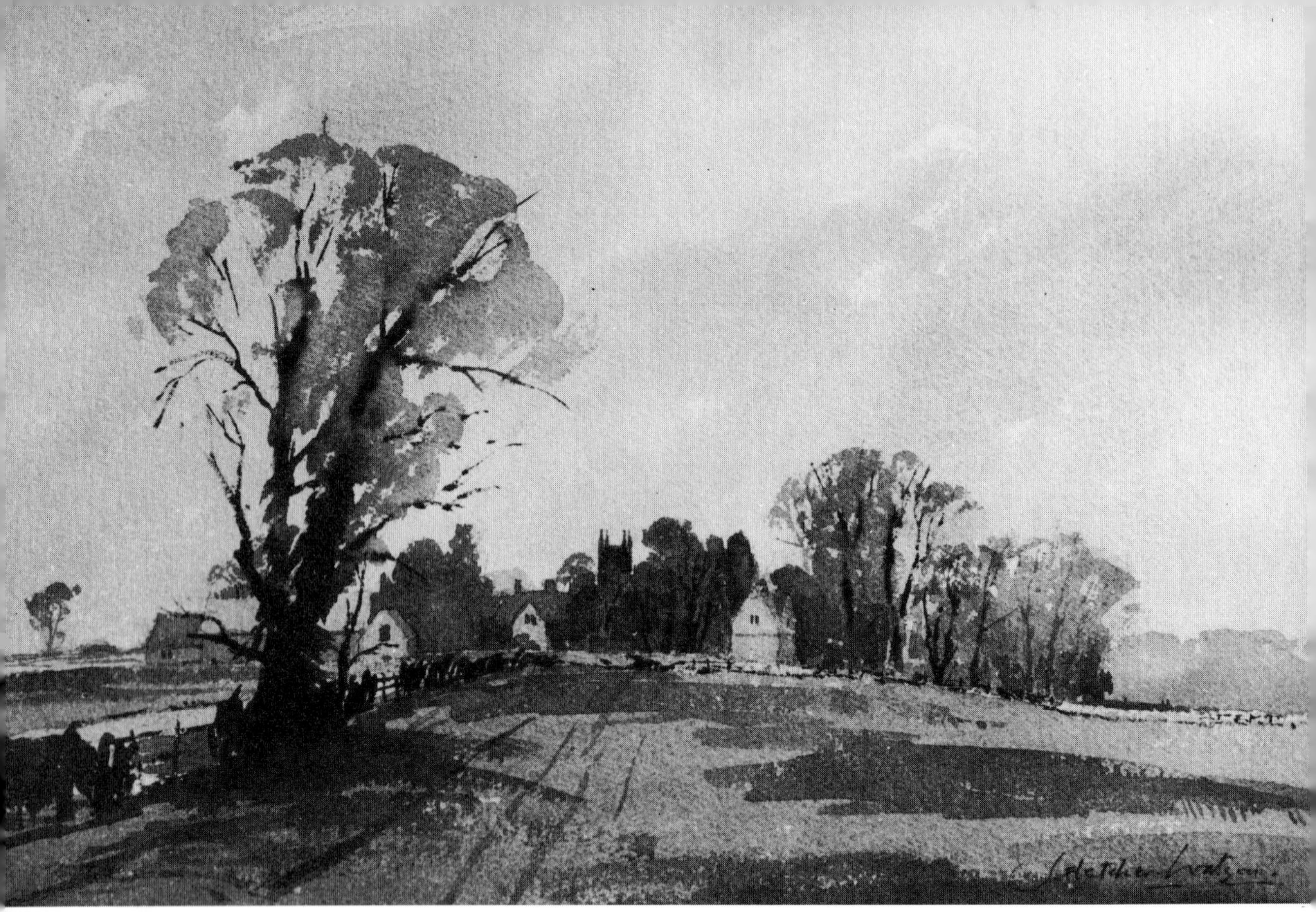

57 Coln St Aldwyn.

caught my eye one day as I passed by on a main road and saw this little view down the narrow side road. Here we can see the backs and fronts of cottages in a lovely jumble, and the large tree to the left of the road is the key to the composition. I tried looking from both sides of the road and the left side seemed the best. The white cottage gable on the right helped counter-balance the tree. It wasn't actually white but very light-coloured yellow stone catching the sun, so I made the best of it as it was such a useful highlight. The typical Cotswold stone wall on the left foreground leads the eye into the picture. You may notice there is pen-work on this stone wall which I found helped the modelling of it. This was added after first having drawn the village in pencil. I then went over quite a lot of the buildings in pen as I wanted them to stand out well, away from the background hills. This pen-work was drawn before I started any painting.

I particularly wanted the large tree to cut into the skyline and at first I was too far away from the village and the top of this tree was below the far hill. As I came closer the height of the tree increased and I eventually found just the right spot so that the tree top was where I have shown it. Sometimes it is worth doing quite a lot of walking about to find the right view-point.

57 COLN ST ALDWYN
30cm × 47cm (12in. × $18\frac{1}{2}$in.)

Another type of village view is this more distant one, painted in late March on a warm afternoon when I was quite happy to sit out of doors. There was a lovely later afternoon light and the whole range of trees were a mellow brownish-blue for which I used Burnt Umber and French Ultramarine. The church tower was silhouetted against the sky, and the house and dovecote were not too clearly defined.

The strong treatment of the foreground tree gave a good contrasting depth to the picture. The ivy clad trunk was a strong dark green and I kept the painting of the whole tree wet and fluid letting the green ivy run into the dark brown trunk, and in turn the dark brown branches run into the wet light brown washes indicating the areas of fine twigs. With half-closed eyes the thinner branches of a winter tree appear as a single mass, best indicated with a wash rather than lots of thin brush strokes which can start to appear laboured.

WINDRUSH MILL
(colour plate 4, between pages 120 and 121)
34.5cm × 47.5cm ($15\frac{1}{2}$in. × $18\frac{3}{4}$in.)

Now I would like to look at a different sort of Cotswold subject, the old water-mill at Windrush.

It is a lovely subject and can be painted from various

angles and, being near my house, I have painted it at various times of year. This was early May when twigs were in bud but no leaves on the trees so far and the grass was not yet a strong green. I will deal with this painting in detail.

Composition

The first thing to decide was how much of the big willow tree on the left to include, bearing in mind that there was a very big ash tree behind the mill showing over the roof. I decided on having just over half the left-hand tree as I wanted the trunk reflection in the water. And then how much water to include and how much foreground bank, and the low trees and fencing had to be considered.

When I was painting this mill the year before in September, the tree foliage was there and I made a rough charcoal sketch on gray Ingres paper before I painted a watercolour. I show this sketch at figure 58 (30cm × 47cm ($12\frac{1}{2}$in. × $18\frac{1}{2}$in.)) as it shows you a slightly different composition. I am closer to the mill and the tree showing over the roof is higher, and the small shed is more to the left and I made this look a little bigger for composition reasons. One does not always have to be slavishly accurate – after all one is creating a picture and not taking a photograph.

This charcoal sketch was high-lighted with touches of white chalk, and, although it was made as a rough guide for the watercolour only, I found it looked rather pleasing in a frame and I later sold it.

Going back to colour plate 4, I was now ready to do a little drawing. I used Arches paper 'Not' surface and with a 2B pencil I sketched in the mill buildings, and with a single outline indicated the various tree groups and the river banks.

Sky

The cloudy sky with blue patches here and there was moving all the time, and it is all part of composition to arrange a sky to suit the picture. I decided that the darker clouds should be on the right to counter-balance the tree shape on the left, and blue sky would be happiest a little to the left.

Having damped the sky area of the paper with clear water and my No. 16 brush, I ran in a little diluted Raw Sienna just over the lower roof. This was followed by a gray wash on the right coming up to what was going to be a white cloud, and a lighter gray at left top of the picture, using Burnt Umber and French Ultramarine. Then quickly, while everything was still wet, I dropped in the blue using Ultramarine forming the white cloud edge. (I had kept this white area dry on purpose so as to get a clear-cut cloud formation.) I brought the blue

58 Windrush Mill, charcoal sketch.

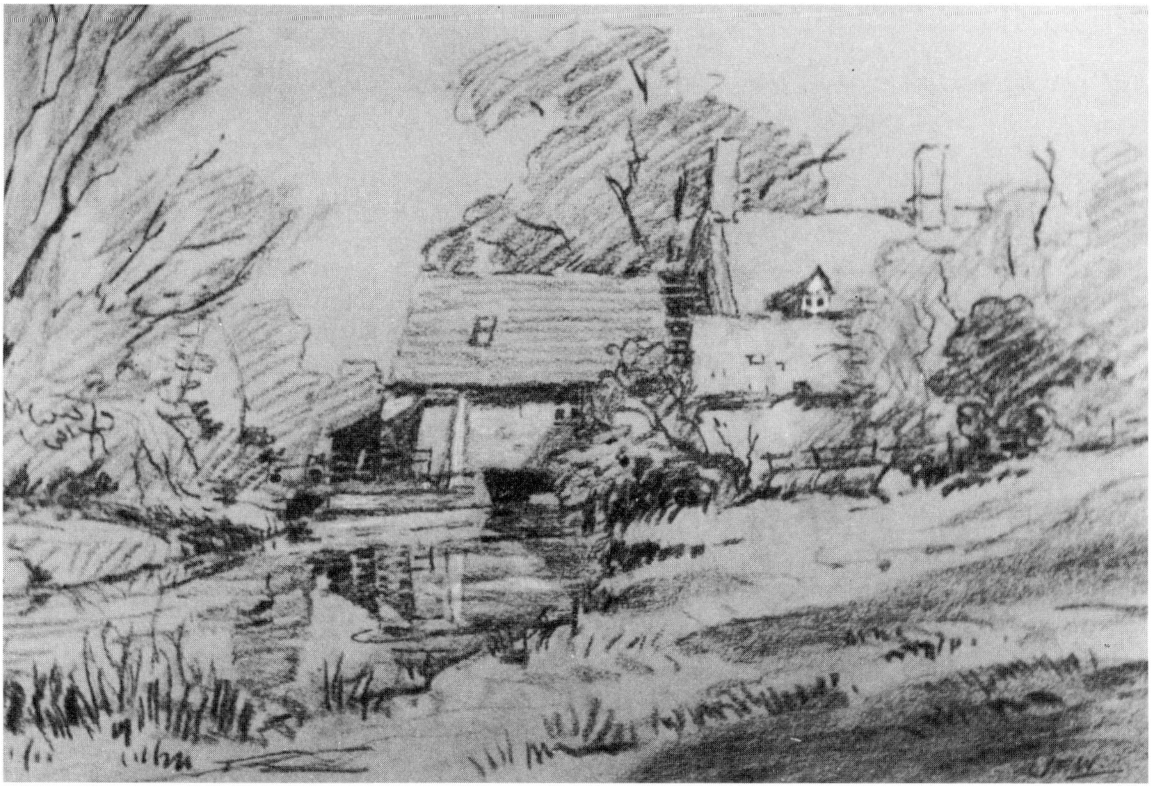

down into the yellow where it ran a little and then merged it into some more light gray which I added at this time.

This light gray was then washed all over the lower parts of the paper, over buildings, trees and banks but *not* over the water, which was left white.

Still using my No. 16 brush, I then painted in some darker gray for the cloud high up on the right; the paper was still damp enough for the colour to run slightly giving the overlaid gray cloud a soft edge. I used the same brown and blue to get the gray colour but added a little Indian Red to give it a warmer darker colour and a slightly purple touch. Indian Red is a very useful colour to bring into cloudy skies sometimes. The sky was now finished and the whole paper was allowed to dry completely.

Middle stage

The next thing was to get the paper covered with the lighter tone colours against which to place darker tones later. Never paint the dark tones first, always *last*.

I mixed Burnt Sienna and Cobalt Blue to give a brownish-gray for the lower mill roof, and by adjusting the mixture I got a bluish-gray for the higher house roof. The chimneys and walls of the mill and small shed were Cobalt and Light Red and a little Raw Sienna. This was also used for roof and walls of the small building behind the tree on the left, leaving the sunny wall a watered-down colour. The buttress against the mill had its sunny facets left uncoloured, and also the window.

The small shed roof was covered in light red flat clay tiles and I used Burnt Sienna and a touch of Cobalt for this. I had been using a No. 7 brush for this work.

Now the grass banks and field were painted with a No. 9 brush and Raw Sienna and a very little Winsor Blue. This was the yellowish-green of the grass but a few areas were darker green and there were some cloud shadows as well, and the same mix but stronger was used with a little more blue than yellow. Also, a touch of Burnt Sienna was added for darker passages including the dark reeds in the foreground and certain tufts of grass, using a No. 5 brush. Some of the grass area was still damp and I obtained the slightly blurred effect that I wanted.

A further stage

Trees could now go in with some of their darker colours together with lighter washes. They had to be painted together and allowed to run into each other.

The low trees on the right were various mixtures of Raw Sienna, Winsor Blue and Burnt Sienna, because winter colours were still prevailing although it was early May. I carefully left the wood post and rails white, using a smaller brush. The bushes to the left of the small shed were important as they were one of the darkest items in the picture. I used Burnt Umber and Cobalt at this stage; darker colour was to come later.

The big tree behind the roof consisted of washes of Burnt Umber and a little Winsor Blue for the twig areas painted in first; and the same two colours more darkly mixed were used for branches put in afterwards with a smaller brush. The willow tree on the left had the twig areas painted first with a No. 9 brush, using Burnt Umber and Cobalt with a watery mix. Then came the creeper of Raw Sienna, Winsor Blue and a little Burnt Umber painted with a No. 7 brush. Then with a No. 5 and No. 3 brush the various small branches were painted with Burnt Umber and Winsor Blue.

Now came the distant trees to the left of the mill, Ultramarine and Light Red and with a touch of Burnt Sienna added for the nearer tree.

Final stage

The lean-to shed to left of the mill was painted almost black with Burnt Umber and Ultramarine. The blue door was light Winsor Blue. The white railings were left white paper colour during the painting of the various washes. The gate and dark hedge on the left was painted in dark brown and the willow tree trunk was darkened with Burnt Umber and Ultramarine and so also were the low bushes in the centre of the picture to left of the small shed.

The shadows under eaves were important and were a mix of Cobalt and Burnt Sienna, and the windows Burnt Umber and Ultramarine. Shadows of chimney and dormer window on the roof were painted a darker tone of the roof colour, and shadows of buttress and small tree near the mill wall were painted a mixture of Cobalt, Light Red and Raw Sienna. The flat arch under the mill was given a dark brown-blue shadow.

Now, finally, the water. This had not been touched as yet and I first mixed a medium tone of gray with Burnt Umber and Ultramarine and painted reflections of mill and left-hand small building leaving light reflection shapes for the sunny wall of this building, the buttress and the window. As this dried I put in darker tones of this gray for the reflection of the big tree trunk on the left and the darker trees beyond, and the blue door reflection also went in. I was using a No. 7 brush and kept a few ripples of white paper showing. The edge of the water wanted strengthening with a dark line of brown in places.

When the reflections were dry I painted a final wash of very light gray over all the water and this completed the picture.

Colours used in the painting were Raw Sienna, Burrnt Sienna, Burnt Umber, Light Red, Indian Red, Cobalt Blue, French Ultramarine and Winsor Blue.

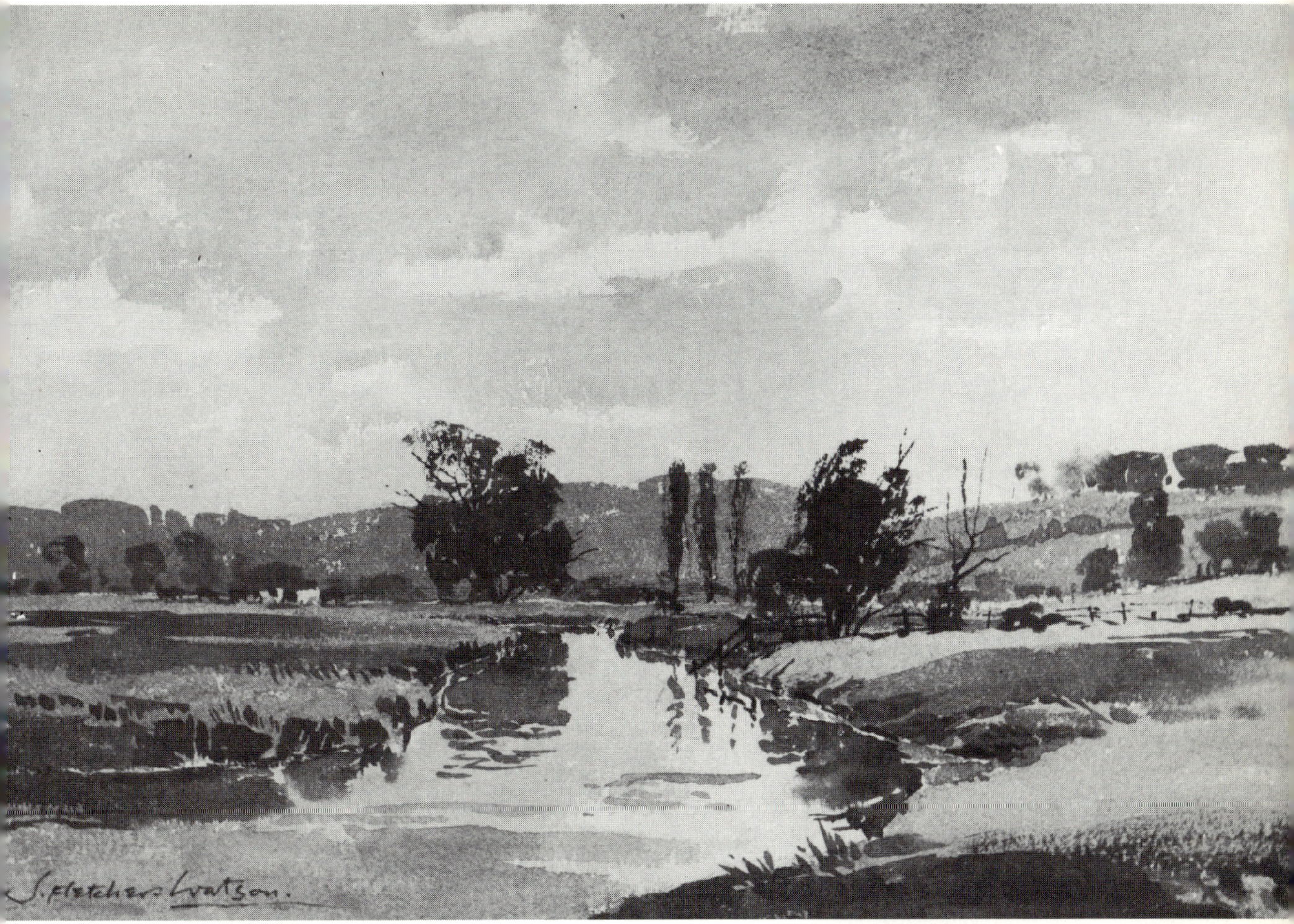

59 Summer on the Windrush.

59 SUMMER ON THE WINDRUSH
31.5cm × 47.5cm (12½in. × 18¾in.)
Whilst we are on the subject of a water-mill and the river, let us look at figure 59 showing the Windrush River in mid-summer. It is a peaceful scene with cattle grazing in the distance and a warm afternoon when it was a joy to be out in the open painting.

This is quite a simple subject really, and the secret of river painting is to choose a spot where there are some good reflections. At this bend in the river the big tree at the end made an excellent reflection and so also did the three poplars and the bit of timber fencing.

With a slow flowing river there is enough movement to cause a slight ripple on the surface, and this is conveyed by making the bottom of the tree reflections separate out with individual brush strokes. The nearer to you the water is, the larger the ripples. On the far away water the ripples are too small to see and therefore your vertical reflections can be painted straighter.

60 A COTSWOLD COUNTRY ROAD
31cm × 47cm (12¼in. × 18½in.)
We have seen one or two road pictures in the Norfolk chapter and the one on the Lake District, and I would now like to draw your attention to the idea of a country road as a subject. There are some good examples in the Cotswolds so let us look at figure 60. This was painted on a late March day with lovely sun and light cloud and the winter colours were quite beautiful. I personally think the Cotswolds is at its best in winter. The distances are very blue and the grass is biscuit yellow and light green and the trees many different shades of brown. In these general terms I have almost described the colouring of figure 60; the distance was certainly a warm gray-blue obtained with a mixture of Cobalt Blue and Light Red.

The road dipped down a little hill and then came up again, more distant and narrower, which carried the eye well into the picture. The distant farmhouse gave a scale to the subject, and the foreground cloud shadows across the road and verges were a help in conveying perspective.

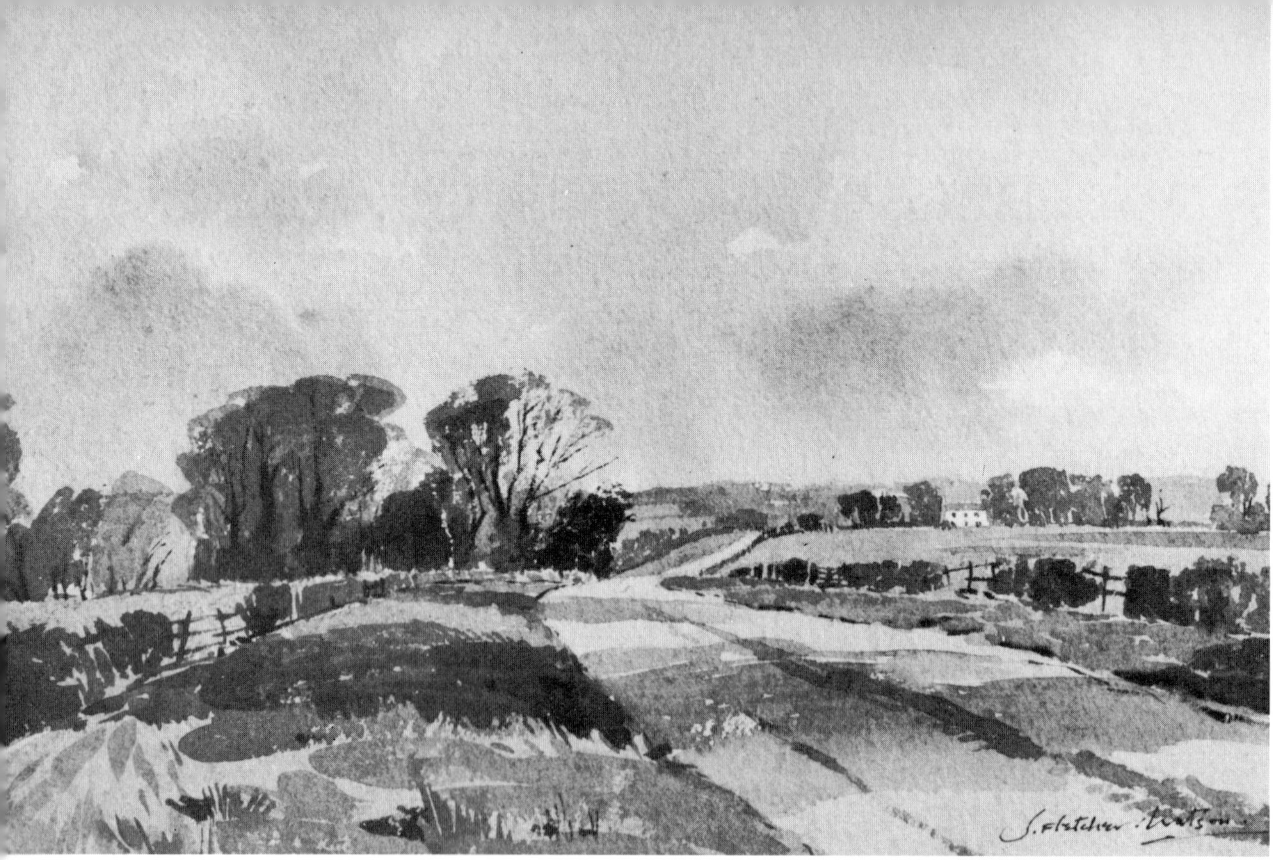

Do try practising road subjects, they are most rewarding and a help when sometimes you are stuck for a subject and don't known what to paint. This picture was painted on Barcham Green thick 300lb paper which is very good to work on.

60 A Cotswold country road.

61 An Oxfordshire farm track.

62 Road near Chedworth.

61 AN OXFORDSHIRE FARM TRACK

30cm × 46cm (12in. × 18in.)

This western part of Oxfordshire is still in the Cotswolds and the picture shows a very lovely rough track not used by cars at all and lined with ancient oak trees, also some very good blackberry bushes. There are not so many of these old tracks left in England these days and it is a real treat when one comes across one.

I felt the need to draw this picture in pen and ink and started straight off with the pen on the clean sheet of paper, using no pencil. The pen is a nice thing with which to draw summer trees when used in a quick flowing manner. I use a broad well-worn relief type nib.

62 ROAD NEAR CHEDWORTH

31cm × 47.5cm (12¼in. × 18¾in.)

There is some lovely undulating country around Chedworth with steep hills and good views of the hills and woods and the village itself. This road view with attractive winter trees was just before you dive down a hill into the village. I was cruising along in the car slowly, hoping to see something that inspired me, and this view struck me at once as perfect for light and colour. When this happens one should always stop at once and get on with it and not go creeping on in case the next corner reveals something better.

The hedge on the left was a kind of bank with biscuit-coloured long grasses all over it; the distance had strong blue which melted into the sky and the dark trees were a lovely foil to this. Note the technique for these small country roads which have rough broken edges and earth showing where the grass verge ends. Put these dark places in with a small brush and Burnt Umber and a little Ultramarine.

SNOW SCENE, WINDRUSH

(colour plate 5, between pages 120 and 121)

31.5cm × 47.5cm (12½in. × 18¾in.)

I have said that the Cotswolds looks good in winter and I would now add that it looks superb under snow. We had our first fall of snow in mid-December in 1983, and I woke up to see bright sunshine and everything white and had a great urge to paint. I ventured out directly after breakfast and it was very cold so I decided to do a pencil sketch only and paint the picture in the studio.

This view of a road looking towards Windrush

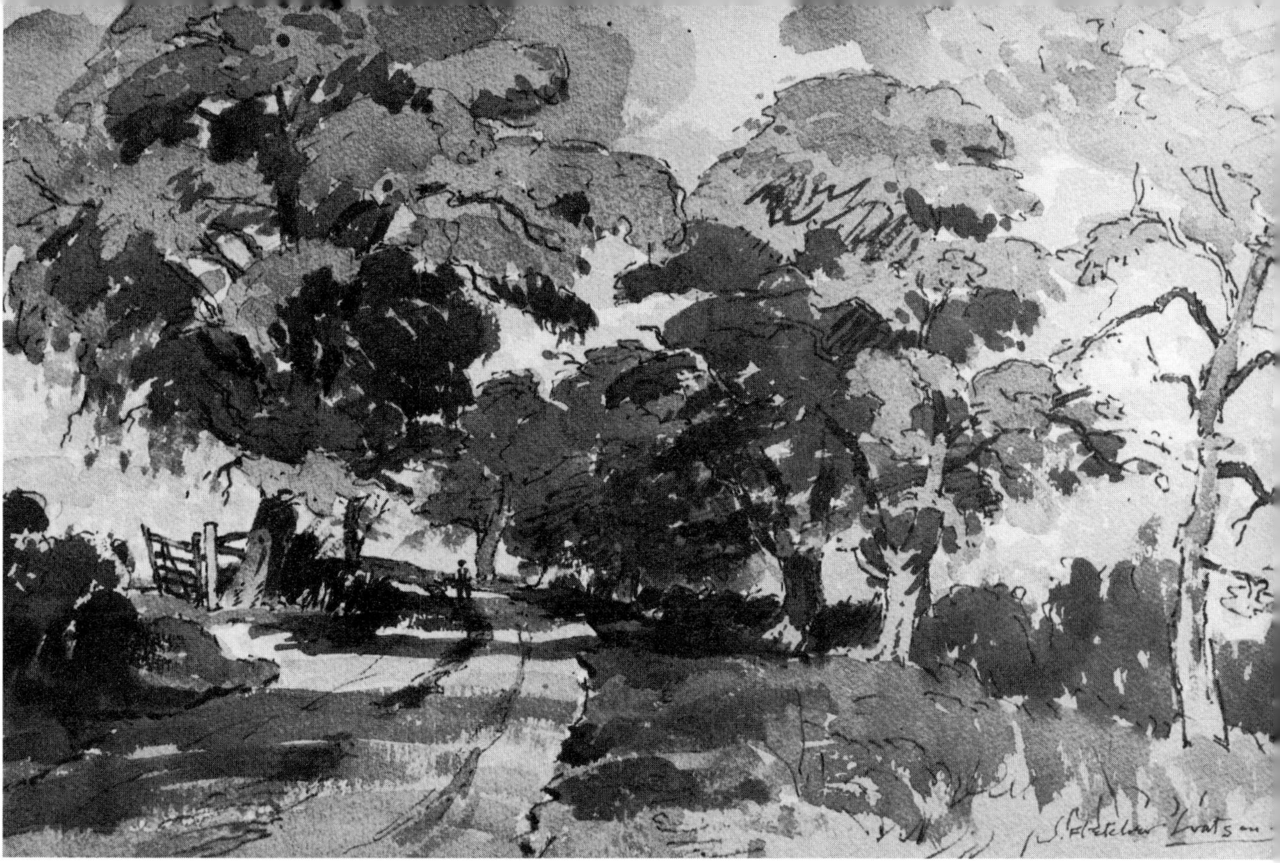

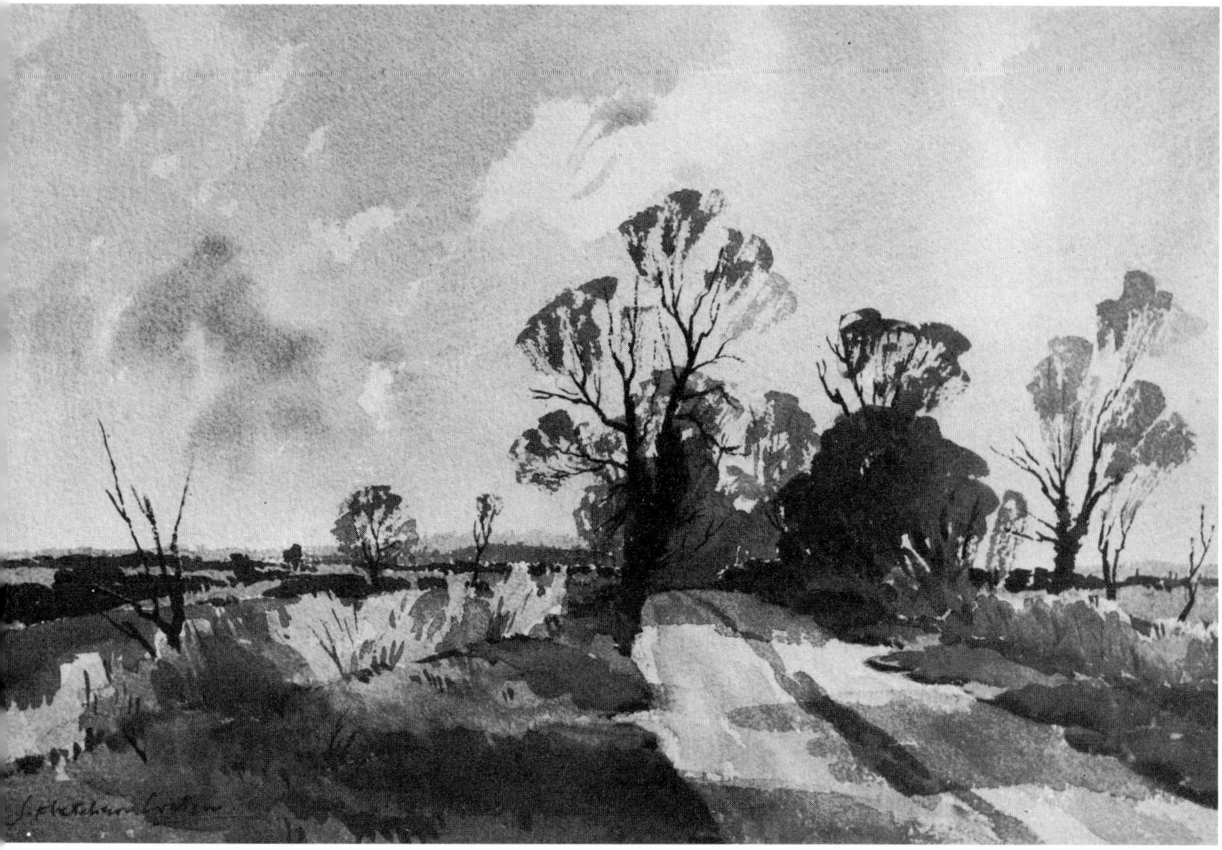

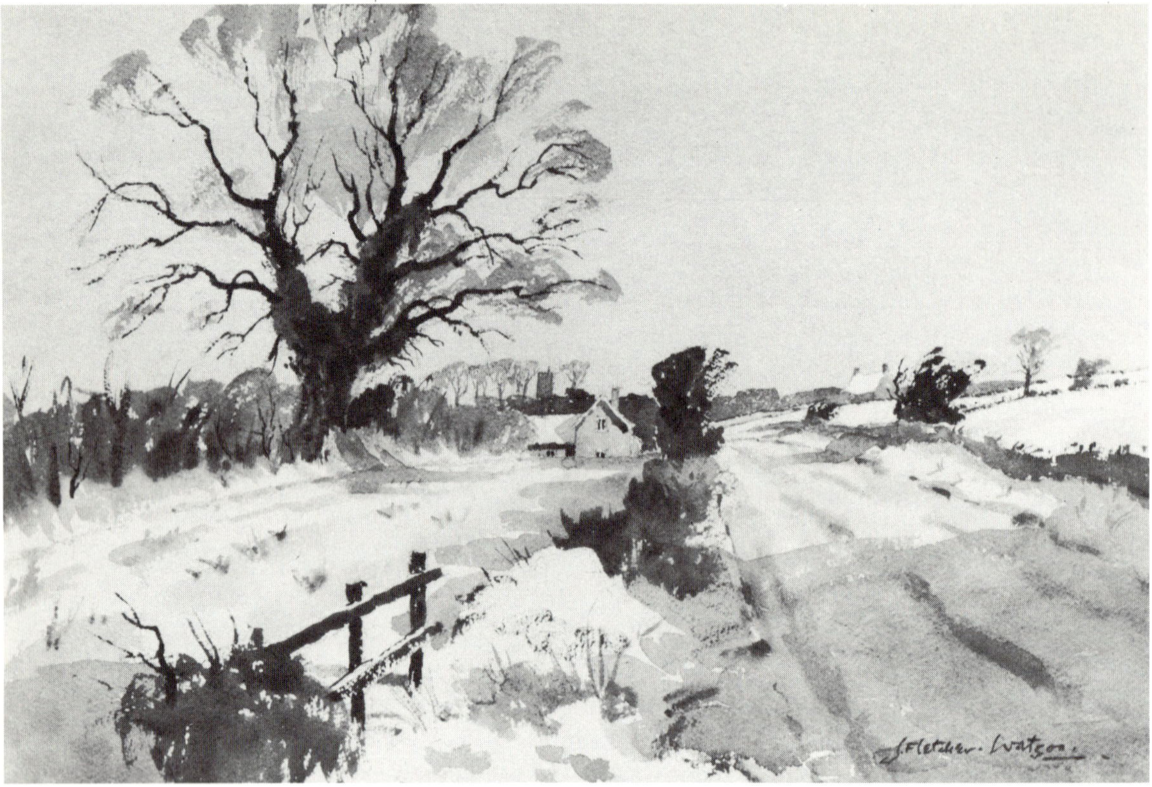

63 Snow scene, Windrush.

village is only a few hundred yards from our house and I quickly decided it was just right for painting. I sat on my usual chair and made a careful drawing in a 23cm × 30cm (9in. × 12in.) sketch book of cartridge paper with a 4B pencil. I was back in the studio in half an hour with the whole colour scheme imprinted on my memory and I started the painting immediately. I used Arches 'Not' surface paper which you will have seen is my usual choice.

I am including a black and white photograph of this picture also (63), as I want you to realize how easy it is to remember *colour* when you are away from the subject, especially when you have been looking at it only minutes before. Looking at figure 63 you can so easily visualize the browny-reds of the winter hedges, the dark green of the ivy on the tree trunk and the blue-gray shadows on the brilliant white snow.

A monochrome picture also has an advantage in telling you if your *tone values* are right. Figure 63 is sharp and clear for the near-to objects and faint and gray for the distant items, which is as it should be.

Now, looking at the colour plate 5, I drew with a 2B pencil the cottage, the road and a rough indication of the big tree with light lines only.

Stage 1

Now I could start on the clear blue sky. What is known as a 'graded wash' was required. They are not always the easiest of things to paint because you must not on any account have brush marks showing. The sky is always a darker blue overhead than it is at the horizon. In winter it is a lighter blue than in summer.

I mixed a pan full of light Cobalt Blue and then left that and mixed a well diluted Raw Sienna. Now, turning the picture upside down and tilting it towards me, I took my big No. 16 brush and started painting the light yellow colour at the horizon line, dragging the brush from left to right and gradually working downwards. After about two inches I washed out the brush and used the Cobalt mixture and joined on the wash to the light yellow one, working my brush strokes across the paper as before. After two or three inches I increased the strength of the colour by adding more Cobalt into the mixing pan. I repeated this process until I had reached the bottom of the paper (i.e. the top of the sky). In this way I had achieved a sky starting as very light yellow at the horizon and grading through light blue to darker blue at the top. I had mixed with the Cobalt a very little Light Red to give a grayish touch and take off the brightness of the blue.

This wash was allowed to completely dry. I now had the rest of the paper the whiteness of the snow. You must remember in watercolour pictures of snow, your white paper is the snow and has to be left unpainted in appropriate places.

Stage 2
Cobalt and Light Red are mixed to give the gray distant trees and the church tower and other distant trees or hills on the right using a No. 3 brush.

Stage 3
I now started on the high left-hand hedge with a No. 9 brush, using first diluted Burnt Umber for the dead grasses at the snow line and then stronger Burnt Umber and a touch of Cobalt for the high thorn hedge, both this side of the big tree and beyond it. While it was still wet I worked in some touches of darker brown of the same mixture and then a very dark bush of neat Burnt Umber just to the right of the tree trunk. Now with a No. 3 brush I put in a few spiky little dark brown shoots and brambles. The hedge area was wet all the time I was doing this painting so that the different browns merged with each other.

And now the main feature of the painting which made it an interesting composition, the big winter tree.

The hedge was still damp and I wanted the tree trunk to merge with the brown hedge so I hastily mixed some Raw Sienna and Burnt Umber and started painting from the bottom upwards with a No. 7 brush. I added some dark green mixing Raw Sienna and Winsor Blue and a touch of Burnt Umber for the ivy growth on the right of the trunk base and then all over the trunk as I painted higher and higher. When I had finished the three main branches in green I went over them again running in some darker green using stronger Winsor Blue and Burnt Umber. Then I wanted a dark brown for the main branches higher up; using the same brush I mixed Burnt Umber and Ultramarine. I changed to a No. 3 brush for the smaller branches.

Now I had to indicate the really small mass of twigs and with a light gray-brown, Burnt Sienna and Cobalt, and with a No. 7 brush I painted in these areas with dragged brush strokes, giving shape to the tree.

I then put in the dark trees behind the cottage with a No. 5 brush and Burnt Umber. This gave clear outline to the snow-covered roof of this cottage.

Now I could put in the fairly dark foreground bush on the bottom left of the picture using Burnt Umber and Cobalt with a No. 9 brush and, while still wet, the post and rail fence with a No. 7 brush and Burnt Umber and Ultramarine, also the small branches coming out of the bush with this dark brown using a No. 3 brush. I was careful to let white snow show on the top of the rails by stopping short the posts. The bottom rail was stroked in rapidly so that the stiff mix of paint allowed white paper to show indicating touches of snow.

I am painting quickly all the time as I want these different passages of paint to run into each other as this gives a looseness to the work and prevents it being a stiff and fussy painting.

I was working my way over to the right of the picture. I had now reached the middle and tackled the centre hedge: first, the nearer line of low-level hedge went in with a No. 7 brush and the same medium tone of brown as the left-hand hedge. Then at the far end I put on a strong amount of neat Burnt Sienna for the very red looking bush; and, while it was still wet, a very strong mix of Burnt Umber and a little Ultramarine in rapid downward strokes so that some paper showed through and gave the *tall* bush a feeling of thinning out.

I now wanted the dark gray stone wall on the right in shadow to take shape, and still using a No. 7 brush I mixed some strong Cobalt and Light Red and dragged the brush a bit to give flecks of white, and with the point of the brush touched in the broken edge of the *top* of the wall where snow lay between upright stones.

I could now put in the dark brown bush just behind the wall and the second smaller bush further away. Then with a smaller No. 5 brush and a medium strength brown-gray mixture of Burnt Umber and Cobalt I painted the thin line of wall far away on the right and the tree and bush.

Stage 4
The cottage walls were light brown-gray stone and again the much in use Burnt Umber and Cobalt was used, and also for the far-away house on the right. When dry, the cottage windows were picked out with a No. 1 brush using a very dark brown mixture. Then the shadows under the eaves of the cottage in a dark blue-brown with a No. 5 brush, and the blue-gray roof shadow using Cobalt and Light Red.

Now the brownish-gray ruts in the road were done, using Burnt Sienna and Cobalt and a No. 7 brush, and some similar gray lines were marked in the small left-hand field.

Some rather strong yellow grass tufts were showing through the snow in the foreground and Raw Sienna was used for this. Various little tufts came through the snow in the field to the left, and they were either Burnt Umber or Burnt Sienna. The snow was wet from the gray wash so they blurred conveniently as they were touched in.

Stage 5
Now all that remained was shadows on the snow. With a No. 9 brush and Cobalt with a little Burnt Sienna these blue-gray washes were brushed in.

There was a shadow from the wall along the road and one from the bush falling across the road. The centre hedge had shadows into the small field and the big tree cast some shadow below, but its main shadow was of course out of sight in the next field to the left. There was

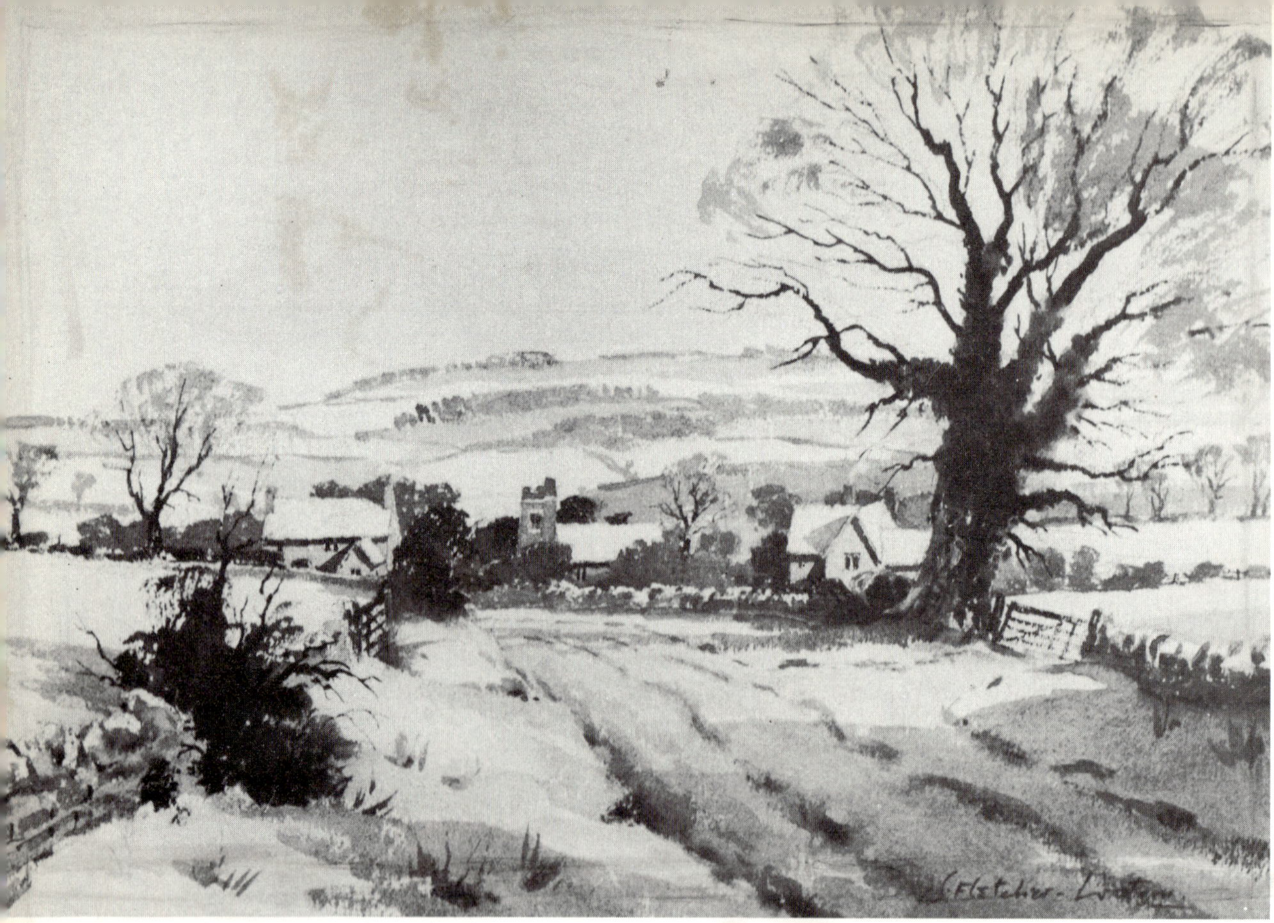

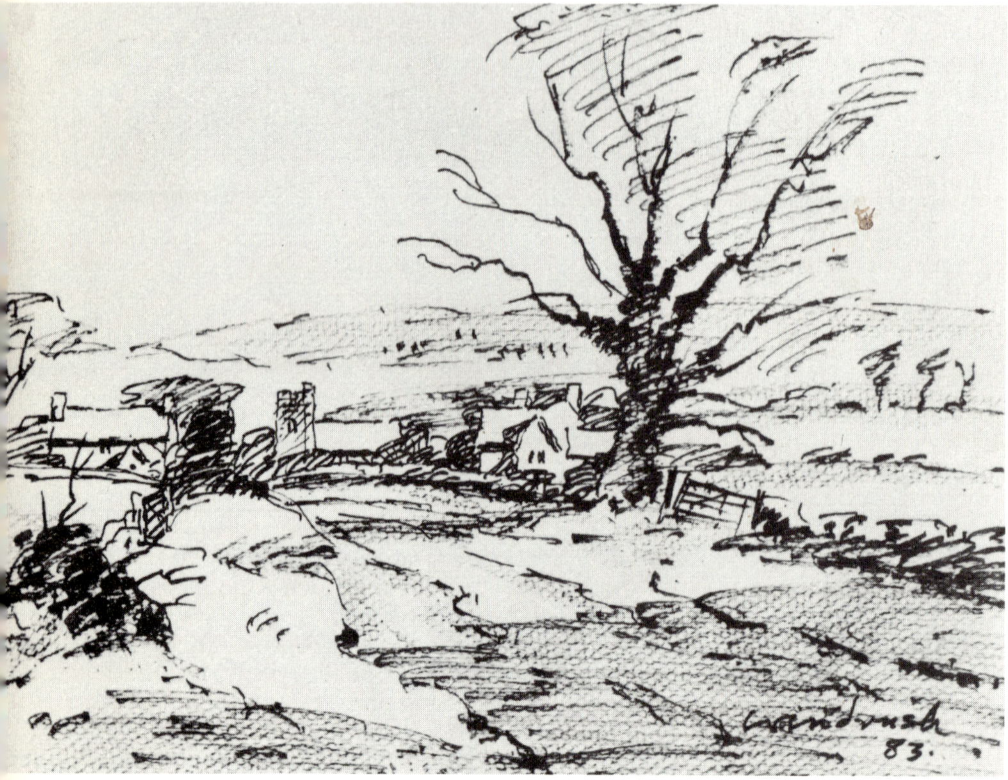

64 Cotswold village under snow.

65 Cotswold village under snow, preliminary sketch.

66 Cotswold village under snow, detail.

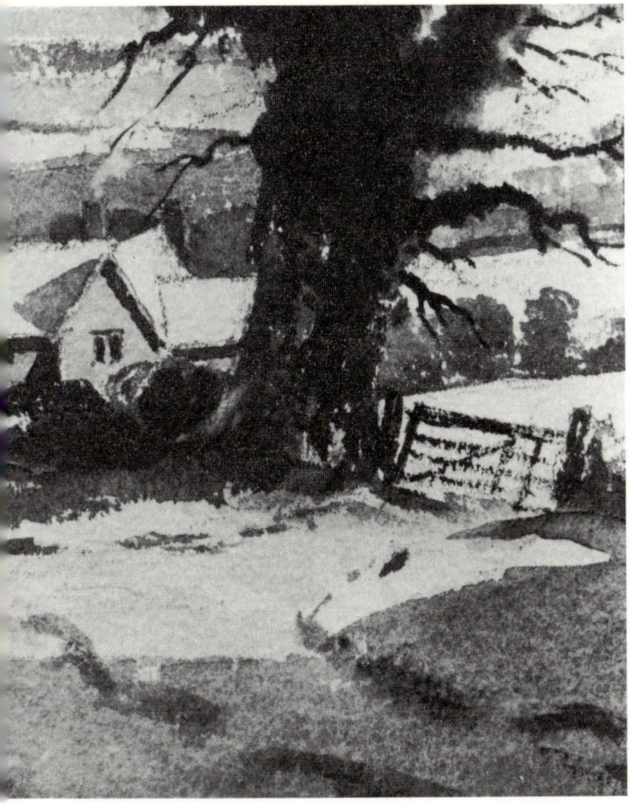

a shadow from the foreground bush on the left and a big shadow across the road in the foreground from trees out of the picture. Into these nearer shadow washes I ran some stronger dashes of almost neat Cobalt. It is surprising how much blue there is in snow shadows on a sunny day.

A few blobs of gray shadow were touched on where there were small dents in the snow. Looking at the picture with half-closed eyes I felt the road required a little more definition, and I put in a light gray wash along the left-hand side where the road camber bent into the verge line. I also touched up the right-hand verge with a little dark brown here and there where earth was just visible.

The picture was now finished and it was time to leave well alone. It had taken me about two hours.

Colours used were Raw Sienna, Burnt Sienna, Burnt Umber, Light Red, Cobalt Blue, French Ultramarine and Winsor Blue.

64 COTSWOLD VILLAGE UNDER SNOW

31.5cm × 47.5cm (12½in. × 18¾in.)

The day after I painted the snow picture shown in colour plate 5 was another day of brilliant sunshine, and I felt it was too good a chance while the snow lasted to miss painting another snow scene. Figure 64 shows Windrush Village as approached from the south. It was a little warmer than the previous day and I decided to brave the elements and paint this out of doors.

I thought I would like to do a quick sketch first to see how the composition went and figure 65 shows this made in a 23cm × 30cm (9in. × 12in.) sketch book using black felt pen and Conte crayon. The composition was in fact a very pleasing one and I was soon at work on the painting.

I was sitting in the snow and I wanted to be fairly quick with this picture. The sky was again a graded blue wash, and I put in the background hills with light grays and browns indicating woods and stone walls. Next came the middle distance of church and houses and darker trees, and finally the strong colours for the foreground walls and bush on the left and big old tree on the right. This had ivy on it again and the detail (66) shows how this was painted on the lower trunk. Part of the bark was showing and then higher up the ivy smothered the whole trunk. Much as I deplore ivy on trees which often kills them, I love seeing it and painting it and of course pigeons love it to roost in at night! Note the simple handling of the five-bar gate in the detail picture – just quick strokes with a small brush is all that is required. The method of painting the house's snow-covered roofs and eaves' shadows and windows can also be seen.

67 SNOW AT WINDRUSH

31cm × 47cm (12¼in. × 18½in.)

One more snow scene before we go on to warmer subjects. This was painted in a previous year and shows a closer view of buildings. Note the quite strong colour given to the stone walls and chimneys which shows up the whiteness of the snow. One soon learns to use the white of the paper and that it is not necessary to think in terms of white paint.

68 GLOUCESTERSHIRE STUBBLE FIELD

31.5cm × 47.5cm (12½in. × 18¾in.)

Going to the opposite extreme of weather to the middle of August and hot sunshine, this picture was painted a few days after the field had been harvested. It was a lovely golden yellow-brown colour; and what a contrast the trees were from the winter ones we have just been looking at.

One can learn a lot from painting a simple subject like this – the distant gray belt of trees, the warm brown shadow in the foreground and the little dark patch at the top right in the sky is actually a strong Ultramarine patch of blue sky which gave a good touch to the whole colour scheme.

To my surprise, the very next day I passed this field and found it had been burnt to a cinder and all dark brown in colour. I was thankful I acted when I did and got my golden stubble picture in time.

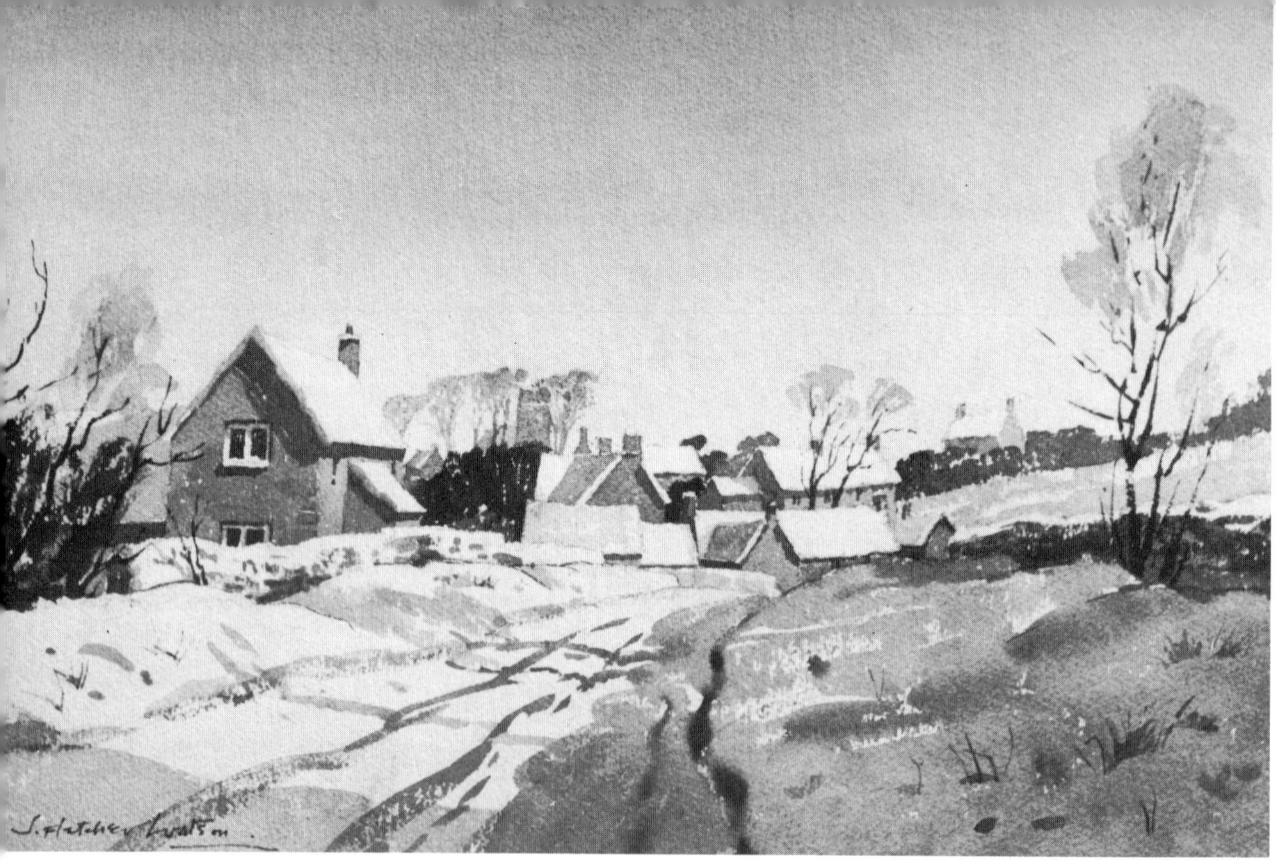
J. Fletcher Watson

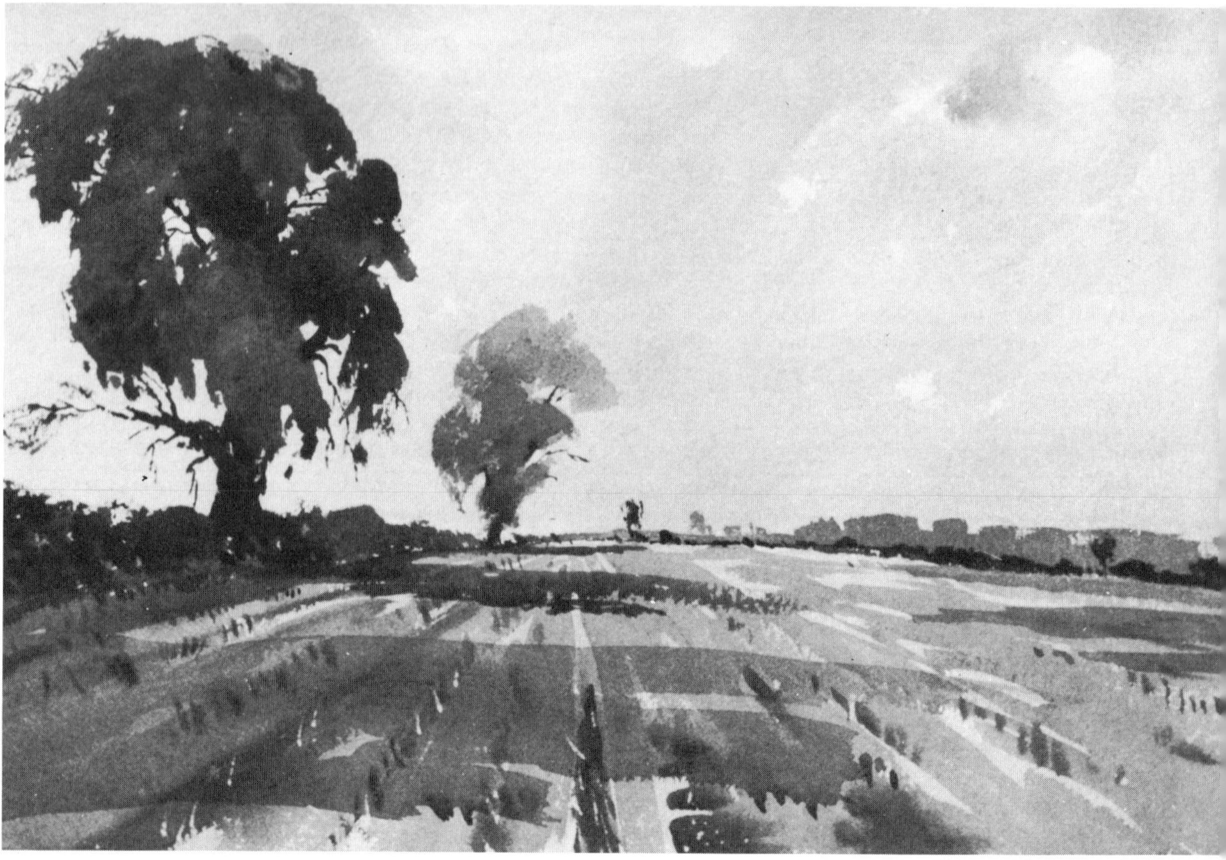

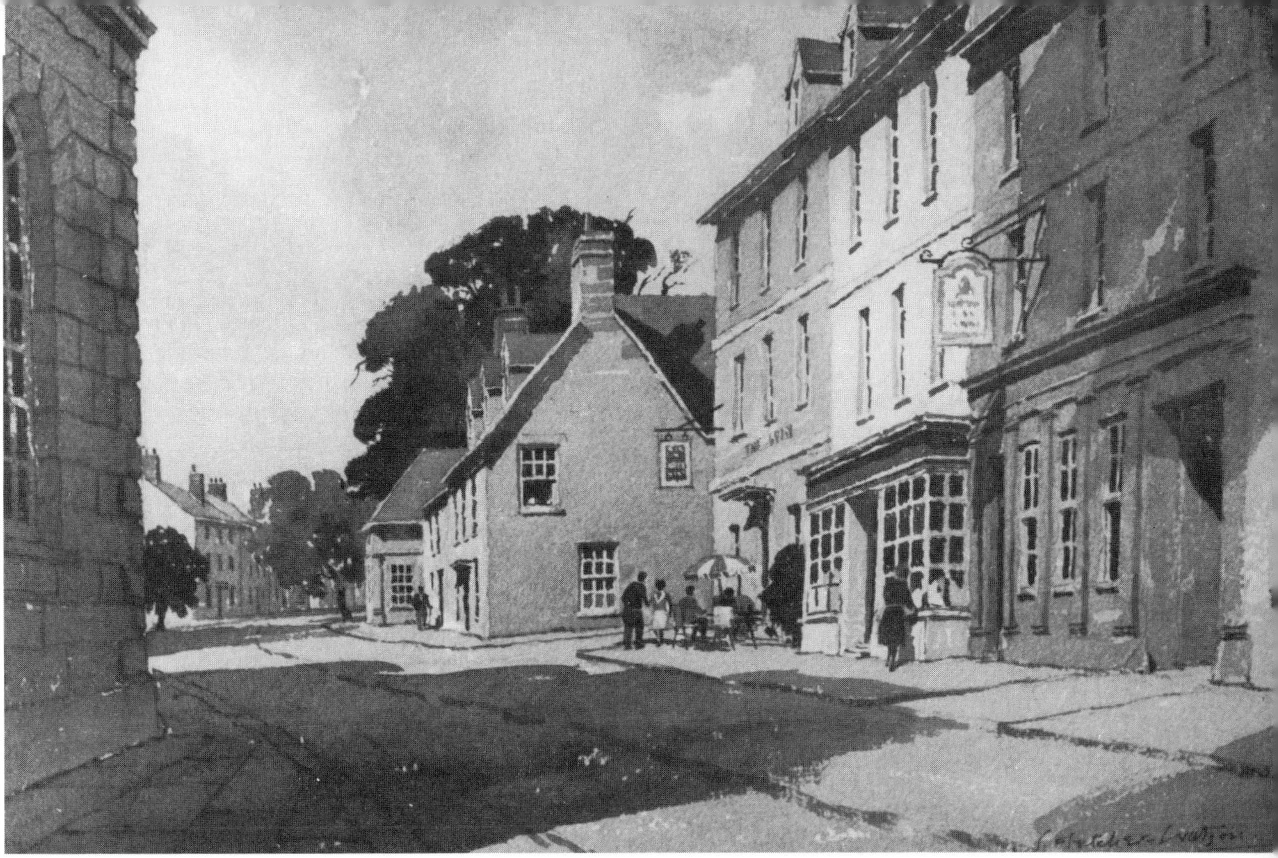

67 Snow at Windrush.

68 Gloucestershire stubble field.

69 Woodstock, Oxfordshire.

69 WOODSTOCK, OXFORDSHIRE
31.5cm × 47cm ($12\frac{1}{4}$in. × $18\frac{1}{2}$in.)
I would like to include a small town which is built largely of Cotswold stone. It lies within the geological belt of limestone which runs diagonally across England for hundreds of miles, starting down in Wiltshire in the south-west and ending up in Lincolnshire in the north-east.

Some of the buildings in Woodstock have been colour-washed over the stone and the town has a charming colour scheme and there are many good architectural subjects for the painter.

This view with the high Town Hall on the left made a good composition and the large tree behind the central group of houses was particularly satisfactory.

Careful initial drawing and a simple knowledge of perspective is rather a must, and be watchful to make figures decrease in size as they go back into the picture.

70 LITTLE BARRINGTON CHURCH
14cm × 19cm ($5\frac{1}{2}$in. × $7\frac{1}{2}$in.)
We have hardly looked at any building subjects where they play the main part in a picture, and this little country church is a very attractive example. It is only a very small picture and it was painted on 140lb Whatman white paper. There is a narrow lane running in front of the church and the white gate opens onto it. Summer trees give it a good setting together with the distant hill behind.

Note how useful the shadow over the porch is, cast from the dark tree close to the churchyard wall, and also note how the pointed Gothic windows are painted with shadows indicating the Label mouldings over the arches.

71 HAMPNETT
23.5cm × 35.5cm ($9\frac{1}{4}$in. × 14in.)
This church with farm buildings makes a very nice rural scene. It is a fairly small picture, what I call my medium size. It is a very good size for beginners, and a pleasing size for anyone to paint. Many of Cotman's and Turner's watercolours were this sort of size, and some of Constable's best oil paintings were this size or even smaller.

Many of the Cotswold villages are on the top of small hills as this one is and very attractive they are. You want to look at the grouping of villages in relation to tree groups. I always try and have a tree or two in a village picture if I can, it gives such a useful contrasting colour and texture.

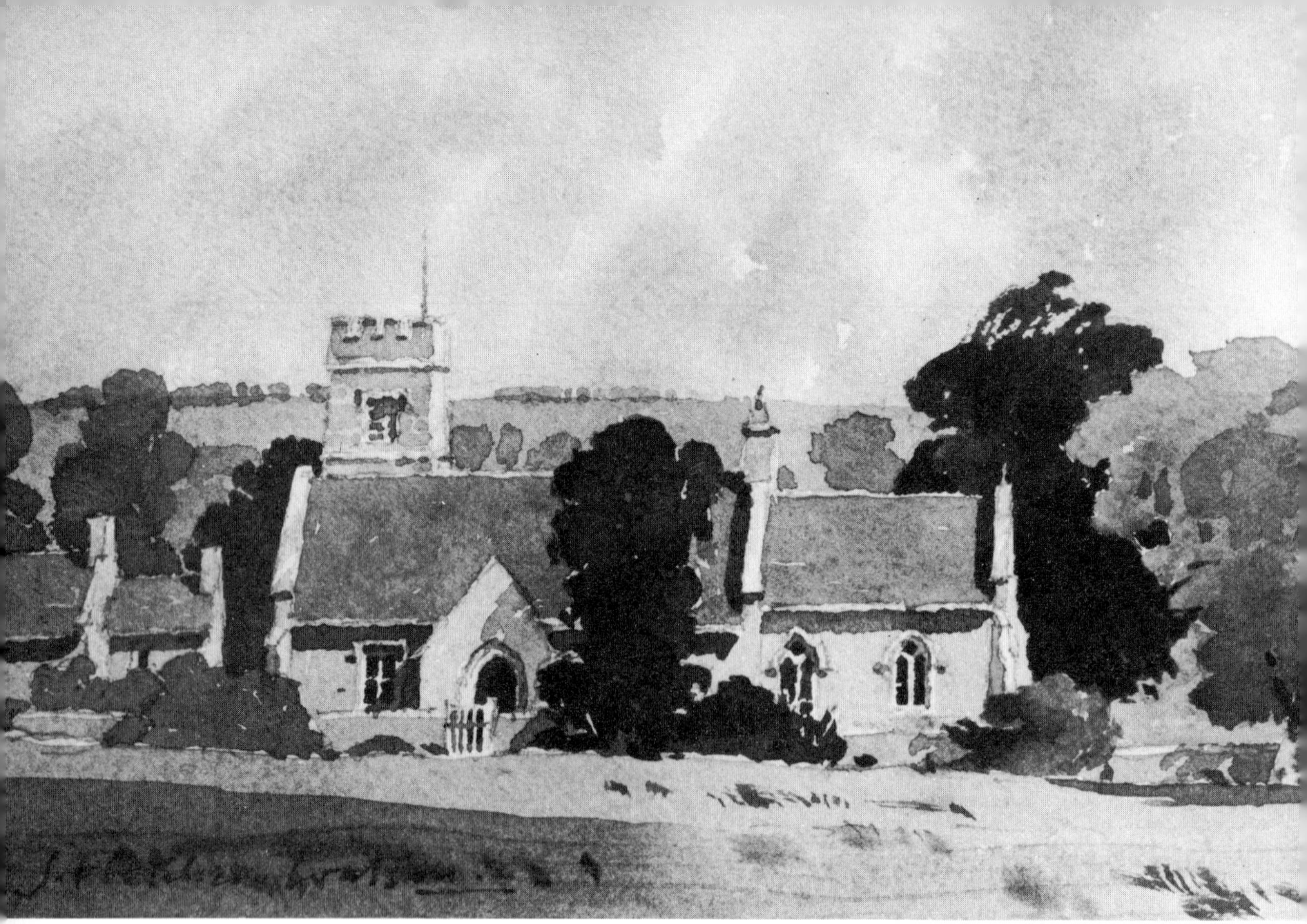

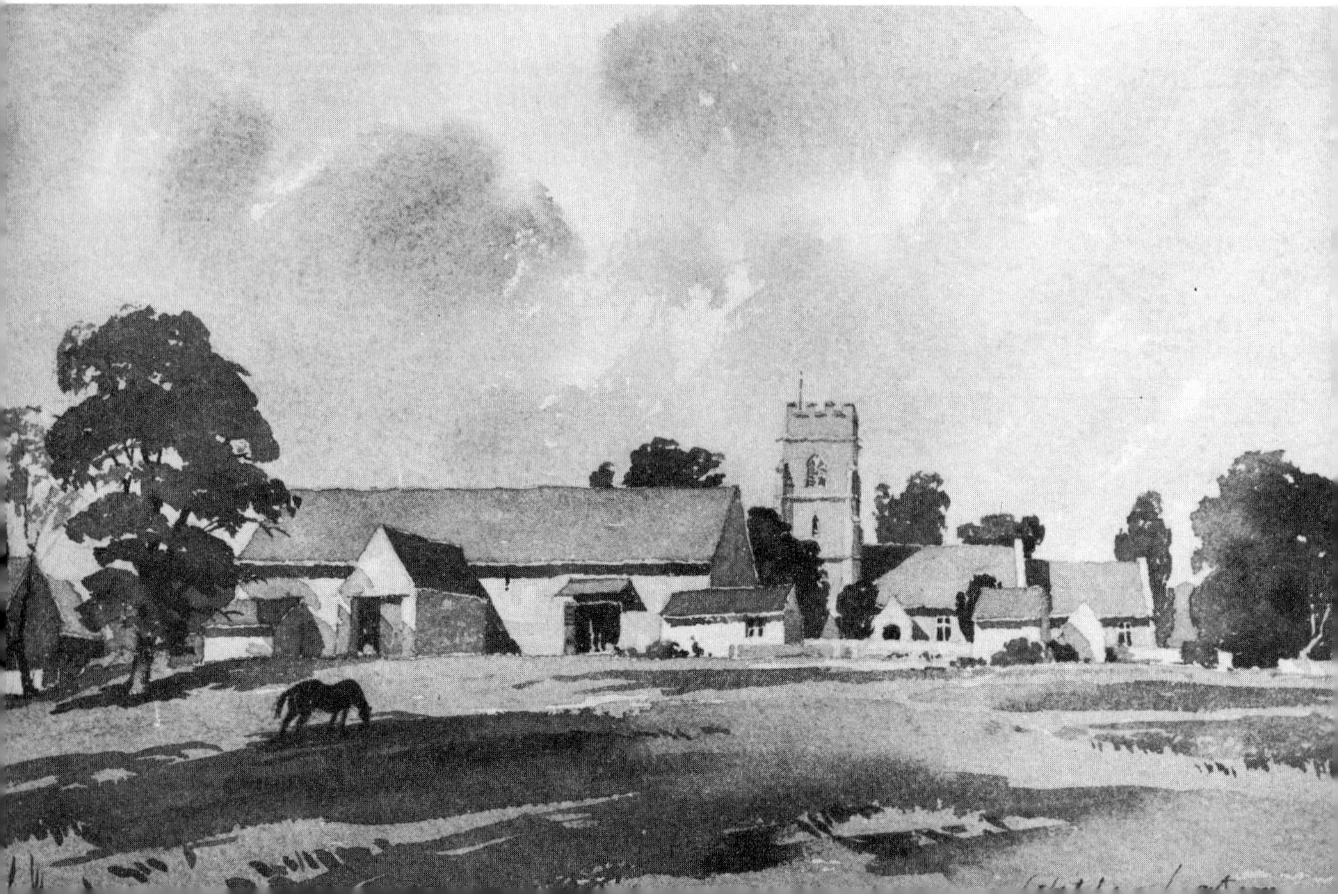

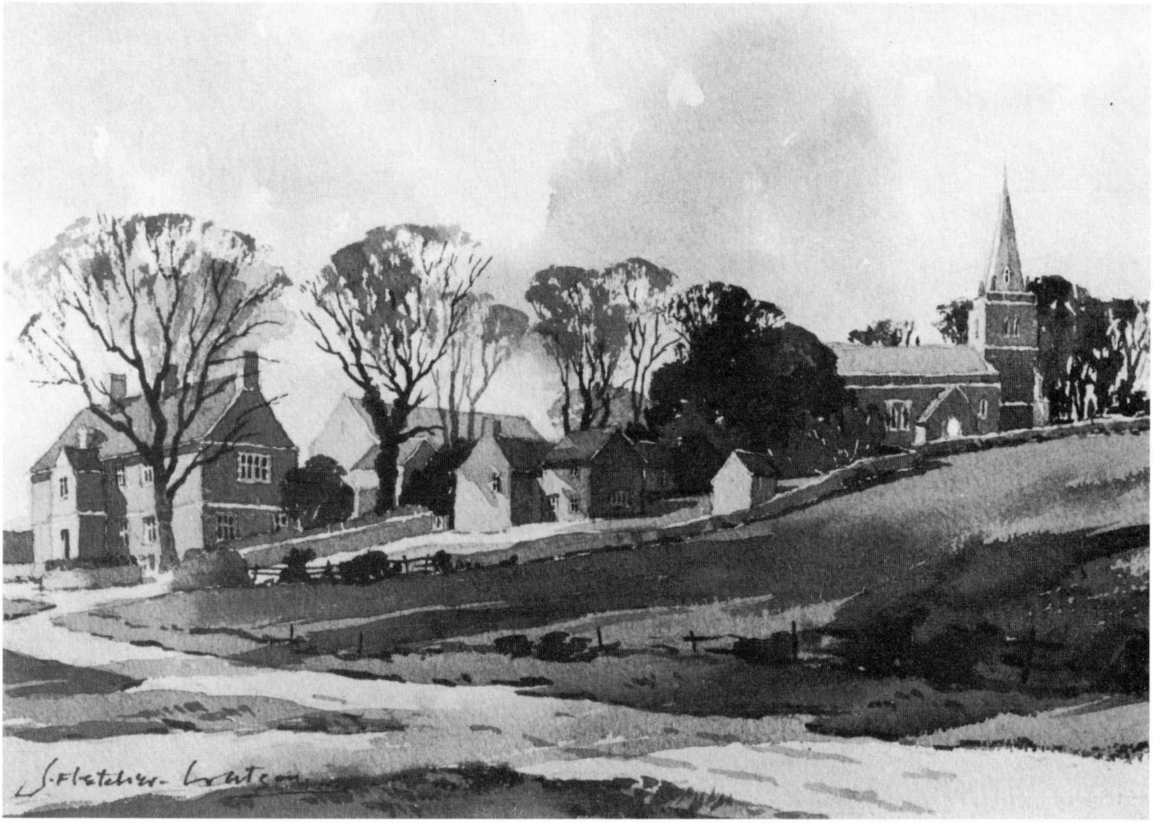

70 Little Barrington Church.

71 Hampnett.

72 Aldsworth.

72 ALDSWORTH
21.5cm × 31cm ($8\frac{1}{2}$in. × $12\frac{1}{4}$in.)
Here is another stone village partly on top of a hill and what a delightful group it makes with buildings interspersed with trees.

NORTHLEACH, FROM THE SOUTH

(colour plate 6, between pages 120 and 121)
31cm × 47cm ($12\frac{1}{4}$in. × $18\frac{1}{2}$in.)
This is quite a large Cotswold village with a big market square through which the main road passes. I discovered this fascinating view one day by exploring up a little side lane leading out of the village to the south. It took me up onto a small hill and from this point one can look across a slight valley to the church on its own hill, surrounded by cottages and the attractive large vicarage on the left. It was an extremely cold day in late February but with a lot of strong sun. I am again including a monochrome print of this picture (73), as I want you to note the tone values. You can see in the monochrome how valuable the dark tree masses are in various places, picking out the buildings in sharp relief.

I used Bockingford paper; it is one I don't often use but I found it was the only one I had with me and it worked very well.

I will go briefly through the painting of this picture.

Drawing
For such an architectural subject quite a lot of drawing was required and I used a B pencil. The composition needed thinking about and I did the forefinger trick, placing the tower well to the left of centre and the big tree with its height was just what was wanted on the right. The houses and cottages would fall into place well with this arrangement and the tree and vicarage to the left of the church were invaluable. The sun was coming from the right and shadows from buildings and trees were excellent.

The drawing took a little time, about three quarters of an hour.

Painting
There was a good mixture of gray cloud and blue sky and I arranged it so that I had some light blue behind the tower and a smaller brighter patch at top right. Always remember the blue is darker as it becomes more overhead and lighter towards the horizon.

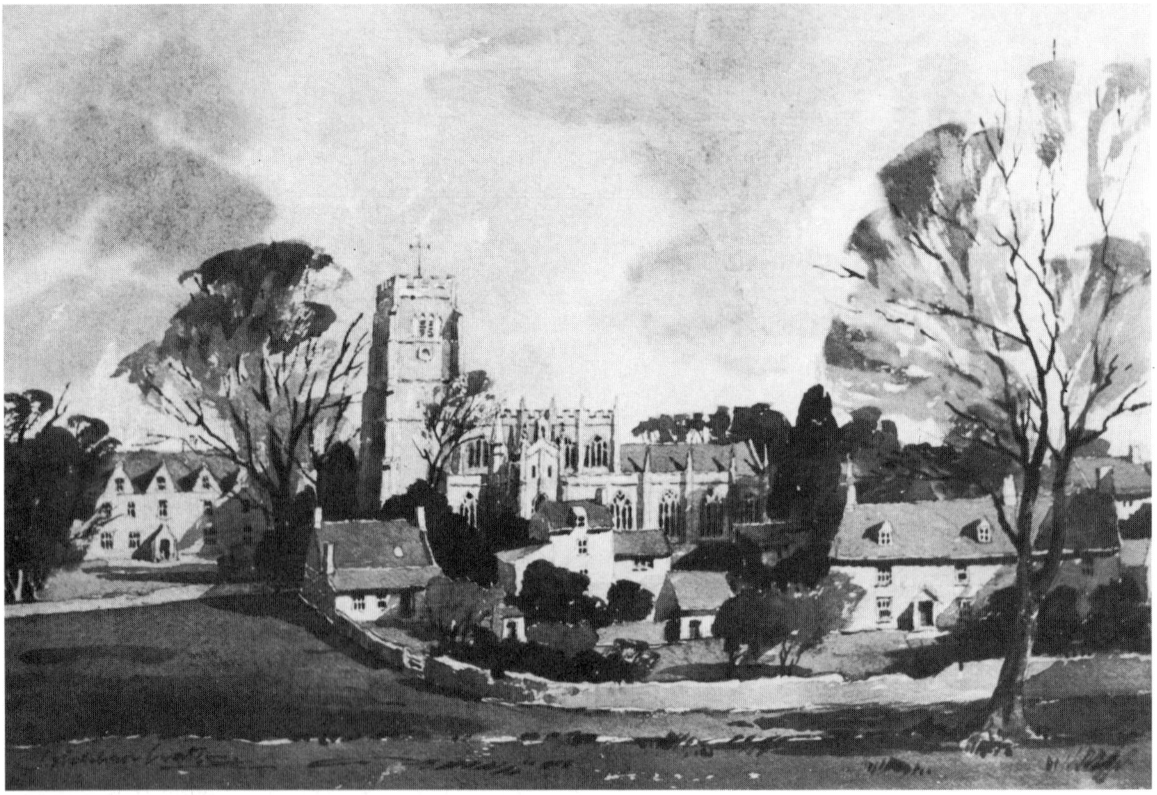

73 Northleach, from the south.

I was using Burnt Umber, French Ultramarine and a little Raw Sienna for the sky.

Now I wanted a warm stone-coloured wash over everything below the sky, and a well-diluted Burnt Umber was right for this. I washed it all over church, trees and grass but left a patch of white for the small cottage in the centre whose walls had been colour-washed white.

My pencil work for the buildings had been with a fairly *strong* line so as to give me something to work to when putting in the dark trees. The pencil would soon disappear with the application of dark colour.

The distant trees went in first, seen over the church roof. They were Ultramarine and Light Red. Then I wanted to deal with the lighter browns of the tall trees, one to the left of the church and the other in the right foreground. The trunks and branches were painted first, followed by washes indicating twigs and the general tree shapes. Colours used were Burnt Umber and a touch of Winsor Blue. The extreme left-hand evergreen tree was also painted at this time, a greenish-brown using the same two colours. I then painted the grass areas in gardens and field with Raw Sienna and a little Winsor Blue and toned some areas down with a touch of Burnt Sienna.

The lighter brown small trees and shrubs were painted next using Burnt Sienna and Cobalt, and then the darker ones with Burnt Sienna and Winsor Blue. The tall yew tree at the right-hand end of the church was painted *mostly* Winsor Blue with only a touch of Burnt Sienna.

The picture was beginning to take shape but I was beginning to get extremely cold and felt that I should finish the picture better at home in a warm studio. So I took a last long look at the scene to memorize the positions of shadows, those on the roof of the church from the pinnacles for instance, and the one on the vicarage from the tree and church. The cottage shadows under the roof eaves were fairly obvious and so were the darks of windows showing up glazing bars. So I packed up and went back home.

Continuing in the studio I next put in all the roofs of buildings with varying mixes of Burnt Umber and Cobalt Blue. Then I started on the windows; there were rather a lot of them. I did the church gothic windows first with a small brush and they were good fun to do. I finished off all windows and doors of the houses and used mostly dark browns but occasional dark blues. I then dealt with the various shadows on all buildings and Burnt Sienna and Cobalt gave me the brownish-blue which was right for Cotswold stone walls. A lot of little

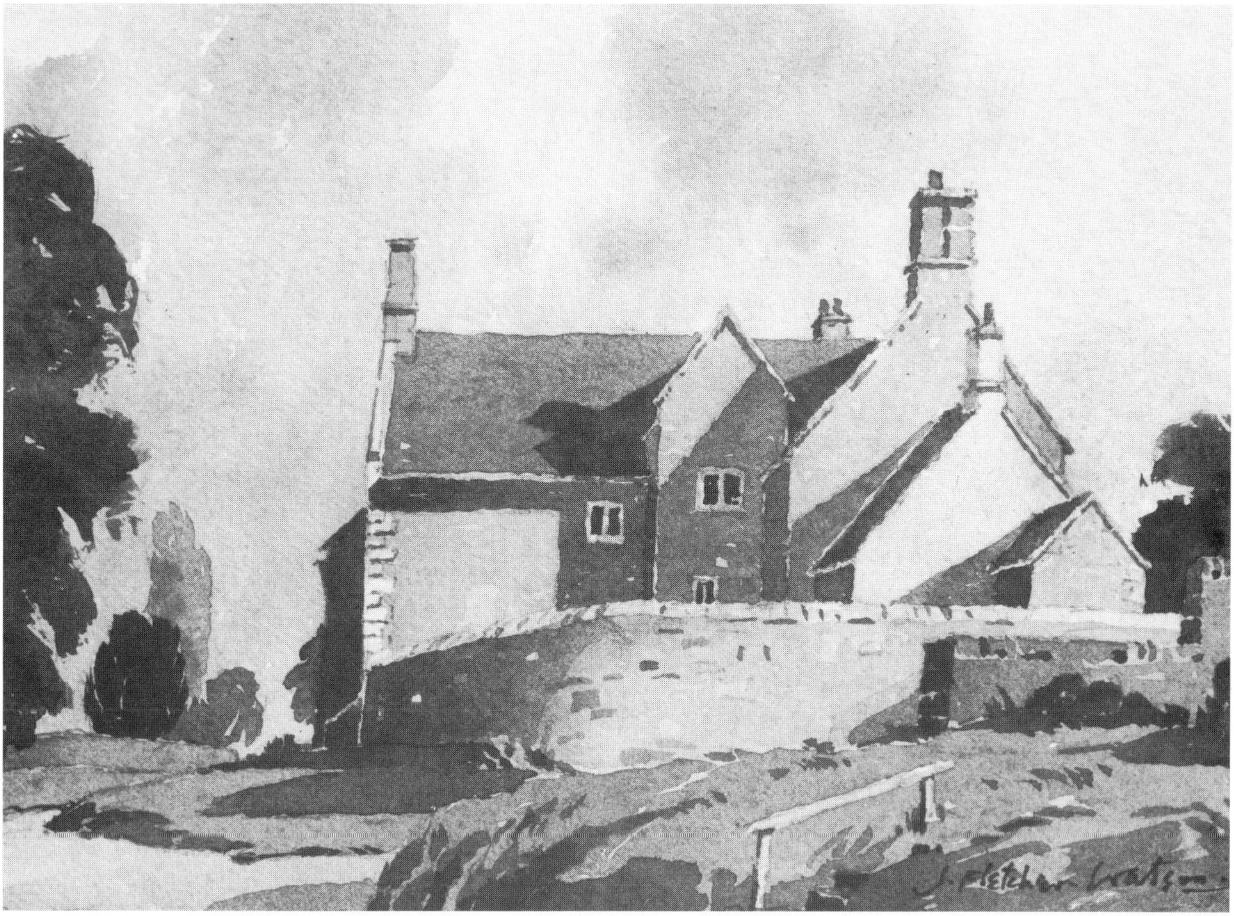

74 Cotswold gables.

shadows were required for buttresses on the church and the eaves of houses. There were some bigger paler shadows from clouds on the right-hand end of the church and the right-hand big house which helped to tie the picture together. The danger of a picture like this is that it *can* become restless and disjointed if you start fiddling with too much detail.

I finally touched in some foreground grass tufts and strengthened up the cloud shadow on the field. The big shrubs just below the church tower were darkened to pull the eye towards the centre. One last item was adding a little warm gray tone to the stone face of the tower near the top and also to one or two cottage stone walls. Cobalt, Light Red and Raw Sienna were mixed for this.

Colours used for the picture were Raw Sienna, Burnt Sienna, Burnt Umber, Light Red, Cobalt Blue, French Ultramarine and Winsor Blue.

74 COTSWOLD GABLES

14cm × 19cm ($5\frac{1}{2}$in. × $7\frac{1}{2}$in.)

Just two more village views to help those looking for building subjects. This old farmhouse stands in the centre of Windrush and was converted a few years ago into a number of small dwellings including large barn conversions. But it still remains unaltered externally, and because of extensions that were made over the centuries the number of stone gables increased and the result of having no less than four gables is rather charming. The tall narrow gable is a staircase. The shadows cast by roofs and gables is always an interesting study, and it pays to watch them carefully when doing a house painting and get them right. This very small painting took about one hour to do.

75 THE FOX INN, BARRINGTON

14cm × 19cm ($5\frac{1}{2}$in. × $7\frac{1}{2}$in.)

This old village inn makes an interesting group as seen from this side view. The front of the inn is on the right where the road runs. It was painted in mid-May when the chestnut tree on the right was out in full leaf, but the two big trees in the centre were only just coming out

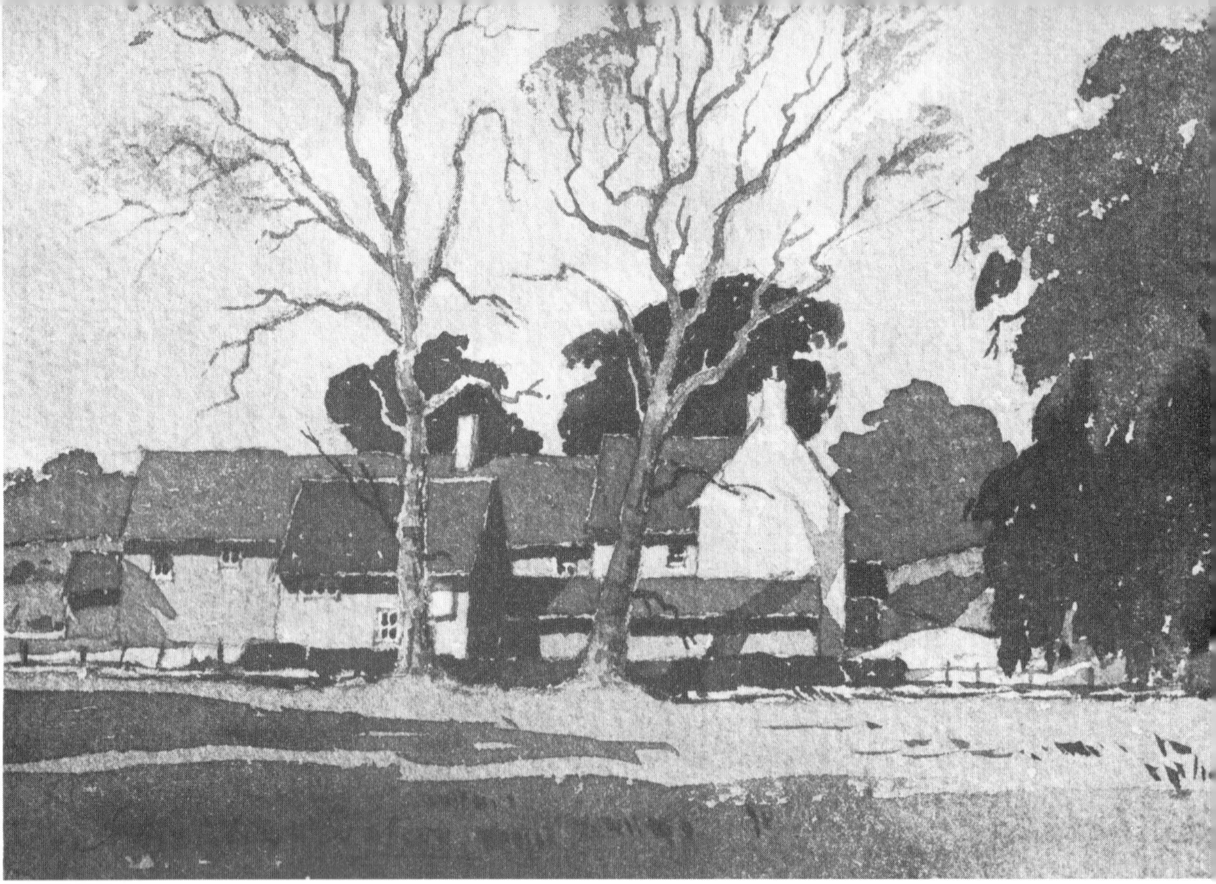

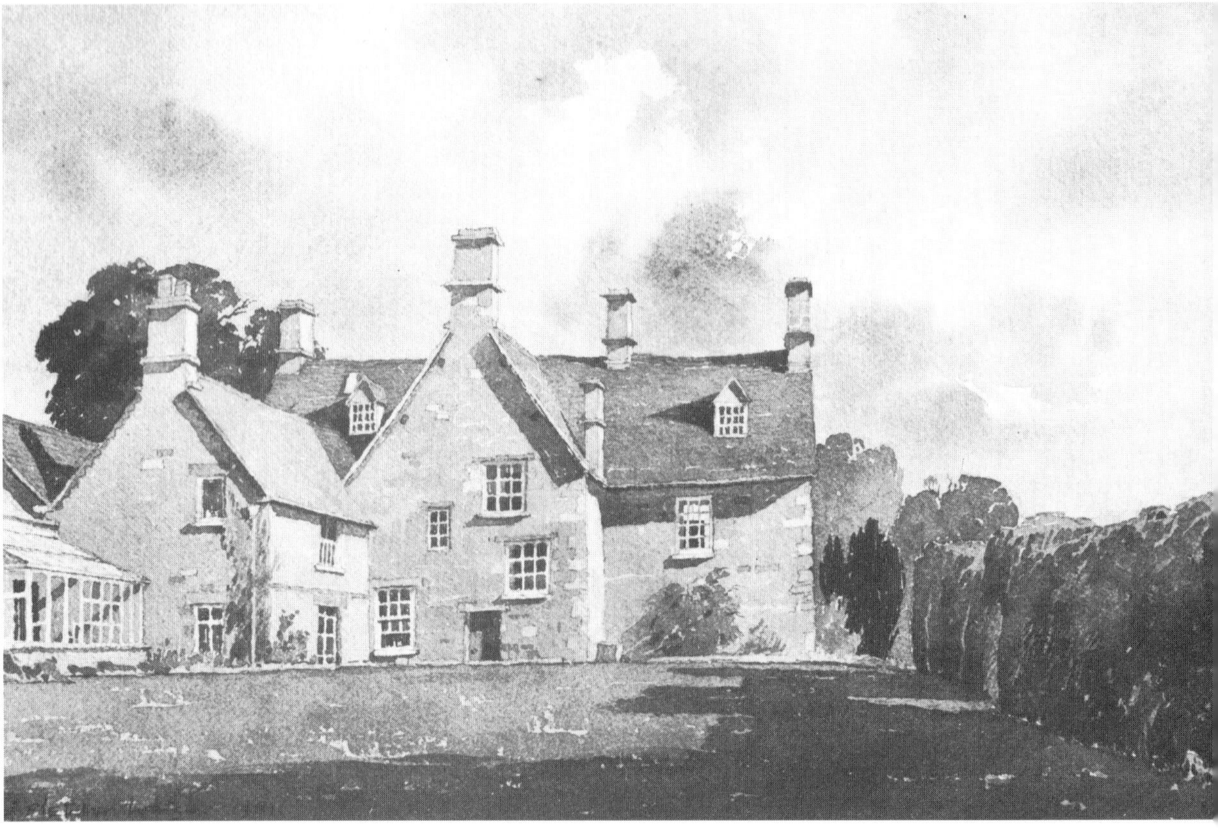

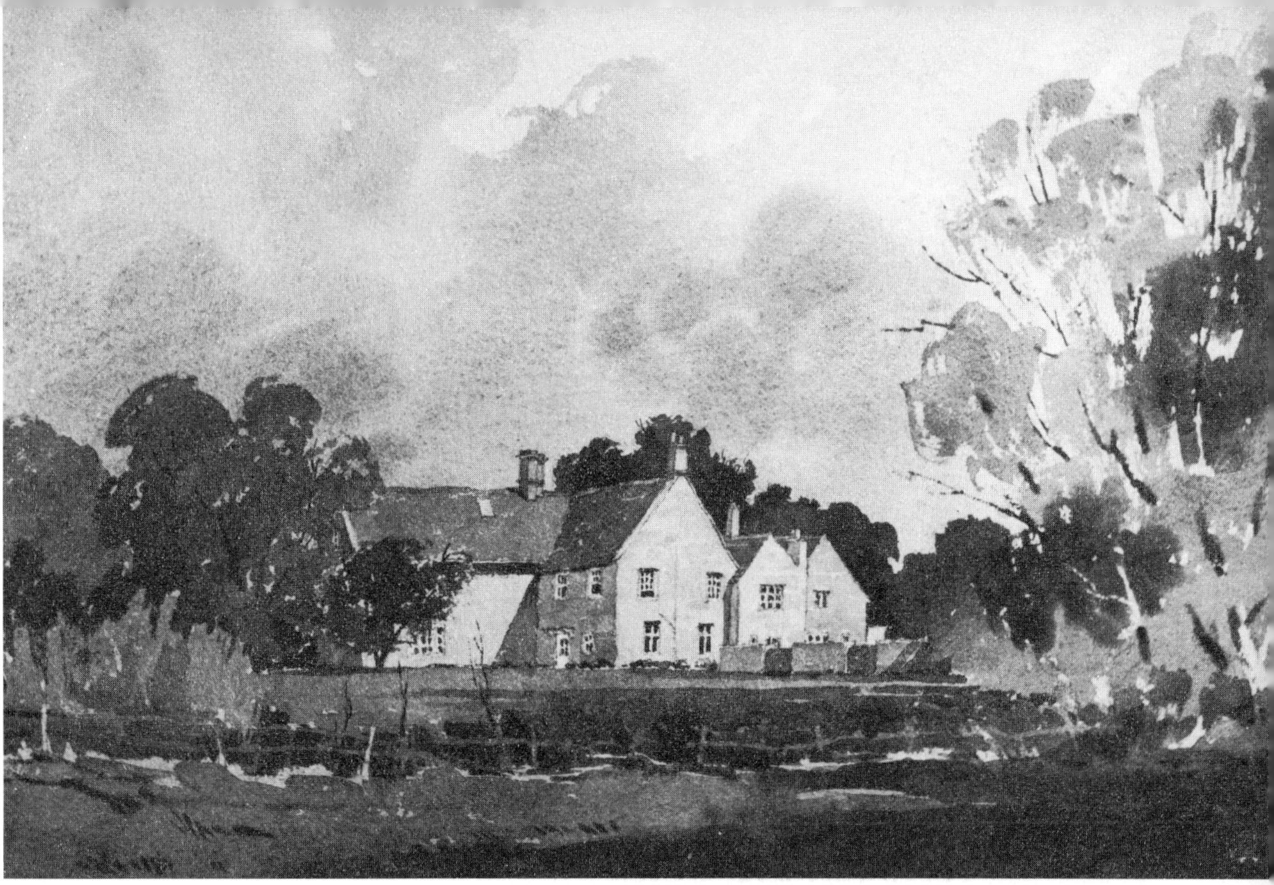

75 The Fox Inn, Barrington.

76 The Old Vicarage, Taynton.

77 Taynton House.

and one was able to see the buildings through them. This was again a very small sketch and a view of buildings across a field which always makes a good subject.

76 THE OLD VICARAGE, TAYNTON

31cm × 47cm (12½in. × 18½in.)

At some time in your painting life you will probably be commissioned to paint a particular view by someone, or to do a portrait of somebody's house. This quite often happens to me and I am going to show you five examples, and I will point out the advantages and also the hazards incurred in doing this.

The old vicarage picture was a view I had known for some time and fortunately I was asked to paint this particular view and not the front of the house which was not so attractive. The owner's wife wanted it as a surprise present for her husband.

I think it is probably a seventeenth-century house with eighteenth-century Georgian sash windows added, and what a higgledy-piggledy arrangement of windows it is but it makes a very nice subject. The dark tree behind the house was very useful in making the building stand out in sharp sunlight.

77 TAYNTON HOUSE

31cm × 47cm (12¼in. × 18½in.)

This second house in Taynton was painted in July and this time the husband wanted to give it as a present to his wife.

We again have dark trees behind the house and the view-point was entirely left to me which was most satisfactory. It is a charming old house in a lovely setting.

78 BARRINGTON DOWNS FARM, ALDSWORTH

31cm × 47cm (12¼in. × 18½in.)

Here is a simple farmhouse in Cotswold stone, like the others we have looked at, and very pleasant colouring. The garden view was asked for and it was agreed to leave out a large foreground flower-bed which would have made the picture fussy.

The fir trees had to be included as they were characteristic of the place, and very nice they were to paint.

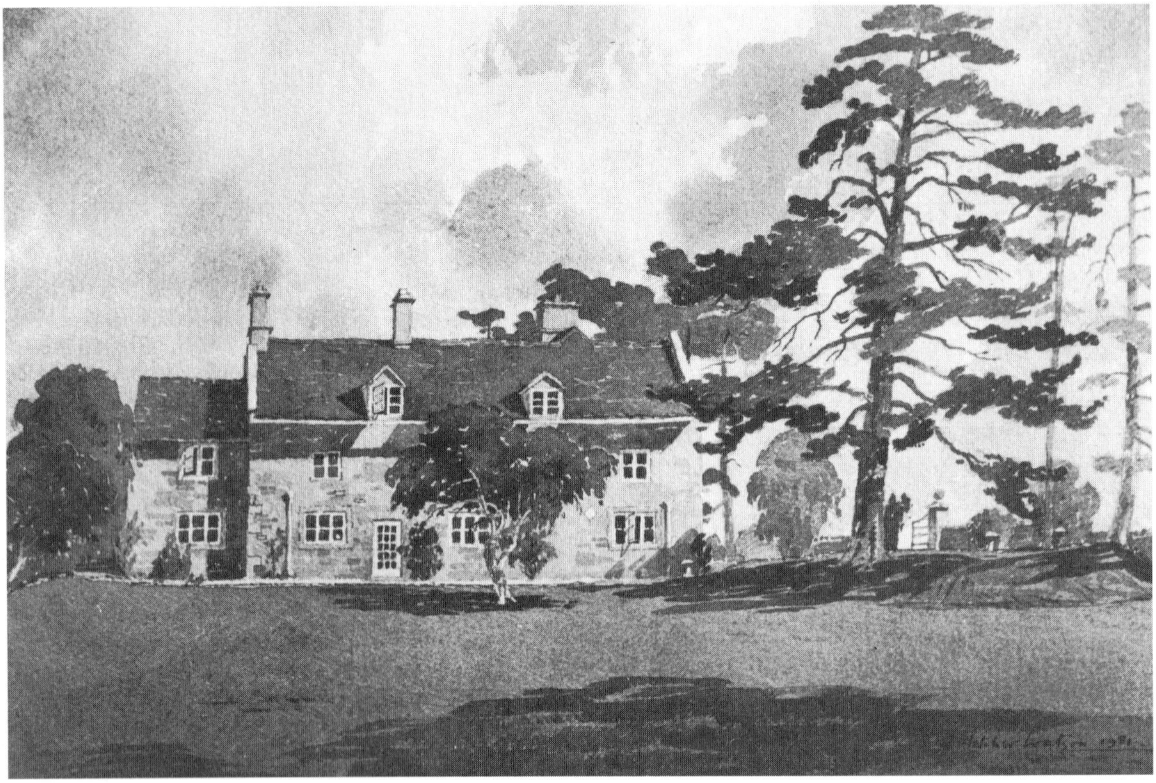

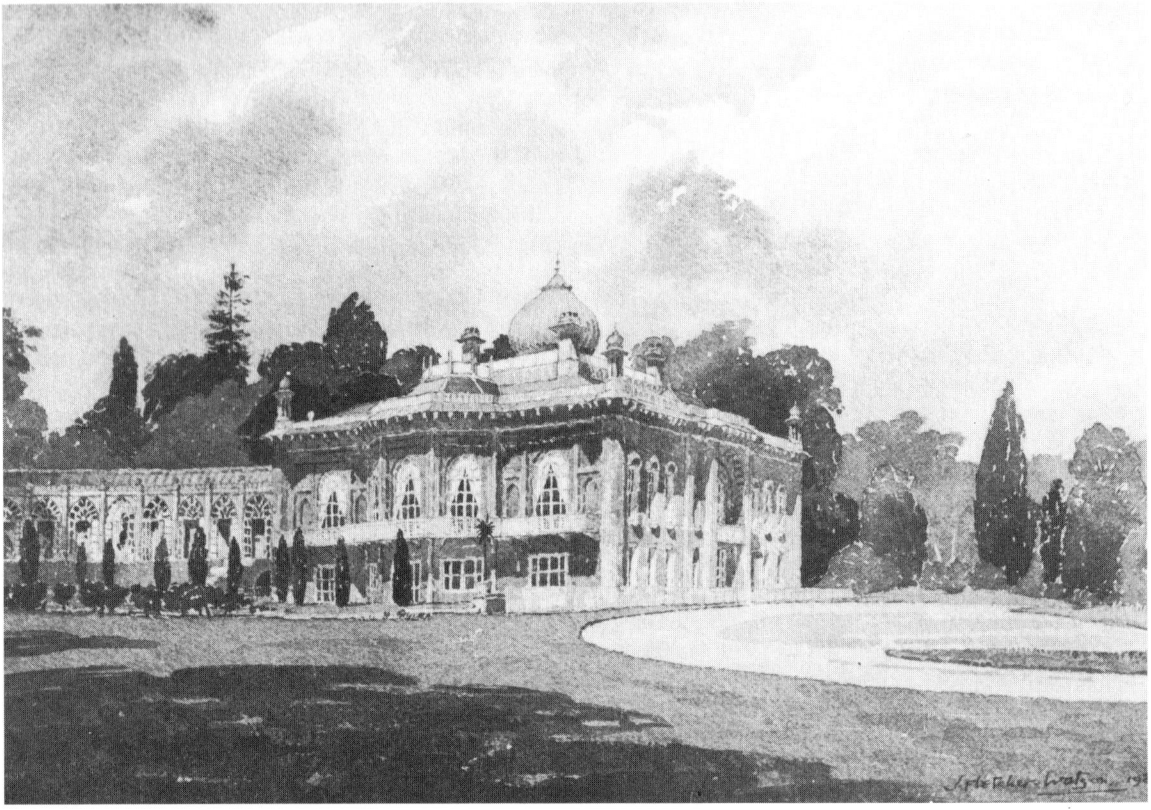

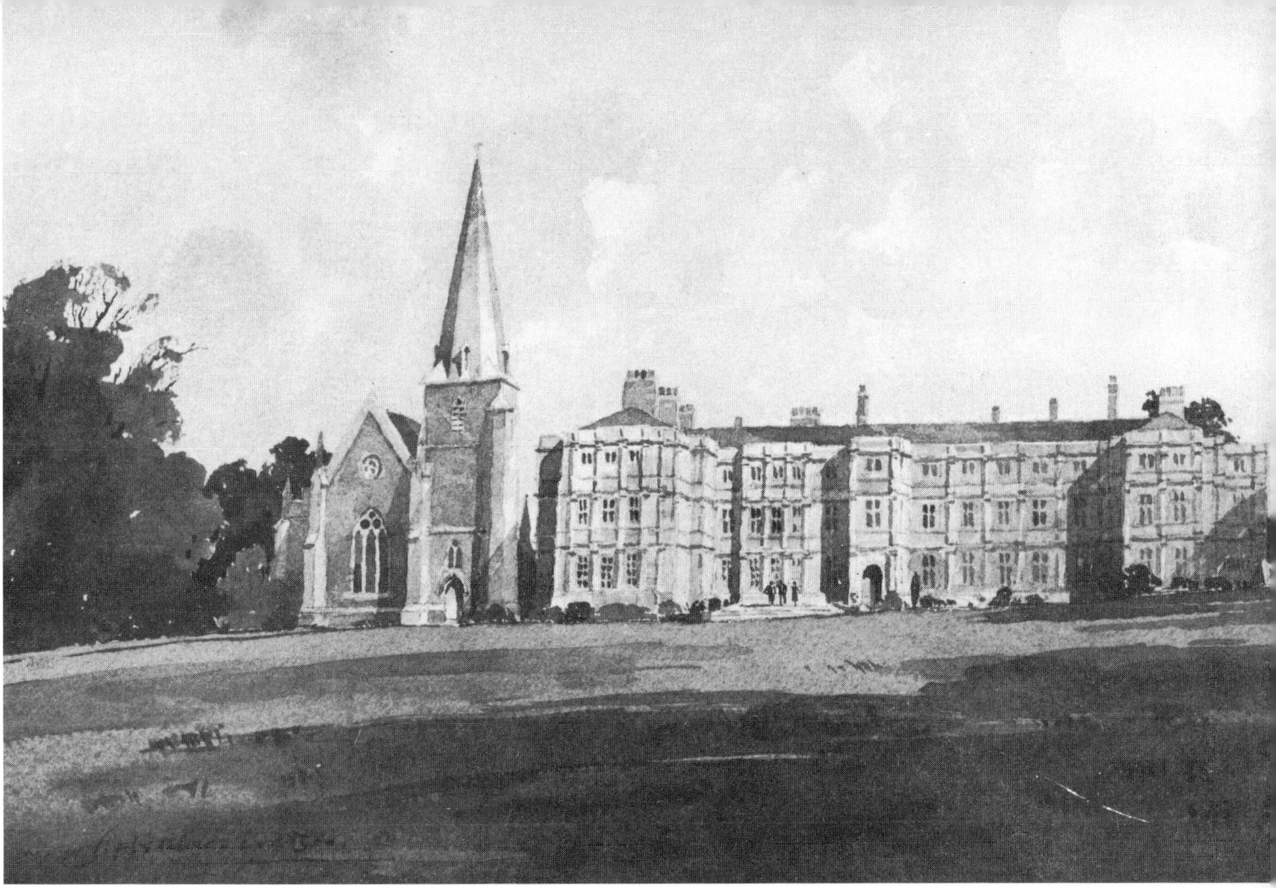

78 Barrington Downs Farm, Aldsworth.

79 Sezincote.

80 Sherborne House.

79 SEZINCOTE

31cm × 47cm ($12\frac{1}{4}$in. × $18\frac{1}{2}$in.)

This is a well-known mansion in Gloucestershire and rather a challenge to paint. It was originally built for Charles Cockrell and designed by his architect brother, Samuel Cockrell. Charles had been in the East India Company and was keen to have his new house designed in the 'Indian manner'. The house was completed in 1805 and in 1806 was visited by the Prince Regent who was about to start building the Brighton Pavilion; seeing Sezincote he was very much encouraged to pursue his idea for an Indian-looking mansion at Brighton.

When the present owners asked me to do a painting, they left the view-point to me. I settled down to making an extremely careful drawing of the dome, pinnacles, ornate cornice and windows and so on. I did some of the painting on the spot and finished it off in the studio. It was rather fun tackling such a detailed architectural subject, and I think it made rather an exciting picture.

80 SHERBORNE HOUSE

31.5cm × 47.5cm ($12\frac{1}{2}$in. × $18\frac{3}{4}$in.)

I was commissioned to paint this other large house recently. It used to belong to Lord Sherborne and then he sold it and it has now, rather skilfully, been converted into a great number of luxury flats. The original house was built in 1650 and then was largely rebuilt in 1830 or so, and it is difficult to tell what is old and what is not so old. However, it is an imposing structure and groups rather interestingly with the church on the left. I was at first doubtful about taking it on, but I then saw it on a sunny day and its attractive cream-coloured Cotswold stone (it had just been cleaned) made it look a pleasing subject.

Again it was a question of careful drawing before starting to paint. If you look closely you will see that the windows and stone columns etc. are not painted too exactly and I managed to give a certain looseness to the treatment. This saved it from being a fussy work.

I have ranged over quite a variety of subjects to paint in the Cotswolds, and I hope you will feel encouraged to visit this lovely part of England and get down to some painting.

4 Painting in France

Last summer I went with my family to Provence, that romantic area of southern France that has attracted so many artists. I was very excited about this combined family holiday and painting trip and was full of anticipation of finding masses of good subjects.

We were staying at a little villa which belonged to some friends and it was built round a small courtyard. I think the building was two or three hundred years old and it had tremendous charm and character.

81 OLD COURTYARD, PROVENCE
31.5cm × 47.5cm ($12\frac{1}{2}$in. × $18\frac{3}{4}$in.)
As you can see from this picture, it was a fascinating place. The sun was on the first floor balcony on the right in the morning, and it worked its way round to the other side in the afternoon when this painting was made. We lived on the first floor in rooms behind the balcony and we had breakfast there every morning. I won't go into details about those lovely breakfasts of coffee and croissants, sitting in the hot sunshine, as it would be too unfair when you are probably reading this on a cold damp day in an English winter!

As a matter of fact on this July holiday the heat in southern France was much *too* hot, even the locals said it was excessive and I found it too hot to paint in the middle of the day.

This courtyard picture was painted on my old favourite Arches paper and the subject was first drawn in with a B pencil. I then followed the usual practice of sky first, which was a glorious blue, and then I applied a light wash of Raw Sienna and a little Burnt Umber all over everything, except the white semi-circular window. Although I was sitting in the shade, the warm air dried the paint very quickly and one learnt to make washes a little wetter than usual if one was wanting to run another colour into the first one.

I gradually built up different washes of Burnt Umber, Burnt Sienna and a touch of French Ultramarine to get the different wall colours and shadows. The roof tiles of the building in the sun and the low building beside it were attractive pinks and yellows and when these had dried I could start on the background trees. These were almost the darkest thing in the picture.

I used Raw Sienna and Winsor Blue for the green and darkened this in places with Burnt Umber.

All that was needed to complete the picture was the dark window and arch openings which were varying tones of dark brown.

Finally, the stone jointing on walls and paving were painted with a very small brush and the balcony railings.

82 UZES, PROVENCE
31.5cm × 47.5cm ($12\frac{1}{2}$in. × $18\frac{3}{4}$in.)
A little way west of Avignon and only a mile or two from where were were staying was the quite remarkable old medieval town of Uzes. This picture is a typical view, and a lot of the town was separated from the main roads by a series of paved courtyards. If only some of our English towns were more like this, we would be saved from looking at masses of cars which detract from the beautiful architecture so much. Mind you, there were a lot of people and children about peeping over my shoulder but I didn't mind that and there was a good opportunity of placing figures where I wanted them in the picture.

In order to get my hand in with these French town subjects I made a rough sketch before starting on the picture proper. Figure 83 shows a very rough scribble in a 18cm × 25.5cm (7in. × 10in.) cartridge sketch book using a black felt pen and Conte crayon for shadows. I always think the *sky-line* is important with a town view, and it helps to have a building going out of the picture at the top, in this case on both sides of the paper. It concentrates the eye on the centre of the view which is a help in the general composition and often leaves an interesting sky shape.

Another reason for the preliminary sketch is to *record* shadows on buildings. They change so quickly when one is painting, and one often chooses the view mainly for the shadows so you don't want to lose them in your mind when you get that far with the painting, and a little reference sketch can be very useful.

81 Old courtyard, Provence.

82 Uzes, Provence.

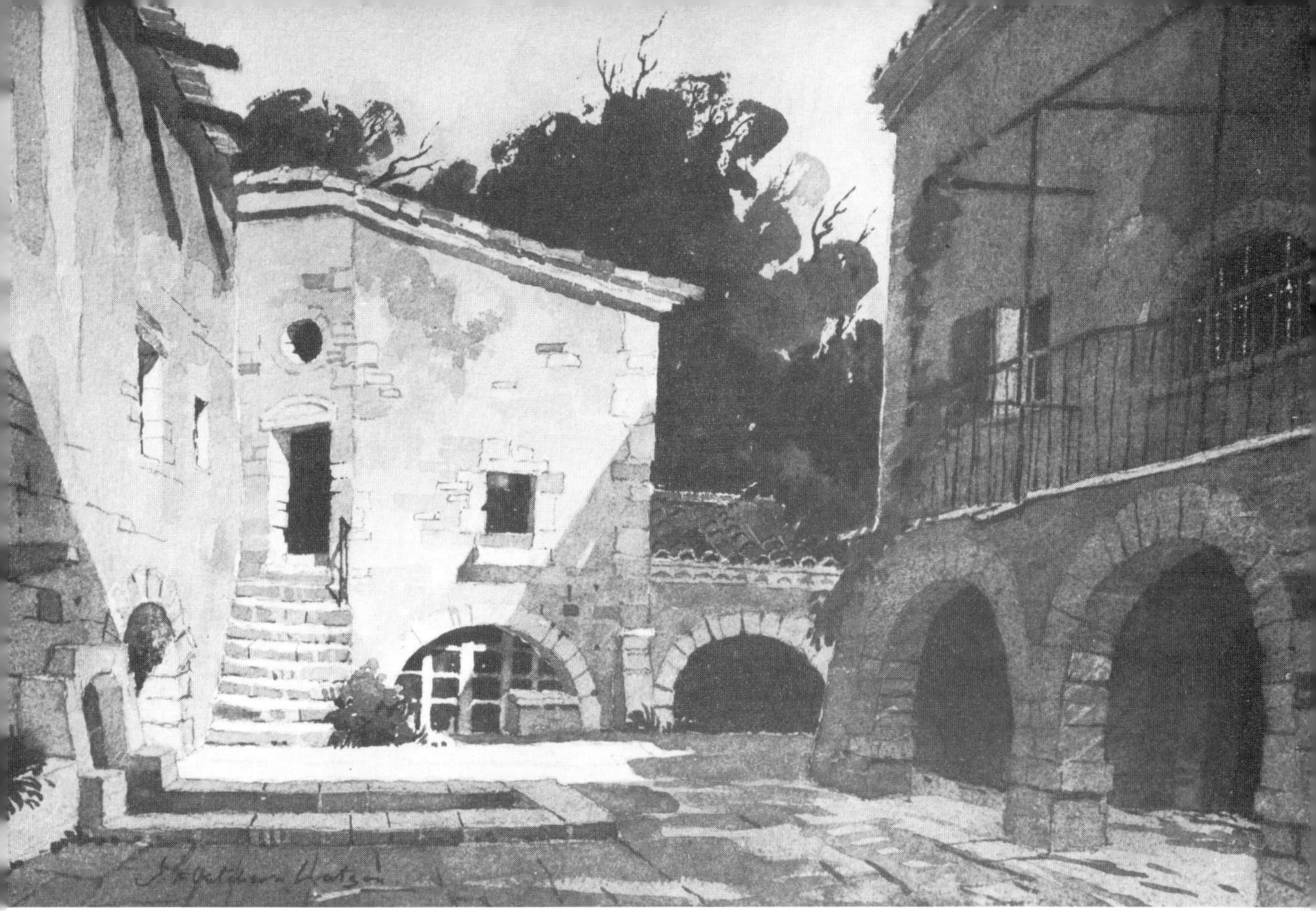

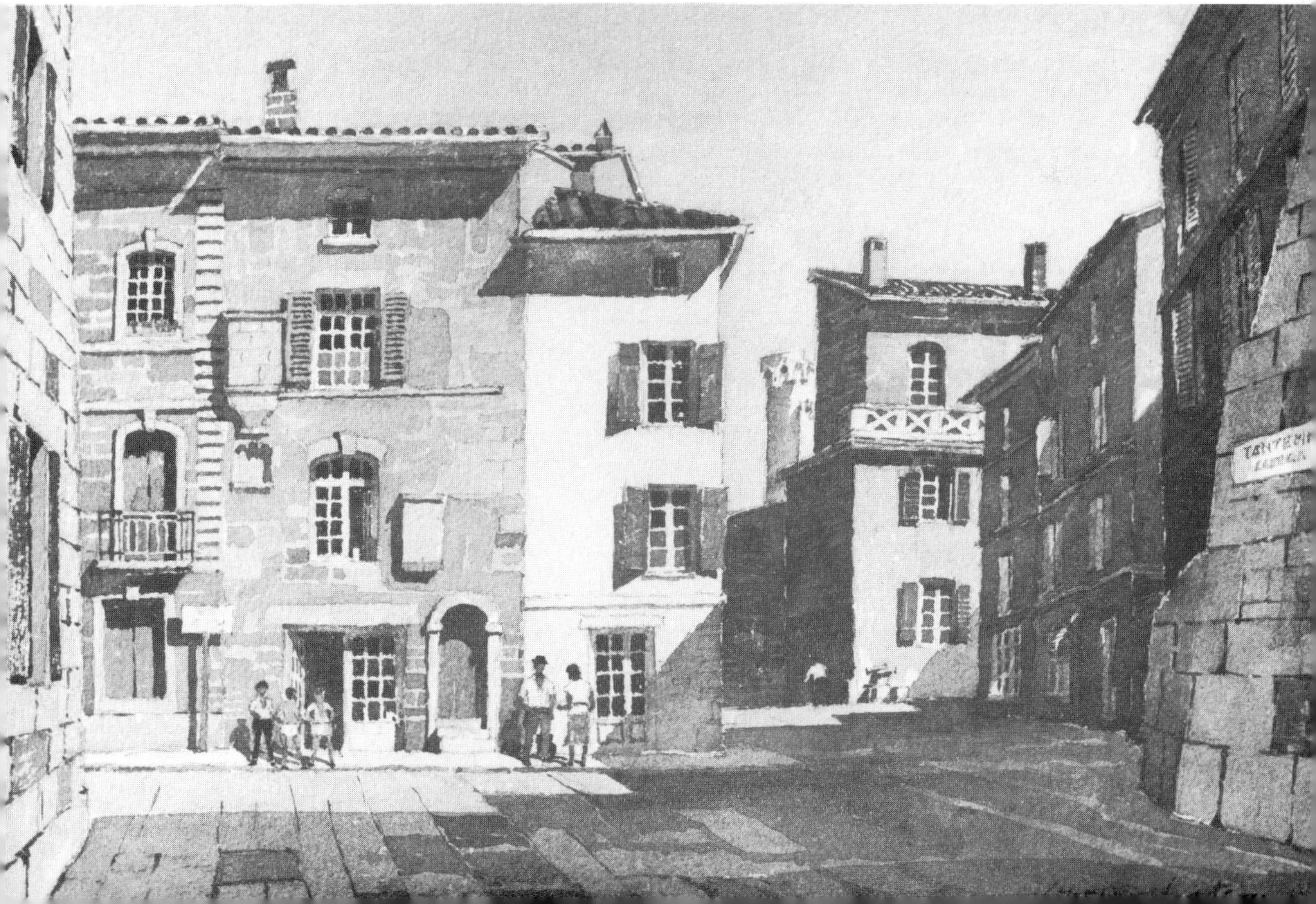

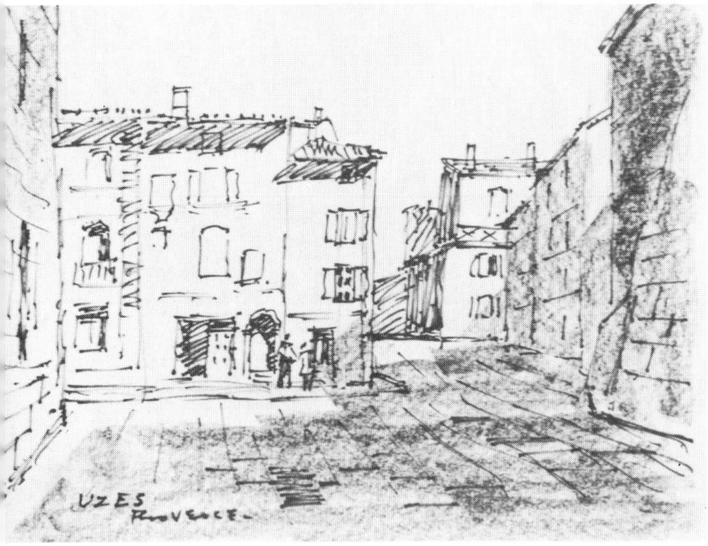

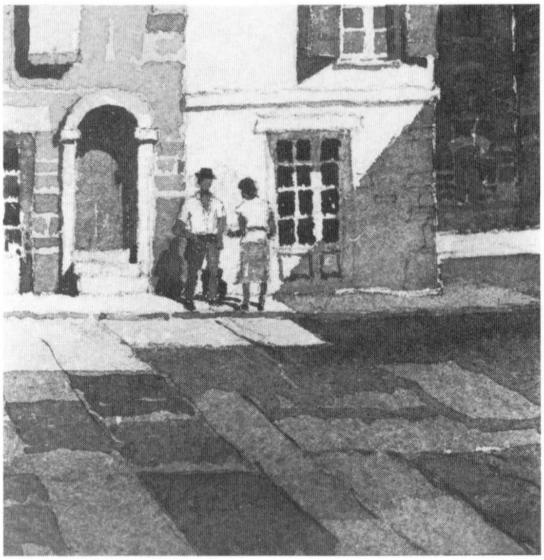

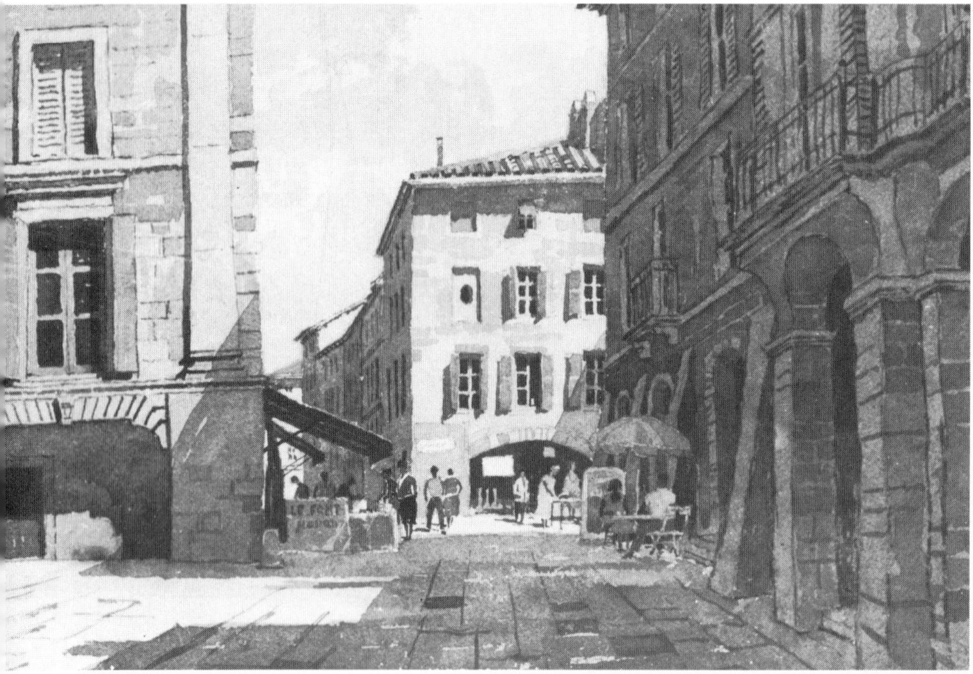

83 Uzes, preliminary sketch.

84 Uzes, detail.

85 Uzes.

Shadows of course are the vital part of most architectural subjects, and in this one the deep shadows under the eaves show what a long way the roofs overhang the walls. Shadows in windows and doorways show how deep the window or door is from the wall face.

The detail (84) shows a close-up of the door and the window on the right, with their strong shadows and up above is a window with shutters which also have shadows which make the shutters stand out from the wall. The shadows of the figures are important and of course the big ground shadow on the paving and the diagonal shadow on the wall both help with the three-dimensional effect and give depth to a picture.

UZES, PROVENCE
(colour plate 7, between pages 120 and 121)
31.5cm × 47.5cm ($12\frac{1}{2}$in. × $18\frac{3}{4}$in.)
Here is another view of Uzes taken from a corner of the big main square, looking towards a walkway going to the left behind the stalls and another one coming in from the right. As bad luck would have it a very large lorry came and parked slap in front of me when I was about half-way through the painting. It unloaded

groceries to a shop through one of the arches on the right, and it was a good half hour before it packed up and went and I could get on with the painting. I will describe the painting work in full.

Drawing

With a B pencil I very lightly sketched in the outline of the main features to see how they were going to fit. I wanted the right-hand foreground building in shadow to be a lot wider than the left-hand building in sunlight which goes out of the picture at the top. There was a nice rectangle of space between these buildings in which to fit the corner building of four storeys and the perspective of the left-hand street. I now used a stronger line and drew in the various architectural details, windows, shutters, roofs, arches and, most important, the figures, which had to be the right height. The ground-lines of the different buildings gave the necessary perspective and recession, especially the joints of the paving stones.

Painting – Stage 1

With this type of architectural subject it is very important to get one's *tone* values correct. It will help me to make the point clear if we look at the monochrome (85). There are *six* main graduations of tone: **1** The sky is the lightest. **2** The corner four-storey building in the middle is a shade darker than the sky. **3** A slightly darker shade is the building on the left running vertically out of the picture. **4** Then the left-hand shadow side of the central corner building. **5** And then the right-hand foreground building. Finally **6** The various dark tones under arches and in windows. If you half close your eyes and look at figure 85 I think you will see what I mean. The foreground shadow on the paving is actually a shade lighter than item 5 and there are of course other intermediate tones. These tone values are not always so apparent when looking at one's subject in full colour. There is such a thing as a 'Tone Value' glass which is slightly gray and when you look through it at your view it cuts out colour and everything is reduced to gray tones. I think it is used by photographers. I had one once but it is lost and in any case I don't think it is really necessary as we ought to be able to train our eyes to assess the tone value in coloured objects.

For once I varied my rule of painting the sky first and I painted it last. It was a very light toned sky with no heavy gray washes required and it would not present any problem to put in after the buildings were finished. I felt that I could design a better sky arrangement of blue with white cloud after I could see the building colours and strengths in position.

So I started off with a big wash of well diluted Burnt Umber and with my big No. 16 brush I covered the whole area except for the sky which was left white. The only other white paper I left unpainted was the rectangular notice hanging in the arch of the central building.

Stage 2

The wash in this hot sunshine only took a few seconds to dry and I went straight on with painting the centre building and the narrow street to the left in full detail. First came the roof in light Burnt Sienna and Raw Sienna with spots of dark Burnt Umber and Payne's Gray mixed for the ends of the rounded tiles as they came against the gutter. The chimney stack was also painted at this time, a yellow-gray colour and darker tones of the same colour for shadows.

Then I painted the shadow on the left side of the building and on the street buildings beyond and also the deep eaves shadow on the sunny front of this building using Light Red, Cobalt and Raw Sienna. I had been using a No. 7 brush for this work and I now changed to a No. 3 brush for painting the windows. I again used Burnt Umber and Payne's Gray and painted in the windows in the side street which were in acute perspective, and they only needed quick vertical brush strokes to indicate them. The lines were made fainter as they went further away. The windows on the front were painted with a little more care. Next I put the green shutters in with a No. 5 brush and a mixture of Raw Sienna and Winsor Blue; they were a bluish-green. Then I did the shutter shadows on the wall using a strong mix of Burnt Sienna and Cobalt, also, with the same colour, the shadows at the top of the windows to indicate the recession of the windows from the wall face. Finally on this building I painted a dark gray-brown in the big archway at ground level using Burnt Sienna and Cobalt, carefully leaving the noticeboard white and some figures who came against the archway.

Stage 3

The extreme left-hand building was now painted. I first drew in with a No. 1 brush the window cornice and architraves using a dark brown mixture of Burnt Umber and Payne's Gray and also stone jointing and the pronounced arch joints of the big archway, and the stone pilaster near the corner with its moulded base. I varied the thickness of the lines. It was like drawing with a pen but it was a paint-brush instead. The top window with its louvered shutters was also drawn in. I then painted the dull yellow shutters of the first floor window with Raw Sienna and a touch of Burnt Umber with a No. 7 brush and also with this brush I touched in the broken colour of stonework on the wall, picking out a few stones individually.

Now the dark shadow in the big arch was painted using Burnt Sienna and Ultramarine, making it darker towards the ground to give a reflected light feeling. This was with the No. 7 brush still.

The dark first floor window was Burnt Umber and

Payne's Gray, picking out the glazing bars carefully, all with a No. 5 brush. The shadows of the shutters and this window itself and the top window were painted with the same colour as for the big archway.

I could now put in the sun blinds and stalls below on the immediate right of this building. The stalls were Raw Sienna and Cobalt, the blinds Burnt Sienna and Ultramarine and a curtain hanging at the side was strong Indian Red. This curtain later got drawn across to keep the sun off the stalls which I think had fruit on them, which of course completely hid stalls and people so I was lucky to have painted it all before this happened.

Stage 4

The building on the right in shadow was now painted and I used the same method of drawing details with a No. 1 brush. You can get a very thin line or a thick line according to the way you press the brush on the paper. Two great watercolour painters, Bonington and later Callow, used this method on their buildings with great success, and I strongly advise you to study their work when you get the chance.

I first put the string courses (the projecting horizontal lines of stonework) in onto the wall face which gave a good perspective guide, and then the windows and balconies. The curved arches of the nearer building were a bit tricky. I was using Burnt Umber and a little Ultramarine giving virtually a sepia colour.

I now washed in with a No. 9 brush a medium brown using those same two colours just mentioned, and took the wash all over everything except the umbrella and figures sitting at the table and the wooden screen behind one of the figures. Then when this was drying I gave the far end of the buildings a wash of Burnt Sienna and very little Cobalt. The stone colour of this building was a little redder. I now painted over the near building some slightly darker sepia mixture and picked out a few individual stones.

A few windows and railings required darkening and the interior of the arches were also darkened considerably, and the cornice at the roof line required stiffening with some dark brown strokes with a small brush. This building had now come well into the foreground and the sitting figure group needed to be dealt with.

The umbrella was Cobalt Blue, the sitting female had a pink dress for which I used Rose Madder and the man's shirt was white so he only required a very light gray tone. The screen was Raw Sienna. The heads, arms and legs were various shades of gray-brown.

Stage 5

Before putting in the ground shadow and certain other shadows I wanted the remaining figures completed. Using a No. 3 brush, the different colours were duly applied, light Winsor Blue, Cadmium Yellow and Burnt Sienna and the woman with the dark skirt by the stall received Burnt Umber and Ultramarine. This mixture was also used in varying strength for the heads and arms etc., making the figures under the stall blinds extra dark as they were in shadow. Little shadows on the ground cast by figures were important and I used Burnt Sienna and Cobalt for these.

Now for the all important ground shadow cast by the buildings on the right. With a No. 9 brush and the same mixture as just mentioned which gave a bluish reddish-brown colour, I painted this shadow making it darker as it came nearer to me. Then with the same colour I painted the two slanting shadows, one on the left-hand building and the other on the central building. You don't always want these shadows to be a flat brown-gray and in the left-hand one I dashed a strong bit of neat Cobalt into it as it was drying. This livens up a shadow and prevents it looking dead.

The joints of the paving stones required strengthening with a small brush and these played a most important part in giving recession to the picture. One or two dark stones were picked out.

The centre house wanted a little stone texture to the wall and a few individual stones were put in with a light mixture of Burnt Sienna and Cobalt. These were *very* light so as not to take away from the brightness of sunlight on this building.

Stage 6

Almost last came the sky. This was not to be a dominating feature like the sky in some wild open landscape.

I first painted a blue area at left-hand top corner with diluted Ultramarine, giving an interesting shape to the white cloud with twisting movements of a No. 9 brush. Then with a gray mixture of Cobalt, Light Red and a touch of Rose Madder I painted in the light gray areas. These washes were not very wet ones and there was no trouble with overlapping buildings and roof lines.

Finally, I looked at the picture with half closed eyes and decided a little more strength was wanted for the dark archway in the centre building. I used a dark mix of Burnt Umber and Ultramarine.

There were eight colours used for the main work – Raw Sienna, Burnt Sienna, Burnt Umber, Light Red, Cobalt Blue, French Ultramarine, Winsor Blue and Payne's Gray.

Then for what is known as 'local colour' used neat without mixing, I used Cadmium Lemon, and Cadmium Yellow for women's dresses, Rose Madder for a dress and a touch in the sky, and Indian Red for the hanging curtain.

So the total is twelve colours which is my full complement.

In describing how a painting is carried out one is bound to miss out a few details, it would become too heavy-going to mention *everything*, but I hope I have included enough to give you a good guide for trying this type of subject yourself. The *best* way of helping someone is by doing a demonstration painting and being watched, and if you do get a chance of going on a demonstration course it can be a very helpful thing to do.

I would also say now that we are at about the half-way stage of this book, that I probably mention techniques which you know about already, but I hope that even for the advanced painters there will be some new point which may emerge which they will find helpful.

86 ST SIFFRET

31.5cm × 47.5cm (12½in. × 18¾in.)

Now I would like to show you views of some of the *open* country that is to be found in this part of Provence. The hill village of St Siffret was fairly typical of a number of little villages built on the tops of hills. There are usually the remains of fortified walls which must originally have surrounded the villages in medieval times to give a defence against attack. One gets the feeling of the very ancient history of France when the many principalities were always warring with each other.

I painted this view in the late afternoon when the heat of the day was cooling off and the long shadows gave a romantic air to the scene. The light is very attractive in this part of France and the colouring generally is very strong, but I did not find that I needed any unusual colours other than the twelve that I always carry, as listed in Chapter 1.

You will notice the proportion of this composition is about one-third land and two-thirds sky. The foreground field was a strong yellow-brown stubble and there were a lot of attractive greens in the village group. The tall dark cypress trees gave a splendid contrast and accent against the horizontal roofs of the houses. The sloping foreground with the distant view to the right and the big tree to the left together made a most satisfying composition.

87 FARM AT FLAUX

31.5cm × 47.5cm (12½in. × 18¾in.)

Flaux was the name of the village where we were staying and this attractive farm was only a few hundred yards down the road towards Uzes. It is very characteristic of the many farms to be seen in the area. The long low proportion reminded one of the Cumbrian farms, but

86 St Siffret.

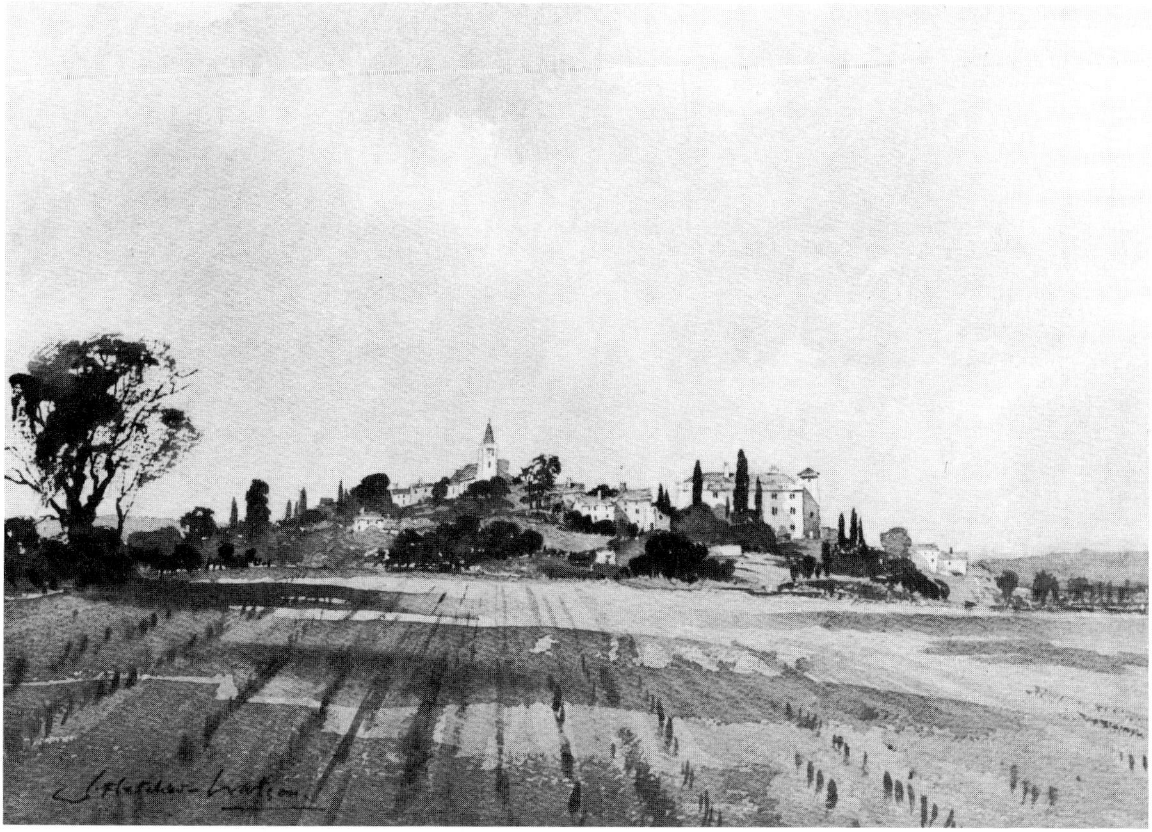

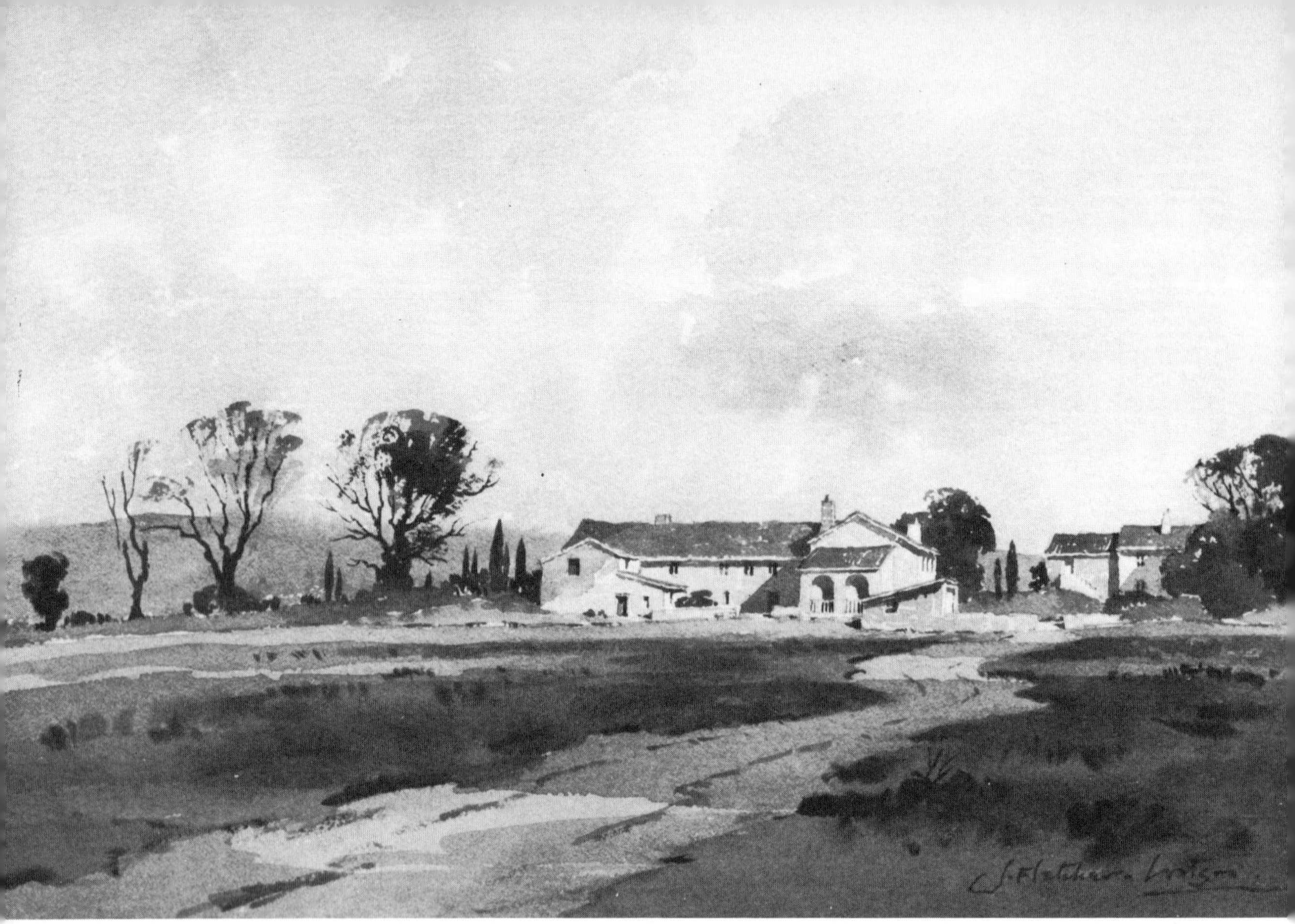
J. Fletcher Watson

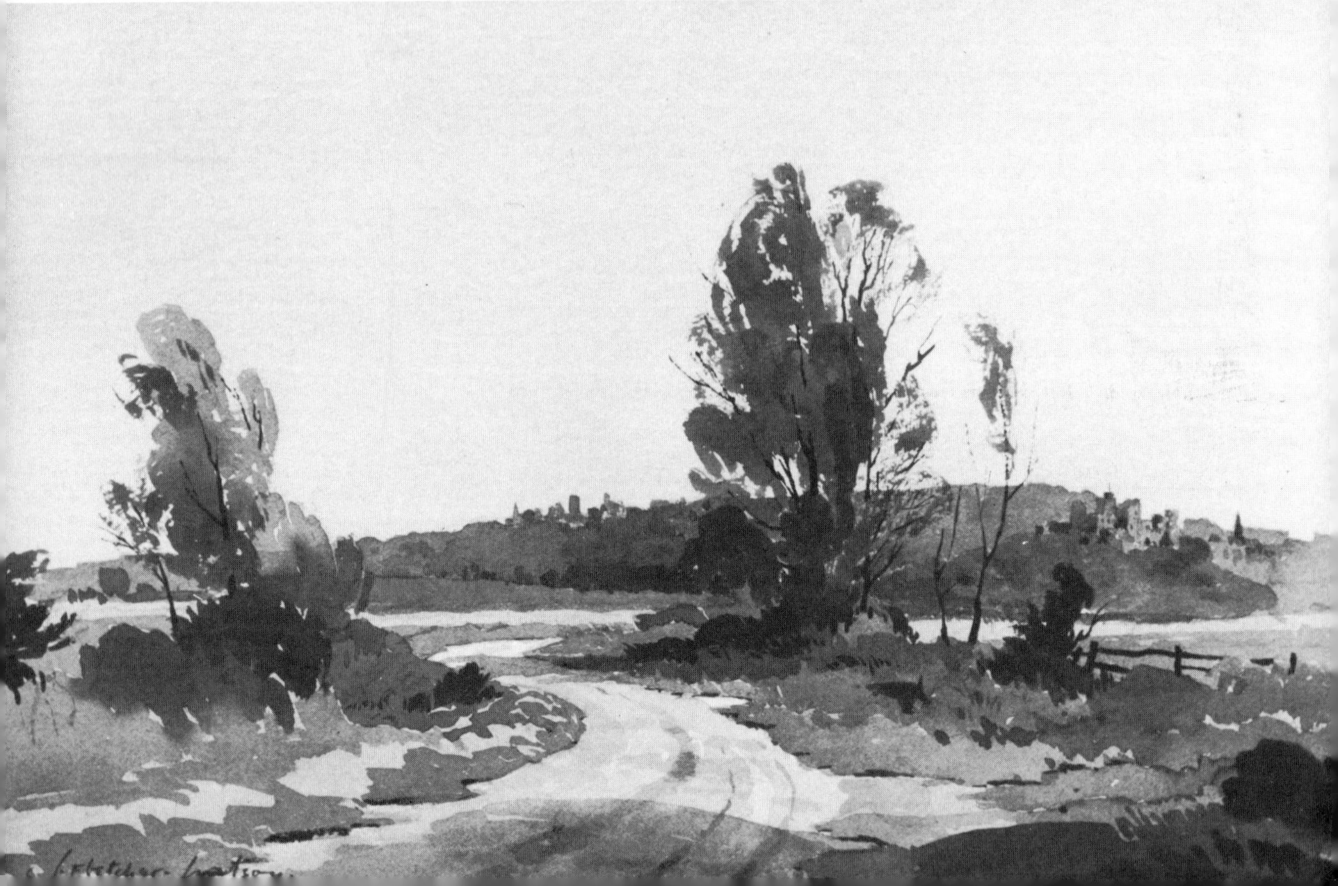
J. Fletcher Watson

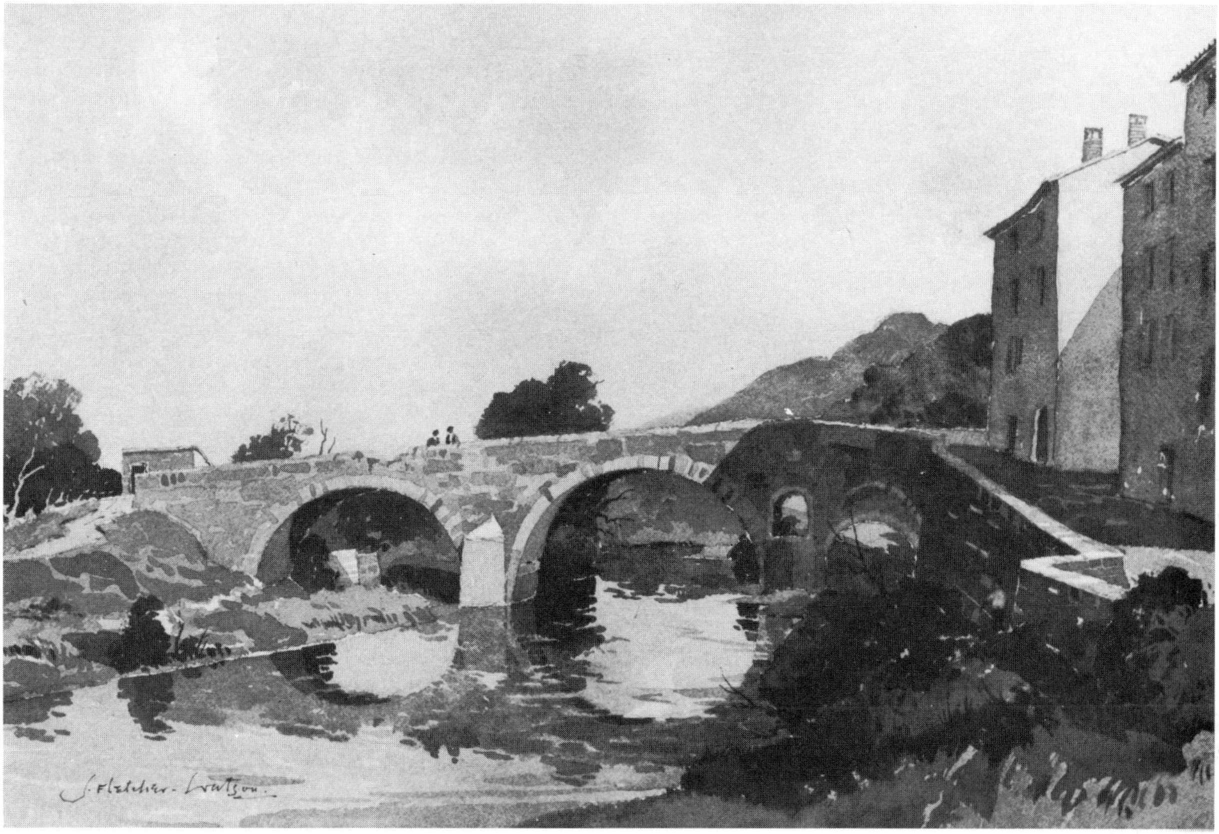

87 Farm at Flaux.

88 Road to La Chapelle.

89 Sauve.

there the resemblance ends. These farms are built of a pale yellow-gray warm looking local stone which has weathered and become rough and the texture and colour is the most lovely thing you can imagine. The roofs are a low pitch and covered with curved brick tiles, and these are also a lovely mellow colour varying from a rusty red to yellow and brown. The windows are usually small because of the bright light and heat, and they often have verandahs and arches as in this case. In the north of France the roofs change to a very steep pitch because of the quite different weather conditions where it can be stormy with heavy rain and snow.

I had unwisely started this picture in the burning sun of the late morning before I had learnt the lesson that the mid-day period is too hot. My son Charles, aged fifteen, was with me doing an excellent drawing of the subject but he kept going to sit in the shade of the car.

The foreground was a burnt-up grass colour of yellows and browns, the trees were a good dark green-brown and the distant hill gray-blue – altogether a lovely colour scheme.

We managed to stick it out to the end and then hurried home to cool drinks and a welcome salad lunch.

88 ROAD TO LA CHAPELLE

31.5cm × 47.5cm ($12\frac{1}{2}$in. × $18\frac{3}{4}$in.)

This was painted one brilliant early morning when the sky was all clear blue and I felt Whatman very white paper would be suitable. The subject was mainly of road and trees but the distant hill village with its towers and roofs made an interesting background, painted a warm pinkish-gray. The old castle on the right was also a nice feature. The picture was painted quickly and loosely, keeping the washes wet, and it was completed in about an hour and a half.

89 SAUVE

31.5cm × 47.5cm ($12\frac{1}{2}$in. × $18\frac{3}{4}$in.)

This village, about twenty miles west of where we stayed, was built on a sloping hill but sprawled attractively down to the river and this lovely old bridge. It is a good sort of view to try and there are plenty of bridges in the district to be found. I always think a bridge and water reflections make an interesting subject and here we had distant hills and tall buildings to the right and a strong foreground, which all built up into a good composition.

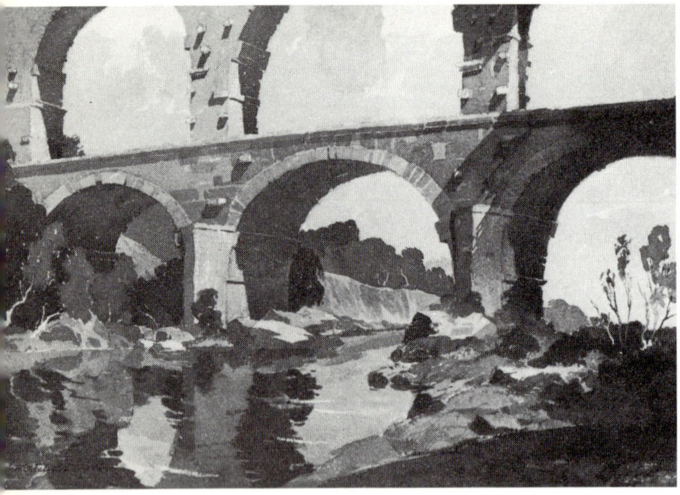

90 Pont du Gard.

PONT DU GARD, PROVENCE

(colour plate 8, between pages 120 and 121)
31.5cm × 47.5cm ($12\frac{1}{2}$in. × $18\frac{3}{4}$in.)
I think my most exciting moment on this painting holiday in Provence was seeing the Pont du Gard. Looking at it for the first time one felt it could have been built only a short while ago. In fact it was constructed in solid stone by the Romans in 18 BC, nearly 2000 years ago, one of the Romans' greatest feats of engineering. It is an aquaduct that brought water across the valley and there are three tiers of arches. At first I thought I would do a distant view of the whole thing, but then I felt a closer view was so intriguing, showing architectural details of the arches and the river reflections, and so I found this angle view which really made a most exciting composition.

View point

It took a few minutes to decide on my exact position; I wanted to include some of the trees on the left and a certain amount of the rocky bank in the foreground. I also wanted the second tier of arches to go out of the picture as this would emphasize the great size of the structure, and I also observed carefully the view through the central arch and how much sky was included above the line of trees. Having got all these things about right I started drawing with a B pencil on Arches paper.

Preliminary work

The drawing-in took me about half an hour; I had to gauge carefully the proportion of the arches and their thickness – the bottom ones were much thicker than the tier above to allow for a road.

The painting work started with the sky and I limited this to within the arch spaces and did not run the colour over the stone areas. There were light gray clouds and areas of blue and I used light washes of French Ultramarine for the blue patches and added Burnt Umber mixed with this for the gray areas. This soon dried; it was early afternoon and the sun was almost too hot to paint but I wanted to catch the shadows in the right place so I pressed on regardless of the heat.

Stage 2

I now put a big wash over all the arches and trees down to the water-line, using not too strong a mix of Burnt Umber and Ultramarine but giving it a brownish colour that was the colour of the stonework when in the sun. I carried this wash down over the right-hand foreshore leaving some of the rocks white where the light caught their upper side. The water area was going to be left until the end.

With the sun being so hot I could carry on with succeeding washes as quickly as I liked. I next put on another brown wash, the same as the last but a little darker on the front facets of stone walling leaving the internal depth of the arches the faint colour as these were all catching the light. The right-hand side of the pointed piers were also left the light colour, of course.

Now I painted the far cliff seen through the centre arch with varying shades of gray-brown using Burnt Umber and Cobalt, and the range of trees above with Raw Sienna, Winsor Blue and softened with a touch of Burnt Sienna. A little area of tree and cliff was seen through the left-hand arch also. For this work I used a No. 7 brush.

I could now paint a light green over the trees to the left, bringing the wash over to the vertical stone pier. I used Raw Sienna and Winsor Blue; I would come back to these trees later. I now wanted to get in the strong shadows under the arches. This was a subtle shadow colour and most important to get right for the whole picture. Cobalt and Light Red gave a basic gray-brown and this was then warmed with Raw Sienna. The top range of arches had a yellowish tinge and the bottom ones were more red, so one varied the shadows considerably by varying the mix. The tone was always darker at the bottom of the shadow owing to the reflected light on the upper part of each arch shadow. I used a No. 7 brush for these shadows and then changed to No. 5 for the shadows of the various projecting stones.

Next, with a No. 7 brush, I painted the far bank and rocks at the water's edge a light gray-green by mixing Cadmium Yellow, Winsor Blue and Light Red for the grass, leaving out the Cadmium Yellow for the rocks.

Now I could come back to my left-hand tree group. With a fairly strong mix of Winsor Blue and Burnt Sienna I painted with a No. 7 brush the darker green-brown trees and carefully left the light green tree shapes. I also left the light coloured tree trunks; when I first painted the light green wash, these twisting old tree trunks were left unpainted. To the right-hand side of this tree group I darkened the trees still more by adding a mixture of Burnt Umber and Winsor Blue and then I painted the *very* dark tree the other side of the central arch with the same colours; this was the darkest item in the picture.

Stage 3
The right-hand bank and the foreground was now dealt with. Various green washes for small areas of grass and shrubs and the small spindly trees were mixed, using Winsor Blue, Cadmium Yellow and a little Burnt Sienna and painting with a No. 7 and No. 5 brush and varying the green for different parts. The rocks were brought to life with dark gray-blue shadows of Burnt Sienna and Cobalt Blue used thickly.

Now I put some big shadow washes over shrubs and ground, cast by trees out of the picture. These were painted with a No. 9 brush and Winsor Blue and Raw Sienna for the green shadow with a touch of Burnt Sienna to stop it being too bright a green, and then adding more Burnt Sienna for the immediate foreground shadow which was cast over light brown rock.

Stage 4
The water could now be painted and I first washed in a light gray-blue, a shade darker than the actual sky, all over the water. With water reflections, the lights are usually a little *darker* and the darks a little *lighter* than what is being reflected. This is particularly the case with rivers when the water may be a little bit muddy.

I had already lightly drawn in some of the salient items of reflection such as where the arch shadows came to in the water. I first painted the *light* greens of trees and *light* browns of the stone structure and followed this up quickly, while all was still wet, with the darker greens and darker browns. I was using a No. 7 and No. 9 brush alternating as necessary and the actual colours were approximately those already described. Some of the thin light ripples on the water were indicated by scratching out with a sharp knife.

I am showing you a monochrome version of this picture (90) as it is interesting to compare this with the colour picture. One can see fairly clearly how the dark and light tones play their part in the picture pattern. I used the following eight colours for the picture – Cadmium Yellow, Raw Sienna, Burnt Sienna, Burnt Umber, Light Red, Cobalt Blue, French Ultramarine and Winsor Blue.

91 BELLEME, SOUTH NORMANDY
37cm × 34.5cm (14½in. × 13½in.)
During our drive back home through France we took a diagonal north-western route on our way to Cherbourg where we were to take our cross-channel boat. We passed many inviting places, but when we came to Normandy we hit upon the most marvellous little medieval town called Belleme. We stayed the night and I had time for a quick pencil and wash picture that evening. I made a firm drawing on Saunders paper as it is lovely stuff for drawing on. The palette was limited to Raw Sienna, Burnt Sienna, Burnt Umber and French Ultramarine. I slapped on the colour quickly next morning before we left. The enormous church was early classical in style which was so unusual with many niches and carved figures. I should say it was seventeenth century.

I shall never forget the evening of arrival: after we had had something to eat we all strolled round, my wife and both children, and once away from the main road we were in a labyrinth of narrow streets and enchanting squares and only a few local people. We exclaimed at every corner which brought a new fascinating group of old buildings into sight, and I remember shouting, 'Oh this is sheer Bonington or pure Callow, we ought to come and stay here a week'.

On our way at last we reached Bayeux where we

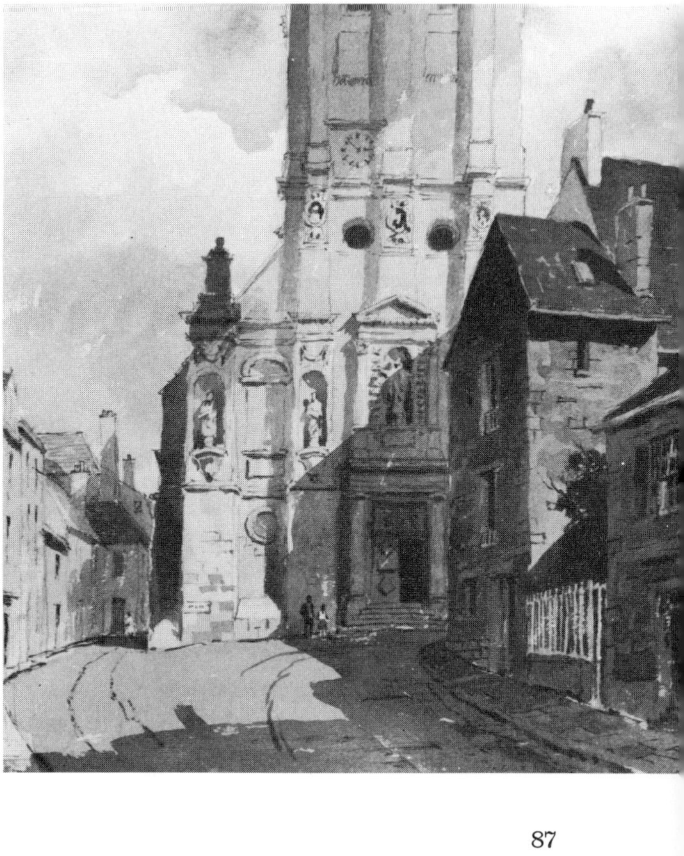

91 Belleme, South Normandy.

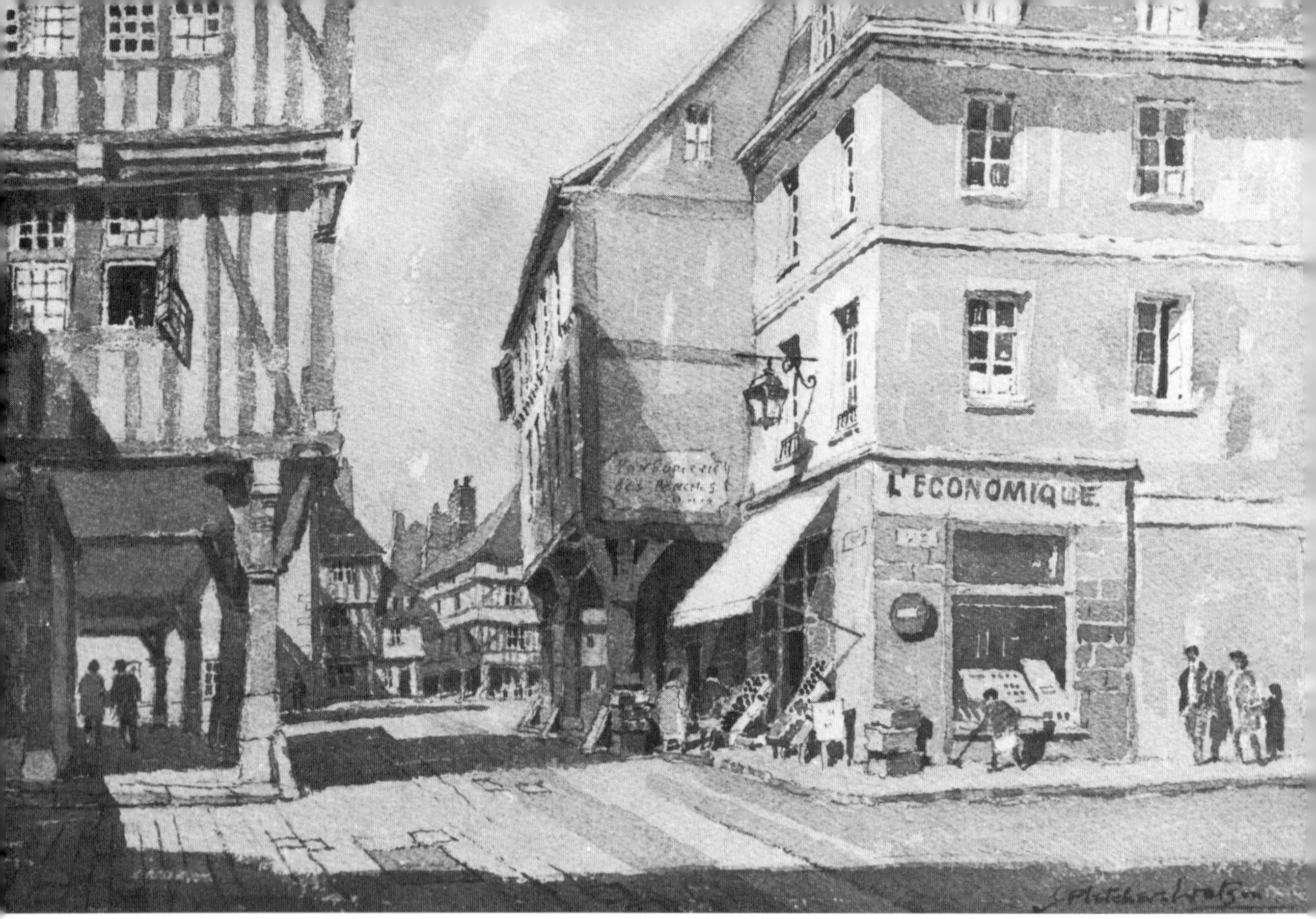
L'ECONOMIQUE

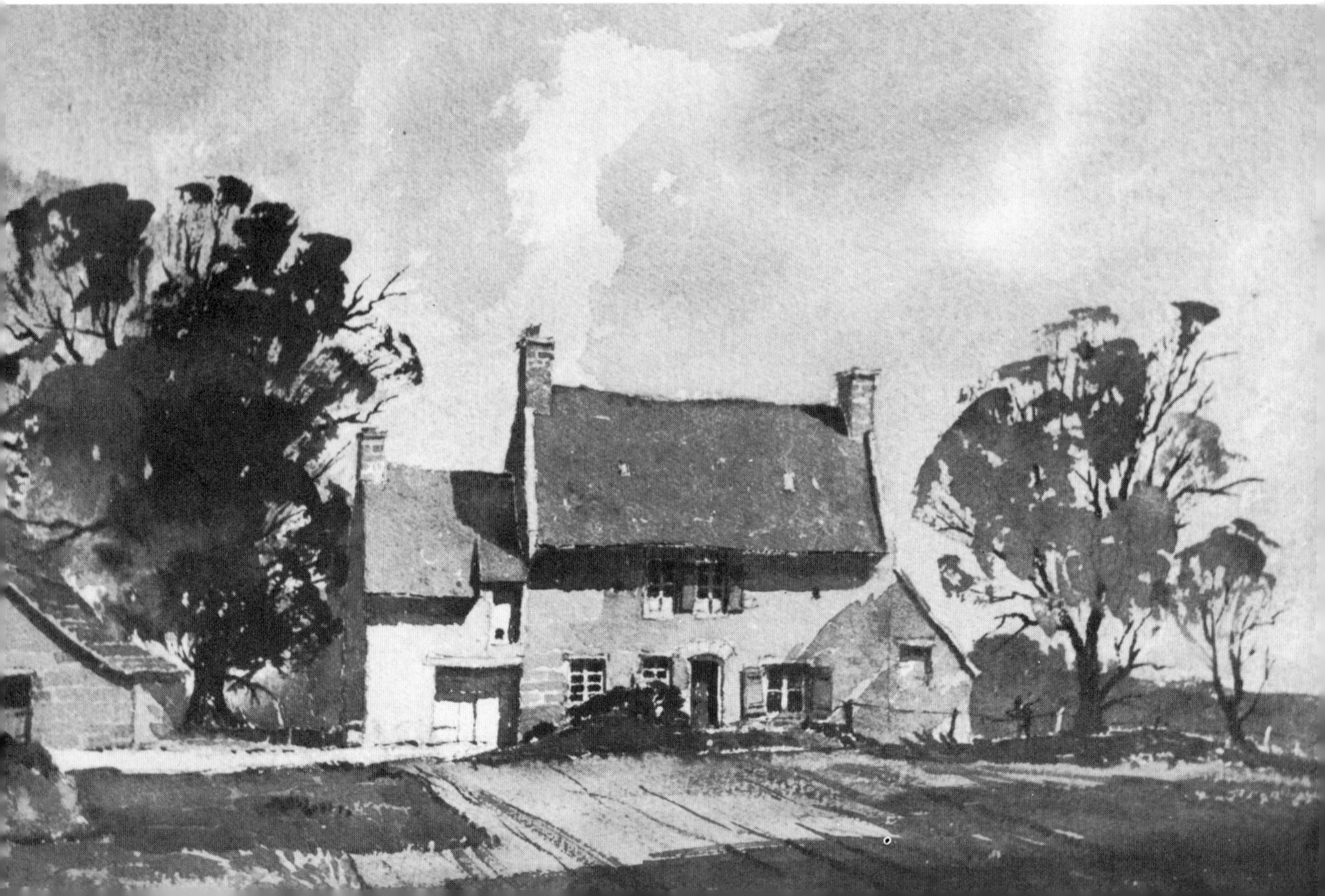

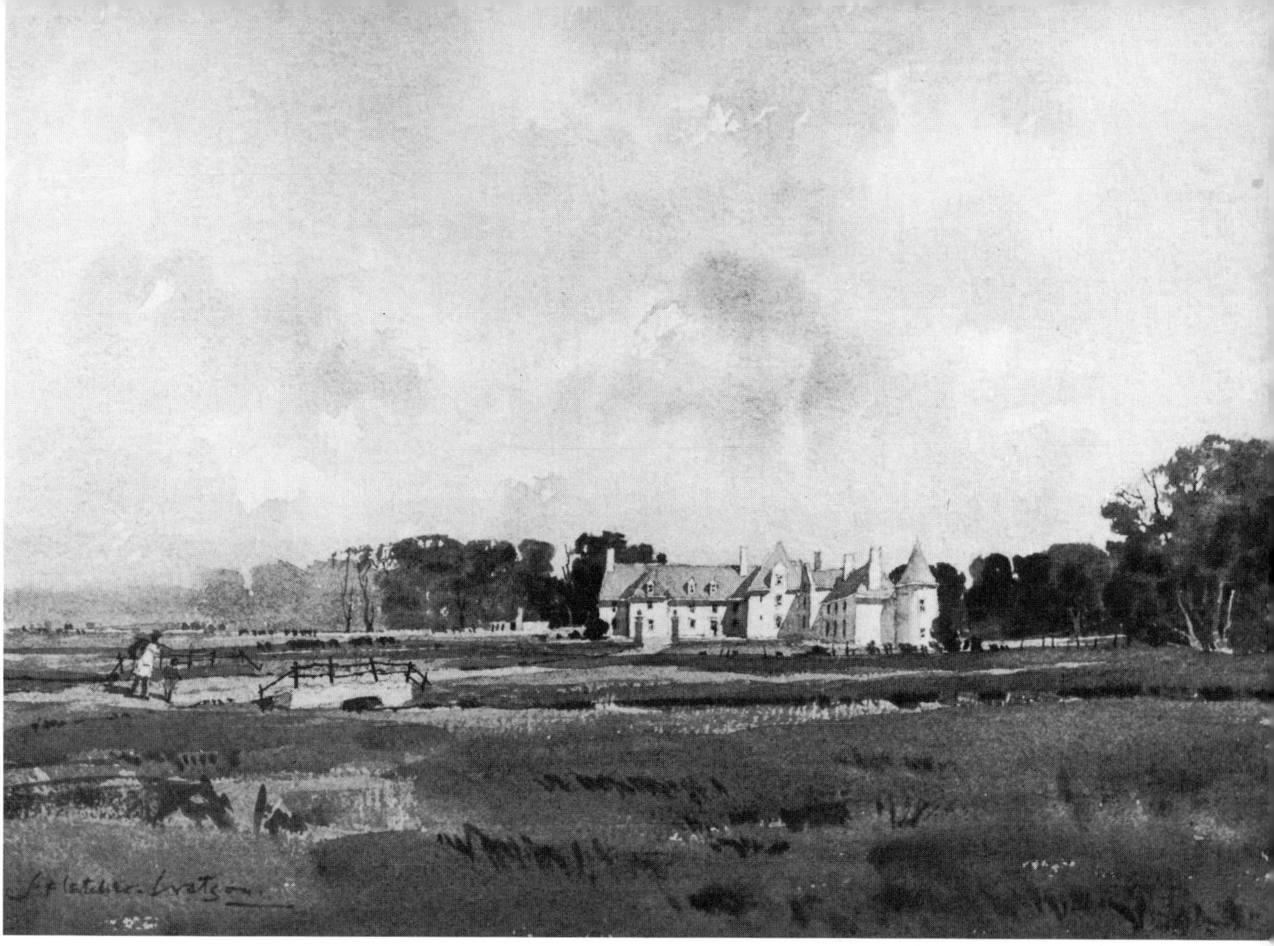

92 Dinan, Brittany.

93 Brittany, farm-house.

94 Chateau near Poitiers.

stayed the final night. This is a beautiful city with a very splendid cathedral and it still has a lot of very sketchable little side streets full of houses with steep roofs. It was lucky to escape with very little damage during the last war and it is well worth a painting visit.

92 DINAN, BRITTANY
31cm × 47cm ($12\frac{1}{4}$in. × $18\frac{1}{2}$in.)
While we are on the subject of old French towns, I visited Brittany on a previous trip to France and I was especially struck with Dinan, not to be confused with Dinard about fifteen miles to the north on the coast.

Dinan has been built up and expanded a lot, but its ancient centre has been beautifully preserved by France's ancient monuments department. It has the finest collection of sixteenth-century half-timber houses I have ever seen in England or abroad.

This picture was painted on the spot with a milling crowd of people round me and I was blocking the narrow footpath with my seat and my paints, but nobody seemed to mind. There were a few cars as well but it would have spoilt the view to put any of them in. This is one more place I must recommend you to visit if you can.

93 BRITTANY, FARM-HOUSE
30cm × 47cm (12in. × $18\frac{1}{2}$in.)
I am afraid I cannot tell you exactly where this charming little farm-house was, but it was somewhere near the north coast of Brittany. There were a number of such farm-houses and cottages in this area, partly built of gray stone and partly plastered.

94 CHATEAU NEAR POITIERS
31.5cm × 47.5cm ($12\frac{1}{2}$in. × $18\frac{3}{4}$in.)
On an earlier still visit to France we were on our way south to the Dordogne and on a little by-road not far from Poitiers we came across this delightful chateau. The mellow cream-coloured stone walls and the light gray-blue steep slated roofs were nicely set off by the mature dark woods behind. I painted this picture quite quickly.

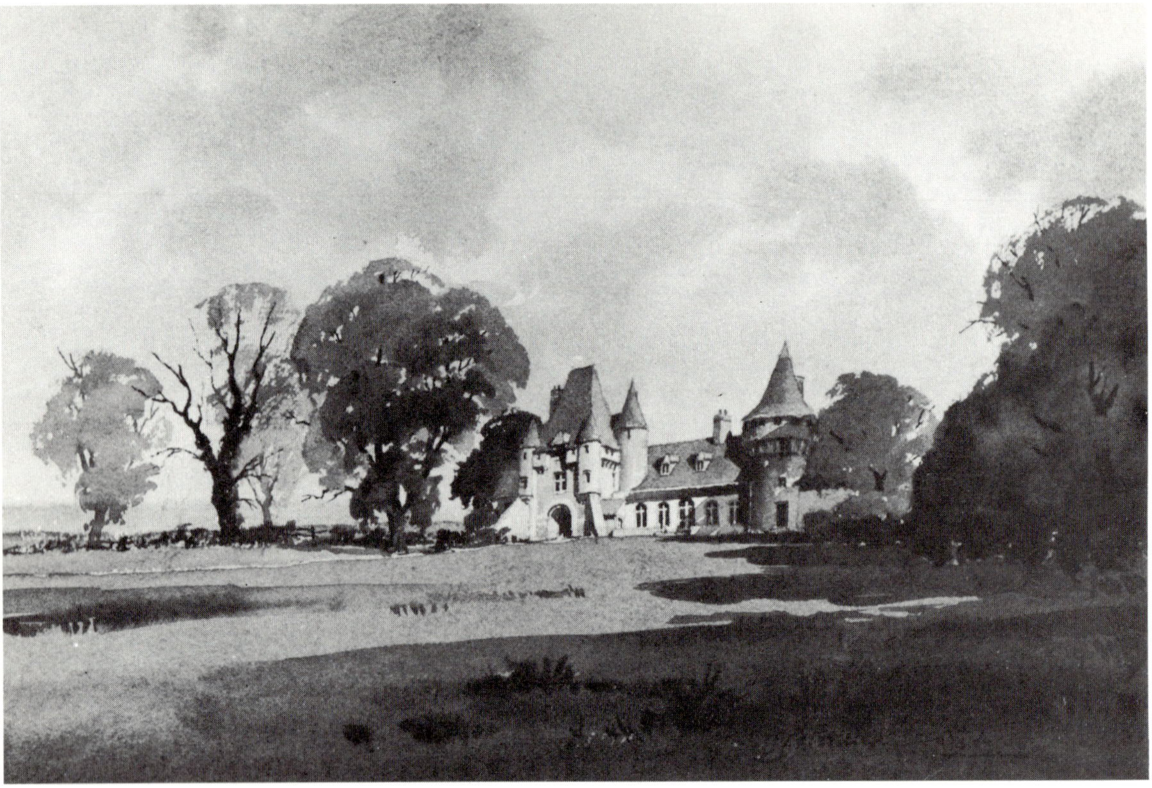

95 Chateau near Chef-Boutonne.

95 CHATEAU NEAR CHEF-BOUTONNE

Farther south on the following day we found this exciting chateau, rather like the ogre's castle of one's childhood. The steep roofs of buildings in this area still persist although it is quite far south. They make lovely subjects for the painter.

Eventually when we reached the Dordogne in the south the character of houses had changed and the roofs were of clay tiles and not so steep. We found many lovely hill villages and old farms in this area, and some of the paintings I made were illustrated in my previous book.

Altogether there is much to explore and to paint in this vast country of France, and I am looking forward to more exploring in the future. I hope I have been able to give you some ideas of where to go and what to paint.

5 Painting in Scotland

One autumn recently we were extremely lucky to be lent a cottage in the West Highlands, quite my favourite part of Scotland and also my favourite time of year for painting. Of all the mountain regions I have known, Wales, Cumbria, the North-West Frontier of India, there is something about the ruggedness and grandeur of Scotland that appeals to me most of all. The cottage was at Shieldaig on the edge of the loch and is in a most central position for getting at a wonderful variety of loch and mountain views.

96 GLEN TORRIDON, ROSS-SHIRE
31.5cm × 47.5cm ($12\frac{1}{2}$in. × $18\frac{3}{4}$in.)
Travelling westwards from Inverness one passes through Glen Torridon and along the south side of Upper Loch Torridon to Shieldaig, and this view is about eight miles before you reach Shieldaig.

It is a lovely twisting lonely road with mountains on each side and the colouring in October was quite gorgeous. The foregrounds are particularly good in the autumn, a lovely rough mixture of small rocks amongst dead yellow and brown grass and bracken and patches of green moss here and there. The roads are never straight but always twisting as most of them are in the highlands, and it was not difficult to select a good composition with a bend in the road and a nice arrangement of mountains overlapping and going away into the distance. The River Torridon can just be seen on the left.

On a cloudy day like this, the shadows on the mountains give them a dark richness which they never

96 Glen Torridon, Ross-shire.

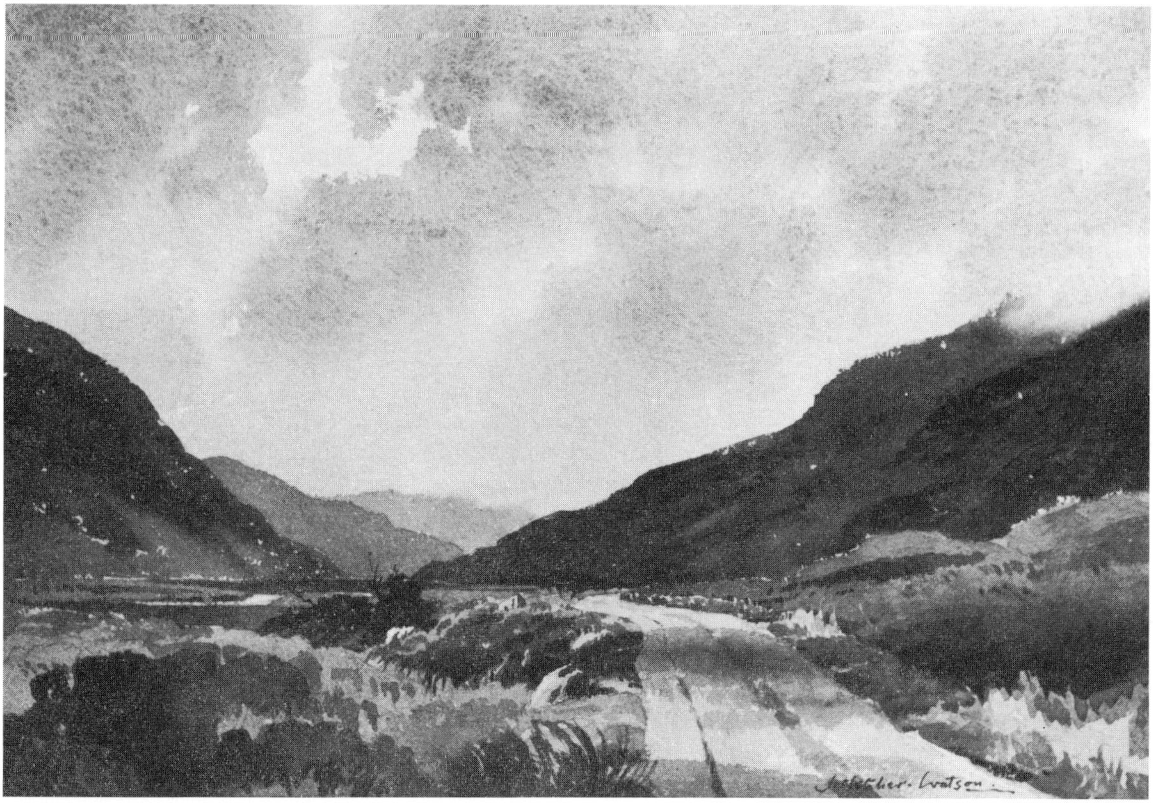

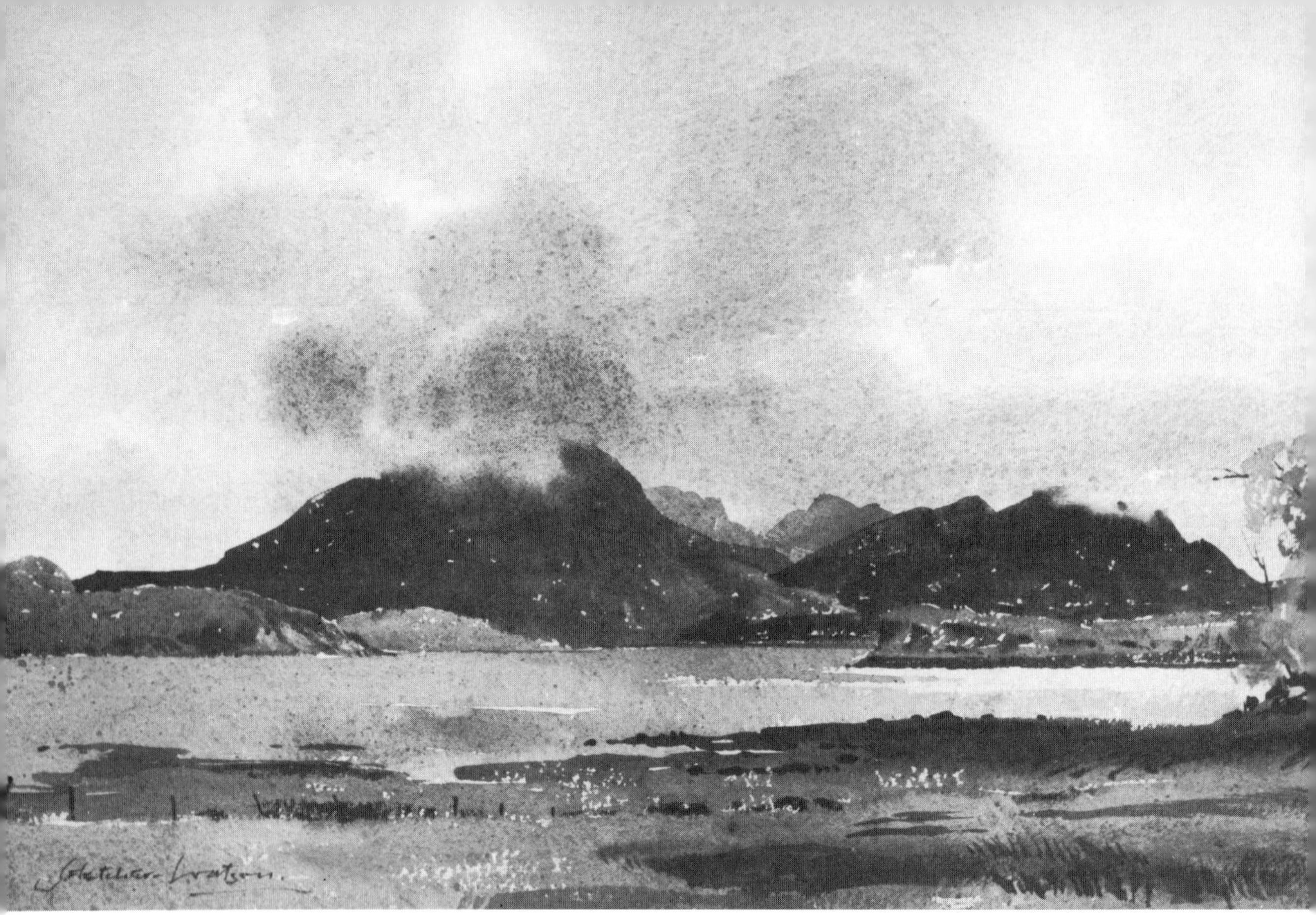

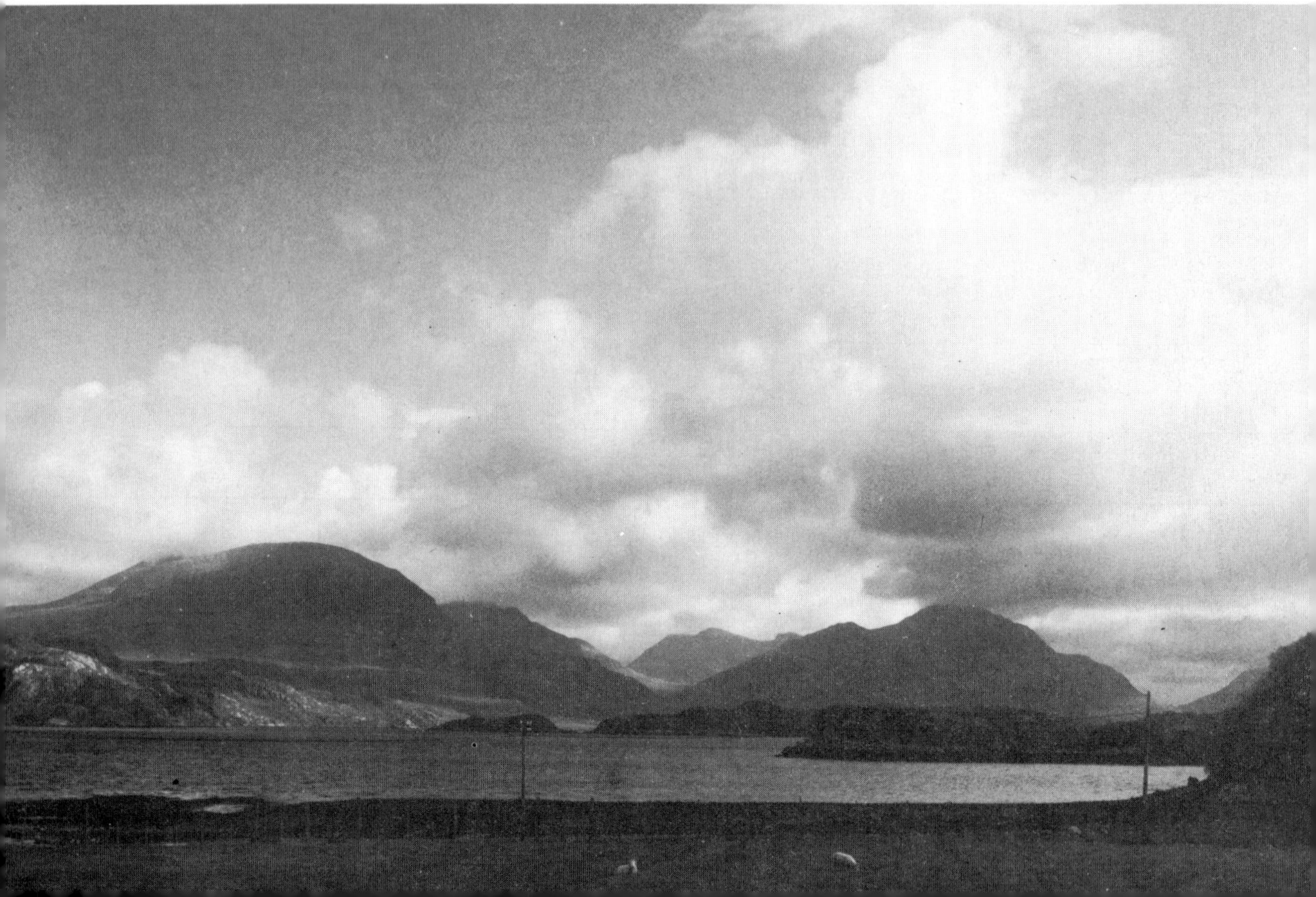

have on a day of plain blue sky. One has to learn to be brave with the way one puts the paint on in this type of country; one must not be half-hearted about it but brush on a dark mixture thick and strong with plenty of water. The low cloud coming over the mountain on the right is characteristic of Scotland at this time of year. I have described the method of producing this before but I will do it again later on.

This simple subject of road, mountains and rough foreground growth was the first picture I painted on this trip, to get my hand in. The great thing to aim at is to achieve atmosphere if you can, because that is what Scotland is all about.

97 LOCH SHIELDAIG

33cm × 49cm (13in. × 19½in.)

A narrow by-road runs west from Shieldaig village along Loch Shieldaig with many lovely views looking right-handed over the loch to mountain ranges the other side.

This is another simple subject where one can use what I call the 'direct method' of painting, i.e. using no pencil guide lines at all, but using the brush only from the word go, straight onto the blank sheet of paper. This method can result in a very fresh spontaneous water-colour and it tends to make you *think hard* before you start as there is no going back or rubbing out once you do start. One may have to sacrifice a little accuracy but with a mountain landscape this doesn't matter very much. What you are trying to do is to capture the *spirit* and *atmosphere* of the scene. You might get the occasional Scotsman who knows the view well telling you that you have got the shape of the foreshore wrong or you have left out a tree, but you must not mind about that as long as you have made a lovely painting.

I am going to ask you to look at figure 98 which is a photograph I took of exactly the same view at the time I was painting. It is interesting to note how far short of making a good picture a photograph usually falls. I may have exaggerated the height of the left-hand mountain a little and improved the water's edge in the foreground, but one's artistic eye tells one to do these things when composing a picture. In the photograph the land is less than one-third of the sky, and in my picture I have made the land about two-fifths of the sky which I think is a much nicer proportion.

I will describe the method of 'direct painting' with the next picture which is in colour.

97 Loch Shieldaig.

98 Loch Shieldaig, photograph.

LOCH TORRIDON

(colour plate 9, between pages 120 and 121)

32cm × 48cm (12¾in. × 19in.)

Continuing along this little road from Loch Shieldaig we come to the big Loch Torridon which opens out into the sea. I painted several views of this loch from further along the road as there were so many wonderful views of the same loch but all completely different.

I also include a monochrome of this picture (99), because it shows the importance of *tone values*. How the light silver birch tree on the left stands out well against the darker trees behind, and how the dark long low hill stands out against the lighter toned far mountain in the background.

There was mainly a blue sky but small white clouds were drifting over the mountain and higher up there were gray clouds.

I decided to use David Cox paper, a biscuit coloured tinted water-colour paper, lovely to work on, but sadly discontinued about thirty years ago. I still have a few sheets left which I use as a special treat on occasions. (You can get a paper which is similar called De Wint paper but it is not quite so good.)

Although this subject is a little more difficult than the last owing to the foreground trees, I wanted to use the 'direct method' again. I was sitting on a patch of gravel beside the road with the paints and brushes carefully laid out ready for quick action, as you have to work quite fast for this type of mountain picture.

Stage 1

First, I did the sky with plenty of pure Cobalt Blue, starting at the top with a No. 16 brush and adding water as I went downwards making the blue a little lighter and *leaving out* the two groups of white cloud and continuing on to the water-line position. I had no pencil guide line for this water-line and I guessed about the right place and painted the sky colour straight across the page. The strong Cobalt took on a slightly greenish tinge as it was painted on yellowish paper; this was what I wanted. If it had been white paper I would have introduced a little Raw Sienna.

I then painted the gray clouds at the top with Cobalt mixed with Light Red and let them merge into the damp blue wash.

I now let everything dry out and then started the background mountain with a No. 9 brush and blue-purple mixture of French Ultramarine and Light Red. As there were no pencil guide lines one could make some lovely clean sweeps with the brush giving the mountain shape. I started the mountain just in the position where the left-hand trees would be coming later and stopped the wash where the left-hand small white cloud came. With a No. 5 brush and *clear* water I wetted a small amount of paper keeping *below* the line of

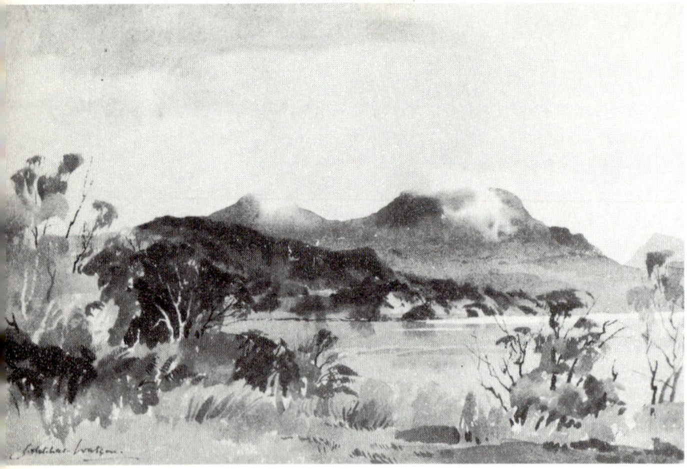

99 Loch Torridon.

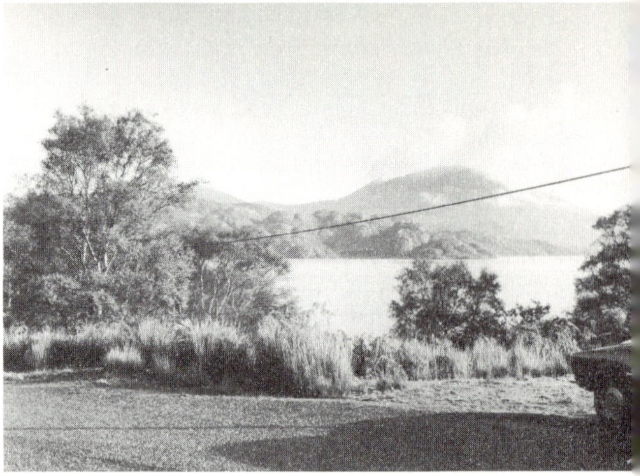

100 Loch Torridon, photograph.

the mountain; that is important. Then with the larger brush I continued painting the mountain colour *into* the clear water and a runny-edged cloud was the result. I carried on with the mountain and did the same thing with clear water for the next white cloud which was bigger, coming down the mountain quite far. I ran the dark bluish colour into the upper cloud and then changed the mountain colour a little using more Light Red, and carried on painting this mountain forming the wispy nature of this cloud. I eventually continued the mountain colour down to about one inch short of the water-line and changed the colour to light gray which would be wanted for the rocky low hill later.

Stage 2

When everything was dry I painted the extreme left silver birch tree. This was a light colour and it was necessary to have this statement before putting in the dark hill. I used medium strong Raw Sienna and Burnt Sienna and a No. 7 brush for the tree leaving some white trunks below. While it was damp I put in the little tree next to it with Burnt Sienna and Cobalt. But not the very dark tree, this would come later.

Now it was time for the dark low hill with the very dark areas of rock and light coloured cliff slopes at the water's edge. I used a No. 7 brush and Burnt Umber and Ultramarine. With a No. 1 brush I drew in the water-line in dark brown colour.

Painting the mountains did not in fact take very long as one had to paint quickly so that the colours would run into each other. But the description in Stages one and two has been lengthy and may have given the impression that a long time was taken for the painting.

Stage 3

It was now necessary to put in the water as this was a *light* tone and dark things had to go against it.

A pure gray was mixed with Cobalt and Light Red and washed all over the water with a No. 9 brush, carefully leaving a white streak of water to the right where the sun was catching it. This was followed by a touch of Ultramarine which merged into the gray. Then as it dried some sideways brush strokes were added of a slightly darker gray under the dark hill and indicating reflection and water movement. There were certainly no definite reflections as there was too much wind on the water.

This water wash dried quite quickly and I could get on with foreground details.

Stage 4

First, a light yellowish-geeen wash was laid across the immediate foreground of Raw Sienna and very little Winsor Blue. Keeping everything damp I added some long grass growths with Cadmium Yellow and Winsor Blue; this give a very strong green but I kept it to medium strength only. Different grass tufts were added in a darker tone by adding a little Burnt Sienna. Then some pure Burnt Sienna to bracken here and there and sometimes darkened with Burnt Umber.

Some dark green low shrubs went in on the left just below the silver birch, giving some sharp edges to the light green grasses. Also a similar dark shrub was painted nearer the centre. This about completed the low level foliage.

The very dark tree to the right of the light brown birch tree was now painted, carefully leaving the almost white thin trunks. I used Burnt Umber and Winsor Blue for this dark brownish-green tree. I think it was another birch tree but being considerably darkened by cloud shadow.

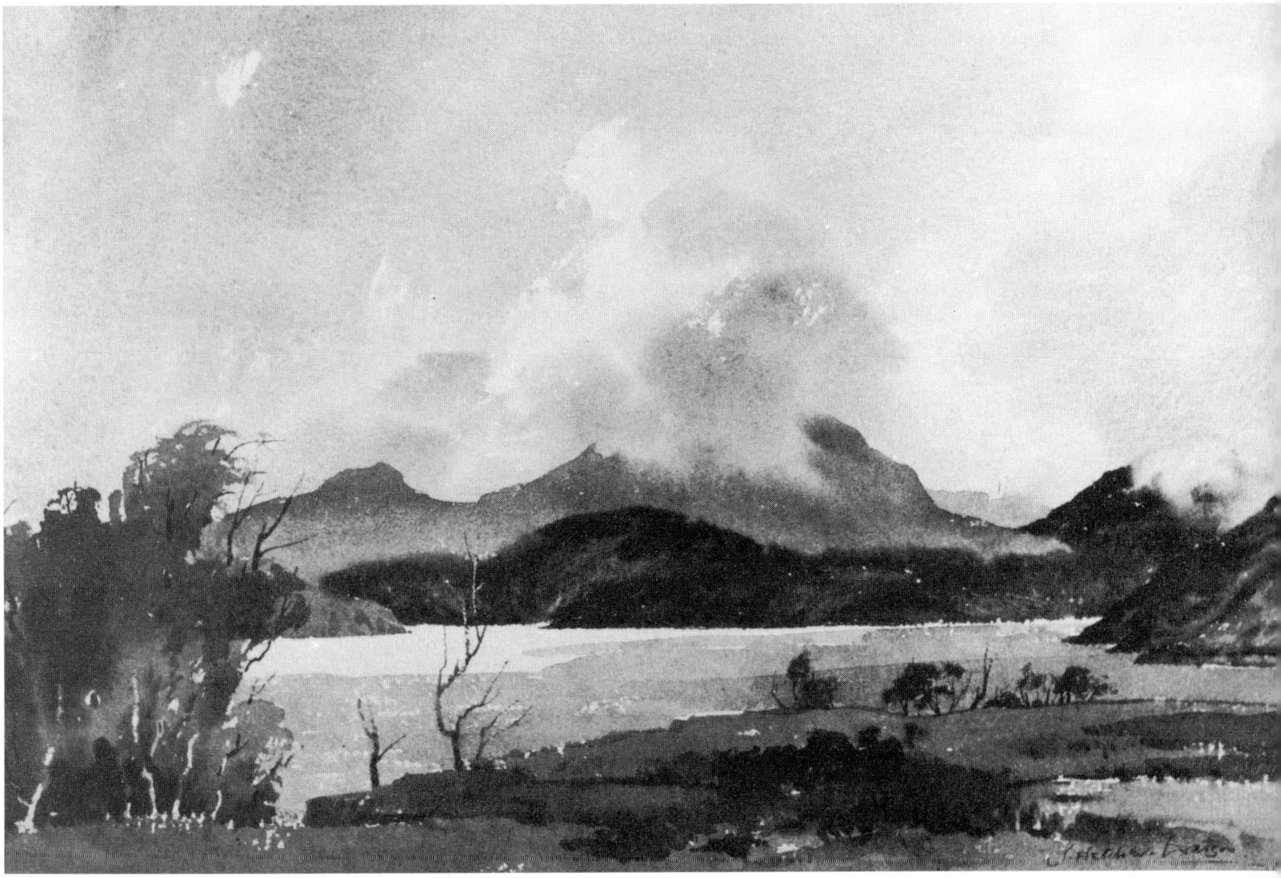

101 Autumn colours, Loch Torridon.

The small trees on the right of the picture had their dull green foliage smudged in with quick sideways strokes of the brush; the colour was a mixture of Winsor Blue and Burnt Sienna. I had been using a No. 7 brush for all this tree work. The dark brown branches were put in with a No. 3 and No. 0 brush while the foliage was still wet.

I touched in a dark brown branch or two on the left-hand tree at this point in the proceedings, and I also scratched out with my knife an additional white branch in this autumn-coloured yellow tree. This about finished the picture.

The colours used were Cadmium Yellow, Raw Sienna, Burnt Sienna, Burnt Umber, Light Red, Cobalt Blue, French Ultramarine and Winsor Blue.

I would now like you to look at a photograph of the actual scene (100). You can see from this to what extent one uses Artist's Licence and alters things a little. I certainly turned the foreground gravel into grass and I considerably simplified the trees. The low long hill did in fact become much darker at times as cloud shadows moved about, and the water looked darker than it does in the photograph. Of course I left out the electric cable running across the sky!

101 AUTUMN COLOURS, LOCH TORRIDON
31.5cm × 49cm ($12\frac{1}{2}$in. × $19\frac{1}{2}$in.)
This picture was painted the day before the one above. It is a little further along the same road with a slightly different arrangement of mountains and trees, but an equally exciting view and full of lovely colouring. Actually on this day I did *three* pictures, one in the morning, this one in the afternoon and a small one of Skye in the evening.

This particular road is one you must discover if you go to the West Highlands, it simply abounds in good subjects. It runs round a sort of peninsula to Applecross.

I show this picture because although it is similar to the last one it shows a good example of a bigger, heavier type of cloud overhanging the mountain, and I do want to encourage you to be able to deal with this type of sky treatment. It is so much a part of mountain scenery, especially in Scotland.

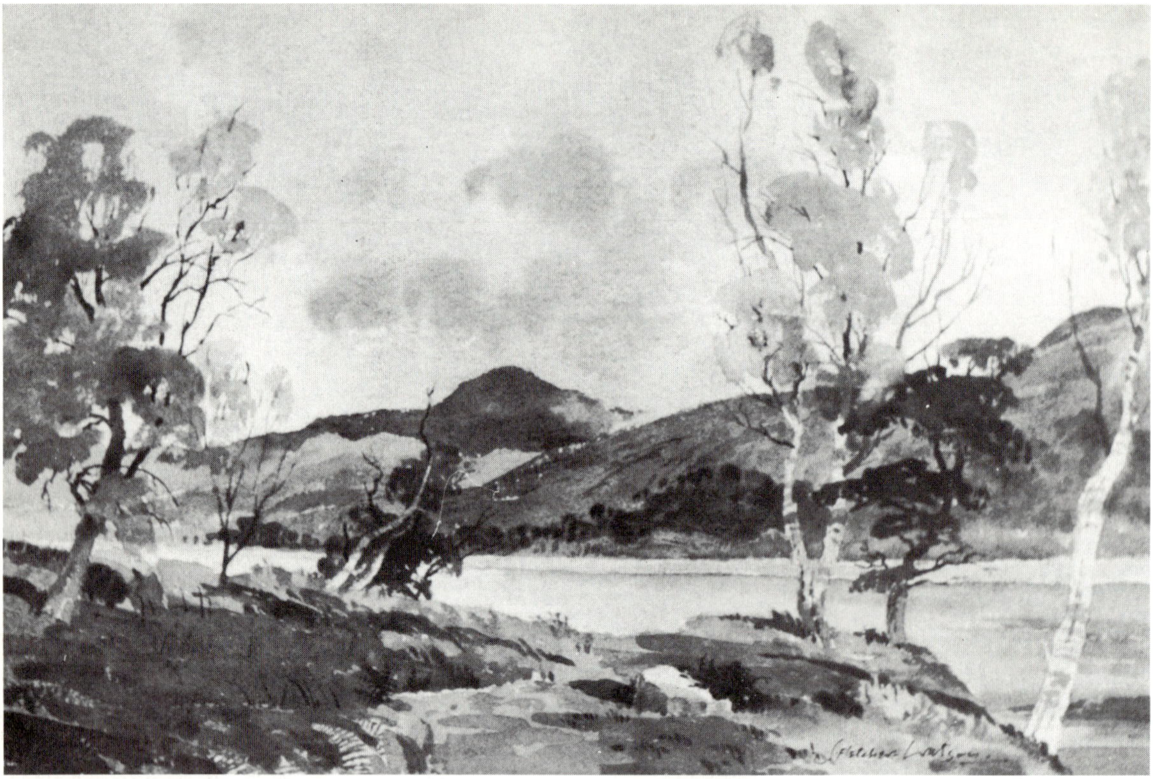

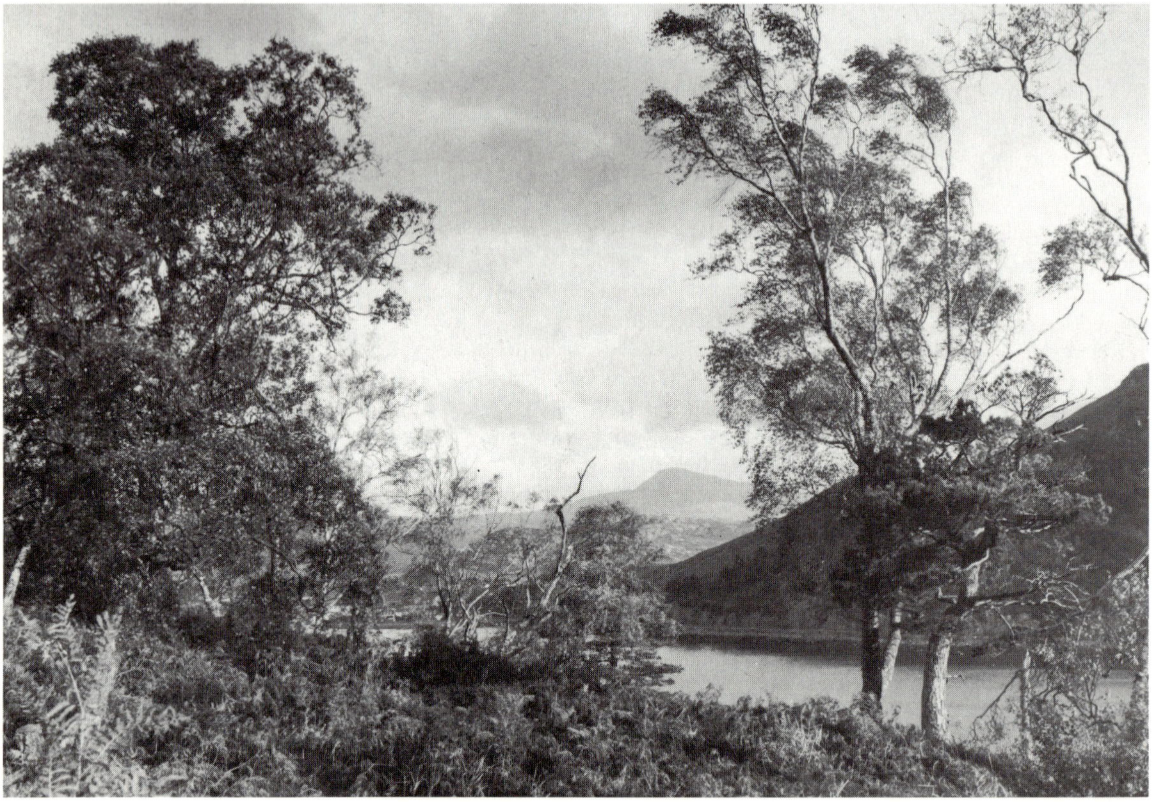

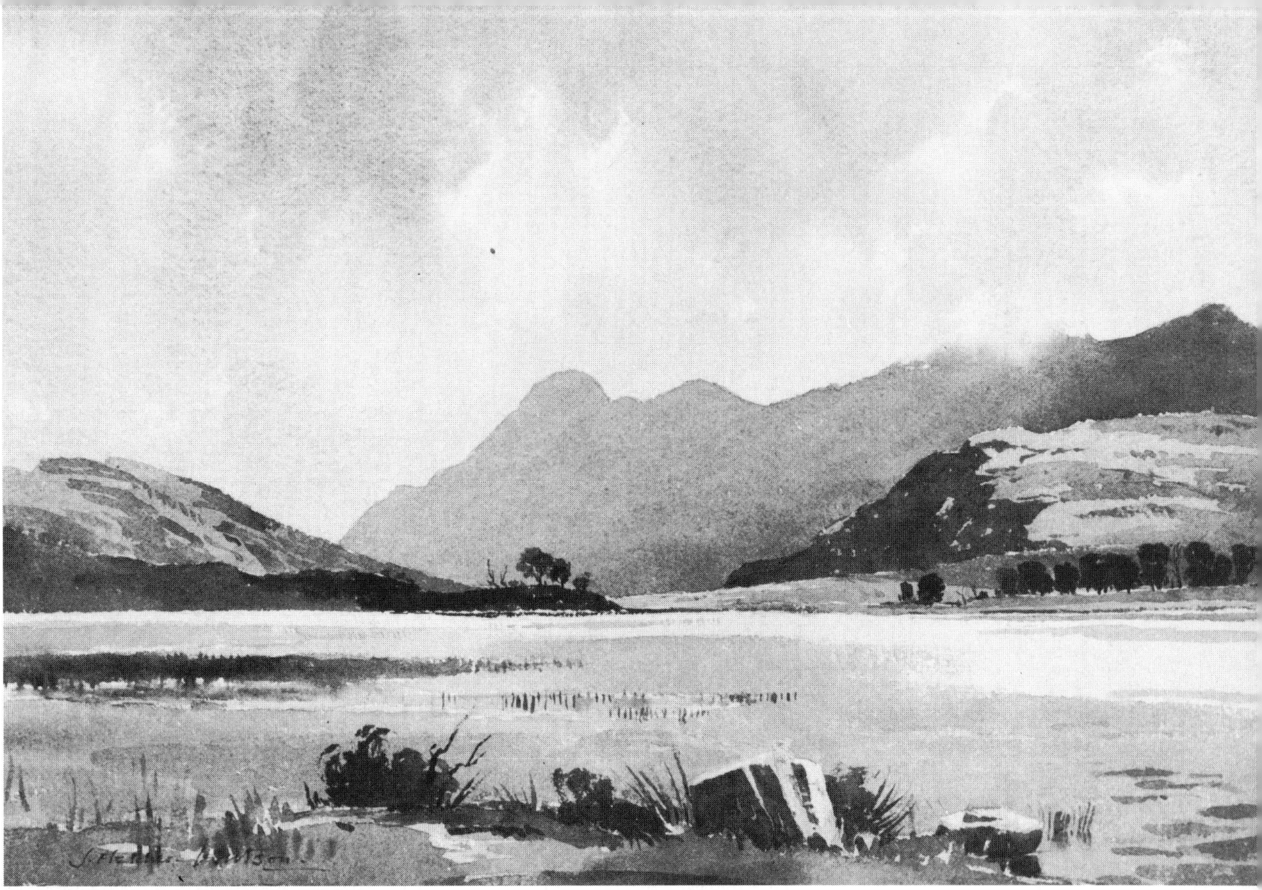

102 Loch Shieldaig, with silver birches.

103 Loch Shieldaig, photograph.

104 Loch an Loin and Beinn Damh.

102 LOCH SHIELDAIG, WITH SILVER BIRCHES
31.5cm × 48cm ($12\frac{1}{2}$in. × 19in.)
Re-tracing our steps a little back to the smaller Loch Shieldaig I found a delightful view looking through silver birch trees. They are very much a feature of Scotland and have most pleasing shapes, especially when they get old. Their autumn colours have lovely strong yellows and browns.

I include a photograph (103) and you can see how I thinned out the trees a bit so that I could get more of the distant view. From memory I don't think the foreground rock was actually there, and this is a legitimate ploy to give extra interest. Foregrounds are so important in bringing the ground right up to the spectator and pushing the background away.

By the way, I tinted this paper before starting, it was Arches and I gave it a flat wash of light Burnt Umber which made it rather like a piece of David Cox paper. For an autumn subject it is sometimes a good idea and it gives a mellowness to your painting. This painting definitely required some pencil work for the tree trunks before starting to paint.

104 LOCH AN LOIN AND BEINN DAMH
33cm × 48cm (13in. × 19in.)
Exploring southwards from Sheildaig one day I spotted a small loch below us which looked as if it might be interesting, so we turned down a very stony narrow track and it widened out onto a grass patch and this glorious view of Beinn Damh mountain opened out before us. It was an absolute 'must' and I set to work while the clouds were good and the light was good. But in fact I did a quick pencil sketch (105) as I wanted to make sure I had got a good view-point. By turning myself fifteen degrees to the right there was another lovely view with a small cottage; I did this one on another day.

I show you also a photograph (106) and it is odd how the camera has a way of pushing distant features further into the distance. I suppose one requires a telescopic lens, but then you would lose some of the side features to right and left. I think this photograph particularly goes to show how the artist scores over the photographer, or at any rate the human eye does.

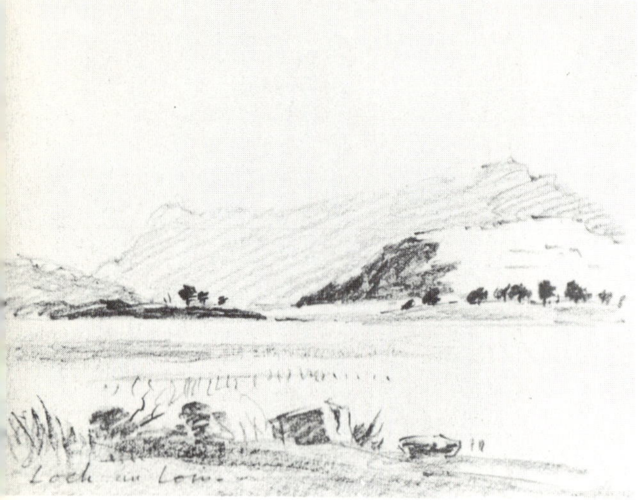

105 Loch an Loin, preliminary sketch.

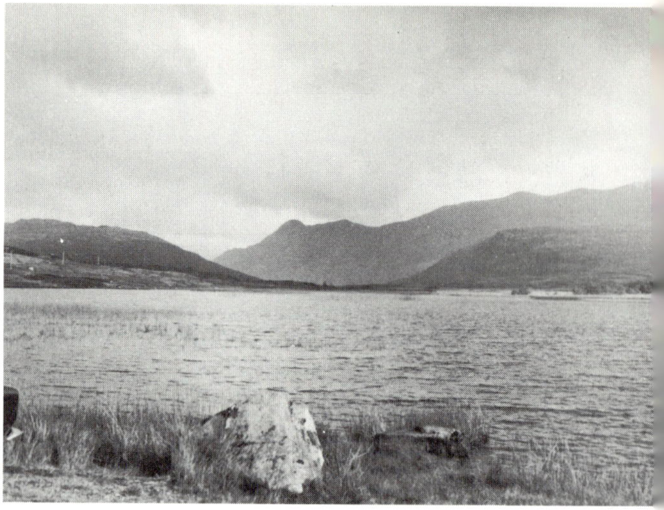

106 Loch an Loin, photograph.

BRIDGE NEAR KISHORN

(colour plate 10, between pages 120 and 121)
31.5cm × 48.5cm ($12\frac{1}{2}$in. × $19\frac{1}{4}$in.)

Driving towards the village of Lochcarron the road twists a lot and rises up through a small mountain pass and we came to a little bridge over a stream. It was nothing to look at from the road but it is often worth having a look at a bridge from below. I was delighted to find this excellent view in amongst the mountains and rocks.

Although it was a very simple bridge to paint, in some ways it was quite a complicated subject and I knew I should have to be careful to simplify the foreground.

Figure 107 shows a monochrome of the painting and you can see the importance of sorting out darks and lights. The mountain on the right was in the sun and was painted in light tones, the one on the left was very much in dark shadow. The arch shadow was dark and made an excellent focal point, and the foreground rocks and clumps of overgrown heather had many conflicting darks which had to be carefully planned and brought together.

Figure 108 shows the actual scene; unfortunately the sun had gone in at the end of the painting when I took it so the darks and lights are not too apparent. But you can see how I sorted out the muddled foreground.

Drawing

A little drawing with a B pencil was wanted for this picture. I first mapped out everything with my finger. The bridge I wanted left of centre and just under a third of the way up the picture. Everything fell into place from this focal point – the stream running to the right foreground, the left-hand dark mountain and the right-hand light mountain made perfect converging slopes down towards the bridge. I drew the bridge firmly and carefully and the mountains were roughly sketched in outline.

Painting

It was a blustery sky with patches of blue and shafts of sunlight; this changed towards the end of the painting to a duller light but I managed to get my shadows in in time. The sky colours used were Raw Sienna, Burnt Umber and Ultramarine and I kept a fair lot of water on the paper, which was Arches, while floating in the grays and blues.

The distant blue mountain was then painted using Ultramarine and only a little Light Red. The left-hand mountain received mixes of Burnt Umber and Winsor Blue and was darkened in places by adding a touch of Indian Red. The little silver birch was catching the sun and was therefore left white until the end and was then painted with Burnt Sienna. The right-hand mountain varied a lot in colour and consisted of different mixes of Raw Sienna and Winsor Blue, adding Burnt Sienna for the darker areas and touches of Indian Red for the rocky places, giving a pinkish-gray.

The foreground had a first wash of mainly Raw Sienna and a little Winsor Blue and the darker heather areas were Winsor Blue and Burnt Sienna, a little burnt Umber was run in as well for the extra dark points. The bridge was a light gray to start with using Light Red and Cobalt, and then Light Red and Ultramarine for the shadow under the arch. For the rocks I used the same three colours as for the bridge. The stream had flecks of white for the rough water and it was mainly a light brown-gray for which Burnt Umber was mixed with Cobalt and well diluted.

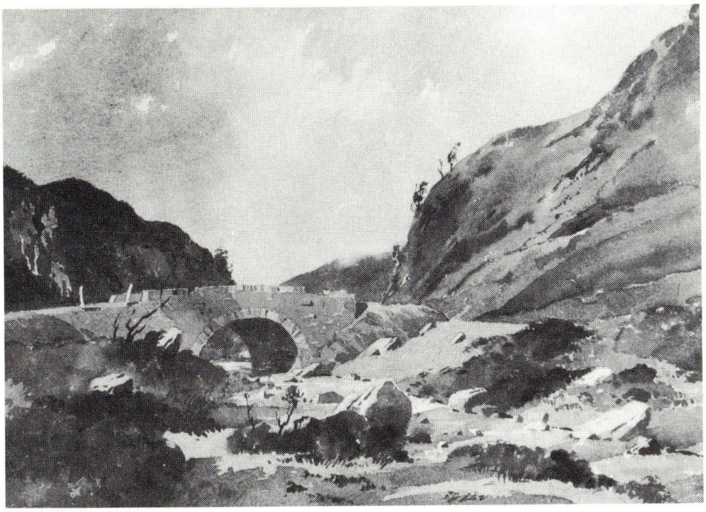

107 Bridge near Kishorn.

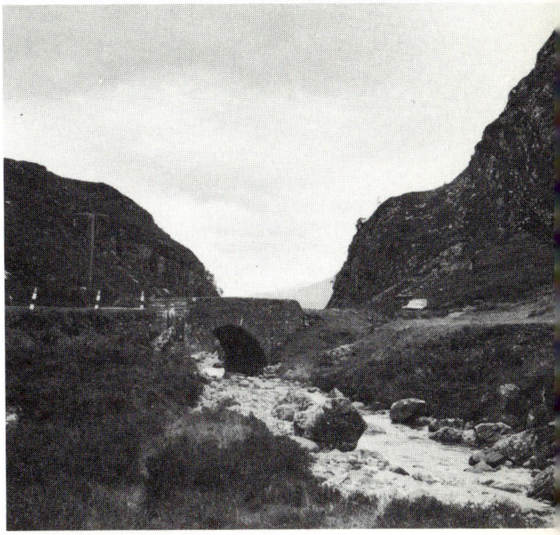

108 Bridge near Kishorn, photograph.

I stood up and viewed the picture from a few yards away and I felt a little bonding together in the foreground was needed. I used Ultramarine and Raw Sienna for a dull green and ran this over the road bank to the left of the bridge; this was a cloud shadow and as it came towards the river I darkened it by adding Raw Umber. Then I mixed the same dull green and continued a shadow up the further bank and also placed a shadow over the immediate left foreground and extended this on over the flat grass.

A blue-gray shadow or two was washed across the stream using Cobalt and Light Red.

Finally some little twiggy bits of bush were drawn with a small brush and some grass texture touched in on the foreground. The small shrubs on the sky-line of the right-hand mountain were also put in.

One thing one learns to do in Scotland is to paint rocks; they are always coming into foregrounds and I have made many rock studies in sketch books over the years. I advise you to do this and learn how to make sharp shadows and cracks on rocks.

I used eight colours for this picture – Raw Sienna, Burnt Sienna, Burnt Umber, Light Red, Indian Red, Cobalt Blue, French Ultramarine and Winsor Blue.

109 EILEAN DONAN CASTLE, FROM THE NORTH

31.5cm × 48cm ($12\frac{1}{2}$in. × 19in.)

One day we ventured about fifteen miles south to have a look at the famous Eilean Donan Castle at Dornie. This is at a junction of three lochs, Loch Alsh, Loch Duich and Loch Long and that is why the castle is so surrounded by big sheets of water: it is on a small island connected to the mainland by a stone bridge.

We were in good time for a morning picture and the tide was high. I took a photograph (110) again in order to show you how the camera pushes the middle distance far, far away, and in making our painting we can bring the castle closer in. The tide was going out and by the time I was half-way through the painting the foreshore was much more interesting than in the photograph.

This subject is a marvellous composition from almost any angle and it is simply a question of choosing which and then deciding how much mountain to keep.

I have painted this castle before and it never fails to inspire me with a great urge to put it down on paper. The building itself is a lovely mellow gray-brown stone, and it always stands out in sharp relief against the backdrop of mountain scenery. Do not miss a chance of painting this great subject if you are ever in the area.

111 EILEAN DONAN CASTLE, FROM THE SOUTH-EAST

31.5cm × 48cm ($12\frac{1}{2}$in. × 19in.)

After painting figure 109 I was having a well-earned picnic lunch and the weather was changing a little and looking rather threatening. I wanted to look at the view of the other side of the castle as I had never painted it from the south-east. I pulled up the car at the side of the road near a parapet wall and a lovely view was obtained, but just then a few drops of rain began to fall. I decided to do a picture from inside the car and hoped the weather would not get too bad. As it turned out we had a series of passing storms which produced exciting gray clouds with sometimes light blue down below and curtains of rain drifting across. The castle looked magnificent in this gray weather and there was the odd glimpse of sun to give a shadow on the building. The tide was very low and the rocky foreground and low hills behind made a lovely composition.

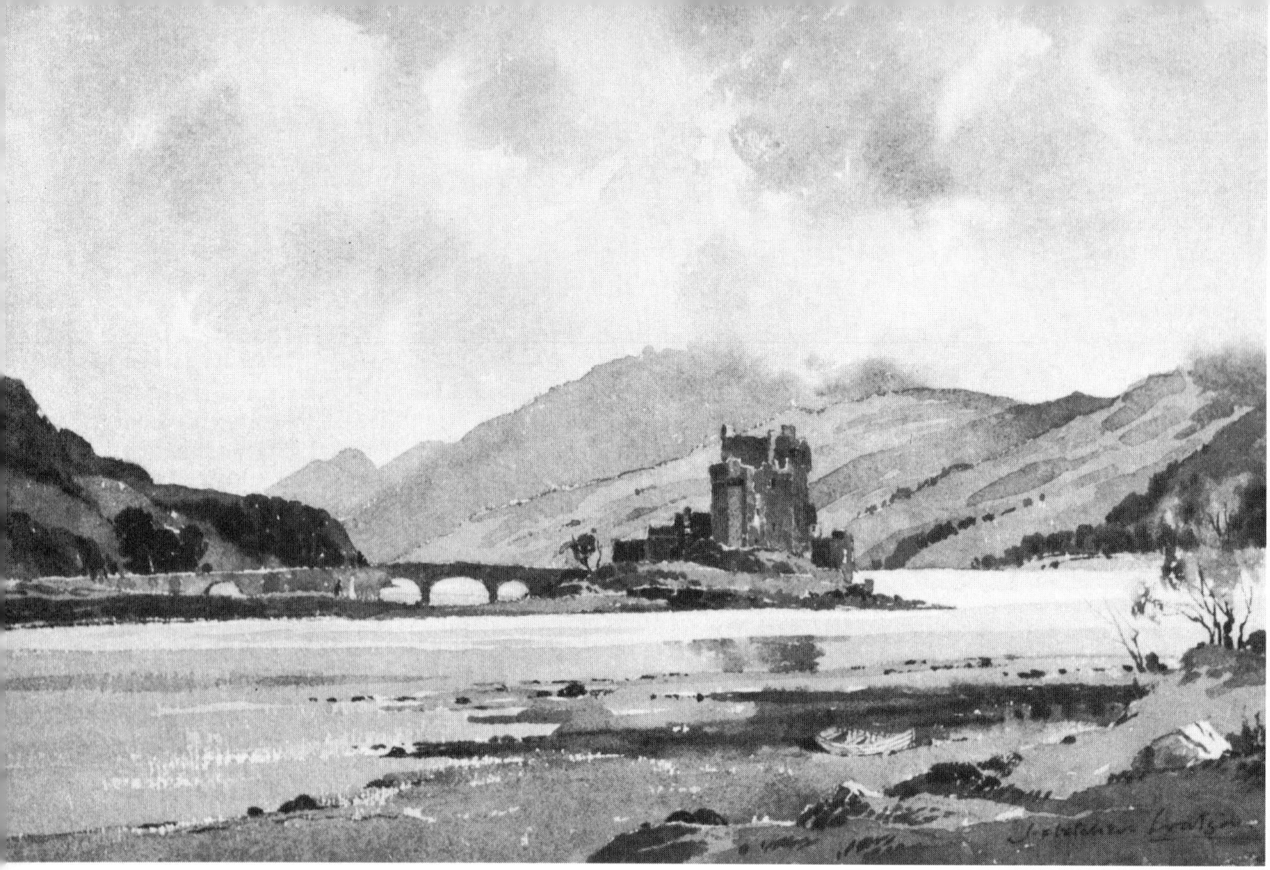

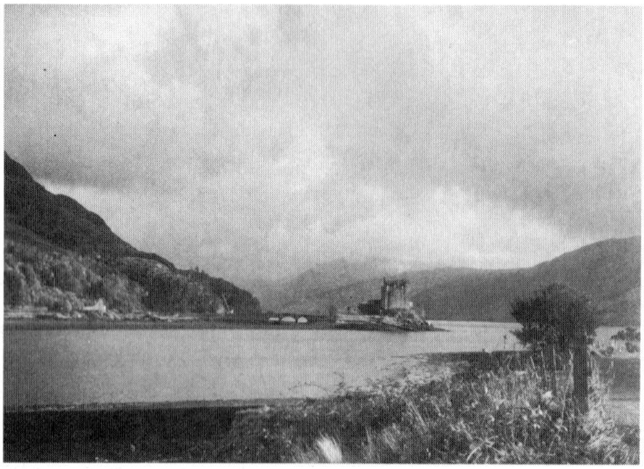

109 Eilean Donan Castle, from the north.

110 Eilean Donan Castle, from the north, photograph.

112 LOCH LONG, NEAR DORNIE

33cm × 48cm (13in. × 19in.)

Just round the corner from Eilean Donan Castle was Loch Long, approached by a lovely little side road wandering along the loch. This perfectly stunning view suddenly appeared as we were exploring and we decided we must stay a night somewhere so that I could paint it the next day.

It is one of those ready-made compositions which I am sure you will not be able to resist, so I do hope some of you will find this view one day.

KISHORN ESTUARY

(colour plate 11, between pages 120 and 121)

31cm × 48.5cm ($12\frac{1}{4}$in. × $19\frac{1}{4}$in.)

Loch Kishorn is a small loch which is to be found a little way south of Loch an Loin, shown at figure 104 with Beinn Damh mountain in the background. Funnily enough the very same mountain is in the background of this picture although it is much further away.

I caught this subject as the tide was coming in and there seemed to be water in all directions leaving little bits of land and mud. The flat land in the middle of the picture was the most gorgeous rich dark green. The day was cloudy and showers kept coming and going and the general ground being very damp the colours were marvellously strong and vivid. It is rather intriguing to paint a wild Scottish landscape when there is no sun; I was, needless to say, sitting in the car for this work.

I chose a sheet of the white Whatman paper as I felt

111 Eilean Donan Castle, from the south-east.

112 Loch Long, near Dorne.

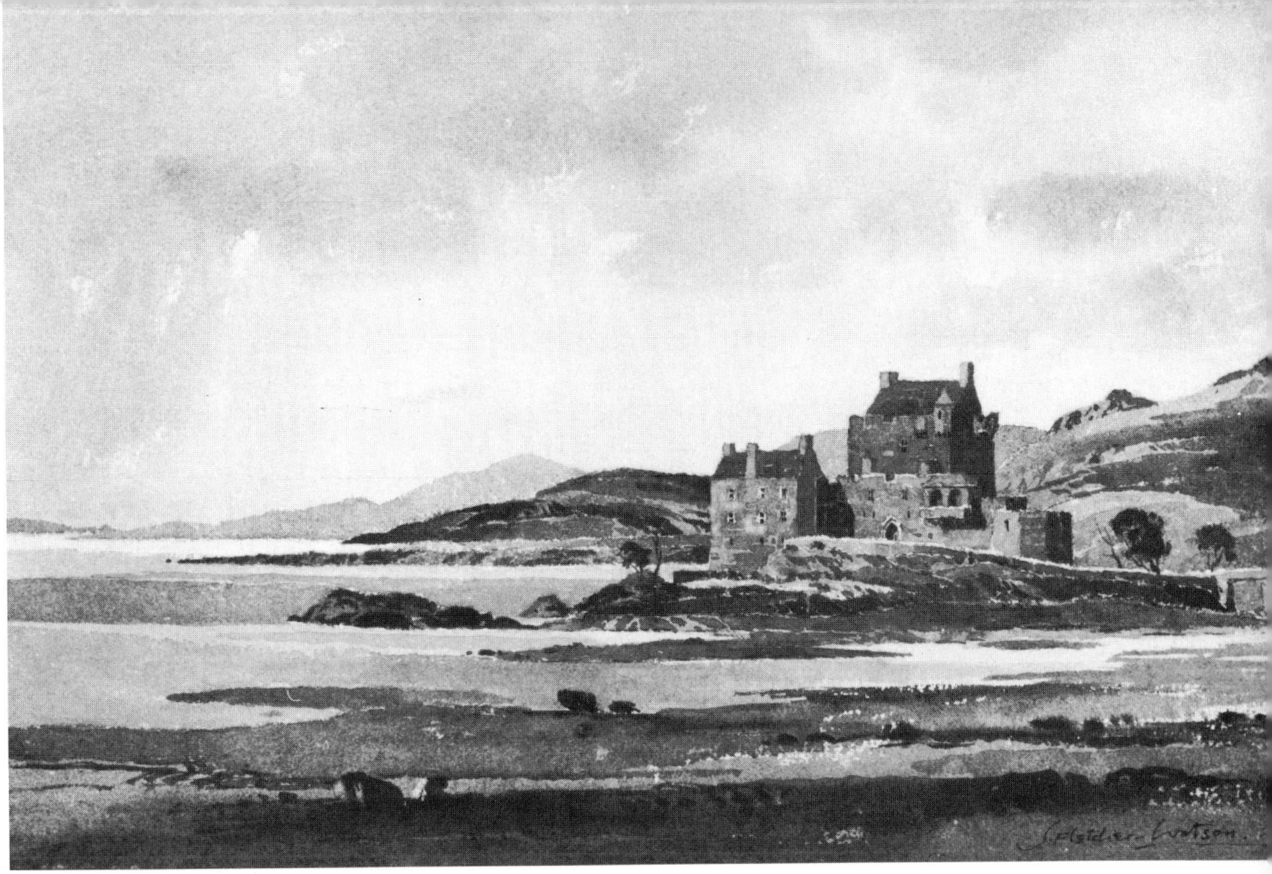

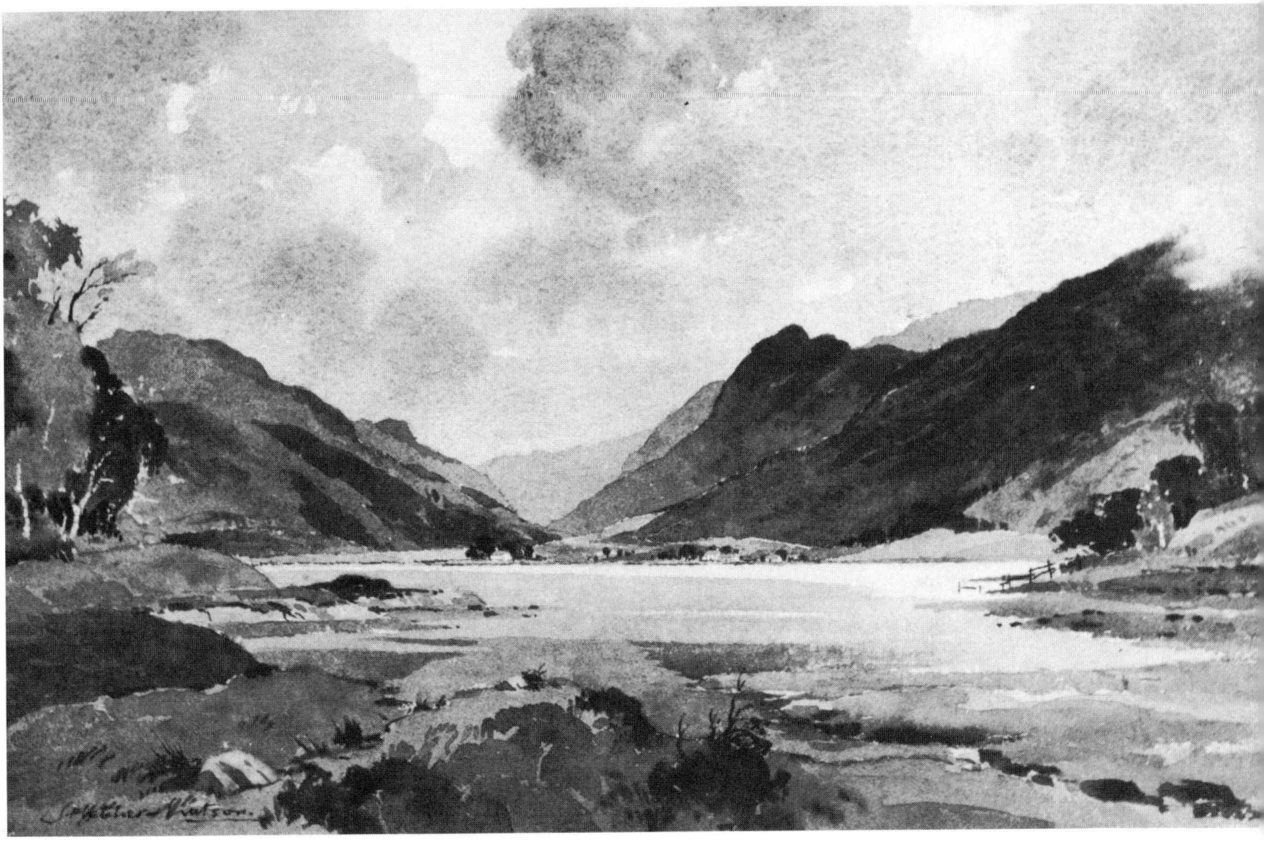

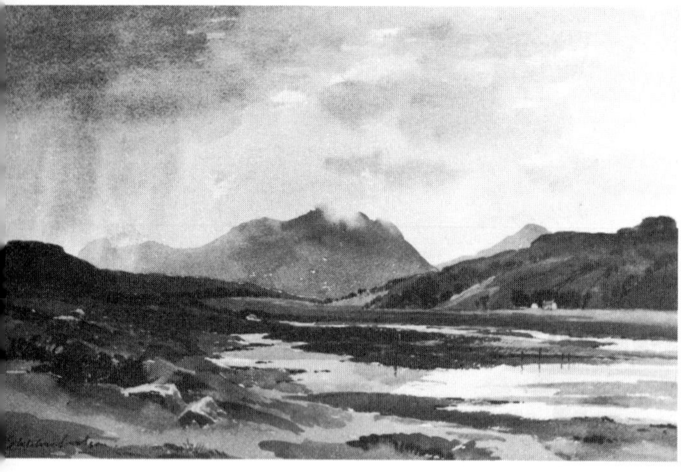

113 Kishorn Estuary.

this would bring out the vivid colours better. I made a few pencil marks to indicate the shapes of the water areas and the middle distance hills but not the far mountain, I wanted this to be pure brush work. I also drew in the farmhouse on the right.

Painting – Stage 1

I first mixed a light tone of gray-blue with Ultramarine and a small proportion of Burnt Umber and washed this all over the sky area, including the background mountain, with the big No. 16 brush. Then as this dried I made a stronger mix of the same two colours and dropped in the darker clouds which had soft edges. Now I dragged vertically the streaks of rain on the left and these ran slightly and gave the impression of rain drifting over from the north-west, i.e. from the left.

Stage 2

This first wash was allowed to dry absolutely and it took time as it was a damp day and I could *not* proceed until it *was* all dry.

Beinn Damh, the background mountain, could now be put in and I mixed a suitable blue-gray with Ultramarine and Light Red. The mountain was a slightly purple-gray actually, and these two colours can give that quite well. The right-hand end was darker than the other end which was further away. I used a No. 9 brush and boldly swept it over the paper, with no pencil guide line, getting a nice clean edge. When I came to the low gray light cloud over the top of the mountain I did the trick I described for colour plate 9 (see page 94), using a second brush and painting the cloud position with clear water before running into it with the gray colour. As the mountain dried out I took a clean No. 7 brush and stroked it downwards over the left-hand end where the rain was falling; this 'lifted' the mountain colour off a little and improved the falling rain effect.

Stage 3

When all was quite dry I could start on the main body of the picture. I mixed up a fair quantity of yellowish-green using plenty of Raw Sienna and a little Winsor Blue and made a big wash with a No. 9 brush all over the land area including hills and foreground and leaving out the water areas, also leaving out the one or two rocks, which I should have mentioned had been drawn in pencil.

From now on I wanted to keep everything *slightly wet and fluid* and I started to mix different colours very quickly. Some neat Raw Sienna was stroked in with a No. 7 brush on the middle background area just above the small bridge. Then some darker greens using Cadmium Yellow, Winsor Blue and a little Burnt Sienna for the hill on the right and the low sloping ground on the left, leaving light green pieces in between. Cadmiun Yellow is a useful colour as it is very thick and opaque and gives a solidity to a mixture which when applied to damp paper is effective.

Then some neat Burnt Sienna on the left-hand side where there was bracken. Now the dark outstanding low hill on the left with Burnt Umber and Winsor Blue: this was an important accent.

Everything was still damp as I had been working quickly and I now took a smaller No. 5 brush and with a darker mix of Burnt Umber and Winsor Blue I painted the various tree groups on the right-hand hill, small ones in the distance and larger ones near-to. The trees behind the farmhouse were almost pure Winsor Blue. The dark rock outcrop at the top of the hill was also painted. And then came the dark tree belt on the other side of the picture, and just to the left of this there was a brown streak of ground for which Burnt Umber was used.

Now I ran in the very dark green of the middle marsh area surrounded by water. This was Cadmium Yellow, Winsor Blue and a little Burnt Sienna. It faded to lighter green at the right-hand end. The little stone bridge, over which I had driven to reach this spot, was painted with a No. 3 brush and Burnt Umber mixed with Ultramarine.

Stage 4

Some muddy patches in the water near the foreground were now required and these were brushed in with a No. 5 brush and a mixture of mainly Burnt Sienna with a touch of Cobalt for the right-hand mud, and for the nearer mud the mix had more Cobalt added to make it gray.

The water so far had been left white and I now added the reflection of the background mountain with a No. 7 brush and a mixture of Ultramarine and Light Red and a few brush strokes of this to the right-hand water.

It only remained to give darker sides to the various rocks using different strengths of Cobalt and Light Red and a few indications of foreground grass with narrow brush strokes of Raw Sienna and Ultramarine and the picture seemed finished. But not quite; the wood posts had to go in with a No. 3 brush and Burnt Umber mixed with Ultramarine and their reflections with a bluish-brown mixture of the same two colours. Also with the dark brown colour I painted the muddy edges of grass showing in one or two places.

On viewing the picture with half-closed eyes I saw that some stronger treatment was wanted for clumps of bracken just beside the foreground rocks, and this was painted with Burnt Sienna and Cobalt.

By working quickly and directly I think I had captured the dampness and soddenness of the subject on such a wet but attractive day.

The monochrome picture (113) shows the tone values and one can see clearly the general dark tone on the left of the picture which is overshadowed by the heavy rain clouds above, also the strength of dark tone on the central marsh area.

Colours used for the picture were – Cadmium Yellow, Raw Sienna, Burnt Sienna, Burnt Umber, Light Red, Cobalt Blue, French Ultramarine and Winsor Blue.

114 UPPER LOCH TORRIDON

31.5cm × 47.5cm ($12\frac{1}{2}$in. × $18\frac{3}{4}$in.)

Going to the other side of Loch Torridon from Shieldaig there is some interesting country to explore. I found this view one sunny morning, with a white cottage by the loch and a very bright tree group to the left of the cottage, with yellows, reds and browns giving a lovely sparkle of colour. Note the dark bush behind the cottage enabling the white building to stand out well. This picture was used by Royle's in colour for their Artists' Scotland calendar and it reproduced rather well.

115 RAVINE NEAR ALLIGIN, SKETCH ON THE SPOT

38cm × 31.5cm (15in. × $12\frac{1}{2}$in.)

Still on the same side of Loch Torridon, Gill and I were having a walk and we stumbled on this dramatic little view. It reminded me at once of Cotman's wonderful water-colour monochrome called 'The Waterfall' painted in 1808. I had to walk perilously near the edge of the ravine to get the view and the ground was sloping quite steeply. It certainly would not do to stumble here as there must have been a drop of over a hundred feet to the stream far below, which I could hear roaring along.

114 Upper Loch Torridon.

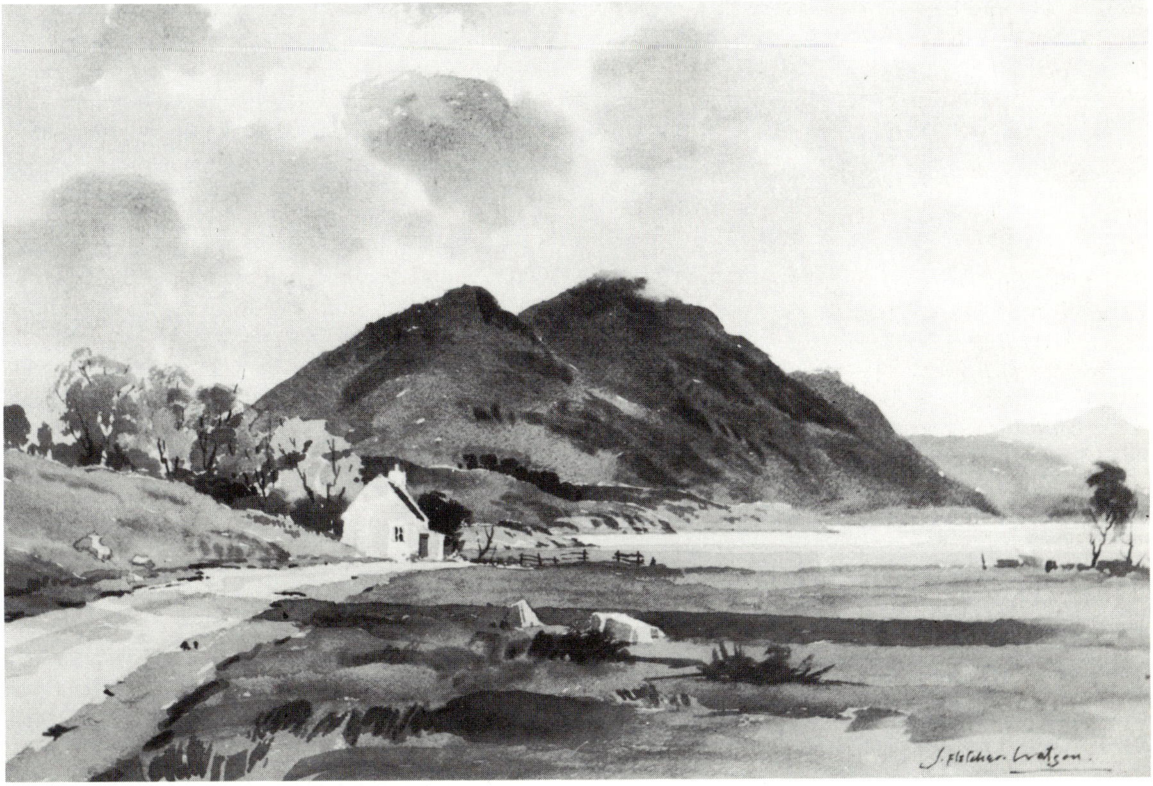

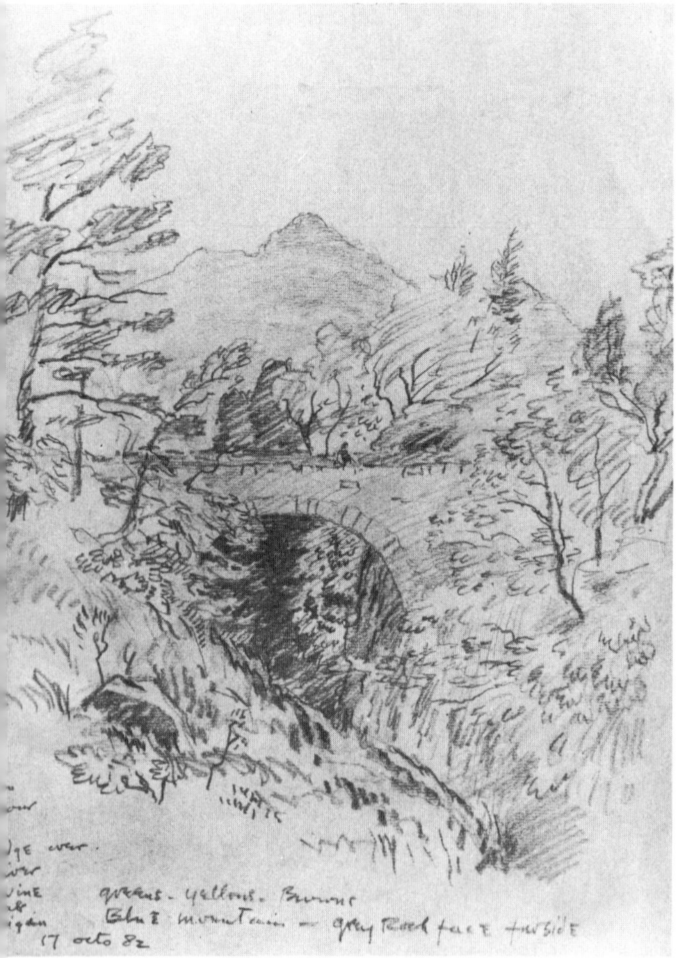

115 Ravine near Alligin, sketch on the spot.

It was an impossible place to sit and paint but I felt I must record it somehow and I came back the following day. I had my board and a piece of gray paper and I set to work with a 3B pencil. I had to stand as I drew which is never easy, but it was well worth the effort. I made a few notes of the general colouring and it took me about three quarters of an hour and in that time one can absorb the colours of a view surprisingly well. Later when we had left Scotland and I was back in my studio I made a painting from this sketch and all the colouring came back to me very well.

116 RAVINE NEAR ALLIGIN, STUDIO PAINTING

37cm × 34.5cm ($14\frac{1}{2}$in. × $13\frac{1}{2}$in.)

It was great fun painting such a naturally good composition. The foreground colours and the trees on the right were a riot of yellows, browns and burnt sienna. The rocky ravine was gray and dull yellow, and the trees behind the bridge were dark greens and yellows. The bridge itself was a warm gray stone and the background mountain a deep blue-gray. A really very exciting subject.

117 LOCH MAREE, FROM THE EAST

35cm × 48.5cm ($13\frac{3}{4}$in. × $19\frac{1}{4}$in.)

Moving back along the road from Shieldaig eastwards and then turning north we came to Loch Maree, a wonderful big loch with fine tree groups at intervals along the side and good views across the loch from the road which keeps near the water's edge.

This view is from the east end showing the loch in the distance and a group of farmhouse and buildings in the middle-distance. The series of mountains on the right are seen from this view-point in echelon getting fainter as they receded into the distance. The strong intrusion of woods on promontories on the left form a nice foil to the mountain range and altogether it makes a lovely scene. Note what a vital part the foreground plays with bushes, rock and rough grass bringing it forward.

118 LOCH MAREE AND SLIOCH

33cm × 51cm (13in. × 20in.)

Here is another close-up view of Loch Maree with the imposing mountain Slioch towering up behind. It is over 3000 feet high and local people say it is hardly ever seen without cloud over it. There was certainly an attractive bit of cloud on it on the day I made this painting.

I had to move about quite a lot before settling on the exact view-point. I wanted the right-hand promontory into the loch with trees on it in a good position, as it was a most attractive feature. The sweeping foreground bay with shingle on the beach was a good shape to include and the left-hand group of small trees was invaluable for the composition. The big mountain wanted to be a little left of centre, and I eventually got all these things about right. The colouring on the mountain slopes was a wonderful mixture, varying from raw sienna to darker browns and grays and a few light greens. Various cloud shadows falling across gave a unifying effect and the dark purple-brown cloud shadow on the right-hand peak was dramatic and helpful in giving a key to the tone values.

KERRYSDALE

(colour plate 12, between pages 120 and 121)

31.5cm × 47cm ($12\frac{1}{2}$in. × $18\frac{1}{2}$in.)

If we continue along the road beside Loch Maree north-west, we come to the hamlet of Kerrysdale and a mile short of this there is a turning off to the left over a small bridge which is seen in this picture. As we were driving slowly along this view suddenly hit one in the eye; it was

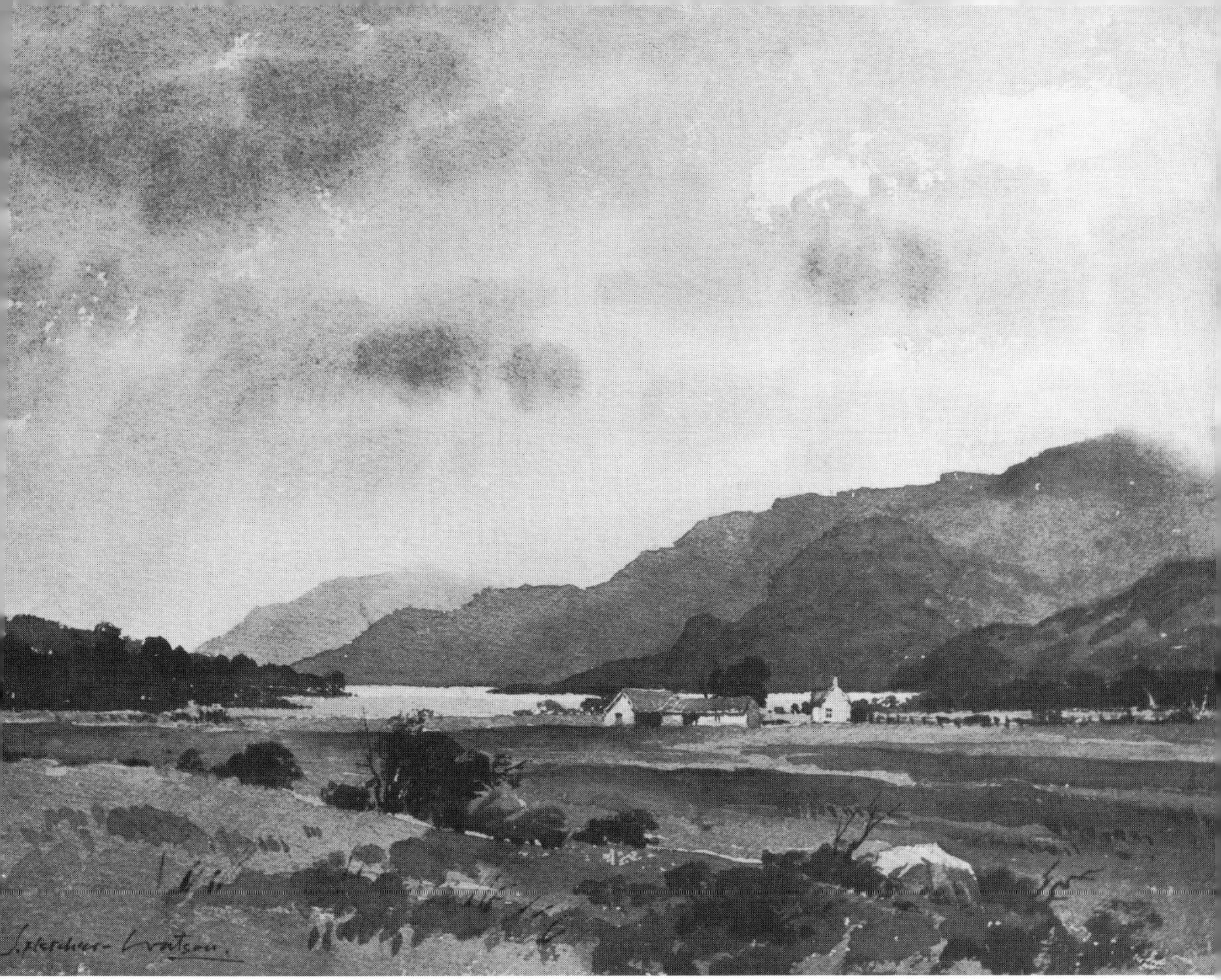

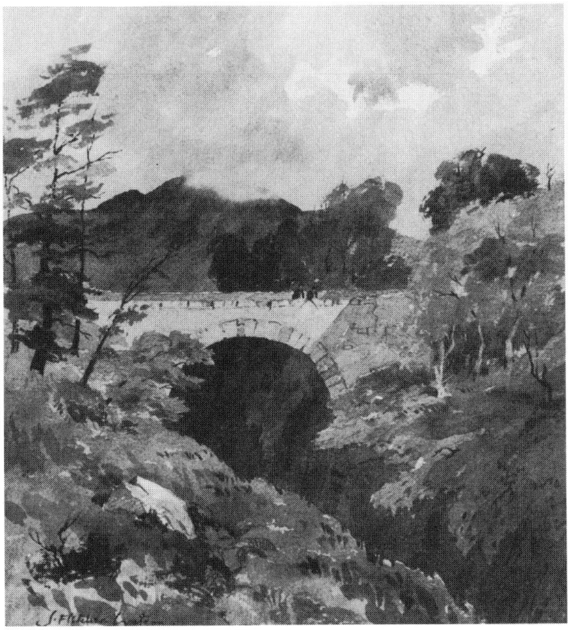

116 Ravine near Alligin, studio painting.

117 Loch Maree, from the east.

a perfect composition on a perfect day of bright light and shadow and I stopped immediately.

It was mid-afternoon; I had been painting Loch Maree (118) all morning, and the sky had developed into something very paintable indeed with contrasting blue and white cloud and very strong gray clouds.

I sat myself down on the right-hand grass verge and got to work with a piece of Whatman paper, as this would help over the brilliance of the scene.

With a B pencil I drew in the cottage and the bridge and road, with a line or two indicating the middle distance hill on the right and wood on the left, but no pencil on the distant mountain. I would have to paint quickly because time was getting on and the light would start going before very long.

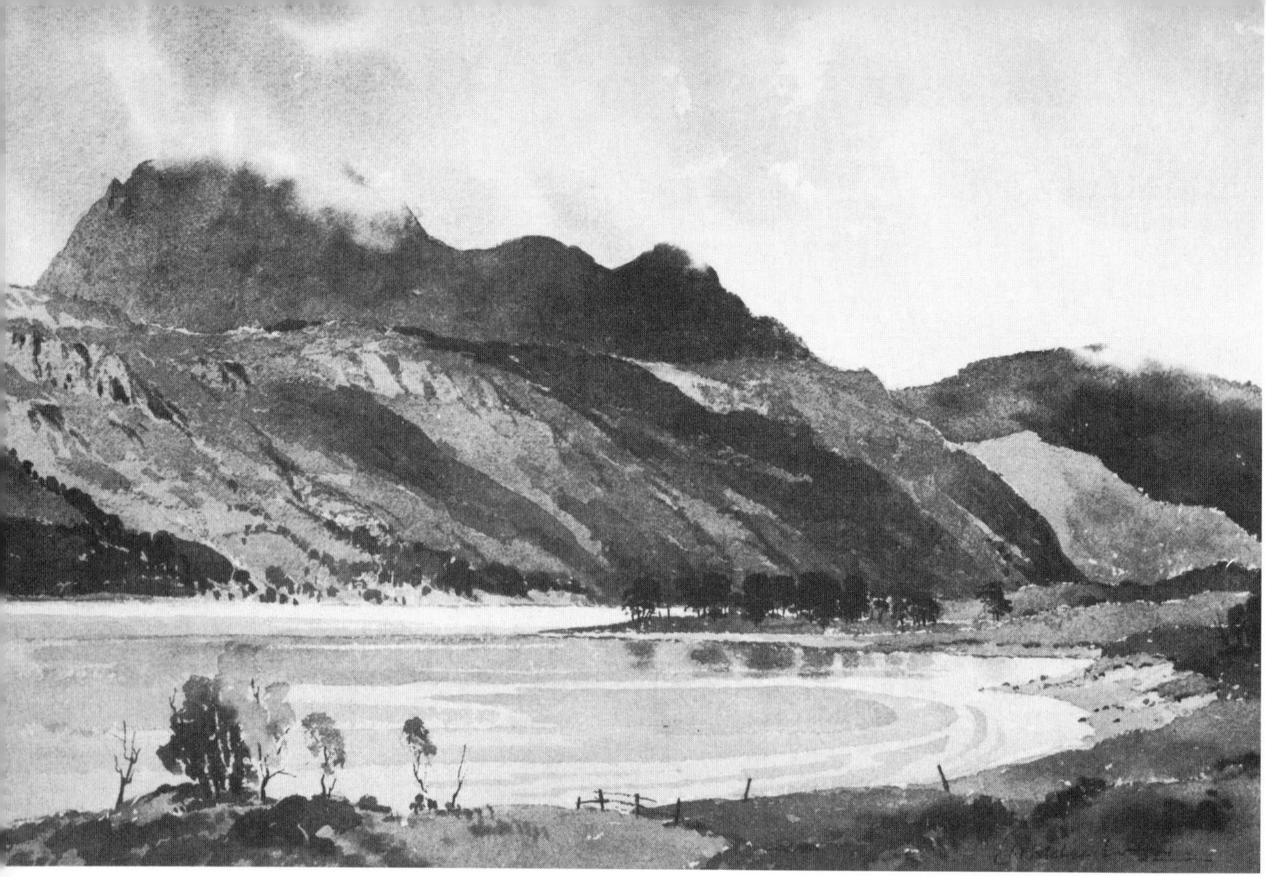

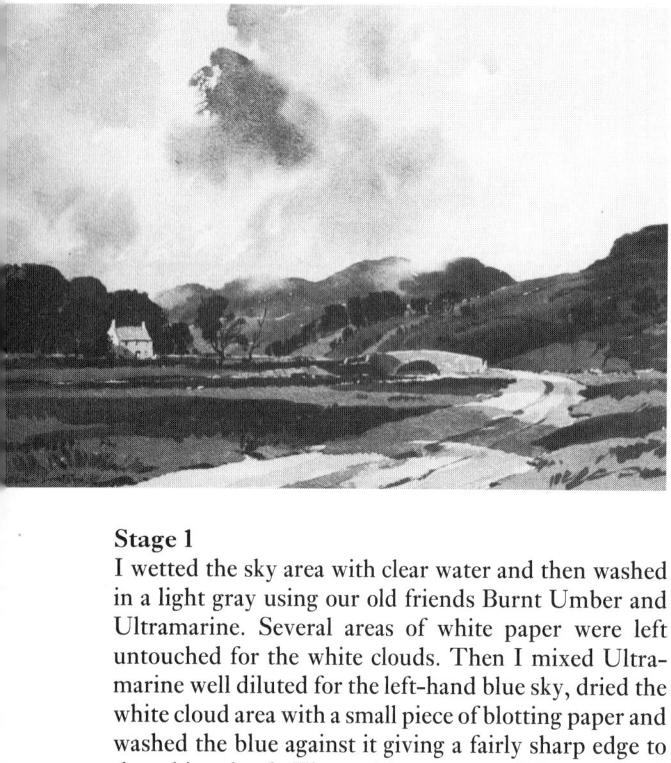

118 Loch Maree and Slioch.

119 Kerrysdale.

Stage 1

I wetted the sky area with clear water and then washed in a light gray using our old friends Burnt Umber and Ultramarine. Several areas of white paper were left untouched for the white clouds. Then I mixed Ultramarine well diluted for the left-hand blue sky, dried the white cloud area with a small piece of blotting paper and washed the blue against it giving a fairly sharp edge to the white cloud. Then with a stronger Ultramarine I painted this *into* the big gray area of cloud to the right and allowed it to run, which gave it the feeling that gray cloud was drifting *over* the blue.

Now while all was still wet I mixed Indian Red with the gray in the palette, giving a strong purplish-gray for the dark clouds in the centre, thinning this out as it dropped downwards. I used the big No. 16 brush for this sky work. A few less dark clouds were touched in at the low left side. Everything was kept wet and loose all the time and to do this it all had to be done quite quickly.

Before going on to the next stage we will just look at figure 119 which shows the picture in monochrome. Because of the very strong light on this day, darks are *darker* than usual and lights are *lighter*. The cloud shadow across the road and field is really strong and the wood behind the cottage is really dark, and these darks show up the brilliance of the sunlight on road and cottage.

Stage 2

As soon as the sky was dry I mixed Ultramarine and Light Red for the background mountain range and then added a touch of Indian Red to give it a slightly purple look which it had on this very bright afternoon. I used a

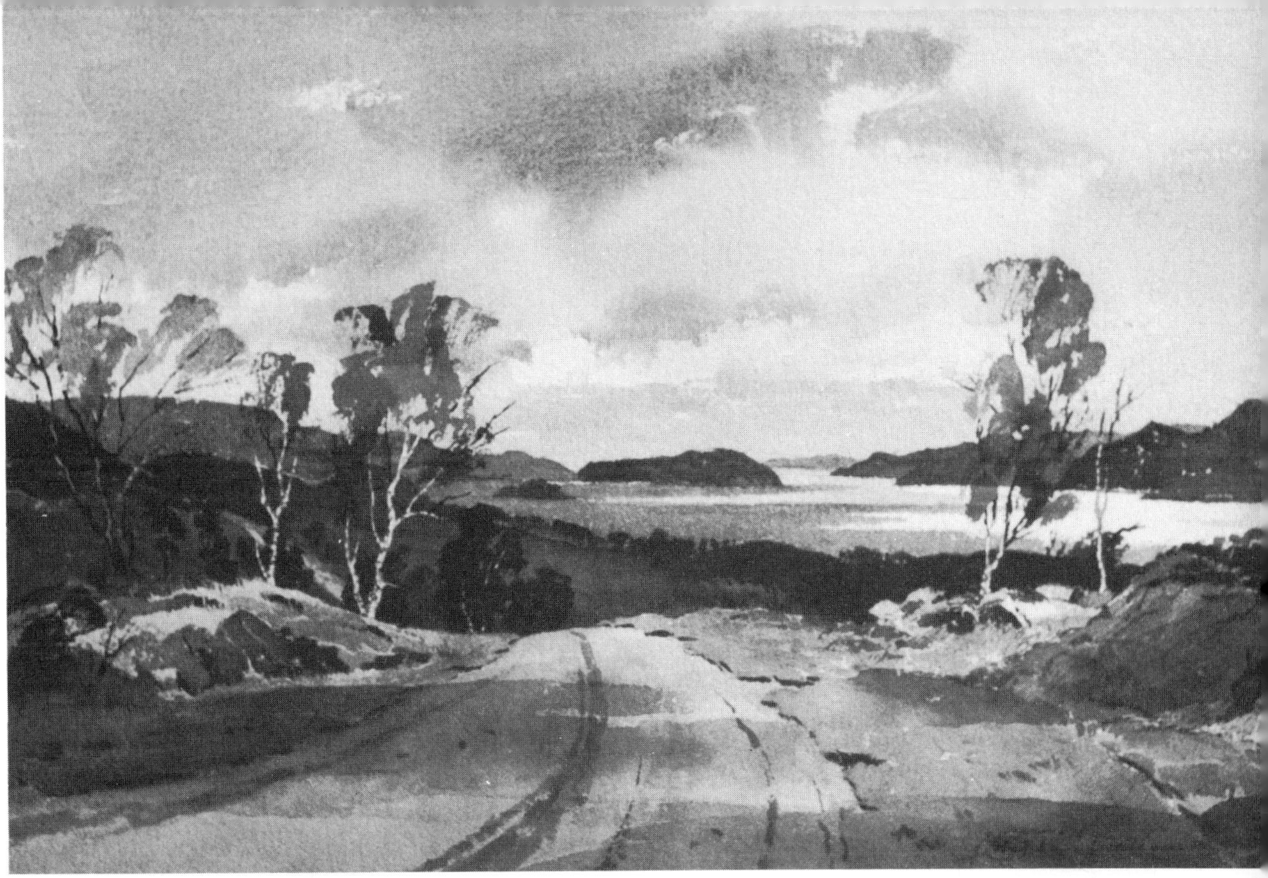

120 Road to Applecross.

No. 7 brush and there were low clouds coming over the mountain in two places which were dealt with in the usual way.

Now I used Burnt Sienna and Cobalt to wash in the right-hand hill from the centre of the picture to the extreme right, and dropped in some Burnt Umber for a darker tone in places. The various tree groups on the sloping ground were painted the same light browns and dark browns using a No. 5 brush and the little trees closer to us on the right were Burnt Umber and Winsor Blue giving a dark green. Small bushes and lines showing the slope of the ground were touched in with a No. 3 brush and a dark brown colour.

I now wanted to cover the flat land with a light green and I used a strong Raw Sienna and a little Winsor Blue for a first wash which included the rising ground on the right; while damp I overlaid this with a darker mix of the same two colours for the top part of the little hill on the right and for the thin lines of cloud shadow across the grass and the wider shadow in the foreground. Burnt Sienna was added to the mixture to darken these washes in certain places.

Stage 3

The wood behind the cottage was painted with a No. 7 brush and Burnt Umber and Winsor Blue was just the mixture for this, but one of the trees was distinctly bluish-green, you will notice. The cottage roof and chimneys were carefully painted round leaving it all white at this stage. The bridge had also been left white. There is an isolated tree between cottage and bridge which I now painted a brown-green colour with this same mixture with a No. 5 brush, and the trunk and also the dead tree beside it with a No. 3 brush.

In painting the wood I left a few tree trunks a light colour and the tops of the trees were outlined with a dragged brush technique, i.e. a stiff mix and dragging the brush quickly over the paper.

Stage 4

We could now deal with finishing details. The cottage had a slate roof; this was blue-gray using Winsor Blue and Light Red. A tone of light gray was put over the front wall with Cobalt and Light Red, the left wall being left quite white. Using a small brush the eaves' shadow and windows were painted with Cobalt and Burnt Sienna . When dry the diagonal shadow cast by a small tree was a mixture of Cobalt and Light Red.

The bridge was now toned down with the same range of colours, giving a light gray to its sunny face and dark gray for the wall in shadow and under the arch.

Cloud shadow was over the right-hand hill top and a strong mix of Burnt Sienna and Ultramarine was painted over this, and an even stronger shadow was painted just to the right of the bridge.

The road was given some light touches of Burnt Umber and a little grass down the middle consisted of Raw Sienna and a touch of Winsor Blue. The road cloud shadows were Cobalt and Light Red with a drop of Indian Red run in while it was wet.

The finishing touch of all was grass texture in the foreground using a No. 5 brush and Winsor Blue and Burnt Sienna and then a darker mixture of the same colours for the few dark muddy edges of the road. The light by this time was fading rapidly.

Colours in use for this painting were Raw Sienna, Burnt Sienna, Burnt Umber, Light Red, Indian Red, Cobalt Blue, French Ultramarine and Winsor Blue.

120 ROAD TO APPLECROSS

32cm × 48.5cm ($12\frac{3}{4}$in. × $19\frac{1}{4}$in.)

This is one of the most beautiful roads I have ever seen in the whole world. It travels along the edge of Loch Shieldaig and Loch Torridon in a north-west direction and then turns sharp left in a southern direction along the inner sound looking across towards Skye. I have already described four views from this road, figures 97, 99, 101 and 102. It is a narrow road that twists and turns and goes up and down little hills and there are wonderful groups of old trees at every corner. This picture is near a cottage or two which the map calls Kenmore, and there is a lovely view of Loch Torridon with rocky islands and the open sea beyond. I must beg you not to miss seeing this road when you are in the West Highlands. You will find many subjects to paint along it. I think probably it looks better in the autumn than at any other time.

I waited until I had nearly finished the picture and put in all the dark shadows before I painted the silver birch trees. Then I scratched out the silvery white trunks of the two trees on the left and the two on the right with my sharp penknife and finally painted the

121 Skye, from near Applecross, evening.

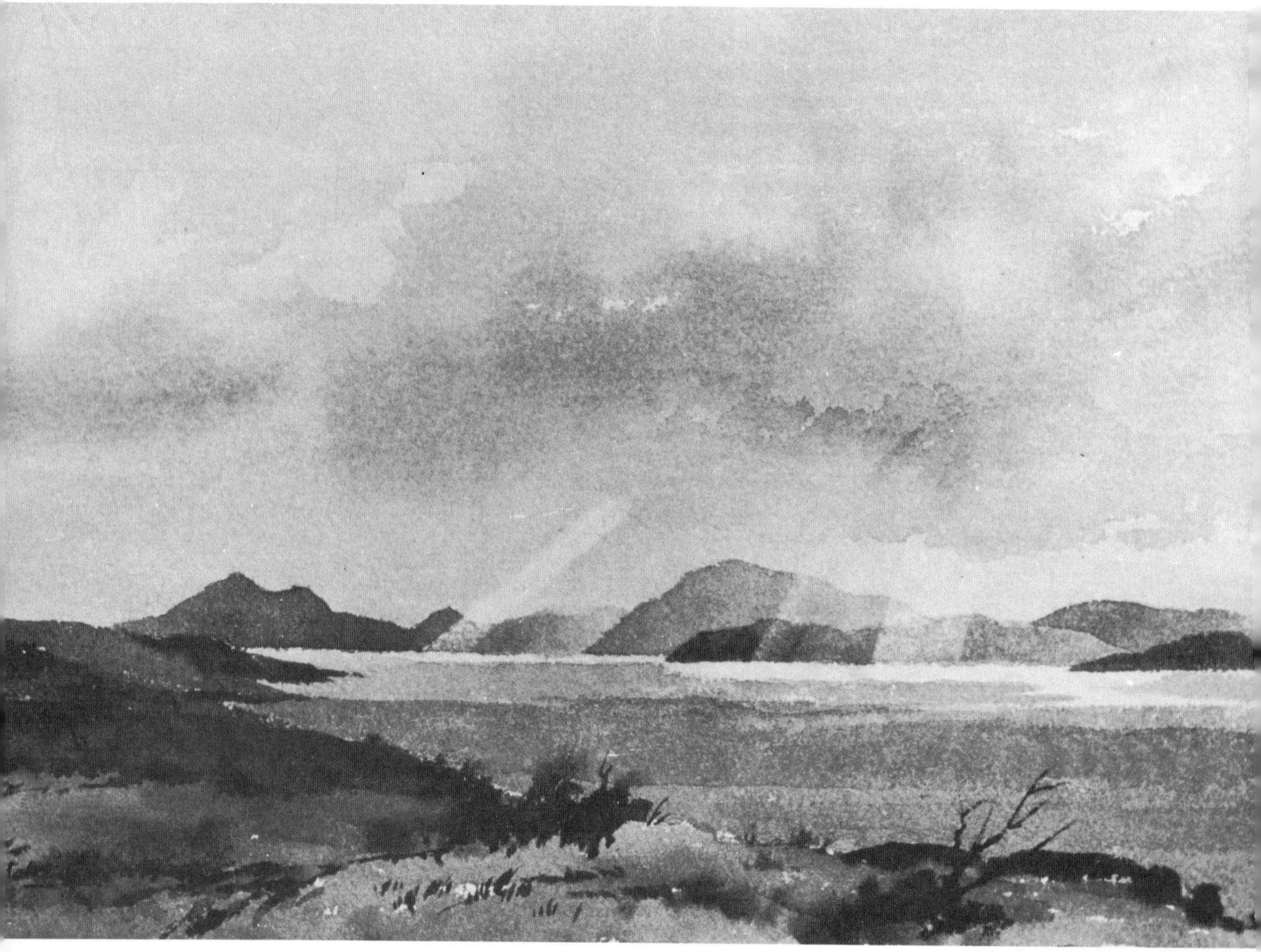

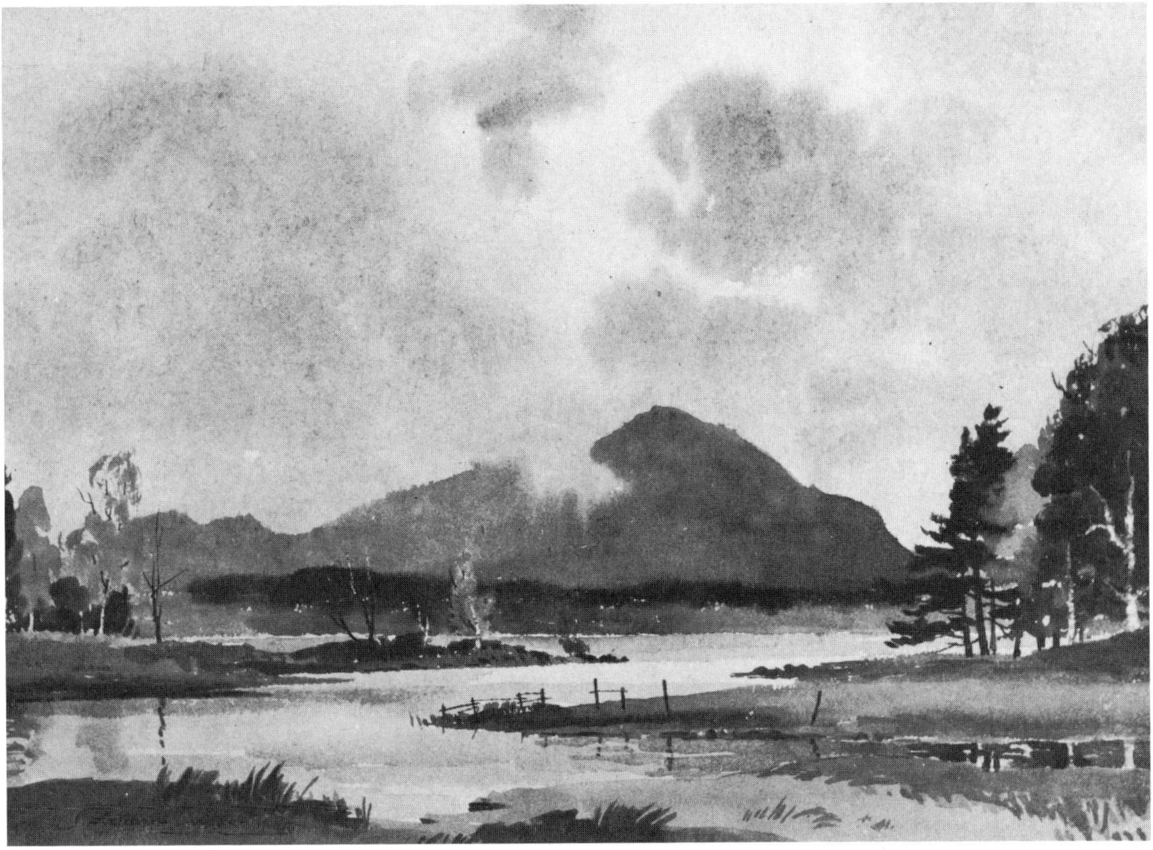

122 Ben Nevis.

foliage. It would have been difficult to do these trunks any other way.

121 SKYE, FROM NEAR APPLECROSS, EVENING

23.5cm × 35.5cm ($9\frac{1}{4}$in. × 14in.)

This little picture was painted later on the same day as figure 120. Having continued along the same road and turned south towards Applecross, the road becomes barren of trees and wild and open, and the views of the Island of Raasay and Skye beyond are very attractive, especially so in this evening light with sun rays lighting up the water. The rays were made with a piece of india-rubber rubbed along the side of a piece of stiff paper. It *can* be done a different way by applying clear water washes with a hog-hair brush.

122 BEN NEVIS

31.5cm × 45cm ($12\frac{1}{2}$in. × $17\frac{3}{4}$in.)

On our way home from Scotland we stopped a night at Spean Bridge near Fort William. Wandering about down narrow lanes through woods we came to a clearing with this view, across some small lochs, of Ben Nevis. The mountain was constantly lost in cloud and little rain showers kept falling but I very much wanted to do this view. I took a chance and sat out, having found this good position.

On two occasions I had to abandon painting and dash quickly with the picture to the safety of the car when a sudden rain-storm came over. But I eventually got the thing done. I was using, once again, David Cox paper and this light brown paper suited the subject very well. If one looks very closely at the original painting one can detect little rain drops, but nothing to worry about. This painting was later sold and no complaints were made!

And so we reluctantly left this glorious country of Scotland with its wonderful autumn colouring – it was quite a wrench.

6 Painting in Venice

I was in Venice last October with Gill and a party of friends, most of whom were sight-seers but some were painters, and we had the most wonderful weather and wonderful time exploring and painting. One week is of course not very long for a painting trip in such a place, one really wants three or four at least.

Venice is so well known in the art world. There have been so many poets who have written about it, artists who have painted it, great architects who have built it, quite apart from its long history going back well over a thousand years, that one might be forgiven for feeling slightly inhibited in visiting it as a humble painter of the twentieth century following in the footsteps of the Great.

They started building the Doge's Palace in the ninth century and then re-built the one we see today in the fourteenth century. The first Doge was elected in the seventh century! At the time that I am writing there is a splendid exhibition going on at the Royal Academy, London, called 'The Genius of Venice 1500 to 1600'. This exhibition is mainly about the great painters of that peak period, men like Bellini, Titian and Tinteretto who painted enormous biblical subjects many of which hang in the Venetian churches.

For the purpose of this book we are more interested in the landscape painters who came later. Canaletto was painting Venice in 1725 and the marvellous thing is that the city has not changed very much in appearance to this day. He was painting in London in 1750 as can be seen in the Queen's marvellous collection of his work; if only London had been preserved as Venice has, what a wonderful City of London we should have today! Of course Venice being surrounded by water could not expand, and as its streets are of water it could not have the invasion of the motor vehicle. This I think is the magic of Venice; you find yourself stepping into the medieval past at its best, with architecture of a very high order and beautiful bridges and canals and squares with statues and trees, so of course it is an artist's dream.

There are many landscape painters it would pay us to study. Turner was painting magical watercolours in Venice in the 1830s and 40s, Ruskin in the 1850s and J. S. Sargent was producing his lovely wet watercolours in the 1880s. We shouldn't forget to look at Russell Flint's watercolours of Venice, some of the best pictures he ever did around the 1930 period.

Well, enough of history, let us get started with painting. I had visited Venice once before when we did a lot of sight-seeing, going into churches and picture galleries and I must just say that the interior of St Mark's is, I think, my favourite church in the whole world. At any rate I felt that this time I could devote my entire time to painting out of doors.

To start with I walked about the narrow streets with a small (15cm × 20cm (6in. × 8in.)) sketch book and made a quick pencil sketch of anything I felt I *must* paint if possible. After a day of doing this with many stops for very expensive but most enjoyable cups of coffee with Gill, I had quite a collection of views to consider. I made a note of position of sun and shadows; this is important in Venice as streets can often be in complete shadow for most of the day.

123 FOUR PENCIL SKETCHES OF GONDOLAS, RIO DI S TROVASO AND OTHER PLACES

16cm × 20cm (6in. × 8in.)

124 SEVEN PENCIL SKETCHES OF S GEREMIA, GRAND CANAL, S MARIA DELLA SALUTE, S GIORGIO AND OTHERS

16cm × 20cm (6in. × 8in.)

I wanted to bring a gondola or two into some pictures and I did several pages of sketches like the one in figure 123 as it was quite difficult getting the shape of the boat right and especially the position of the gondolier as he made his skilful manoeuvres with his single long oar.

Some of these sketches took five minutes, others took about quarter of an hour, but I found them all extremely helpful.

125 RIO DI S TROVASO

23.5cm × 35.5cm ($9\frac{1}{4}$in. × 14in.)

This small little painting was one of my first. It is a simple view with *trees* as well as buildings which was an asset and a bridge and of course water reflections. I had

123 Four preliminary pencil sketches, Venice.

124 Seven preliminary pencil sketches, Venice.

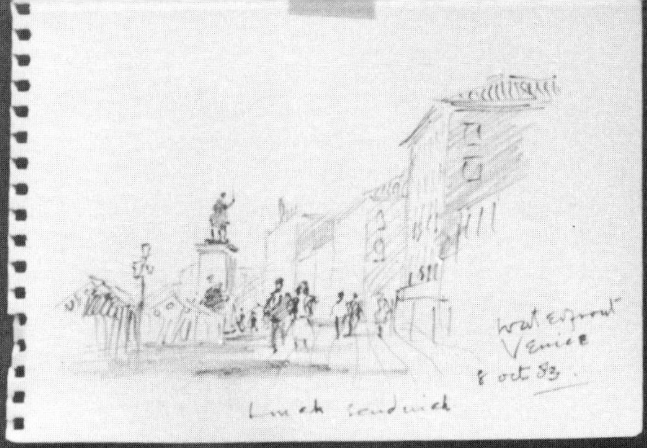
Waterfront Venice 8 oct 83
Lunch sandwich

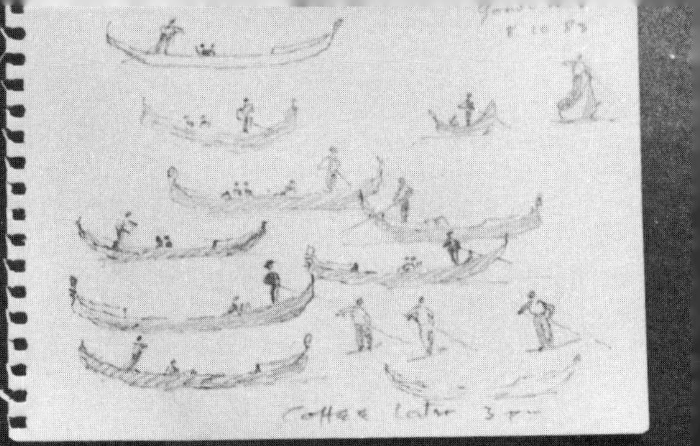
Coffee later 3 pm

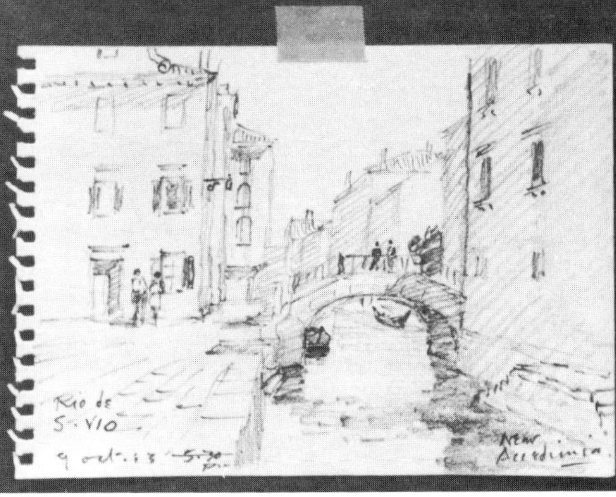
Rio de S. Vio
Near Accademia

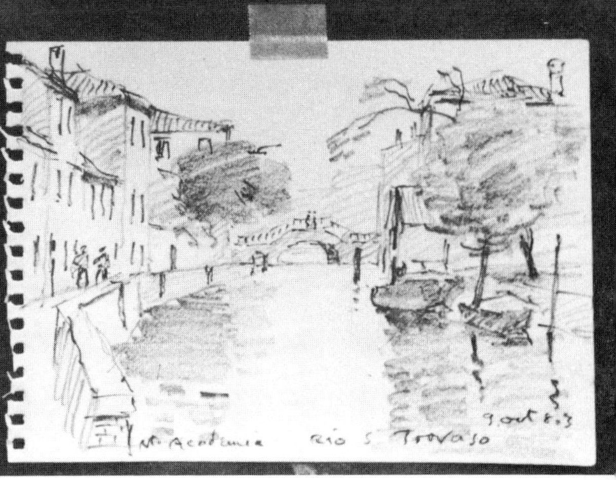
9 oct 83
Rio S. Trovaso

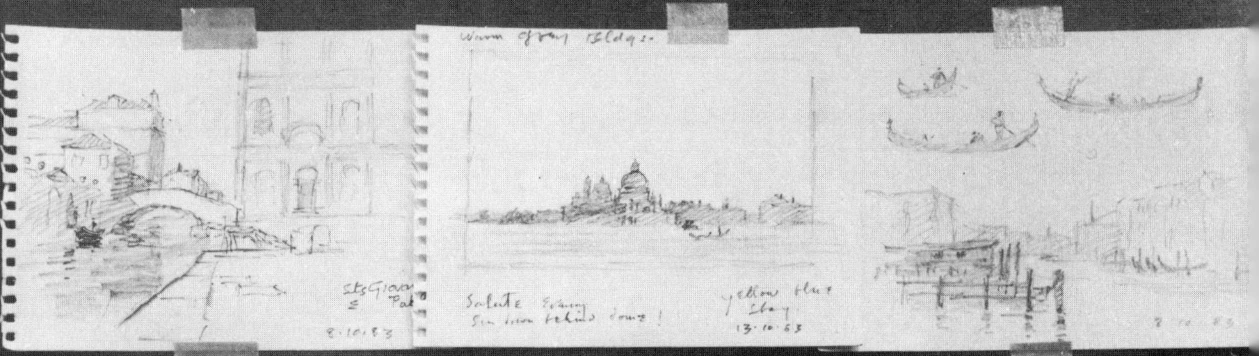

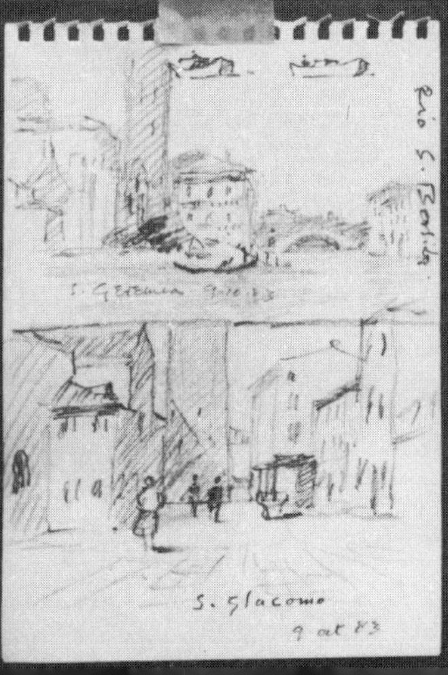
S. Giacomo
9 oct 83

13.10.83

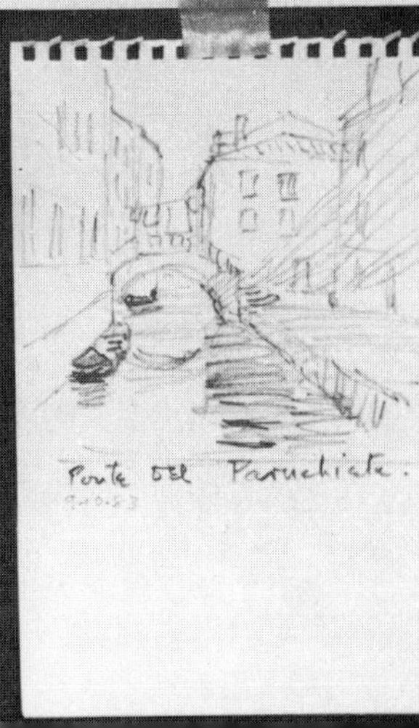

to stand up for this one with my paints and board on top of the parapet wall along the canal as I couldn't find a suitable gap in the wall to see from the sitting position.

Figure 123 shows the rough sketch of this picture at bottom right. It was a perfect composition with dark buildings on the left in shadow and sunlight on the right-hand buildings.

126 RIO DI GARZOTI
23.5cm × 35.5cm (9¼in. × 14in.)
Here is one of the narrow side canals near the big Frari church. The Venetians have an ingenious way of hanging their washing out to dry. Two wires are fixed on pulley wheels across the canal and by pulling one wire you can feed the washing back and forth. I was sitting on a dead end path-way so I was not bothered by passers-by. It lead to the archway on the left which gave entrance to a delightful small garden and a large mansion beyond.

I managed to include two gondolas, one coming towards me and one going away. The perspective of these craft is quite tricky. Note the interesting shadows cast by one building and falling across another.

RIO DI S BARNABA (colour plate on front cover)
31.5cm × 47.5cm (12½in. × 18¾in.)
Let us look now at a more ambitious subject. This canal is on the west side of the Grand Canal and we are looking east towards it; in the centre of the picture is the campanile of San Samuele's church on the far side of the Grand Canal.

I felt I would like to make a quick sketch of this view to check the composition, and this is shown in figure 127. This was done in a larger sketch book 18.5cm × 25.5cm (7¼in. × 10in.) and I used a 5B pencil and Conte crayon for some of the shading. This only took a few minutes but it reassured me that the composition was going to work out well. I also show a monochrome illustration (128) as this will save you referring too often to the front cover and give you an idea about tone values. The light in Venice is very bright and this monochrome shows how the dark shadow tone of the buildings on the right-hand side dominates the picture and the strong tone of the boat on the left is able to counterbalance this.

Dealing now with the actual painting work, it was important to do *some* drawing with a pencil first. But I did not want to have *too* much pencil work, only enough for guidance as I wanted to draw with the *brush* as much as possible such features as windows and roof cornices and balconies.

125 Rio di S Trovaso.

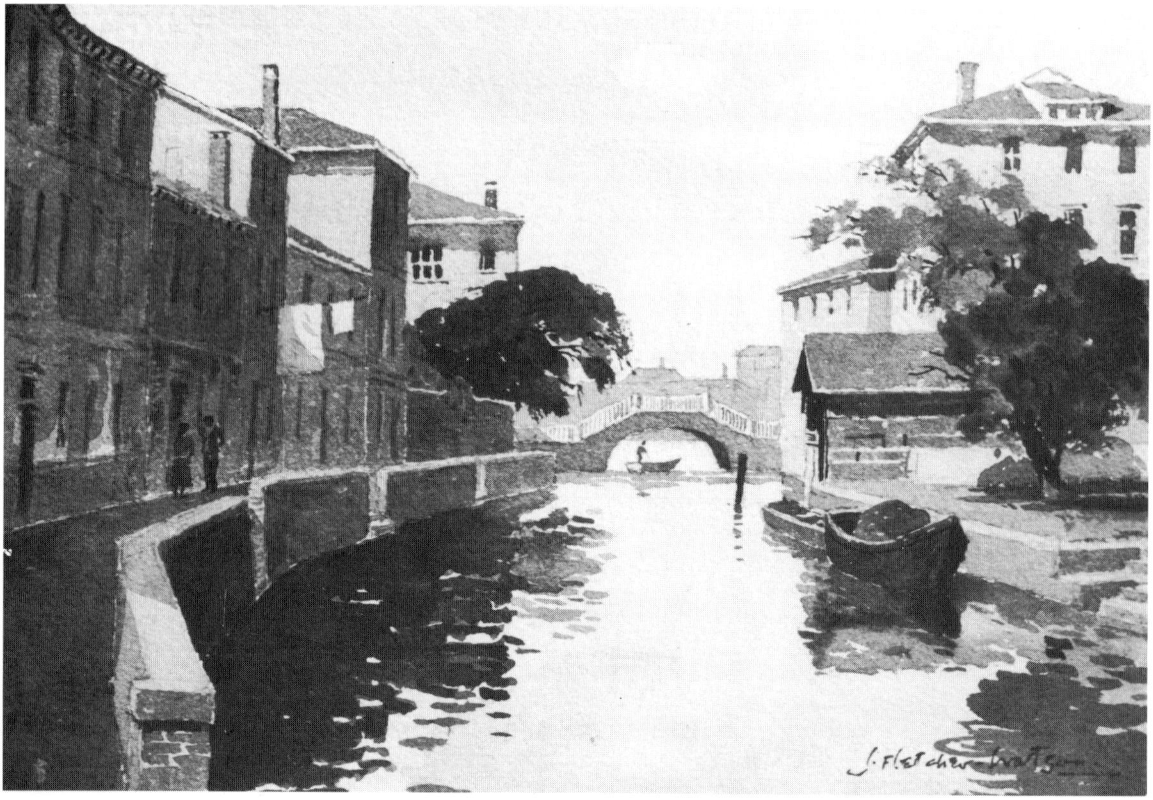

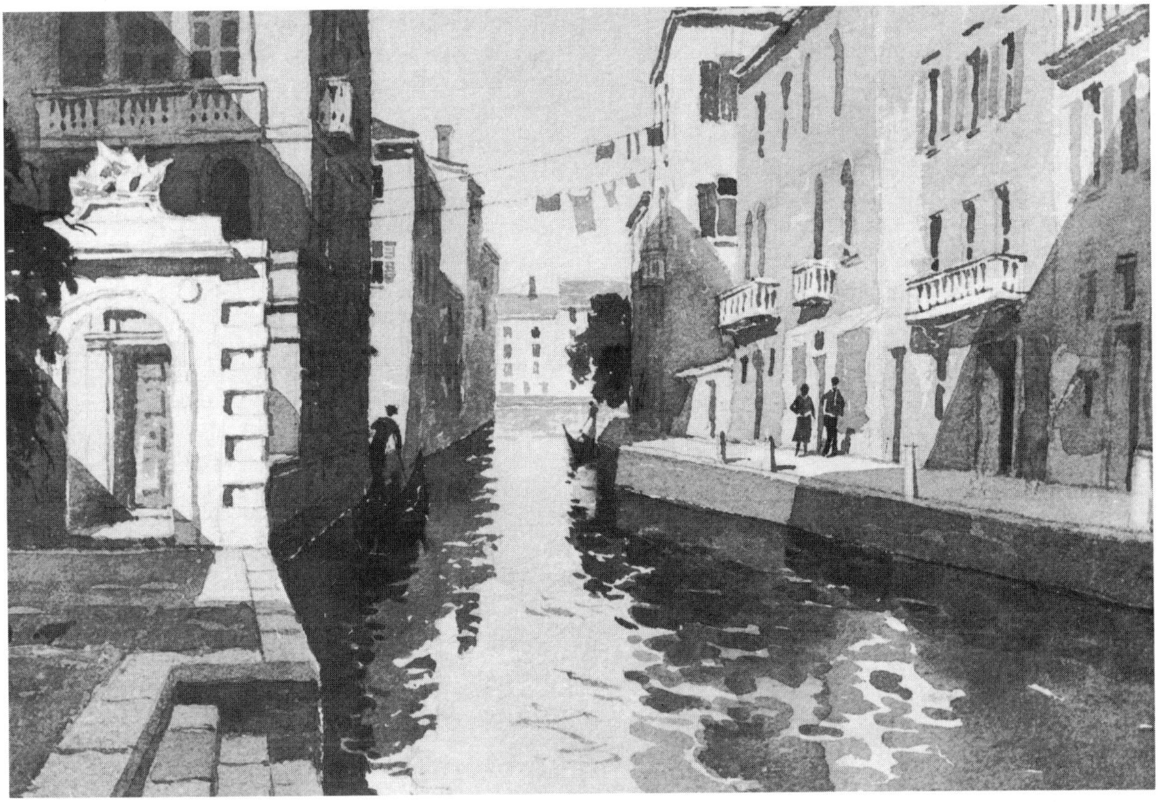

126 Rio di Garzoti.

The basic drawing outlined the footpath lines on both sides and the roof lines and eaves sloping in the right direction for proper perspective. The sides of the canal and the bridge were drawn in and the campanile in the background. Also the big canvas sun-shade which was shielding a fruit stall in a large barge below. I was using a 2B pencil and Arches 'Not' surface paper.

Stage 1

The sky had quite a warm yellow glow on the light clouds and I used Raw Sienna for this, washing it in for the lower clouds as soon as I had damped the sky area with clear water and a No. 16 brush. Then followed a light gray wash using Ultramarine and a little Burnt Umber, and then while still wet some diluted Ultramarine was washed in which formed the right-hand white cloud. We were getting some very nice cloudy sunny skies during our week in Venice and it is all part of composition to arrange the clouds and blue areas to suit the building sky-line.

I now continued the sky wash of light gray, adding a touch more Burnt Umber, down over the whole picture but leaving untouched certain items I wanted to be *white*. These were the second house from the left and another one a little further along and also the white washing hanging out on a stick. The house just below the campanile was also white and the canvas awning was left white. This awning was later painted light green with a darker green shadow. The canal itself was included in this gray wash except for one or two small patches of water which were left white.

Now that the whole picture had a tone of colour all over it I found it easier to think about the next stage of the painting.

Stage 2

I wanted to apply the lighter tones of buildings first, remembering that we must always work from the lightest to the darkest colours when painting watercolours.

I mixed a dull yellow with Raw Sienna and Burnt Umber and a little Cobalt and washed this over all the right-hand houses with a No. 9 brush, including the wall faces catching the sun. I added some diluted Indian Red to the extreme right-hand sunny wall. This wash included the right-hand canal footpath etc. and also the bridge and the flat roofed building immediately above the bridge.

Next I painted the bright yellow house on the left with Cadmium Lemon and a touch of Light Red and then the third house along with Rose Madder and Raw

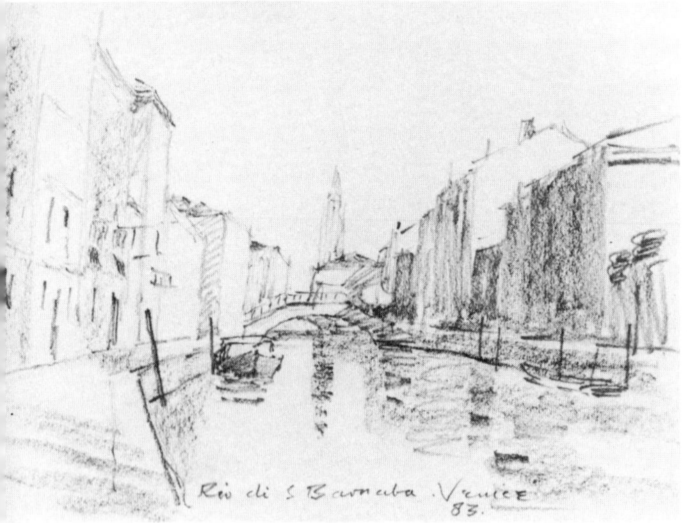

127 Rio di S Barnaba, preliminary sketch.

128 Rio di S Barnaba.

Sienna. These colours were not quite so vivid as they sound as they had the under-wash of gray put on at the beginning.

Further along this side some buildings jutted out and the sides were a little darker than the fronts facing the canal. These sides received washes of Burnt Umber and Cobalt and Raw Sienna. The same colour was painted on the left-hand paved footpath leaving out the smooth lighter stone top of the canal wall.

I now went back to the right-hand buildings and still with a No. 9 brush I painted the shadow walls in various colours, dark yellows, dark reds, dark grays, using different mixes of Burnt Sienna, Light Red, Raw Sienna and Cobalt.

The campanile was painted with a No. 5 brush a warm light gray with Burnt Umber and Cobalt, and the shadow walls of the small buildings below had Burnt Sienna and Cobalt applied to them. The roof of one of these buildings was the same colour but not too dark. Other roofs were now touched in using the same two colours but mostly Burnt Sienna.

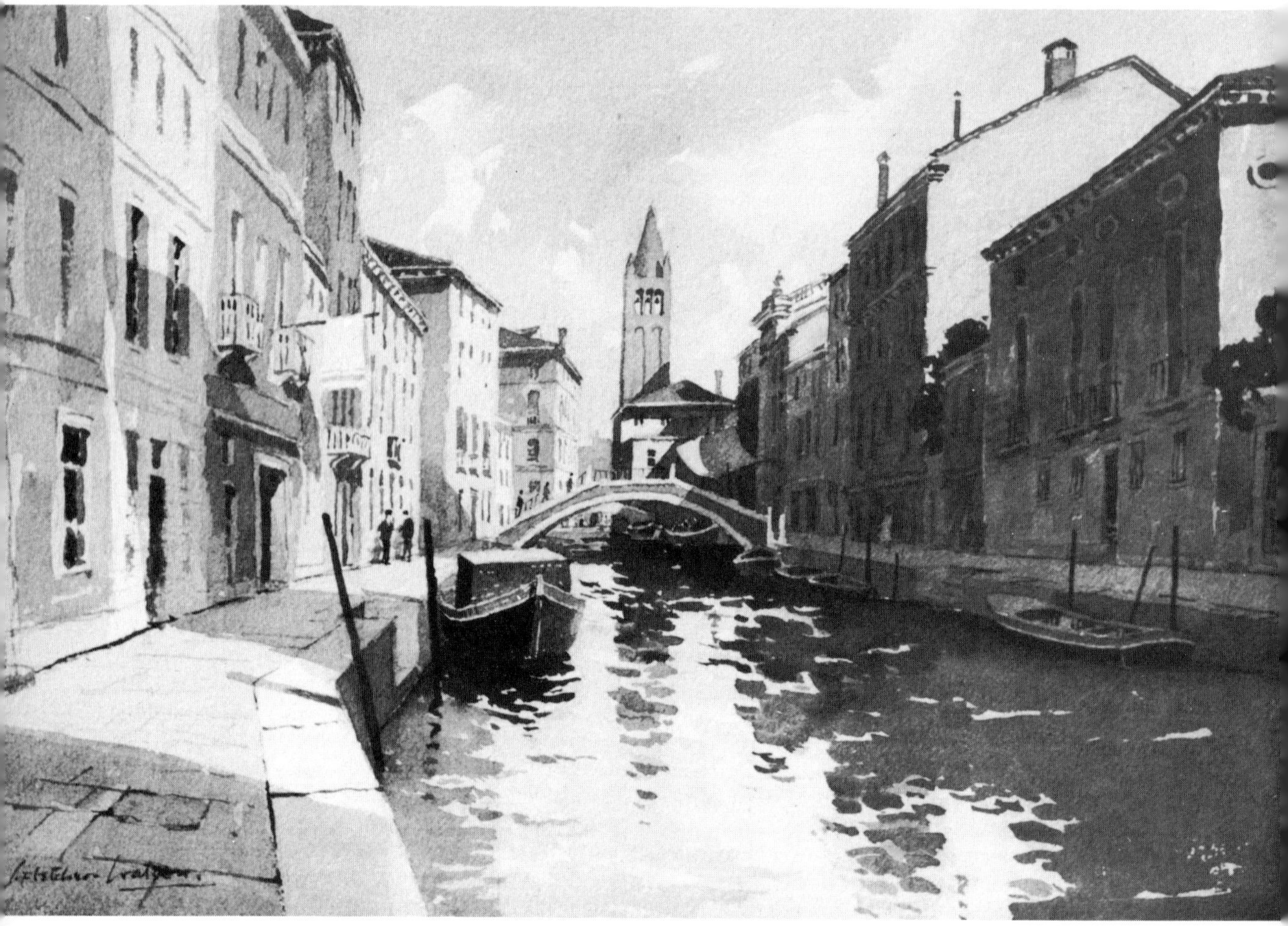

The bridge was built of brick and stone and I used Light Red with very little Cobalt for this.

Stage 3
The basic washes were now done and it was time to bring out a bit of detail with a small No. 3 brush. I used various mixes of Burnt Sienna and Cobalt making my lines sometimes brownish and sometimes bluish. I started at the left-hand side *drawing-in* string courses and cornices and windows and balconies, sometimes changing to a larger brush No. 5. I started putting shadows under the eaves and under balconies more or less at the same time. I had to change the colour to pink for the eaves shadow on the pink house and for under the two balconies. I gradually worked down the street to the distant houses making the colour a little less strong for the far away details. There were green shutters to the windows in the white house on the left and I used Raw Sienna and Winsor Blue for these.

I could now work over the right-hand buildings in the same way putting in cornices, balconies, windows and doors. It is very important to keep an eye on perspective while you are doing these items. Windows must get smaller as they go further away, and they must follow an imaginary line going to a vanishing point somewhere vaguely in the middle of the picture in your mind's eye.

I now put in the various boats which had been drawn in pencil. I used neat colour in some cases such as Cadmium Yellow and Ultramarine and Light Red and Indian Red. Burnt Umber mixed with Ultramarine was used for darker boats and shadow places in the boats, and this mixture was also used for the dark brown posts in the water to which boads were tied up.

I wanted the small bits of tree hanging over walls on the right painted in next, and I used a No. 7 brush with Burnt Sienna and Winsor Blue for these.

Stage 4
I now had a coffee break and stood back and studied the tone value position and the general state of the picture. I was not ready for the water yet; that must come last. The buildings in shadow on the right wanted to be considerably darker, but first I put in the cast shadows on the small buildings under the campanile with a small brush and Burnt Sienna and Cobalt, and also the green shadow on the canvas awning using Raw Sienna and Winsor Blue; and then the slanting shadow across the bridge using Light Red and Cobalt.

Then I mixed a lot of Burnt Sienna and Cobalt for an all-over wash on all the right-hand buildings and this sharpened up the feeling of sunlight. This wash included the canal wall.

Cloud shadows were falling across the canal and onto the left-hand footpath and houses, and I used Indian Red and Cobalt for these and a little Raw Sienna to take off the purple look. These shadows were very useful in holding the picture together.

Stage 5
Now the water could be tackled. The water in the Venice canals appeared to be a muddy green for the reflections, except when a building in bright sunlight was being reflected and this was the actual colour of the building itself, but this did not apply here. Out in open water the tone could take on the colour of the sky and on the right day it could be quite blue. The sky was in fact reflecting blue-gray in this case; but the shadowy buildings were reflecting a definite green tone.

I found that Payne's Gray and Raw Sienna gave just the right colour. I started with the reflections furthest away using a No. 7 and later a No. 12 brush. I did *not* damp the paper first as reflections from clear-cut building shapes are pretty sharp and clear-cut themselves. I worked my way down the right-hand side, breaking the wash where the top of a building was reflected and making it a little less strong at that point.

The left-hand reflection was much lighter as it was reflecting light coloured buildings. The boat reflections were strong and dark. When all this was dry I washed in a little light blue and gray for the sky reflection.

I now put in a few figures, watching their height carefully in relation to doorways and the bridge railings. The pink lines on the washing were touched in and also the stone jointing to the foreground footpath, using Burnt Umber and Ultramarine with a No. 3 brush.

One or two windows and doorways wanted stiffening with dark brown and that was about the completion of the picture.

I used quite a lot of colours for this picture, in fact all the twelve that I carry in my box – Cadmium Lemon, Cadmium Yellow, Raw Sienna, Burnt Sienna, Burnt Umber, Light Red, Indian Red, Rose Madder, Cobalt Blue, French Ultramarine, Winsor Blue and Payne's Gray.

129 VENICE, FROM THE GUIDECCA
31.5cm × 47.5cm ($12\frac{1}{2}$in. × $18\frac{3}{4}$in.)
The Guidecca is a long thin strip of land to the south, separated from Venice by a wide strip of water known as the Guidecca canal. From a point a little south-west of St Mark's Square I found this lovely view with the great Campanile, St Mark's Basilica and the Doge's Palace forming the centre-piece. Of course dozens of other artists have painted this view, not the least being Turner. I suppose it is as typical of Venice as almost any other view and it was rather fun to be painting such a well-known subject and to interpret it in one's own way.

Venice being so flat as seen from a distance one had a big sky area of two-thirds the picture height compared with one-third for the water. With this big expanse of water the colour was greenish-blue and although there was movement of water, there were partial reflections. I 'lifted' the lighter reflections of buildings off the paper by damping and working it with a No. 5 brush and then blotting it.

I chose the morning for this painting so that shadows would fall from right to left and this I knew would help in giving St Mark's Square some recession. There were water buses and gondolas moving about on the water all the time and it was easy to place these where one wanted them for the composition.

I started by drawing with a B pencil on Arches paper the outline of the main buildings and I took the trouble to count the seventeen arches of the Doge's Palace and get them right!

130 SIDE CANAL

23.5cm × 35.5cm ($9\frac{1}{4}$in. × 14in.)

This charming little backwater was found somewhere in the central area north of St Mark's Square. It made an interesting composition and the pattern of reflections was pleasing. I found myself choosing a subject very much for the arrangement of water reflections and shadows on buildings.

RIO DI BRAGADIN

(colour plate 13, between pages 120 and 121)

31.5cm × 47.5cm ($12\frac{1}{2}$in. × $18\frac{3}{4}$in.)

This view is at first sight similar to that of the St Barnaba canal (128), but on closer inspection it will be seen that it is a rather more simple subject with less detail, but I liked it equally as much. It took less time to paint.

This time the sun comes from the left-hand side instead of the right and the general colouring is slightly warmer than the other one, and for some reason I only needed *eight* colours instead of *twelve*. The colours used were Raw Sienna, Burnt Sienna, Burnt Umber, Light Red, Cobalt Blue, French Ultramarine, Winsor Blue and Payne's Gray.

I will run over the painting work in rather less detail.

Stage 1

Composition. There were tall buildings on each side in the foreground and I let them both run out of the picture at the top. The big side view of the building on

129 Venice, from the Guidecca.

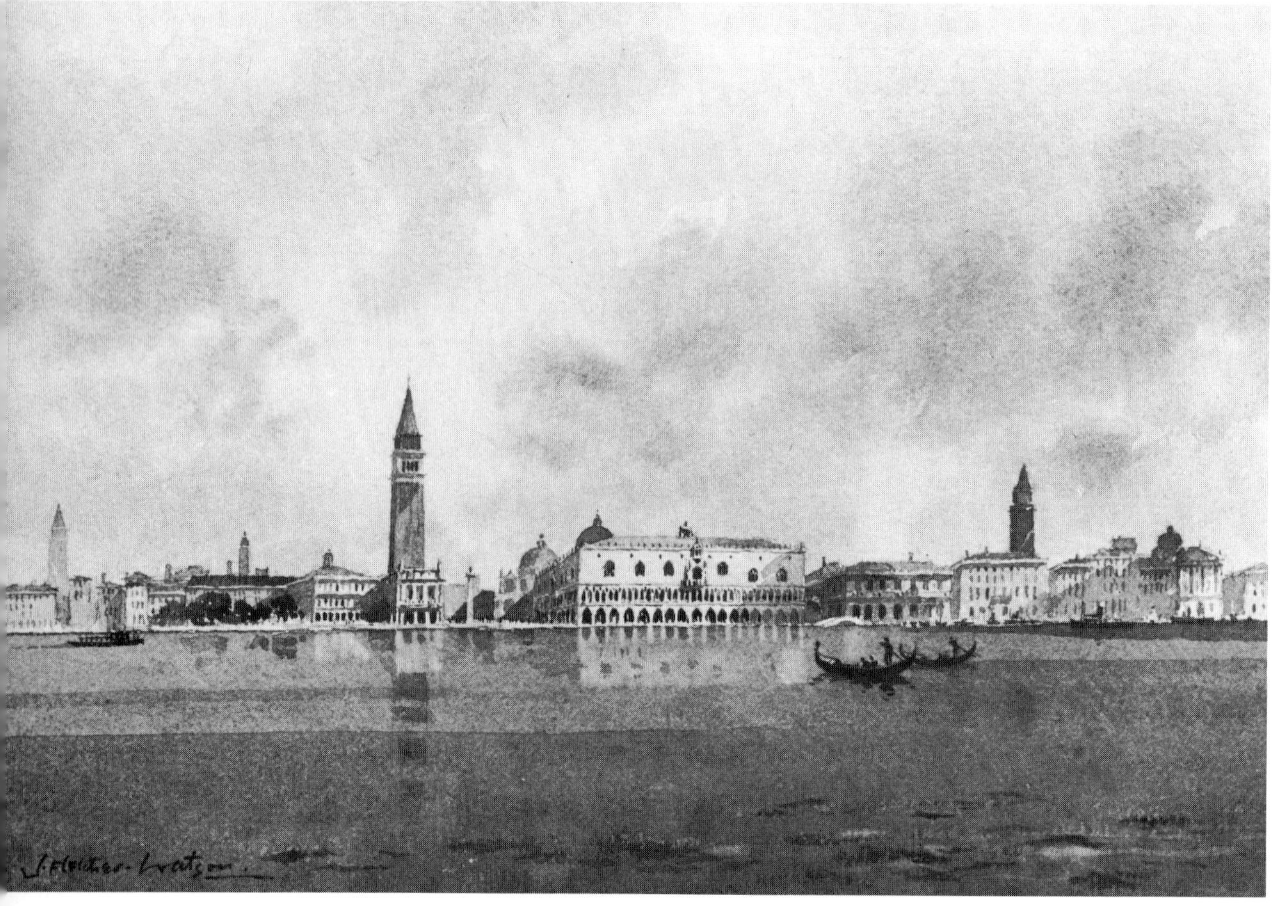

the right helped to give an unsymmetrical look to the picture and the tree coming over the railings was useful. The bridge and buildings far beyond gave a nice feeling of distance. The several boats on the right were a useful group of detail combined with the foreground stonework and steps.

Talking about the foreground, an unfortunate thing happened when I had just finished drawing and started painting. A very big builder's barge arrived and put itself right in the foreground on the right. It had a small crane on board with a noisy little engine that went 'chug chug chug' all the time, puffing out a very smelly exhaust. The crane was loading barrows with sacks of cement and men were walking backwards and forwards to the house on the right where evidently building alterations were going on inside. This disturbance and blocking of my view went on for three-quarters of an hour. This is one of the hazards of painting in a town, but somehow one does not expect it to happen in Venice of all places!

I was again using Arches paper 'Not' surface and I drew with a 2B pencil the essential skeleton of bridge, buildings, water-line and boats. This took about half an hour. I was sitting in my usual sketching chair with paints laid out on my rug on the stone paving.

The sky was one of light gray clouds and plenty of blue openings and sunshine on the buildings. The gray clouds were Ultramarine and Burnt Umber, and a little Raw Sienna was dropped in to give the white clouds a slight warmth. Some diluted Cobalt was used for the blue sky area and a very small touch of Light Red was added to this to prevent it being in any way a *sharp* blue.

I carried these sky colours down over the water area and the gray sky colour was washed over all the buildings adding in a little Raw Sienna to warm it up. I did leave one little bit of white building the colour of the paper in the middle distance on the left.

Half way through these washes my friends the builders arrived with their crane but I found I could manage to look past them without too much effort.

I now had a much needed cup of coffee or two and allowed these first washes to dry out.

Stage 2

I mixed a good quantity of Raw Sienna and Burnt

130 Side canal.

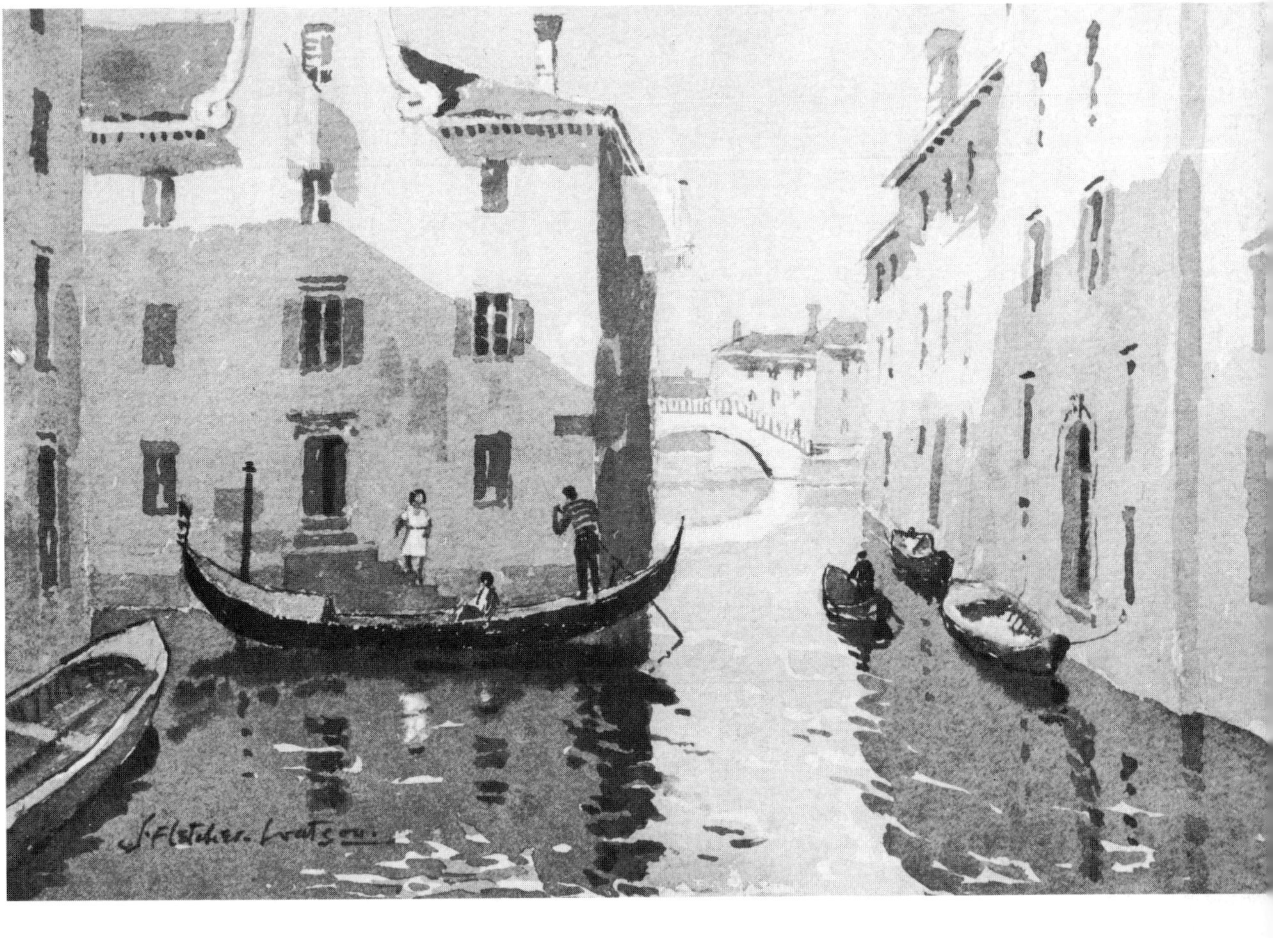

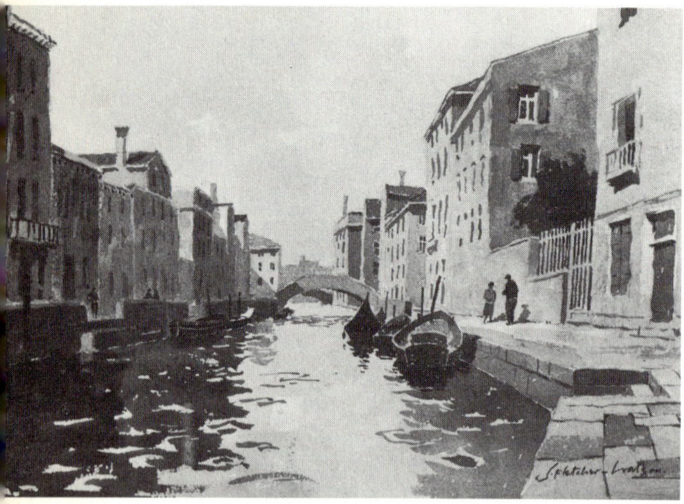

131 Rio di Bragadin.

132 San Giorgio Maggiore at sun rise.

Umber well diluted to give a very light yellow-brown colour and washed this over all buildings including the bridge and stone paving on the right. The later morning sun was giving a warm glow over everything.

This quickly dried and I could start on the left-hand buildings in shadow with some darker tones. Using five colours, Burnt Umber, Burnt Sienna, Light Red, Raw Sienna and Cobalt, I mixed these in different ways to give the various wall colours – some were quite strong yellow, others were fairly strong red as you can see. These colours were suitable for the red roofs also.

The right-hand buildings require the same colours for their shadow walls but less red and more yellow; the sunny walls were left untouched. I was using a No. 9 and No. 7 brush for all this building work.

With a No. 5 brush I put in the distant gray buildings beyond the bridge using Cobalt and Light Red.

Stage 3

I could now proceed with windows, doors and cornices using a No. 5 and No. 3 brush and dark mixtures of Burnt Sienna and Cobalt or Burnt Umber and Cobalt.

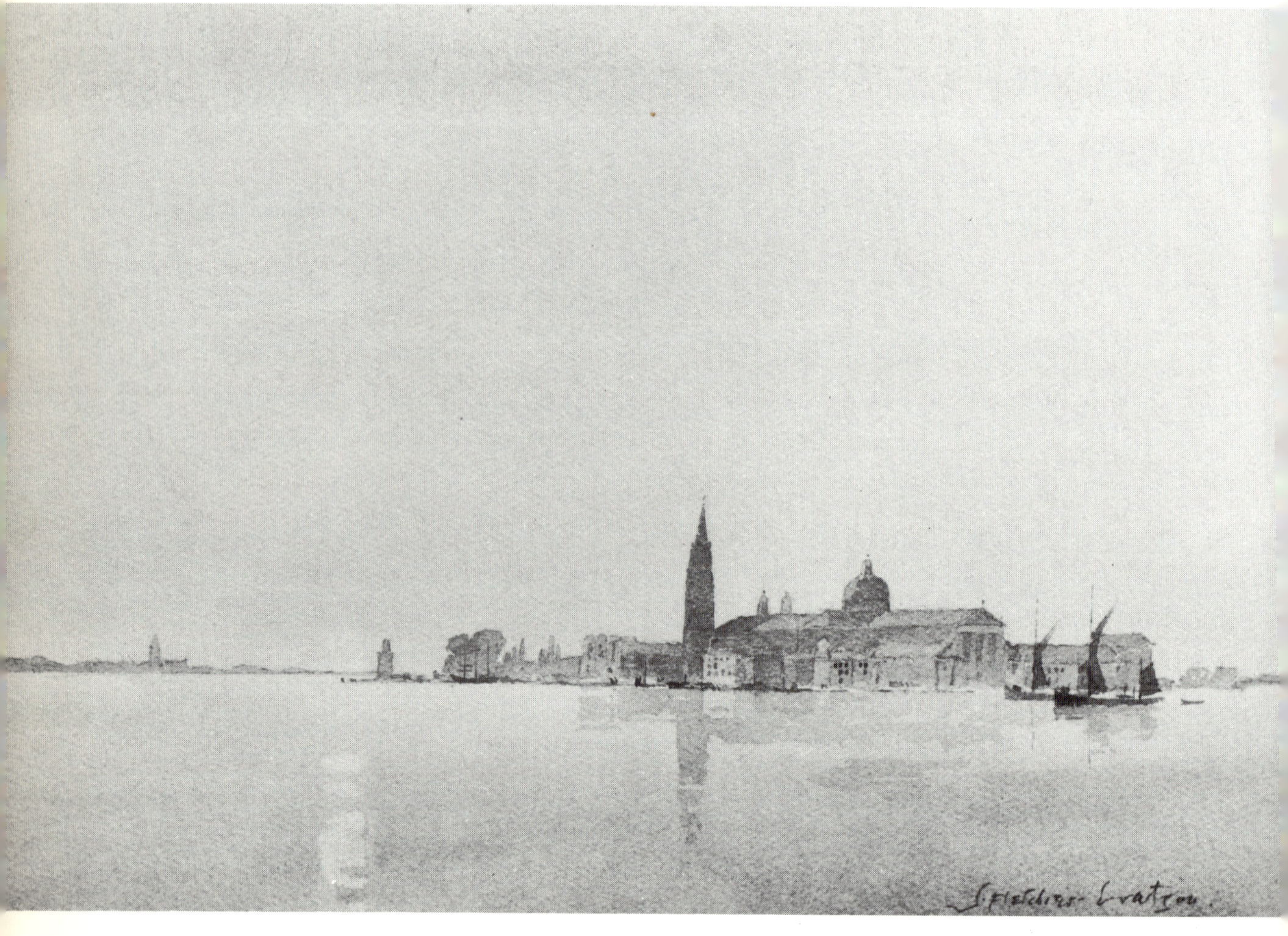

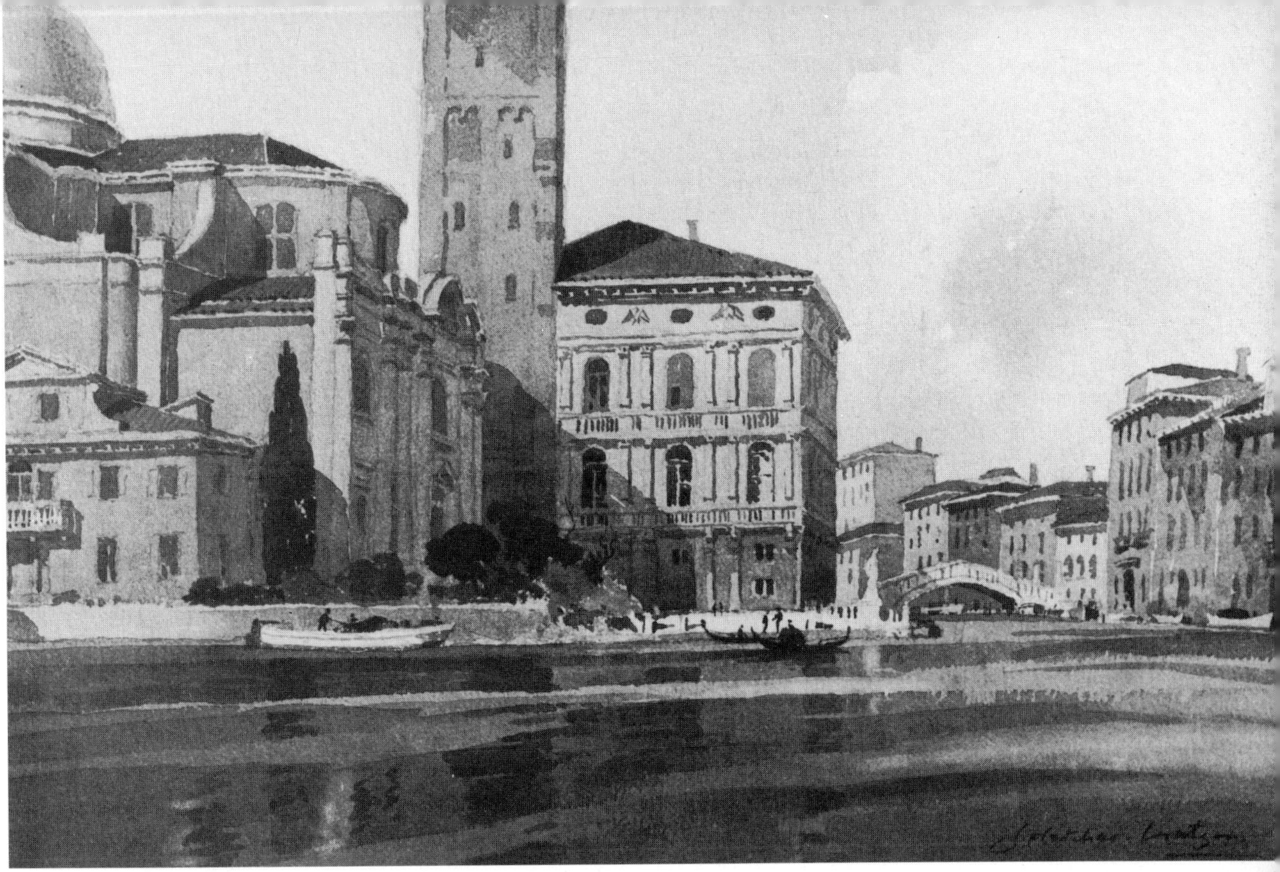

133 S Geremia, Grand Canal.

At the same time shadows were painted falling across the building by the bridge and on the bridge itself and under eaves of various houses. Balconies were indicated with the smaller brush.

The dark tree on the right was painted with Burnt Umber and Winsor Blue and a touch of Raw Sienna and the spaces between the railings underneath.

The various boats came next using some strong Ultramarine for the nearest one, and for its darker parts I added Burnt Umber. Gondolas are always black and you can see one with the sharp pointed bow; I used the two colours just mentioned to obtain this black colour. Burnt Sienna and Cobalt were used for the other boats. One or two posts were painted dark brown.

The parapet wall to the left-hand footway wanted to be darker and so did some of the buildings on this side near to me. For these I used strong mixes of Burnt Sienna and Cobalt.

Stage 4

The water was practically the last thing to be done and again the muddy-green reflection of buildings was a mixture of Payne's Gray and Raw Sienna. I used the same technique as for figure 128, using a No. 7 and No. 12 brush and starting at the far end of the canal and working gradually downwards. The boats' and posts' reflections required darker tones of the same dull green.

Finally, figures were painted with a small No. 5 brush and joints of stone paving in the foreground with a No. 3. A few final shadows were wanted, such as the boat shadow against the quay and shadow to the foreground steps and figures standing on the quay. A few doorways and window shadows required stiffening up; I noticed this after standing a little way back from the picture, and I used Ultramarine and Light Red for this final item.

The picture had taken just under three and a half hours whereas figure 128 (and on the front cover) took about four and a half hours.

Before leaving this subject it is just worth observing it in monochrome as shown in figure 131. We can see here clearly that the darkest tones are the dark water reflections, the boats and the tree. Then come the buildings in shadow, and finally the lightest tones are the sunny side of buildings and the sky and the water reflecting the sky.

132 SAN GIORGIO MAGGIORE AT SUN RISE

31.5cm × 47.5cm ($12\frac{1}{2}$in. × $18\frac{3}{4}$in.)

This is one of the most lovely views in Venice looking across the big stretch of water from a broad quay called Schiavoni. It was in a Pension at the east end of this quay that we were staying, and we saw this view from our bedroom window on many fine early mornings.

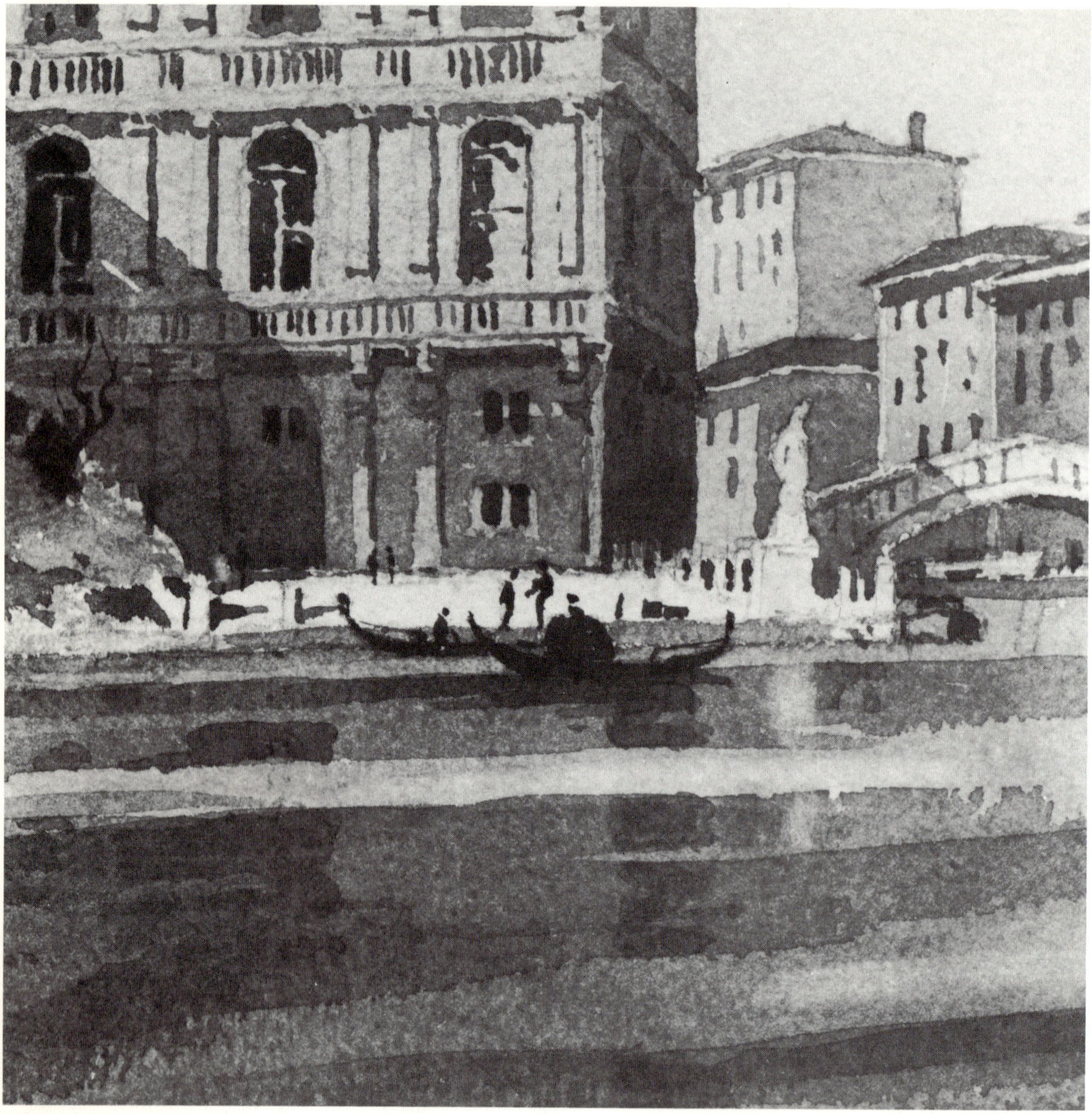

134 S Geremia, detail.

I made this painting one morning from near the St Mark's Square end of the quay. The sky was blue above fading to yellow on the horizon and the water was pale green. The group of buildings and trees were blue-gray with a touch of pink.

This is not a difficult subject but it requires delicate painting to capture the rather ethereal atmosphere. The sky was of course a graded wash. With the picture upside down I started at the horizon with Raw Sienna and a touch of Light Red and gradually changed this to Cobalt Blue as I got near the top of the paper.

133 S GEREMIA, GRAND CANAL

31.5cm × 47.5cm (12½in. × 18¾in.)

At the northern end of the Grand Canal is this great church of S Geremia, making a lovely group with its campanile and large palace beside it and the little side canal going away to the right with its stone bridge. It was a fascinating composition to play with. One was tempted to get more of the church in on the left, but then one would have lost the valuable line of houses running down the side canal to the right. The very tall cypress tree at the corner of the church was a valuable dark vertical feature to echo the campanile tower, and the small dark trees and shrubs were equally helpful in giving contrast to the architectural detail behind.

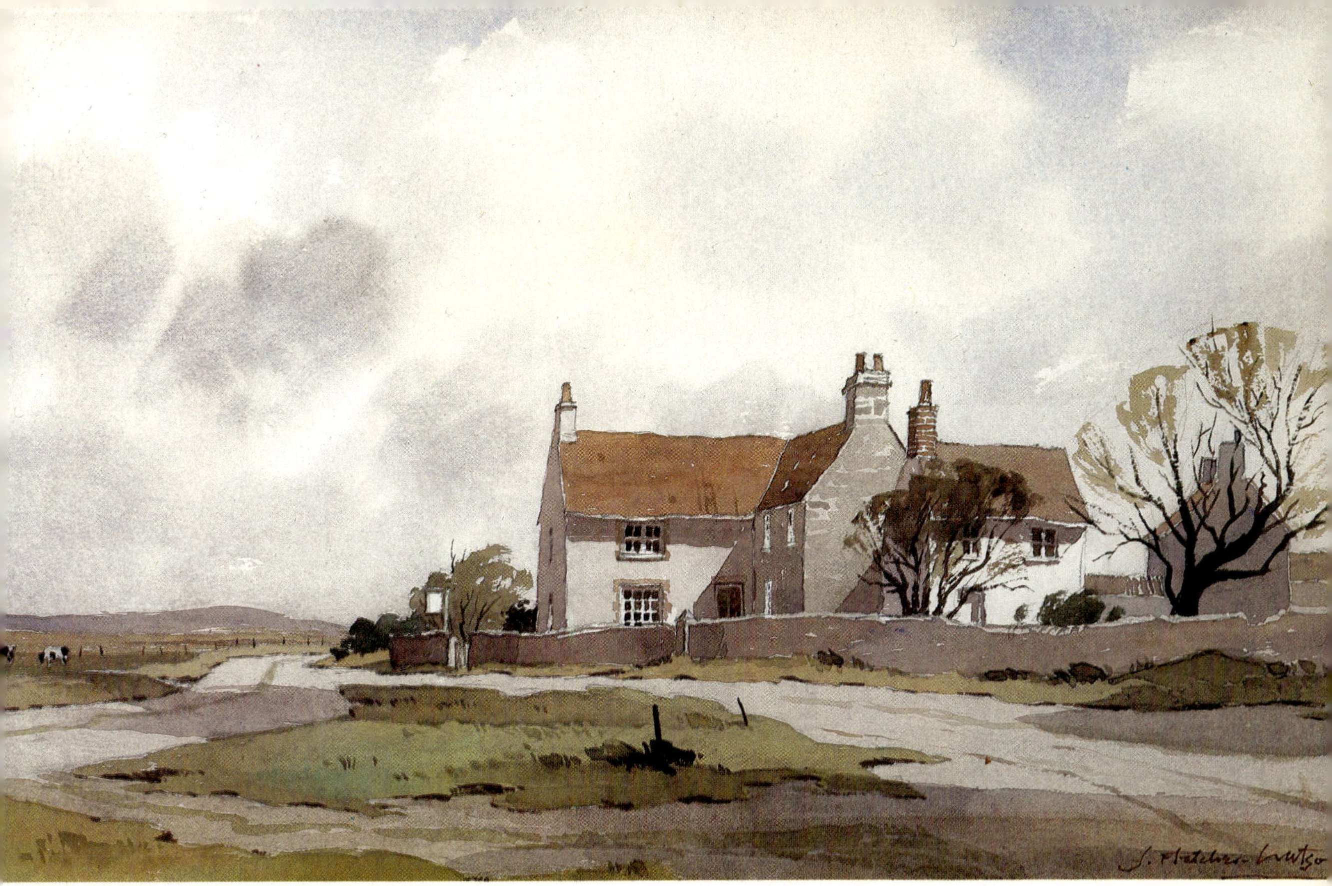

1 Fishermen's cottages, Salthouse. 31.5 cm x 47.5 cm (12½ in. x 18¾ in.)

2 Flood tide at Morston Quay. 31.5 cm x 47.5 cm (12½ in. x 18¾ in.)

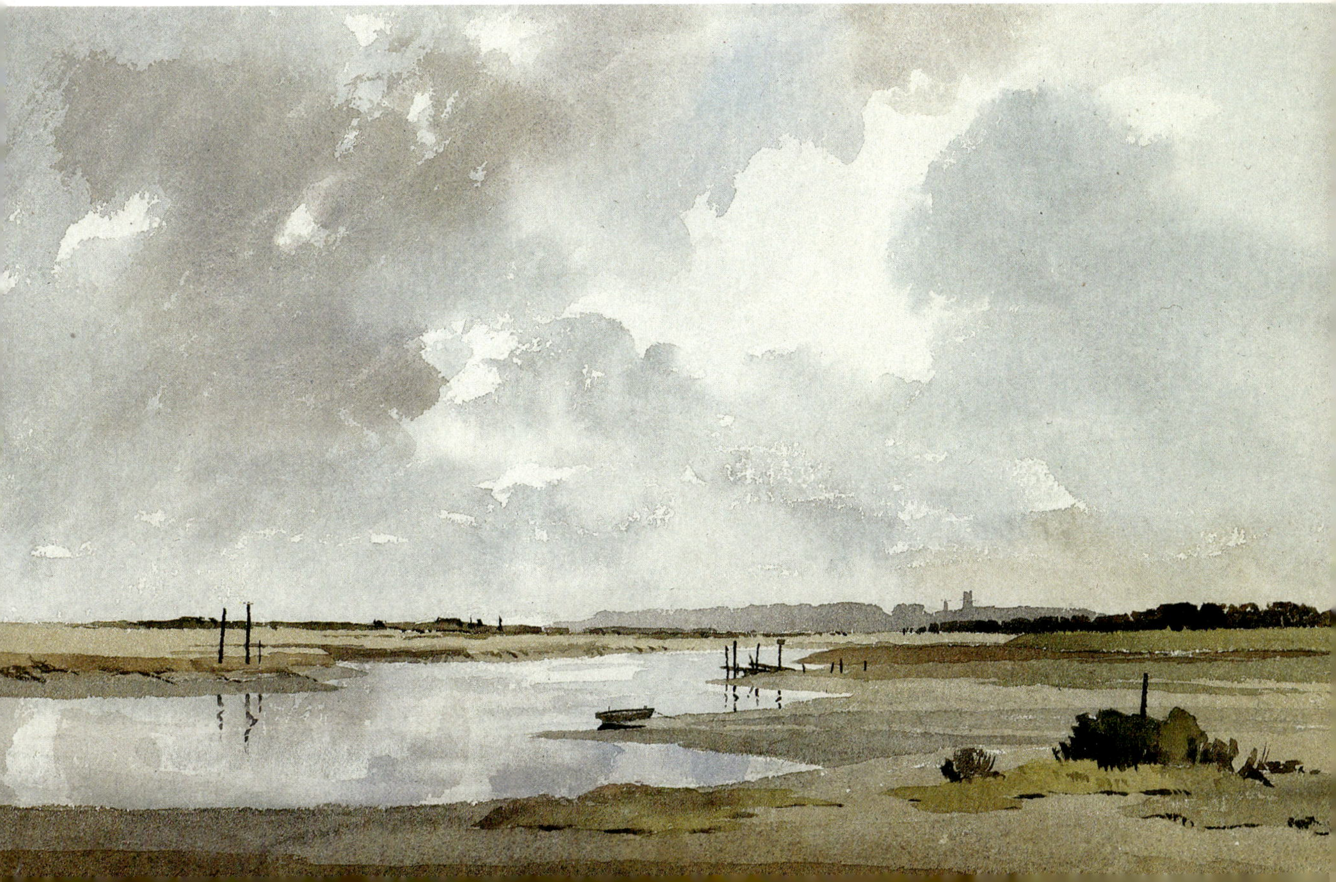

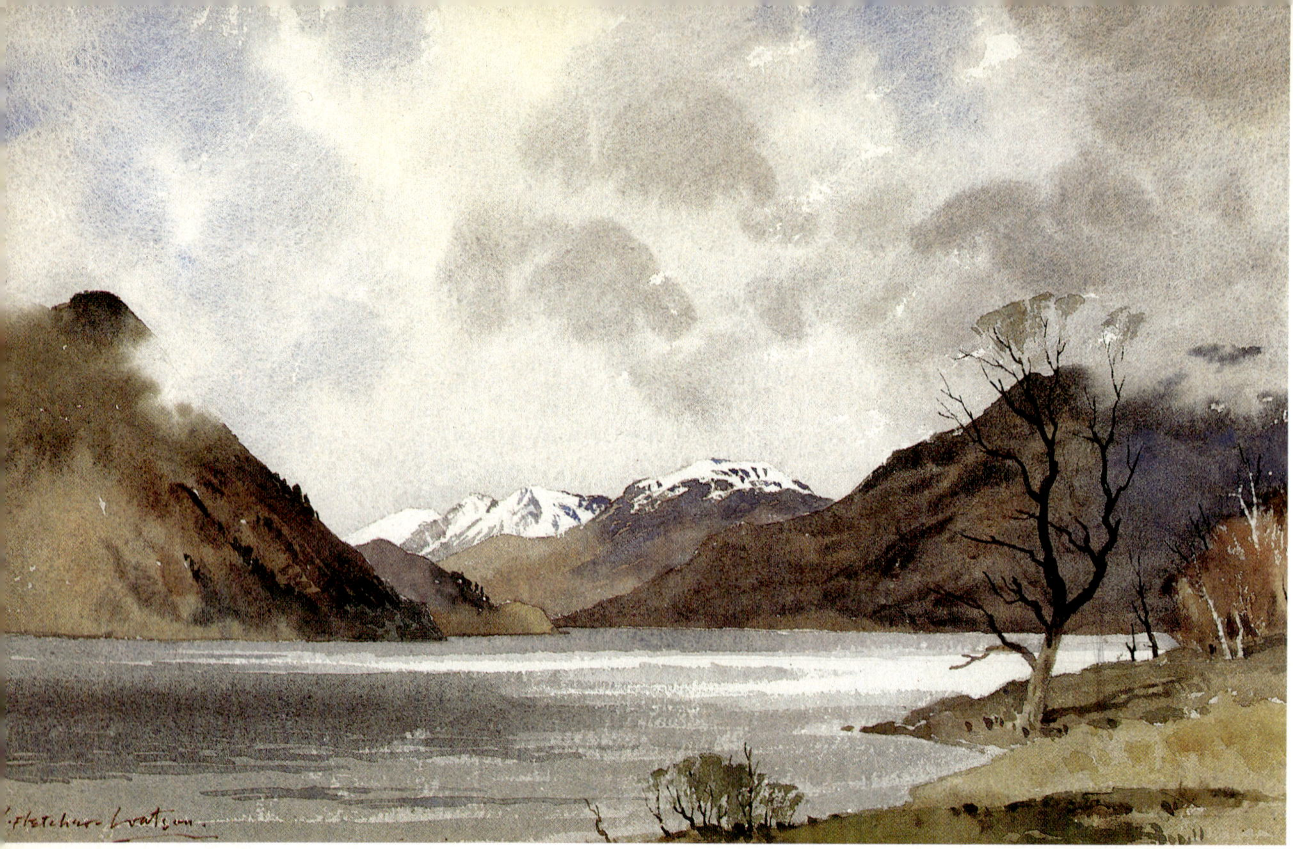

3 Ullswater. 31.5 cm x 48 cm (12½ in. x 19 in.)

4 Windrush Mill. 34.5 cm x 47.5 cm (15½ in. x 18¾ in.)

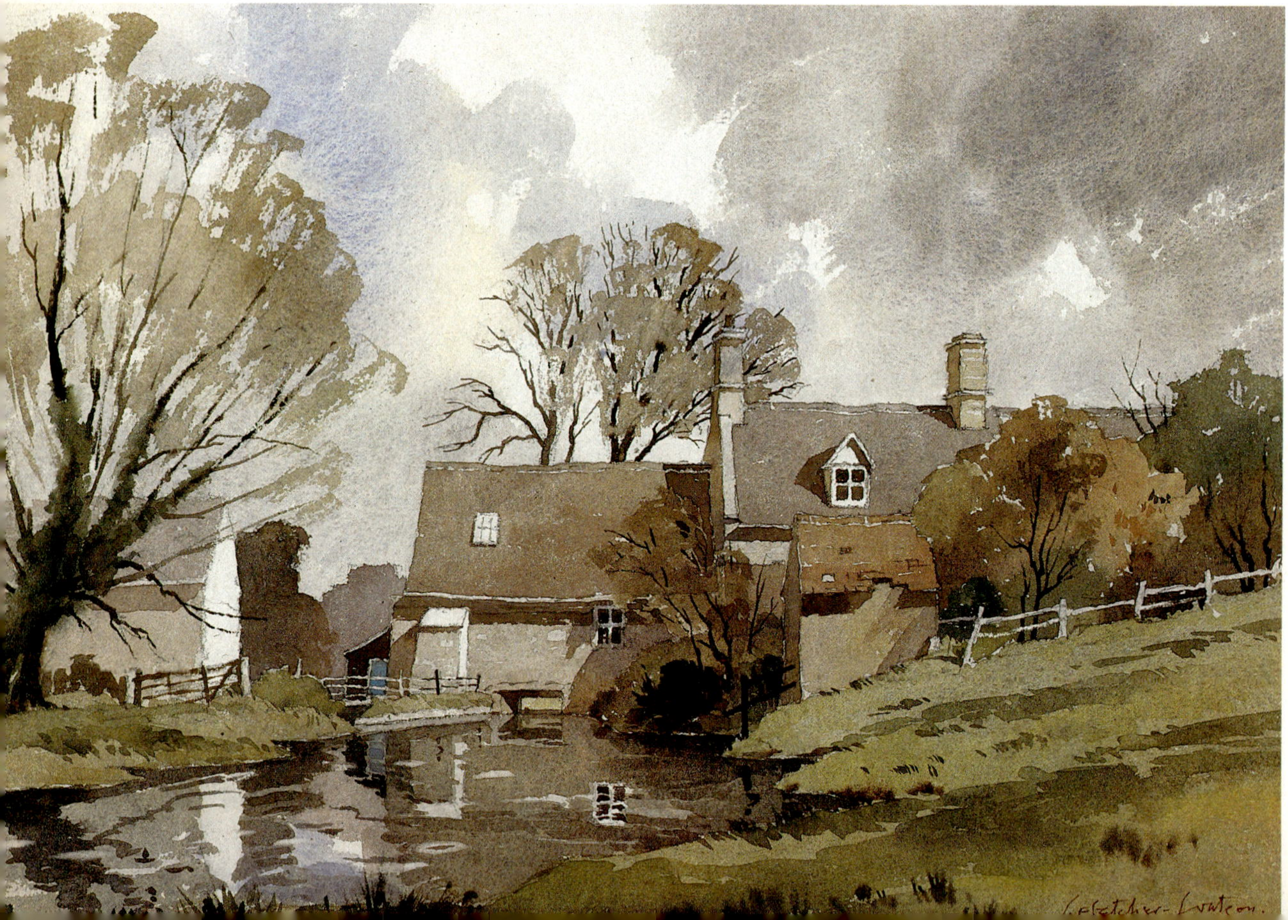

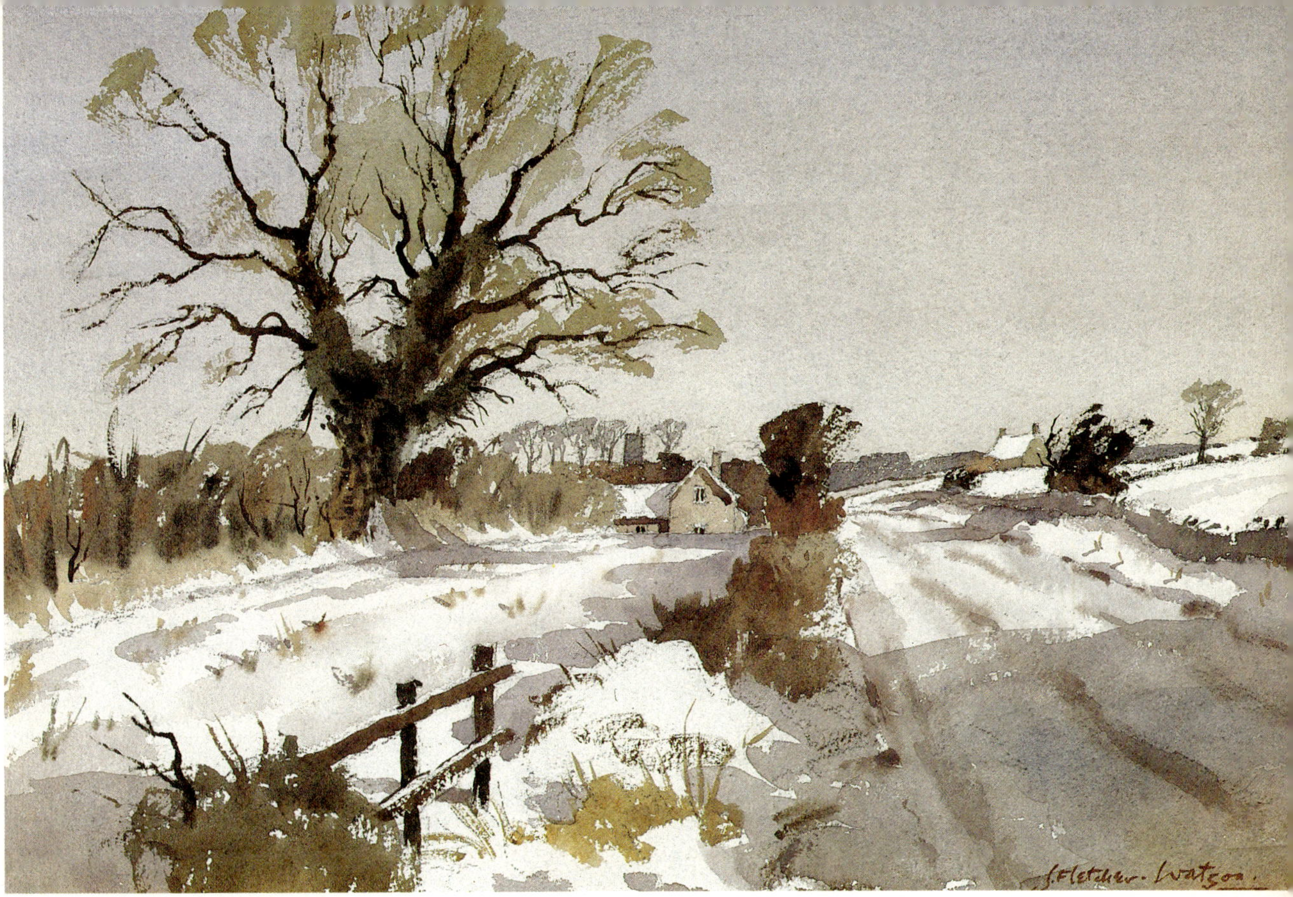

5 Snow scene, Windrush. 31.5 cm x 47.5 cm (12½ in. x 18¾ in.)

6 Northleach, from the south. 31 cm x 47 cm (12¼ in. x 18½ in.)

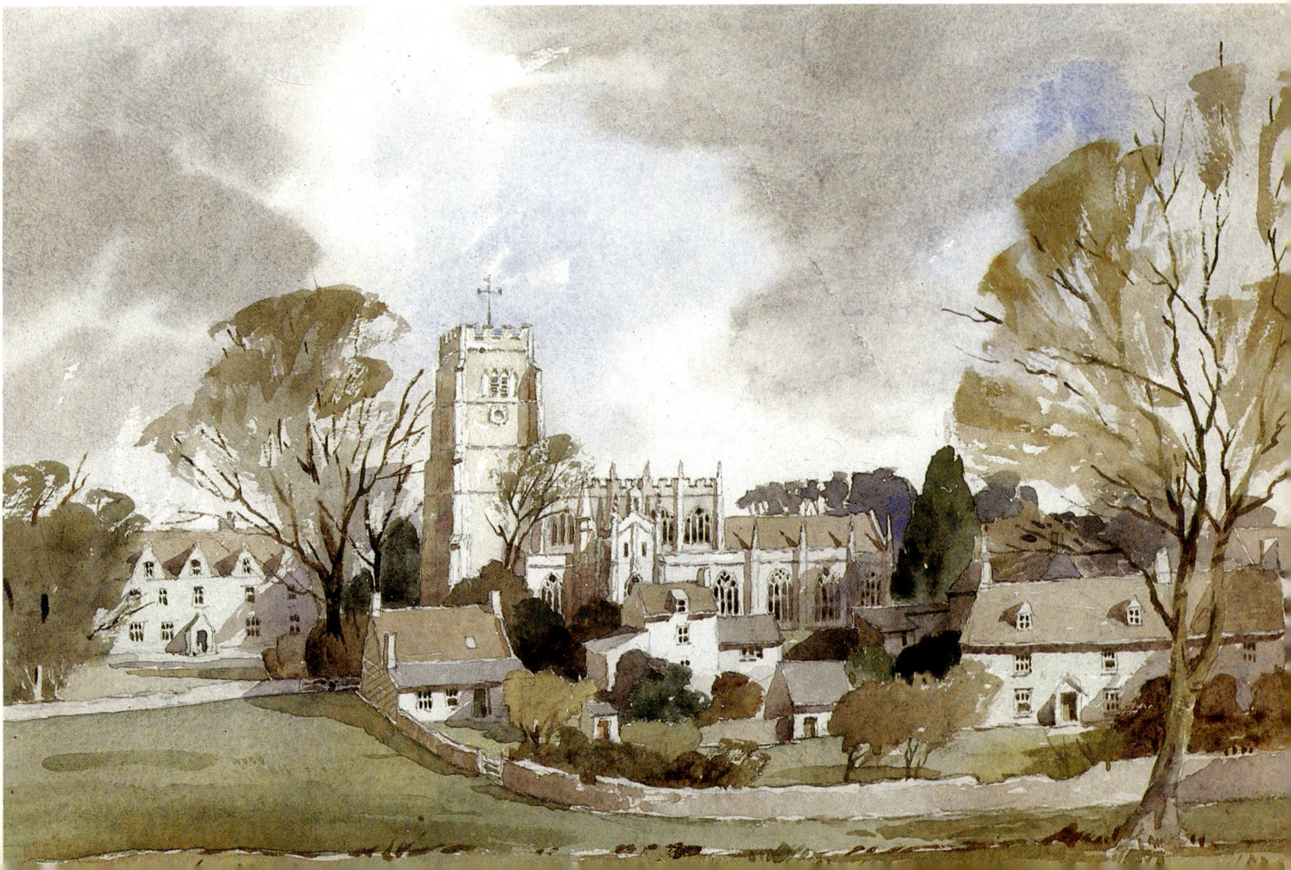

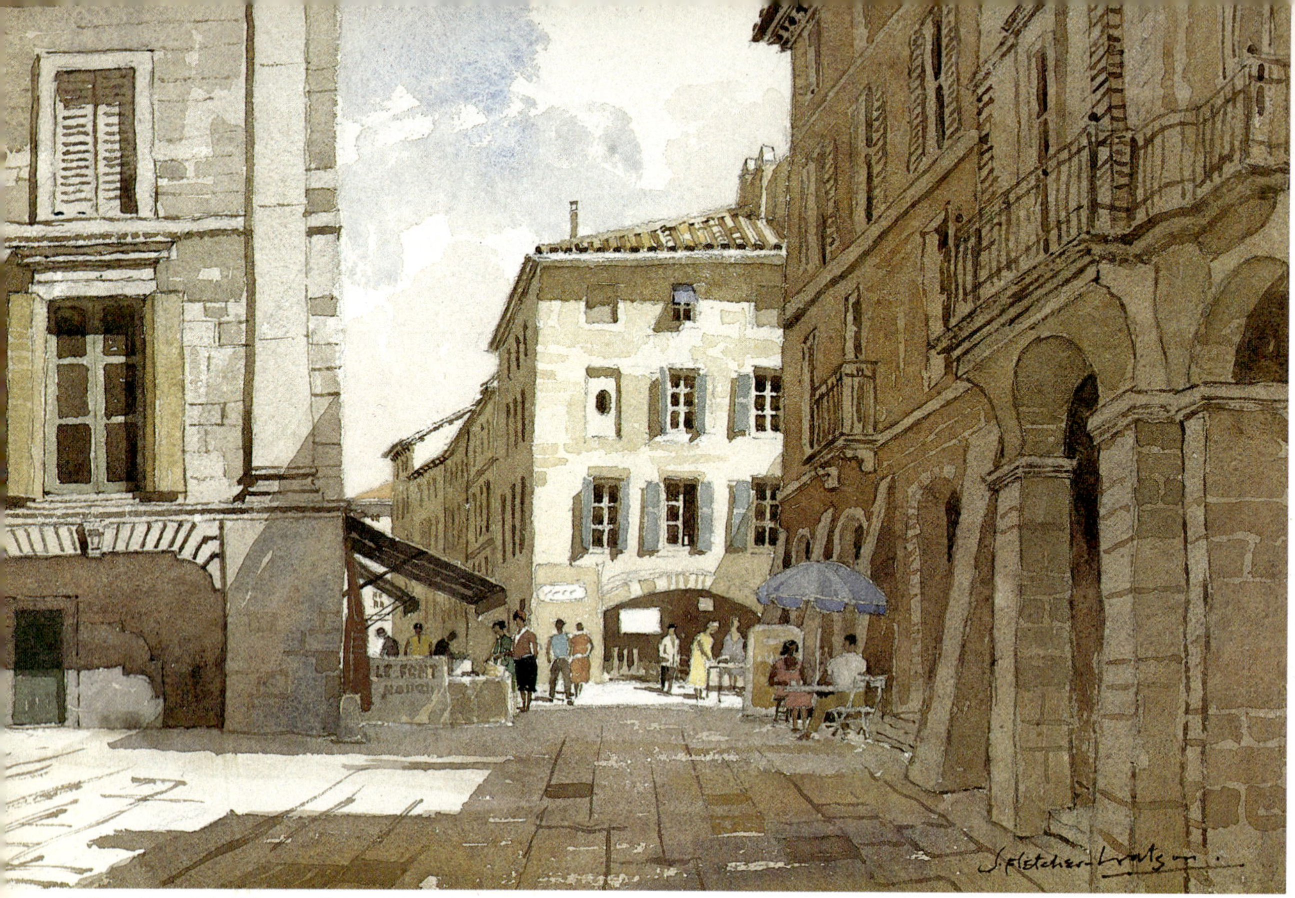

7 Uzes, Provence. 31.5 cm x 47.5 cm (12½ in. x 18¾ in.)

8 Pont du Gard, Provence. 31.5 cm x 47.5 cm (12½ in. x 18¾ in.)

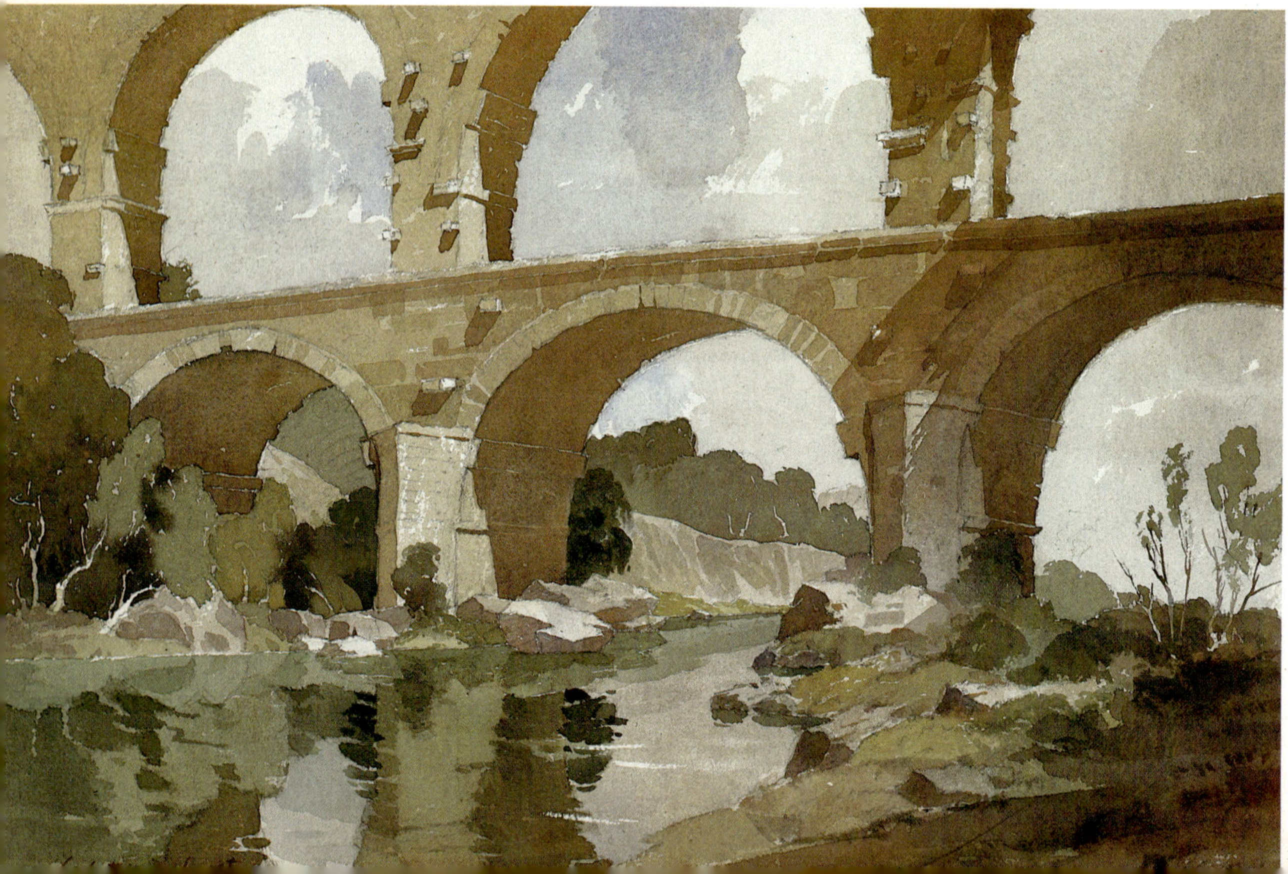

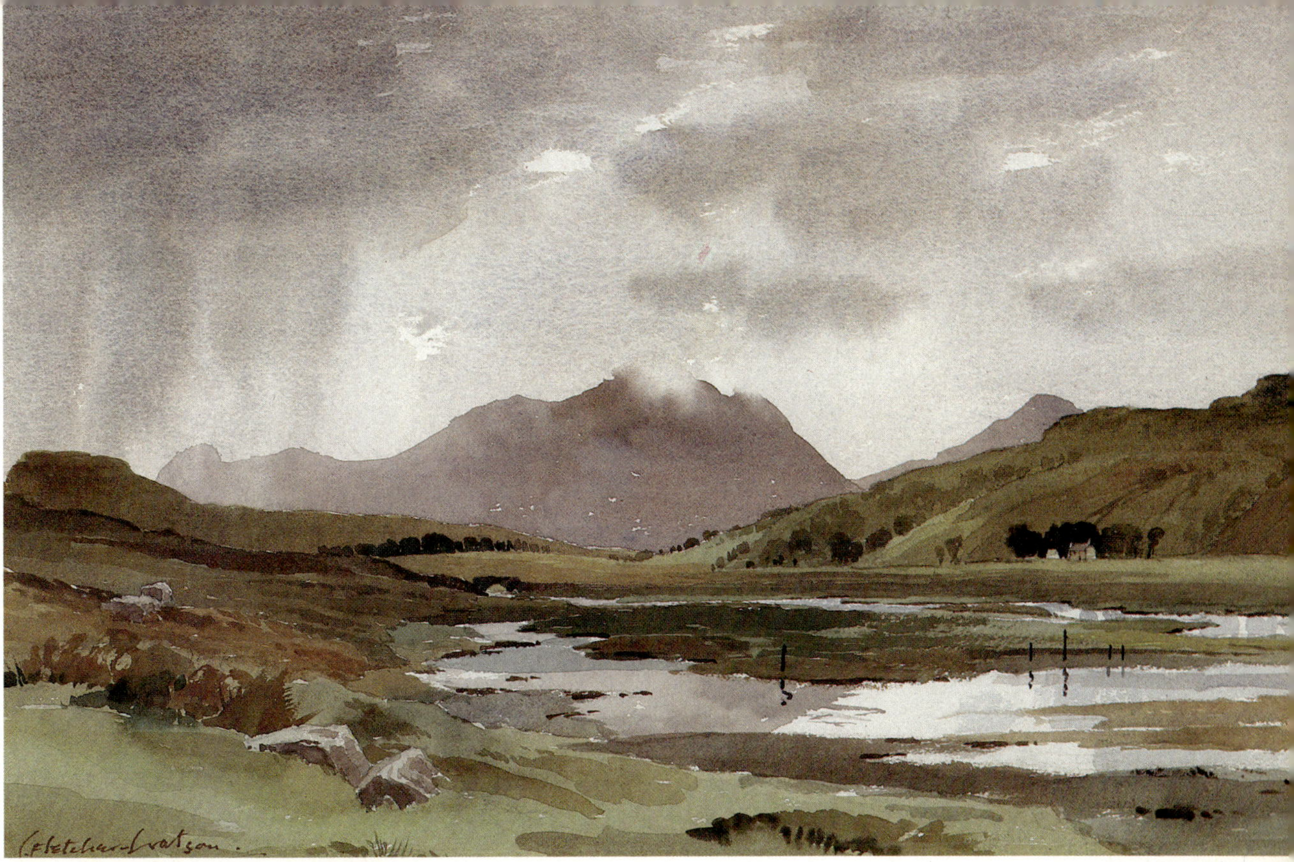

9 Kishorn Estuary. 31 cm x 48.5 cm (12¼ in. x 19¼ in.)

10 Bridge near Kishorn. 31.5 cm x 48.5 cm (12½ in. x 19¼ in.)

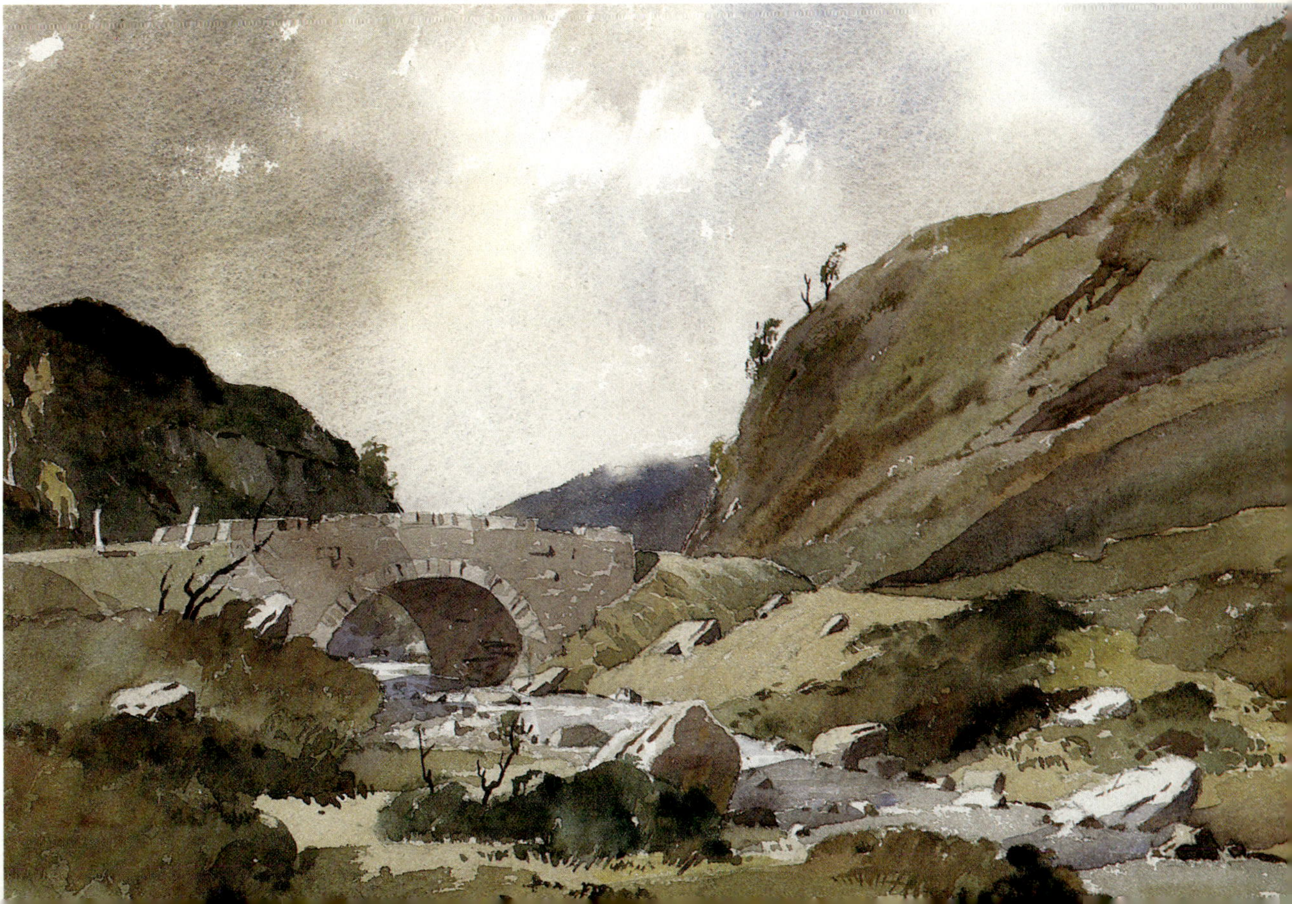

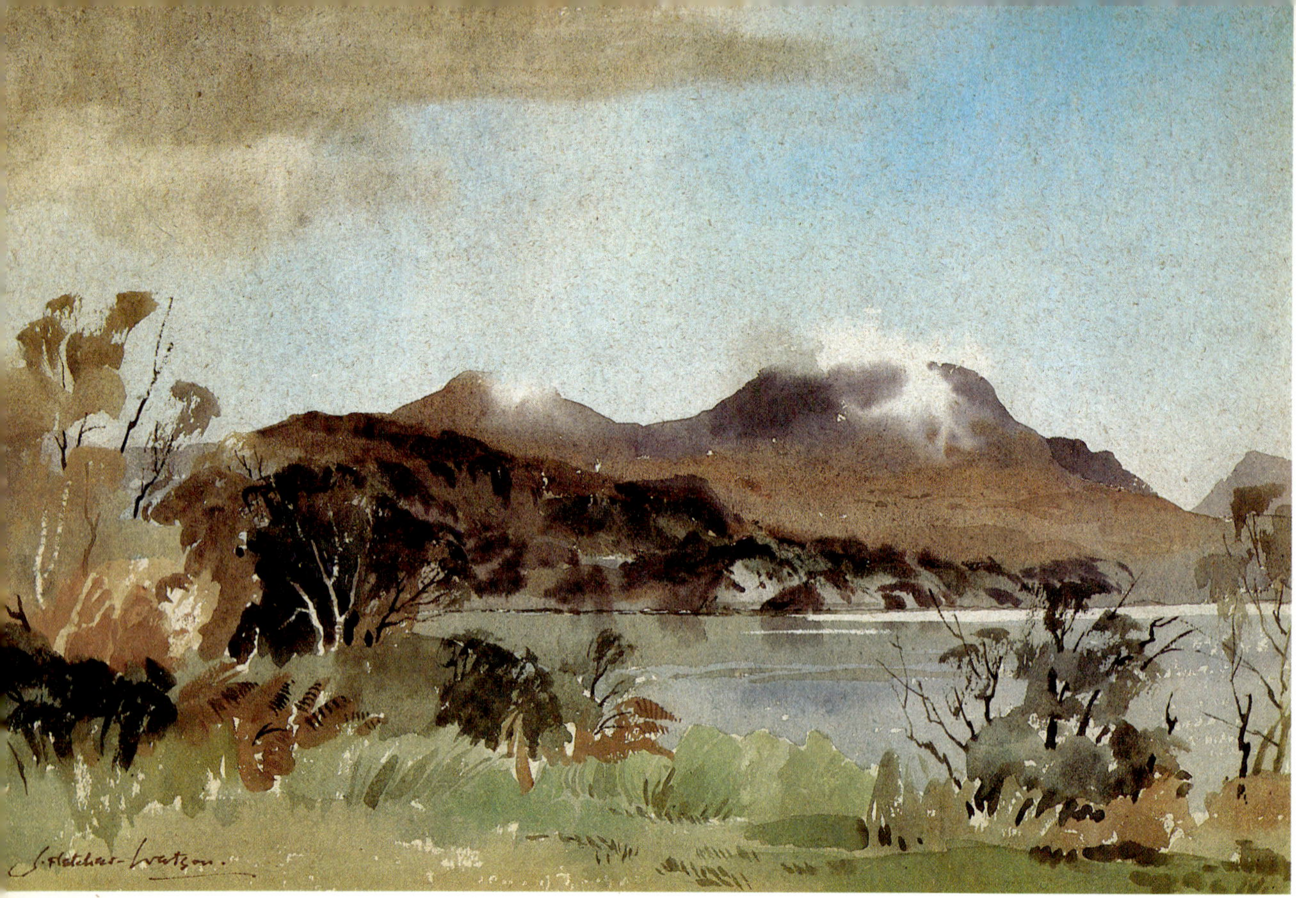

11 Loch Torridon. 32 cm x 48 cm (12¾ in. x 19 in.)

12 Kerrysdale. 31.5 cm x 47 cm (12½ in. x 18½ in.)

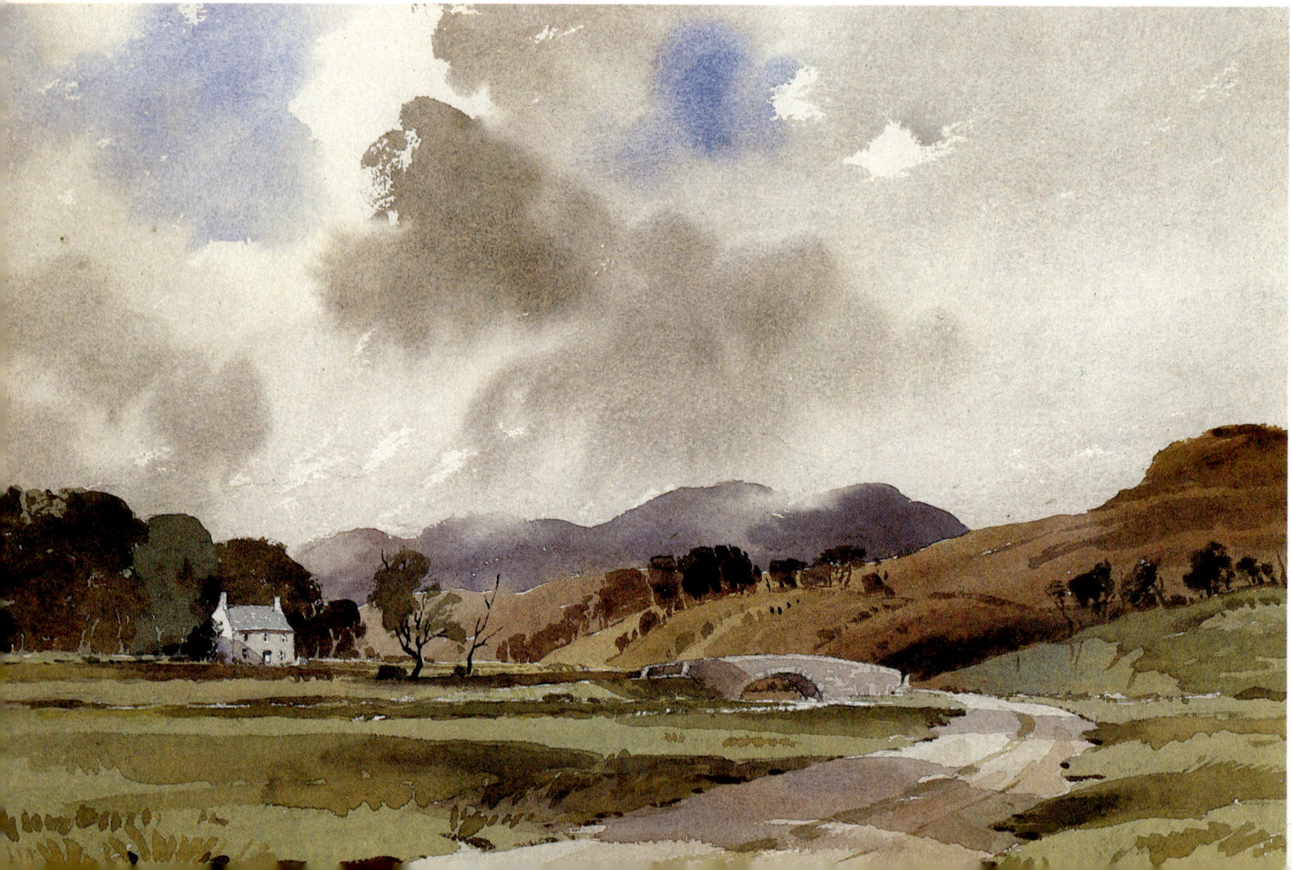

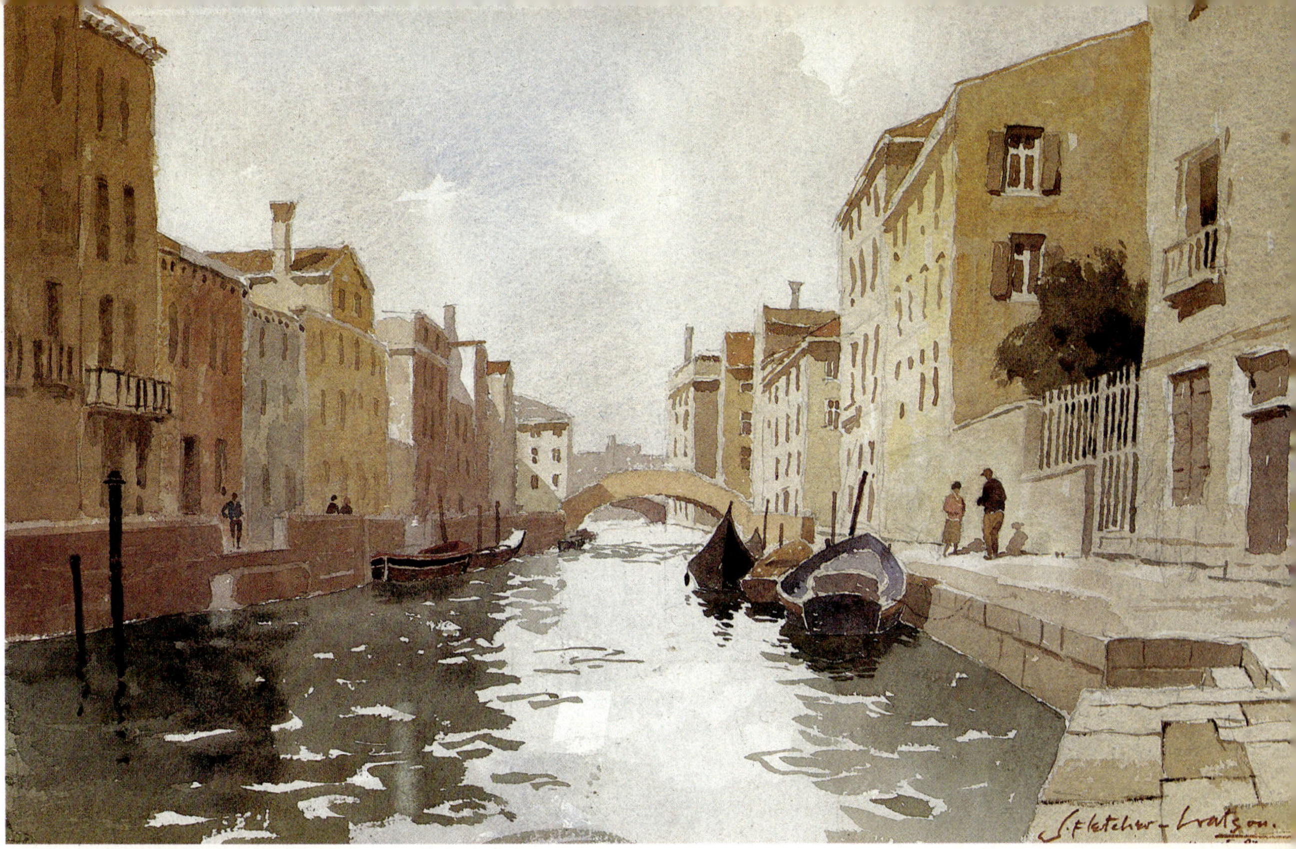

13 Rio di Bragadin, Venice. 31.5 cm x 47.5 cm (12½ in. x 18¾ in.)

14 Wylye. 31.5 cm x 47.5 cm (12½ in. x 18¾ in.)

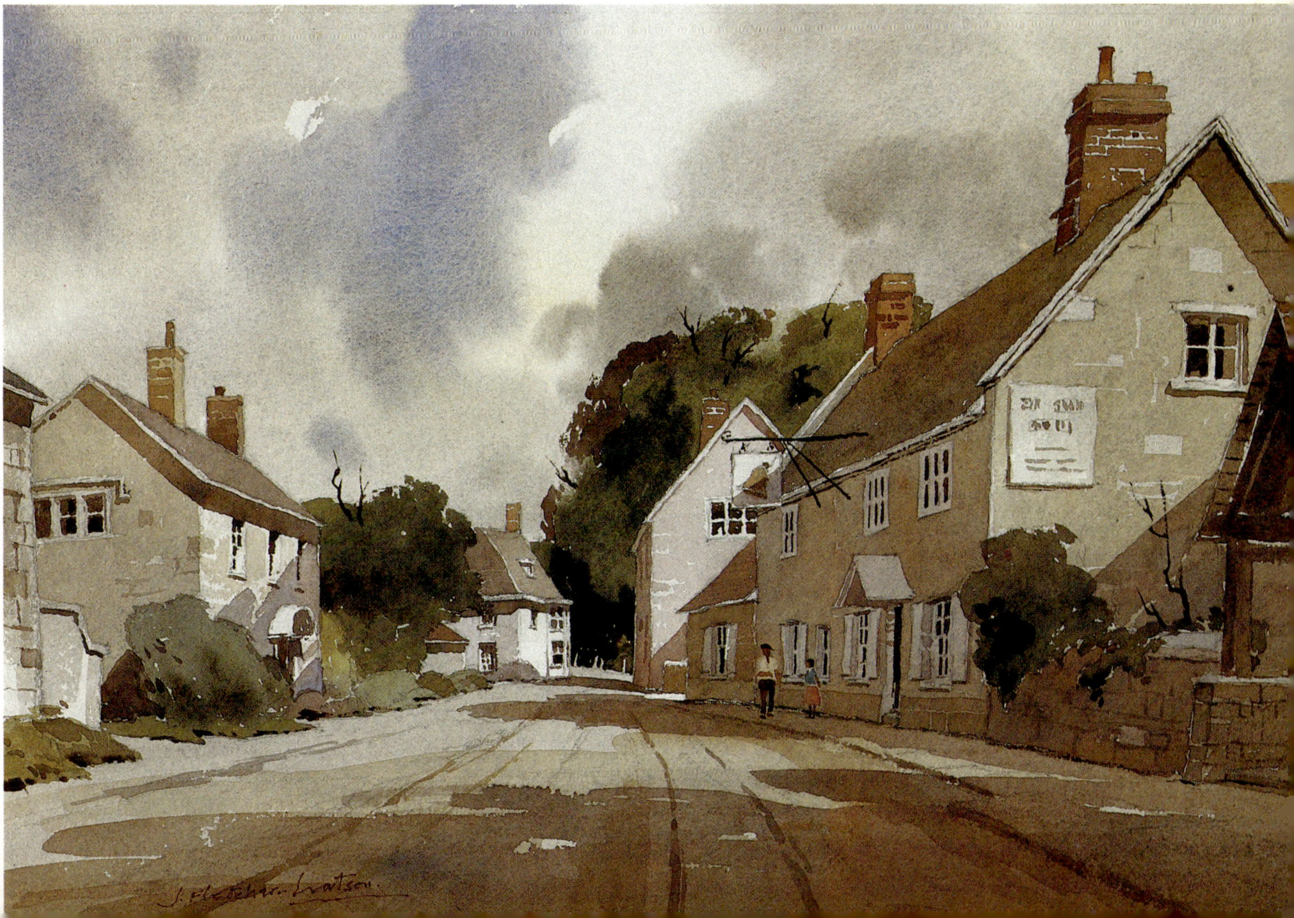

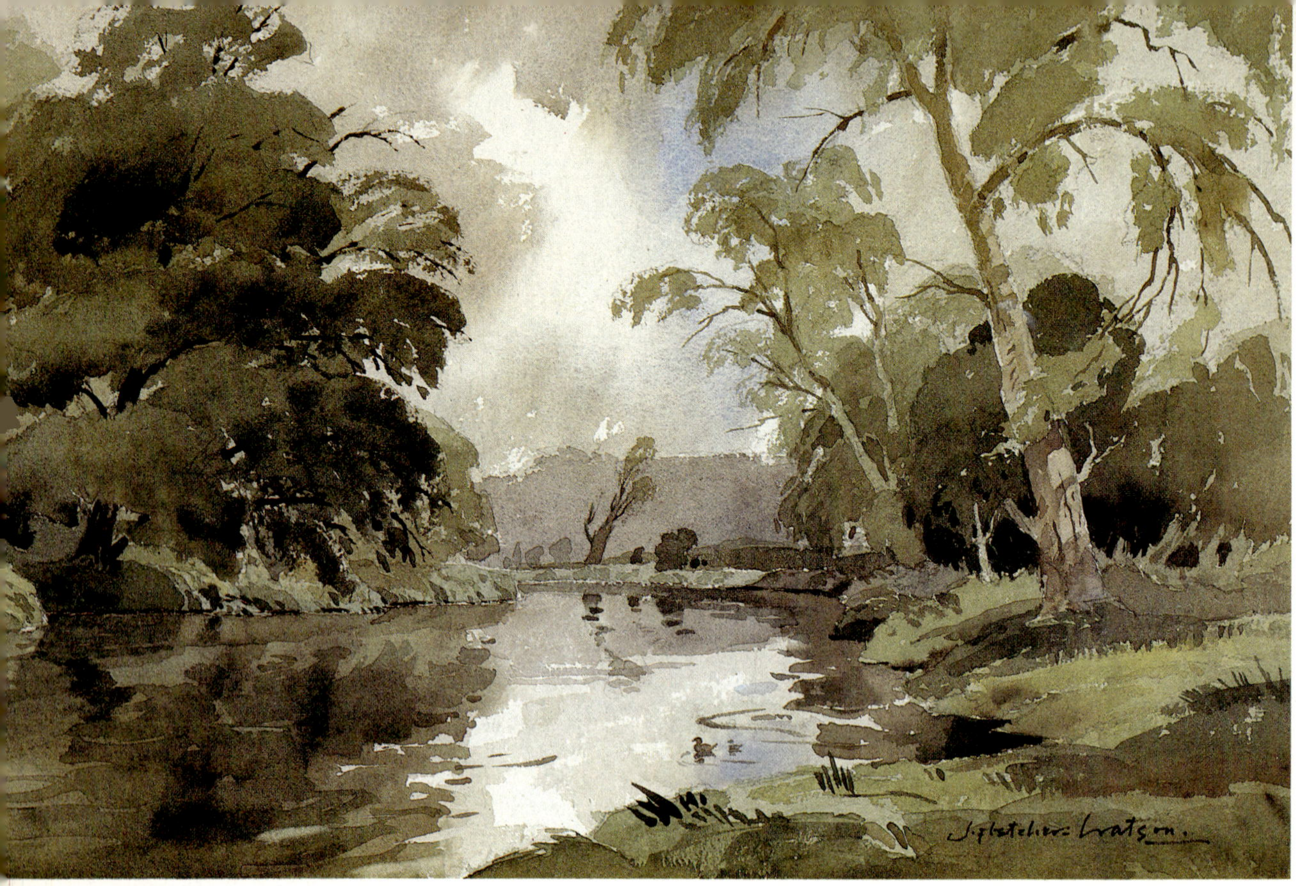

15 River Avon, Middle Woodford. 31.5 cm x 47.5 cm (12½ in. x 18¾ in.)

16 New End Square, Hampstead. 23.5 cm x 35.5 cm (9¼ in. x 14 in.)

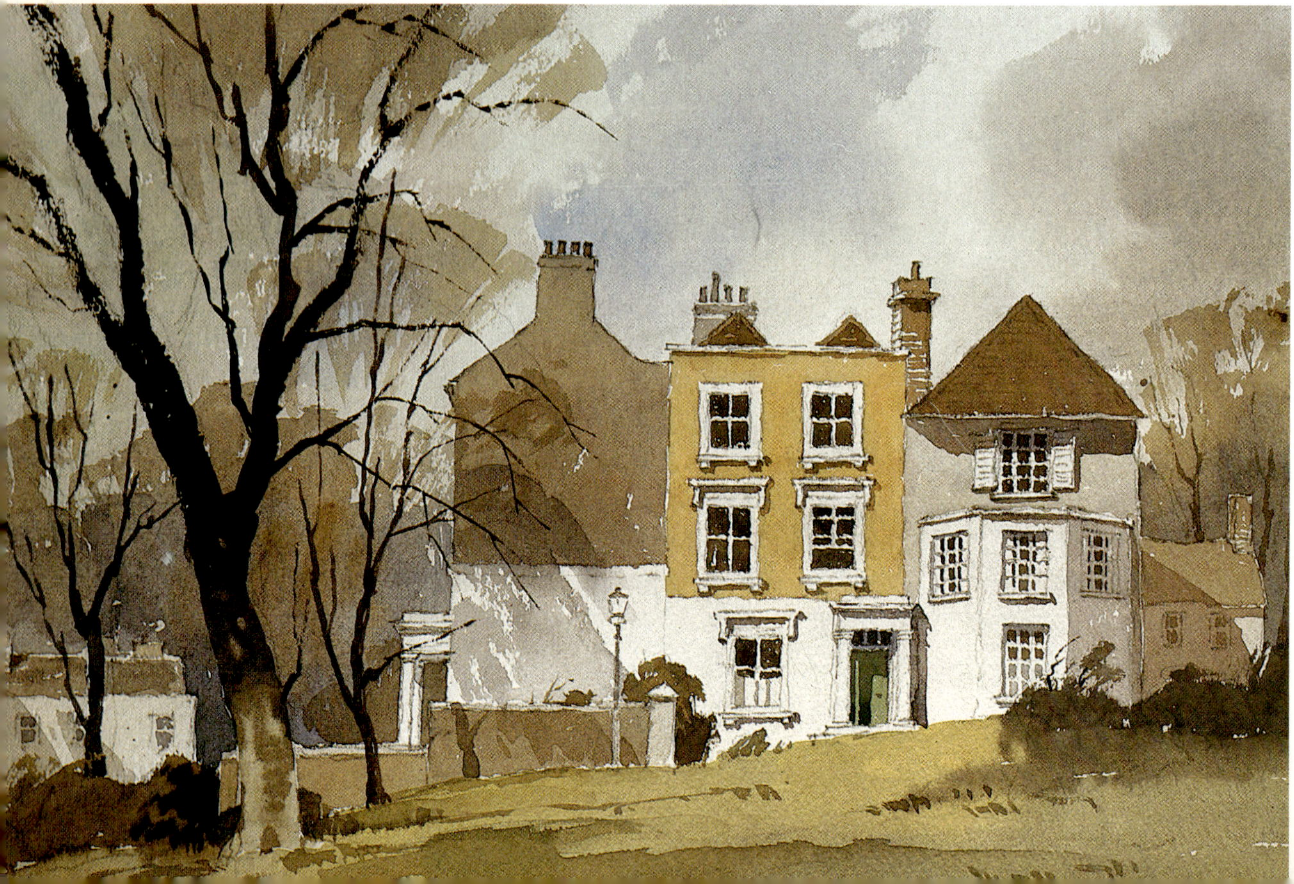

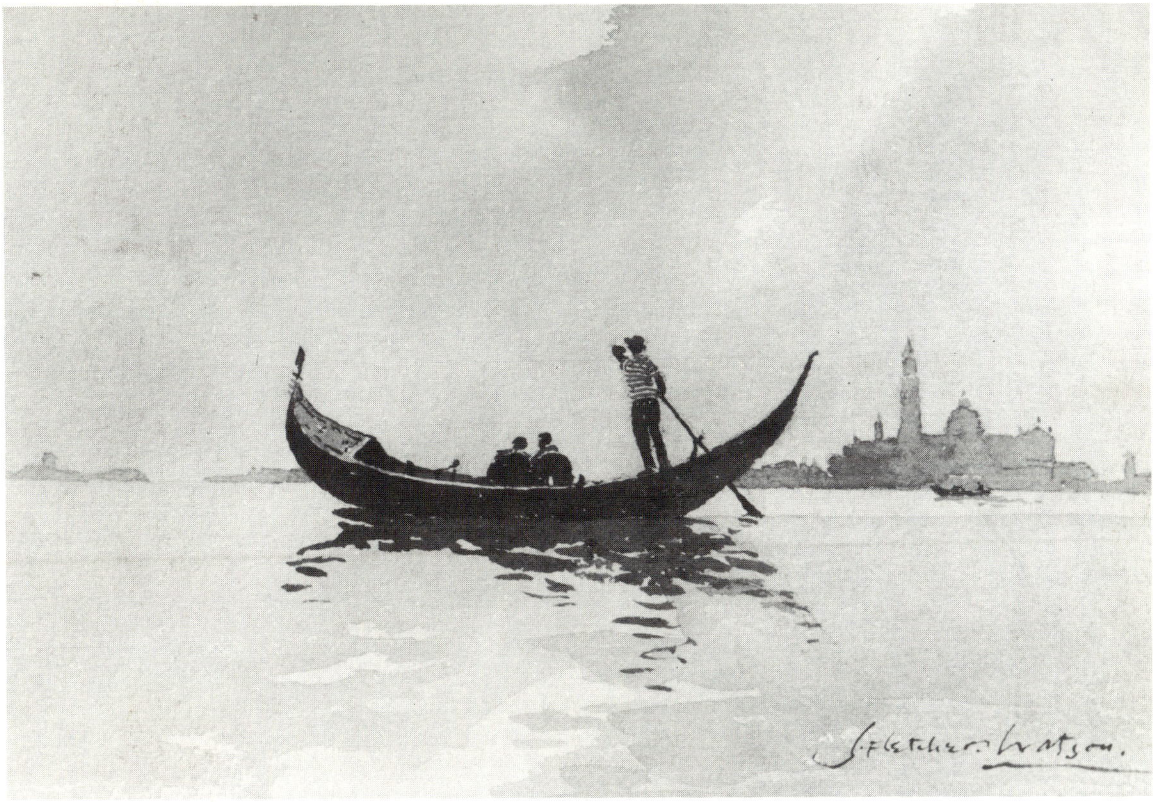

135 Gondola, with S Giorgio in background.

Gondolas are nice things to place at strategic points to focus interest and give scale to the enormous size of the buildings.

The detail (134) shows the brushwork handling of the gondolas and figures and the fenestration of the building in the background.

135 GONDOLA, WITH S GIORGIO IN BACKGROUND

23.5cm × 35.5cm (9¼in. × 14in.)
This study of a gondola is an irresistible subject to paint as it so typifies Venice. Of course the boat was moving slowly past me and I had to quickly draw it in my sketch-book and then paint from that onto the picture with the view of San Giorgio in the background.

Note the sharp reflections one usually gets from boats. Quite quickly and strongly brushed in on *dry* paper not wet.

This seems a suitable picture to end this chapter on the most beautiful city in the world. I would like to have shown you far more examples of watercolour subjects, but alas there was no time for more in one week.

7 Painting in Wiltshire

Now we move to south-west England and the lovely county of Wiltshire, to a particular part of Wiltshire west of Salisbury. The area is around the village of Dinton and a little north to include the beautiful Wylye Valley. This part of Wiltshire abounds in unspoilt sleepy old villages, beautiful farm buildings in fine rural settings and a mixture of arable and grazing land, which gives the artist plenty of scope for various types of landscape subject.

The chalk belt runs across Wiltshire here and consequently we find houses built in the light-coloured chalk limestone, and sometimes it is mixed with flints giving a chequer-work wall which, when mellowed with age, can be a most attractive architectural feature.

I take watercolour painting courses in August at Philipp's House, Dinton, and some of the pictures shown in this chapter were carried out with painting friends on the courses, and a lot of fun we have on these joint painting expeditions.

136 MANOR FARM, STOCKTON
31.5cm × 47.5cm ($12\frac{1}{2}$in. × $18\frac{3}{4}$in.)
This first picture is of a typical Wiltshire farm with a large thatch-roofed barn; the house behind and other out-buildings had brownish-red clay tiles to the roofs. There is a lovely grouping of trees to the left and in the right-hand distance is a sight of the downs. The foreground stubble field had been cut some time and there was a pleasing mixture of yellow and green colouring to it.

This is a good subject for anyone to try and there

136 Manor Farm, Stockton.

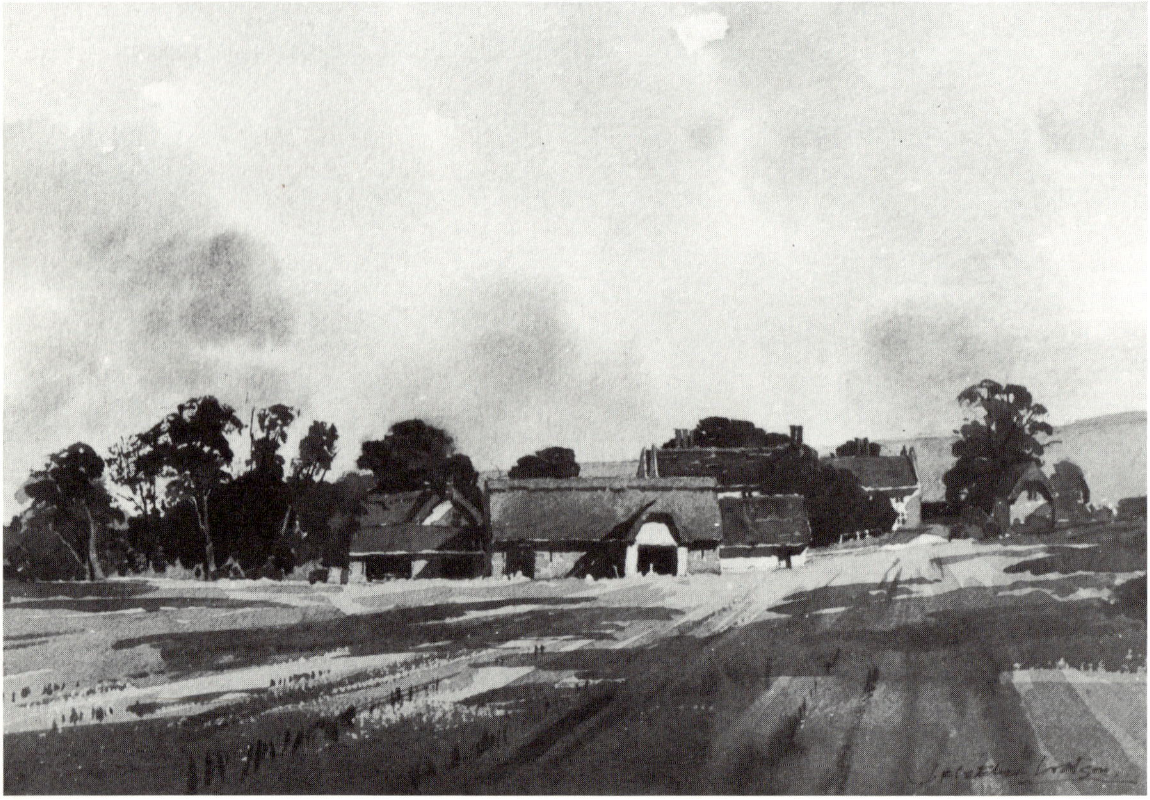

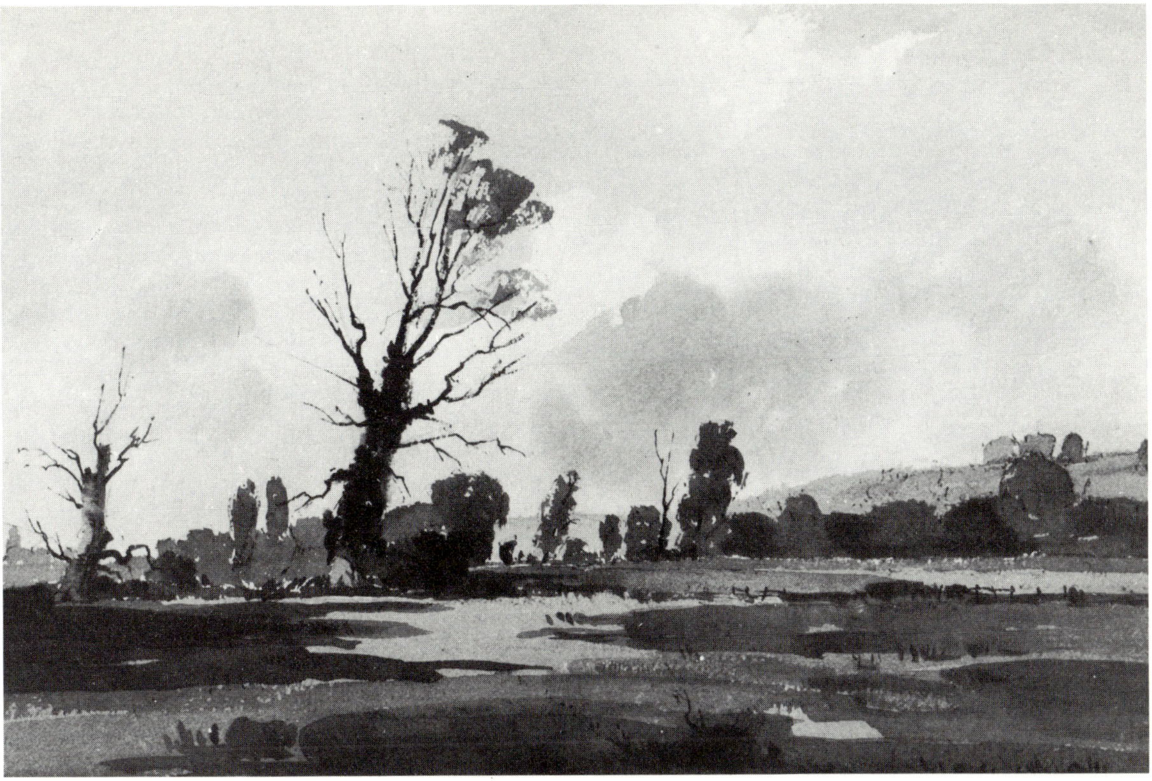

137 The dying tree, Wylye.

were a number of view-points from which it could be painted, all giving good compositions. Note how helpful the lines of stubble are in giving perspective to the foreground, leading it into the middle distance. Cloud shadows are helping to break up the expanse of field.

137 THE DYING TREE, WYLYE

31.5cm × 47.5cm ($12\frac{1}{2}$in. × $18\frac{3}{4}$in.)

In this picture of water meadows near the Wylye river there is a nice uncomplicated landscape for the not too advanced painter. The rising ground in the background received a simple wash, and the tree groups against it were painted in strong tones.

The fields received various washes, light to start with and then darker shadow washes and some grass textures. The fine old half-dead tree was fun to paint with heavy cladding of dark green ivy and then strongly painted dark brown branches emerging at the top.

A good sky is essential for a simple picture like this; a white cloud, some blue sky and light gray clouds forming an interesting pale summer sky pattern was what was wanted, and of course was put in at the beginning.

Wiltshire has very fine woods and trees dotted about the farming land as we shall see in further illustrations.

138 WYLYE

31.5cm × 47.5cm ($12\frac{1}{2}$in. × $18\frac{3}{4}$in.)

We will now paint a village subject and I will give full details of the technique, but first let us look at the black and white picture (138). The composition and tone values are so important and we can see them well in this monochrome picture.

With the composition I had to decide whether to have more building space taken up on the right or the left of the road. As a rule one does not want it to be equal both sides. I decided to have most of the building weight on the right and that meant that as the road disappeared round the small white house at the end, this strong focal point of light house and very dark trees would be a little off-centre to the left. This was satisfying to the eye.

The Bell Inn on the right had a pleasing steep gable roof and chimney which I wanted to include as a good foreground shape. The dark bush against this gable wall was useful and it counter-balanced well with the other two *dark* areas in the picture, the large tree group in the centre distance and the smaller dark tree to the left. These three dark foliage masses were very vital to the composition and their tone values were important too.

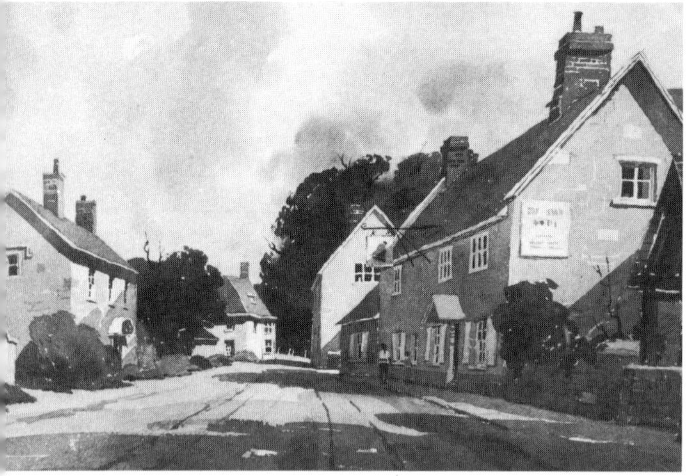
138 Wylye.

WYLYE

(colour plate 14, between pages 120 and 121)
31.5cm × 47.5cm ($12\frac{1}{2}$in. × $18\frac{3}{4}$in.)
Now I would like you to look at the colour reproduction of Wylye village. Having decided in my mind on the arrangement of the composition as just mentioned, I could start to draw the scene, using a B pencil on Arches paper. I usually find that it helps to draw in the road first with a village view and then build up on that. Having got the houses with roofs and chimneys well defined, I lightly outlined the tree groups and I was ready for painting.

Stage 1

I am not going to mention the exact size of brush I use as I think we have had enough variety of subjects by now for you to know what size I am using. However, I will mention size if it is something out of the usual.

Sky of course comes first and we had a really lively cloudy sky this day of strong sunlight. When clouds are moving about you can settle the sky pattern as you wish it to be, as I have said before. I rather wanted a good blue patch to the left so I mixed up my medium gray with Burnt Umber and Ultramarine and washed this over to right and left, leaving a big area of white in the centre. I then ran in some clear water over part of the white and dropped some Raw Sienna into the lower central area. Now I could use my Ultramarine rather strongly from the top of the paper downwards forming a nice white shaped cloud as I came down with the large brush and diluting the blue a little towards the bottom. Next I ran some more of this blue into the gray area on the left, giving formation to gray clouds. As everything became fairly dry I could paint the *dark* grey clouds on the right using the same gray mix, but adding Indian Red to make it a *warm* dark gray.

Now I mixed a quantity of brown-gray in the palette with Burnt Umber and Ultramarine and continued the sky wash down over the whole picture. This brownish colour would be suitable as the final colour of the road. I left one or two areas the white of the paper as this wash was applied, namely the left-hand little porch roof, the white house at the far end of the road and the white inn sign on the right. This was a convenient time for a mid-morning cup of coffee while the wash was allowed to dry out completely.

Stage 2

I now painted the house walls that were catching the sun a very light stone colour using Burnt Umber and Cobalt but not the house on the right immediately in front of the big tree mass; this house was a very light pink and I used a diluted Indian Red. When these were dry I painted the *shadow* walls of the houses. The inn shadow wall was a rather subtle stone gray and I used Cobalt and Light Red giving gray, but warmed it with Raw Sienna. I dropped the Raw Sienna in after applying the gray so that the yellow showed through. The low building beyond the inn, which was in shadow, was painted Burnt Sienna and Cobalt, but the pink house received a mixture of Indian Red and Cobalt; only a very narrow bit of shadow wall showed in acute perspective on this house. I carefully left all windows white at this stage.

Now roofs were painted with Burnt Sienna and Cobalt, some being made bluish-gray which were slate roofs and others of tile were brownish-gray.

And now the various brick chimneys were painted. Incidentally, most of the houses had stone walls but some were plastered and colour washed. If this had been in the Cotswolds the chimneys would have been in stone as well as the walls.

I used various mixes of Burnt Sienna, Cobalt and Indian Red for chimneys. Using a small brush, brick jointing could be indicated.

The right-hand low wall and lych-gate to the church were now painted with suitable grays and dark browns.

The road was given another light wash of Burnt Sienna and a little Cobalt.

Stage 3

The various trees, shrubs and grass were now tackled. At this time of year in mid-August the greens were a superb dark colour, but varying in tone from light to very dark. I first painted the big tree group in the centre and used Raw Sienna and Winsor Blue basically; at top right it was mostly all Raw Sienna, and then lower down it became more Winsor Blue and for the very lowest part next to the white house I added Burnt Umber which gave the *extremely* dark green that was required. The trees were kept wet all the time so that the different colours ran into each other, and while still damp I

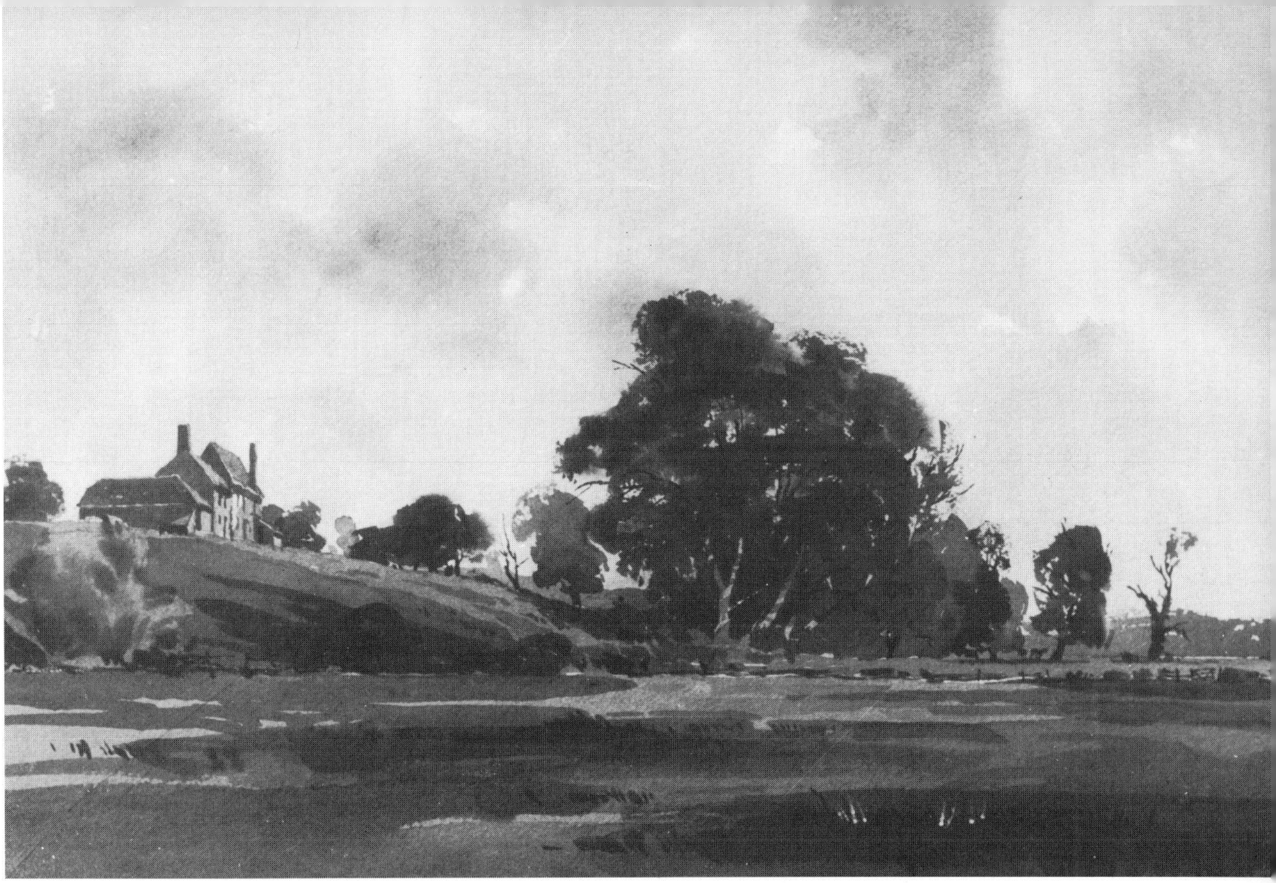

added the copper beech tree nosing its way over the top, using Rose Madder and Burnt Umber.

Where foliage comes against the skyline it is usually broken and you can see between leaves, and one can get this effect by using a stiff mix of colour and dragging the brush sideways.

Now the lower tree and shrubs to the left of the white house were painted, using the same dark green but dropping in neat Cadmium Yellow to mix with it at the left-hand bottom corner; this was for a bright green bush at this point. Next the bush near the lych-gate on the right was added, using the same greens again, with variations.

The grass verge on the left side of the road was a mixture of Cadmium Lemon, Winsor Blue and a touch of Indian Red. The latter is a very nice colour for toning down a green if it is too vivid. The gray-green bush against the house on the left was Raw Sienna and Ultramarine and the further away verges were variations of these two colours.

Some branches of the different tree groups were added while the greens were still damp. A small brush was of course used and Burnt Umber and a little Ultramarine gave the dark brown required.

Stage 4

The finishing items were now dealt with. Windows first, using the dark brown mixture just mentioned. Painting little glass rectangles and leaving glazing bars white can be a fiddling job, I prefer to use a rather *old* small brush which doesn't have too good a point to it, you can fill in a square shape rather easier with this.

After windows came the *cast* shadows under the roof eaves and shadows thrown slanting onto walls, and shadows in doorways and window openings. Most of this was done with Burnt Sienna, Cobalt and a small amount of Indian Red.

The cast shadows across the road from buildings or in the case of the foreground from trees, were painted with the three colours just mentioned, but with various mixes so that sometimes the blue shows quite clearly and sometimes the Sienna.

Finally, some wheel marks were painted on the road with a few brush strokes of light brown, the right-hand curb was painted with a darker brown and a few touches were given to the edges of the left-hand verges with dark brown.

Here and there on stone walls, some stone jointing was indicated and that completed the picture.

Quite a lot of colours were used, eleven in all – Cadmium Lemon, Cadmium Yellow, Raw Sienna, Burnt Sienna, Burnt Umber, Light Red, Indian Red, Rose Madder, Cobalt Blue, French Ultramarine and Winsor Blue.

139 Burcombe.

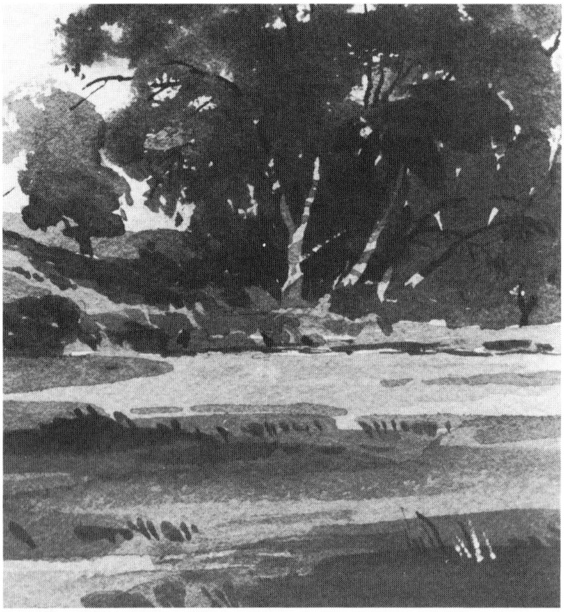

139 BURCOMBE
31.5cm × 47.5cm ($12\frac{1}{2}$in. × $18\frac{3}{4}$in.)
Motoring along from Dinton towards Salisbury you arrive at the village of Burcombe and turning right here you come to the River Nadder and a whole host of attractive river views and other good subjects. Several of us wanted to enter a field by the river but there was a very large flock of sheep all over it. At that moment the farmer came along with dogs and we saw a good demonstration of sheep being herded out into the road. The farmer kindly said we could go anywhere we liked in the field to paint.

I was rather taken with this group of trees and the farmhouse up on the hill.

The mid-morning sun was attractive, shining from right to left across the trees and catching some of the trunks. The picture detail (140) shows the treatment of

140 Burcombe, detail.

141 Above Teffont.

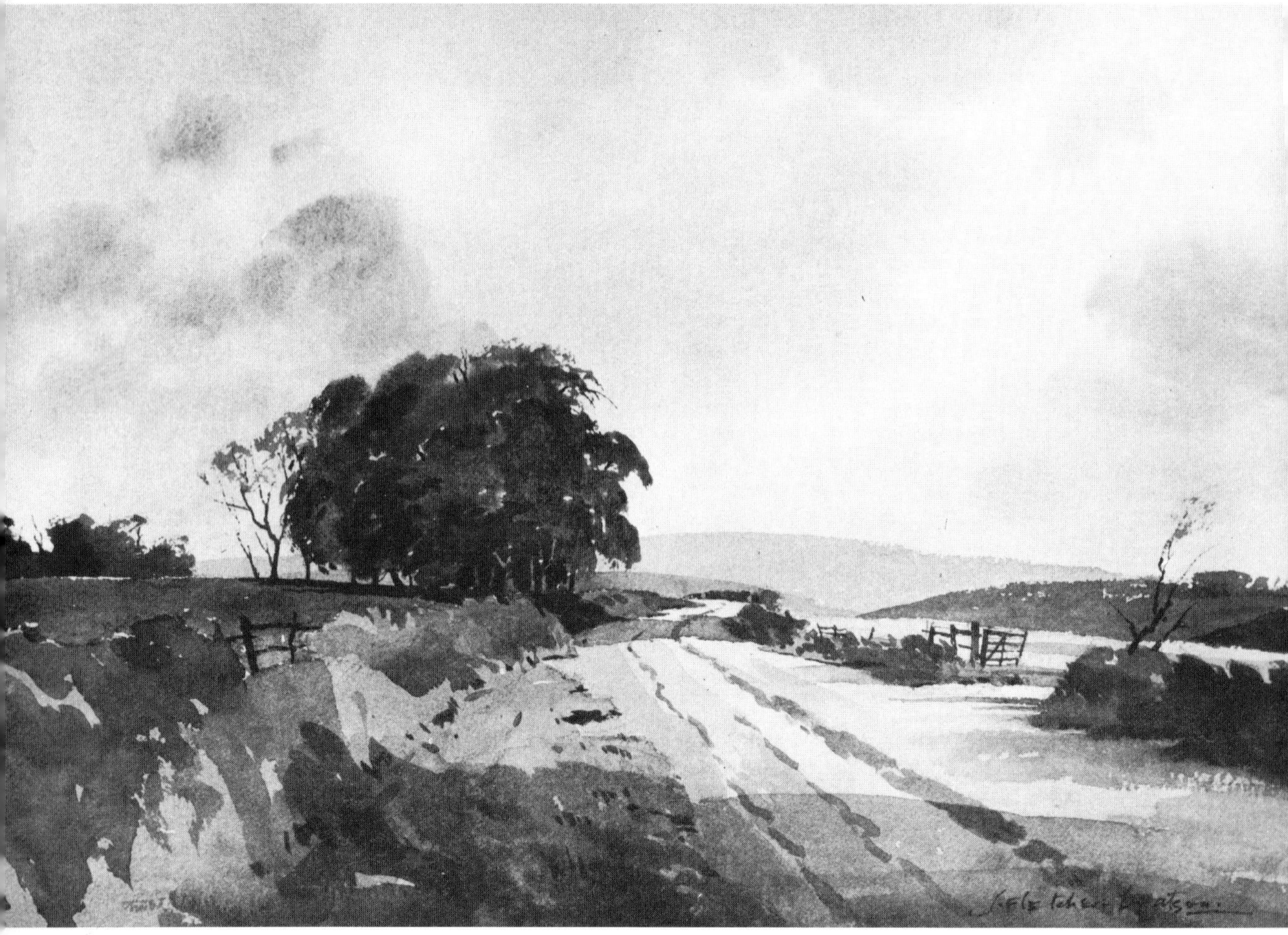

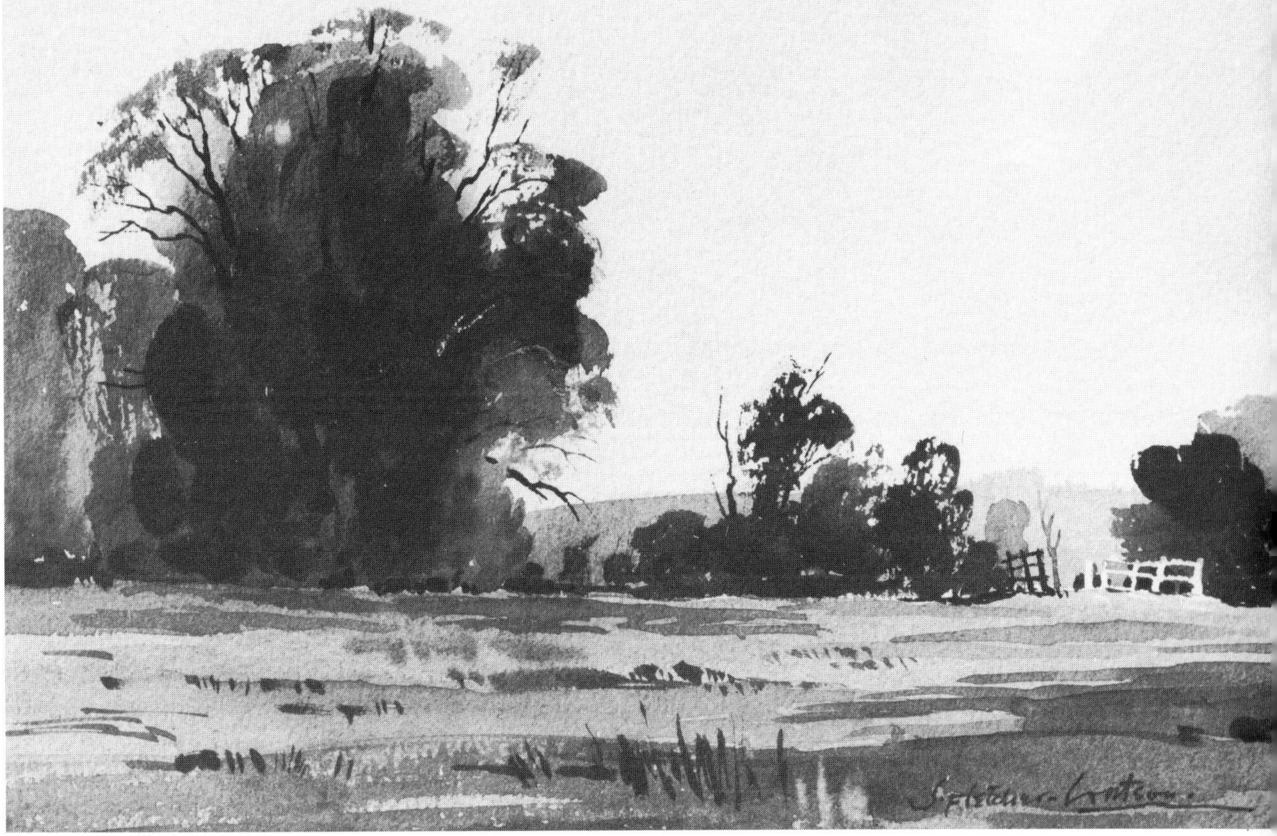

142 Summer trees, Wylye Valley.

these trunks. I first gave the whole tree group a wash of greenish-gray, the tree-trunk colour. After this had dried I got going with the greens of the foliage with different tones of dark yellow-green and brown-green and changed to a small brush for painting round the trunks, leaving them the light gray colour. Later, when all was dry, I put in the diagonal shadows across the trunks using a blue-gray mixture.

You will notice the outline of foliage against the sky is again painted with a broken intermittent wash as mentioned for the last picture (138). In addition to the dragged brush treatment, I made some of the foliage green *run* into the sky a little by adding clear water using a second brush. One of the low level thin branches is scratched out with a knife. This picture was painted on Whatman paper.

Whilst I was sitting in this spot, I noticed to my immediate left across the river a lovely view of the beautiful little church of Burcombe, standing on a rise in ground. Really very paintable. I made a mental note to come back and paint it another day.

141 ABOVE TEFFONT

31.5cm × 47.5cm (12½in. × 18¾in.)

Exploring one day a little to the west of Dinton, I passed through the village of Teffont Magna and went right-handed up a steep hill to a glorious high point overlooking Wylye Down and the river valley beyond. There was a narrow little-used side road and along this I found the view shown here.

It made an excellent composition with the lonely tree group and the open gate to the right. The left-hand field was dark brown and the right-hand one was golden stubble.

I used the same technique for tree trunks as for figure 139.

142 SUMMER TREES, WYLYE VALLEY

23.5cm × 37cm (9¾in. × 14½in.)

This small picture is a good example of making something out of nothing. We do not always have to seek out a great view or important focal point. Sometimes the most simple subjects can make delightful pictures.

Here all we have is a grass field, a dark tree group and the distant downs. This spot was just behind Wylye village and the light was attractive with long shadows and a pale blue-gray sky. What I like about Wiltshire is the untidiness of some of the farmland; no offence meant to the farmers, far from it. They are not cutting down their fences ruthlessly but leaving them high and ragged as in this case, where birds can nest and cattle can find shade.

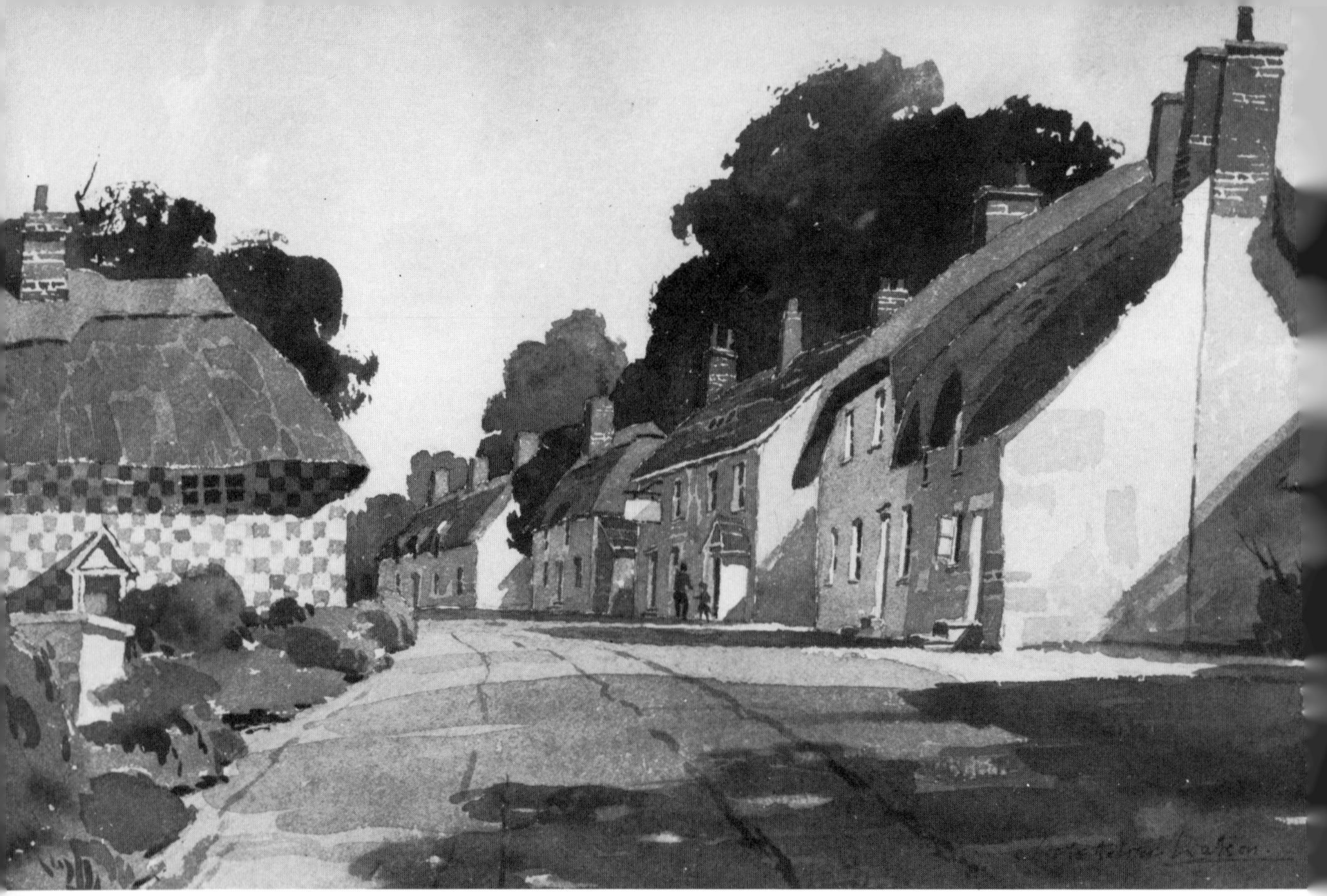

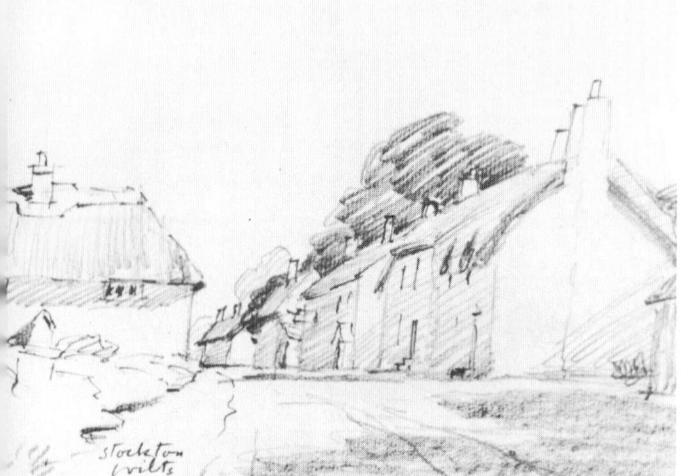

143 Stockton.

144 Stockton, preliminary sketch.

145 River Wylye, Great Wishford.

143 STOCKTON

31.5cm × 47.5cm ($12\frac{1}{2}$in. × $18\frac{3}{4}$in.)

At the beginning, I mentioned the sleepy old villages of Wiltshire and here is an example. There seemed to be no traffic, and people were sauntering down the middle of the village street with not a care in the world. We were a party of painters doing this subject and we were straggling into the road quite a lot but nobody seemed to mind.

It was mainly a thatched village and the cottage on the left had fascinating chequer-work walls with pink brick and square blocks of white chalk-stone. I would put it as late Elizabethan in date.

I made a quick preliminary sketch first shown at figure 144 (18cm × 25.5cm (7in. × 10in.)) using a 4B and Conte crayon for this. Here again we have big mature trees the same as in figure 138. They are a splendid back-up to cottage buildings with tall chimneys, and they help so much in giving dark tones to a picture. They also help in giving an interesting sky shape. Always pay special attention to the shape of sky you are going to have in a landscape.

The general colouring of this subject was most pleasing with dark gray-brown thatched roofs and warm yellow stone walls. There is always a convenient pub in the centre of these delightful villages!

145 RIVER WYLYE, GREAT WISHFORD
31.5cm × 47.5cm ($12\frac{1}{2}$in. × $18\frac{3}{4}$in.)
There are numerous rivers in this part of Wiltshire and lots of paintable views which make excellent subjects for water-colour.

This view of the Wylye was from the east bank looking upstream; it is a slow moving river giving good reflections.

You will note the dark tone tree group has reflections a little lighter and the sky reflection is a very little darker in tone than the sky itself. The water was kept fluid during painting so that reflections could be slightly blurred, which gave the feeling of movement.

RIVER AVON, MIDDLE WOODFORD
(colour plate 15, between pages 120 and 121)
31.5cm × 47.5cm ($12\frac{1}{2}$in. × $18\frac{3}{4}$in.)
I will next give you a detailed description of painting a river scene and the colour plate of the Avon river at Middle Woodford is a lovely subject. This was a demonstration painting for the Dinton course and it was a perfect place for everyone to sit along the river bank. Later on people did their own paintings.

This was very much an all green picture and it was important to sort out the tone values carefully. The monochrome picture (146) shows how the main dark mass was on the left and smaller dark areas on the right behind the light tree trunk. In-between tones of shadows were on the foreground grass and a really light tone for the background belt of trees in a gray-blue colour.

Stage 1
I chose the rough surface Arches paper, as this texture would help in painting the tree foliage.

Not a lot of drawing with a pencil was required but I did want the shape of the river drawn in with the far bank about one third up from the bottom of the paper. The big tree on the left was drawn in rough outline only and the several tree shapes on the right were pencilled in with the leaning trunks which were a nice part of the composition.

I wetted the upper half of the paper for the sky and then ran in gray clouds using Burnt Umber and Ultramarine. The blue sky area was diluted Ultramarine. I pulled the gray wash down over the whole sheet of paper including the water area, leaving one or two white bits and a touch of blue for cloud reflections.

Next came a wash of blue-gray for the distant line of trees, using Ultramarine and Light Red with a No. 12 brush.

Stage 2
All was allowed to dry while we had cups of coffee and a gossip. It was late morning and the sun was shining

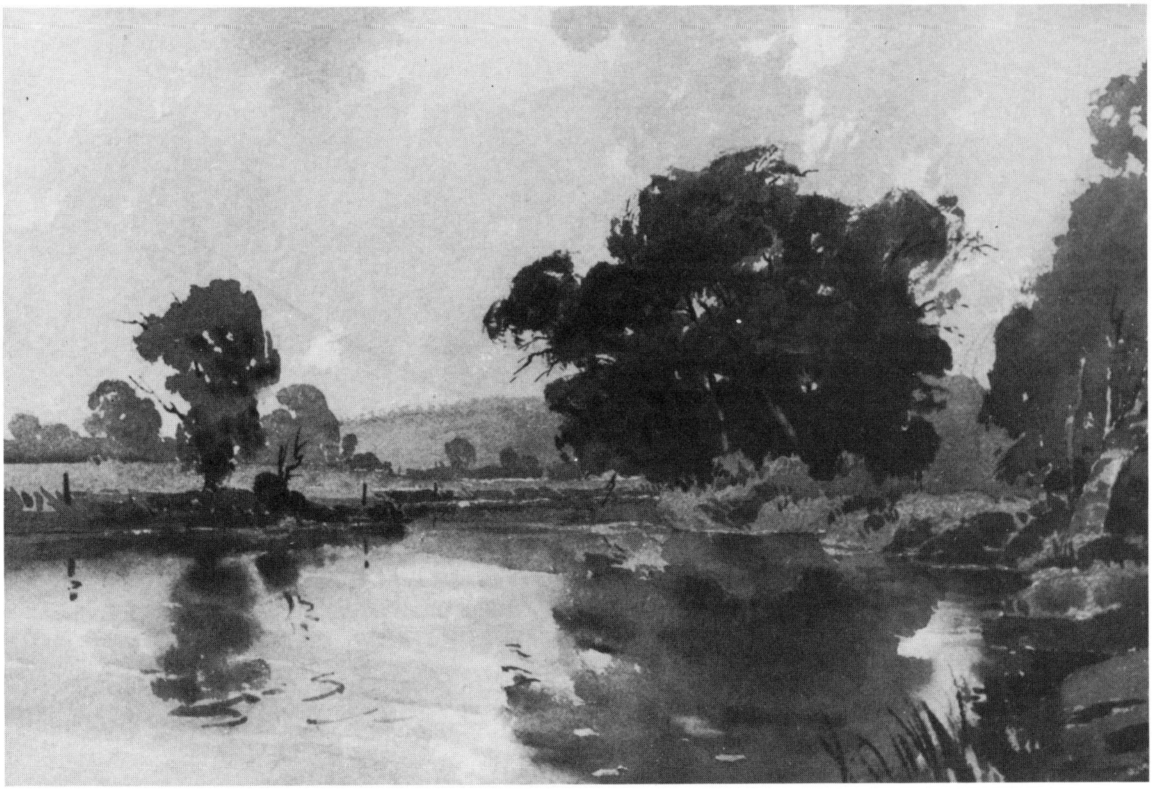

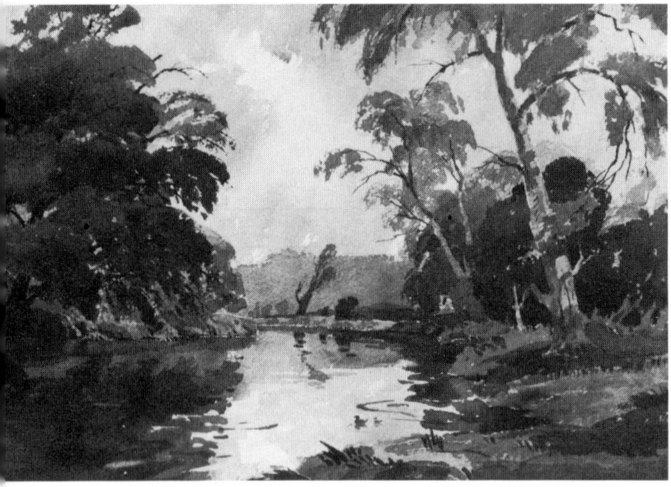

146 River Avon, Middle Woodford.

from the right side and filtering through the trees.

I now mixed quite a lot of light green so that I could get the tree masses and grass river banks toned in for a start. I used mostly Raw Sienna with a little Winsor Blue giving a good yellow-green, and with a large brush I covered all the trees and grass areas with this wash. While it was still wet I painted the big left-hand tree with dark green using Burnt Umber and Winsor Blue. The lighter green trees behind were allowed to show through in places. While this was still wet I ran in a few darker groups of foliage that were overhanging the water with a smaller No. 9 brush. Then I dropped in a yellowish part of the tree low down by adding some Cadmium Yellow to the existing wash and letting it run and mix in. Now, quickly, while the tree was still damp, I mixed a dark brown with Burnt Umber and Ultramarine and with a small brush painted in tree trunk and branches. It is important that the branches are allowed to merge with the green.

I could now give some attention to the various right-hand trees. The far leaning tree was a brownish-green using Burnt Sienna and Winsor Blue not too strong in tone. Then lower down and further back the trees were Raw Sienna and Winsor Blue. They were dark enough to show up the trunks of the far leaning tree.

Now the big foreground tree was painted, again with Burnt Sienna and Winsor Blue, rather a stronger mix with a touch of Raw Sienna added. And next some really dark green for the low trees behind the very big foreground trunk; these were painted with Burnt Umber and Winsor Blue. I painted carefully round the light gray trunk, which was the original wash colour, and I left a light coloured sapling sticking up in the background. This dark green was lightened a little as it was painted towards the right side.

The trunk of the big tree was touched with a little light Burnt Umber and branches were painted with a small brush and a mixture of Burnt Umber and Cobalt. Also, the branches of the farther back leaning tree were painted.

The river banks were now painted, they were various shades of light greens and darker greens. I used Raw Sienna and Cobalt for the lights and Raw Sienna and Winsor Blue for the darks. Some very bright green grass on the foreground bank on the right was Cadmium Lemon and a touch of Winsor Blue. Some strong tree shadows fell across the foreground bank which were Raw Sienna, Winsor Blue and a little Burnt Sienna.

The far distant bank and field and bushes were painted with light washes of Raw Sienna and Cobalt, making the mixture stronger for the bushes. The old leaning willow tree was also painted at this time, with the same colours.

Stage 3

Now at last we could paint the water. First, I damped the water area as I wanted a *slightly* blurred effect to reflections but not too much. Then I painted the reflection of the distant tree belt using the same colour mix of blue-gray. Now I painted the green river bank reflection on the left and next the big tree reflections, using very much the same greens as for the actual tree but half a tone lighter. As the wash was brought down to the bottom of the paper the edge of the reflection wash was opened up to indicate ripples on the water. I used a No. 9 brush for this work.

The right-hand reflections were next dealt with. These were approximately the same green as the trees they reflected but with some Ultramarine added to give a bluish tinge. Reflections of the far-off leaning tree and small bush were added and this completed the water.

There were several ducks swimming about with young ones and I put in a couple of these to give the right atmosphere. I also touched up some of the foreground grasses with a few strong green brush strokes. A shadow was painted on the ground behind the near-by big leaning tree, using Burnt Sienna and Cobalt.

The painting of this fairly complicated picture in actual fact went quite smoothly, and the process of dealing with different statements of wash over wash followed systematically. The whole time I was simplifying fussy groups of foliage and assessing tone values with half closed eyes, to arrive at a homogeneous result in the end.

Colours used were as follows – Cadmium Lemon, Cadmium Yellow, Raw Sienna, Burnt Sienna, Burnt Umber, Light Red, Cobalt Blue, French Ultramarine and Winsor Blue.

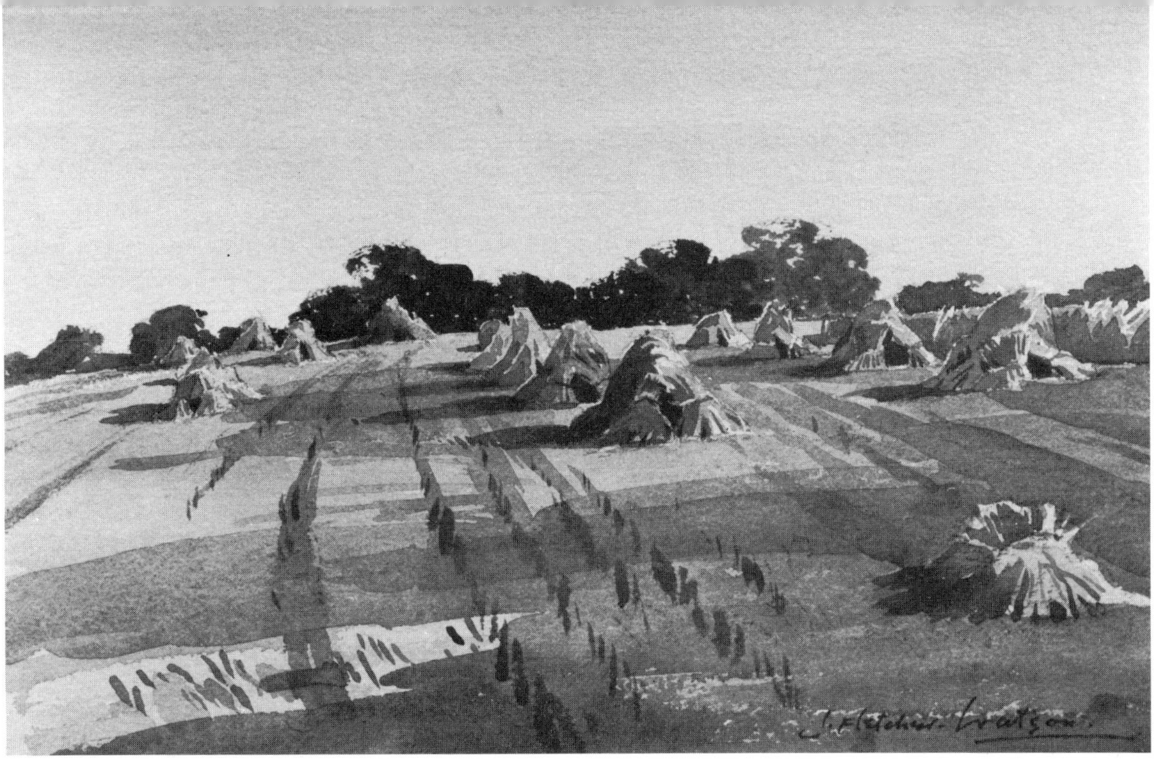

147 Stooks at Chilmark.

147 STOOKS AT CHILMARK

24cm × 35.5cm ($9\frac{1}{2}$in. × 14in.)

One day a report came in that a local farmer had actually piled his newly reaped corn into *stooks*. I was mad keen to see this rare event and some of us went rushing off to find the farm which was near the village of Chilmark. It was a beautiful sloping field and farm workers were already carting the corn away. It was late afternoon and we were told that a few stooks would be left till the following day so we found ourselves suitable viewing points and got to work straight away.

It was a beautiful sight and one felt that here was the old England that David Cox and Peter De Wint had painted 170 odd years ago.

The last time I had painted stooks was some twenty years ago in Scotland and so I was not very familiar with the necessary technique.

I drew one or two of the stooks carefully showing each of the sheaves which were tied together and propped up against each other, looking rather like an Indian wigwam with dark shadows in the middle. They made good lines of perspective as they went away towards the end of the field decreasing in size as they went. The lines of stubble helped the perspective also.

If you ever see a field of stooks, don't miss the chance of making a painting; they make a delightful picture.

148 SALISBURY CATHEDRAL, FROM THE WEST

31.5cm × 47.5cm ($12\frac{1}{2}$in. × $18\frac{3}{4}$in.)

What amazed me about this distant view of Salisbury Cathedral was that it was *still possible* to get such a view when most of our old towns and cities are so surrounded with modern suburbs. There is a housing estate on this west side but fortunately it is hidden in the trees. Long may this open view with lovely big fields of cultivation be preserved. If you want to find this view point you must go to the small village of Netherhampton and it is not far from there.

With this morning picture the sun was shining from the right glinting on the white lead roofs of the cathedral. It was a breezy day of wonderful passing clouds which were casting interesting shadows on the stubble field.

Several other views could be obtained by going closer to the Cathedral and there are also good views of it to be had in the city itself close to an old water mill.

One final word about the foreground. I used my flat $\frac{1}{2}$in. brush for some of the upstanding stubble and grass; this type of brush is very handy for obtaining very thin lines. I mentioned this brush in Chapter 1. I also have a $\frac{1}{4}$in. flat brush which can be very useful.

149 STORM AT STONEHENGE

28cm × 61cm (11in. × 24in.)

I painted this picture some years ago before there was any fence round Stonehenge. Now of course there is a high wire fence all round and car parks and lavatories and crowds of visitors. But it is still possible to find some sort of view for a painting I think.

It is the most dramatic subject and amazing to think that it is about 4000 years old. I made a pencil and wash

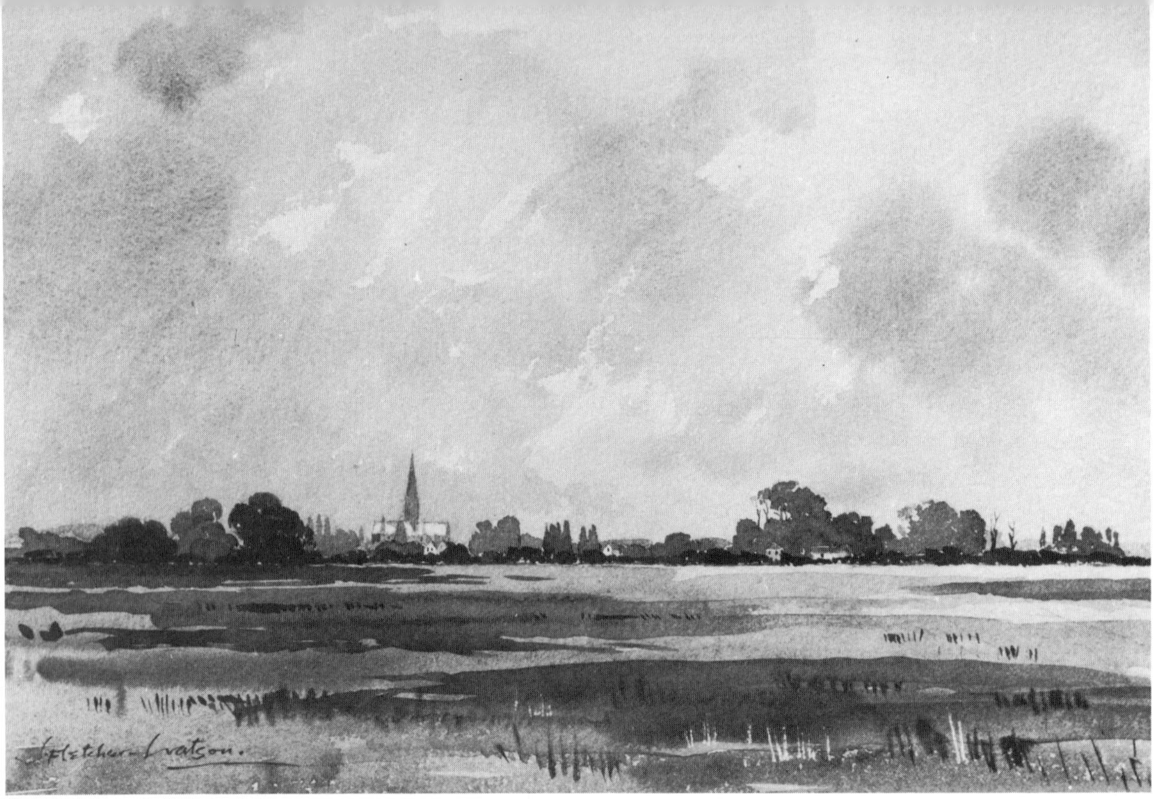

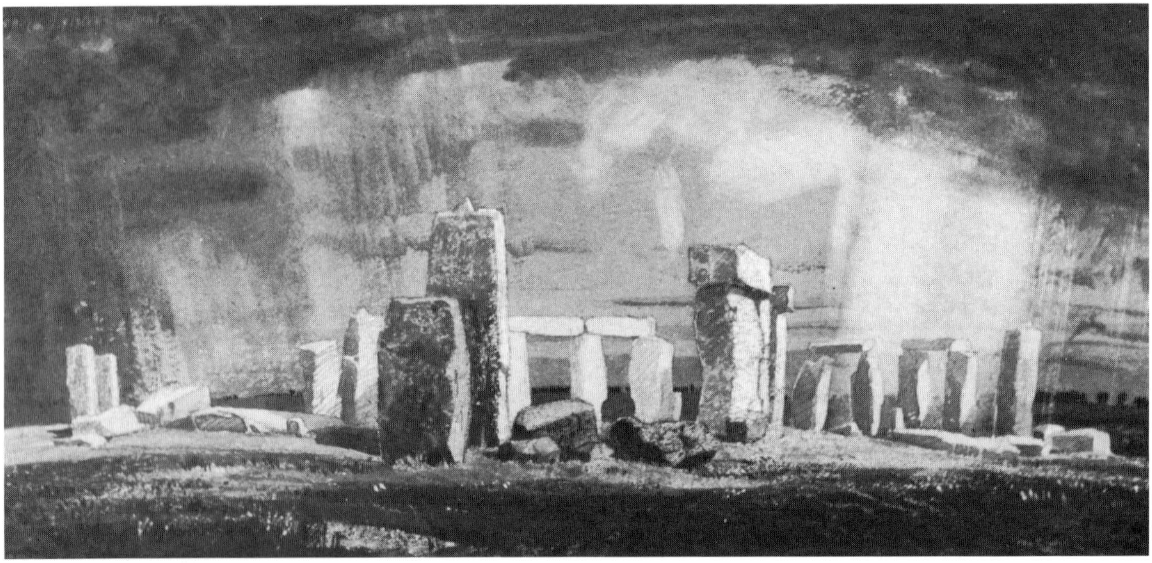

148 Salisbury Cathedral, from the west.

149 Storm at Stonehenge.

drawing on the spot and then did a larger water-colour in the studio giving it a dramatic sky of rain and shafts of sunlight.

I was particularly interested in the texture of the massive great stones and this was indicated by dry brush-loads of colour dragged over the paper.

Wiltshire has much to offer the painter and Stonehenge is one of the most ancient prehistoric sites in Britain and certainly the most dramatic.

I have only dealt with a quite small district of Wiltshire, mainly around the Wylye Valley, and I hope I have been able to show you what an attractive range of subjects there are in this part of the county. Wiltshire is a big county and there are many exciting views to be found on Salisbury Plain and further north near Marlborough and Malmesbury, so try and find a chance to explore this part of England if you don't already know it.

8 Painting in London

One of the difficulties of painting in London is the traffic problem. I am always particularly thrilled with the London parks and the Regency houses that are near to so many of them. There is a magic about these places with their great mature plane trees and somehow one is able to forget the traffic.

150 QUEEN'S GATE, KENSINGTON GARDENS

29cm × 49cm (11½in. × 19½in.)

Here we have a delightful subject which includes a lovely little Regency lodge with iron railings and surrounded by big trees. There are the massive wrought iron entrance gates into Kensington Gardens on the left with graceful stone piers surmounted by bronze sculpture and these gates give a useful foreground feature to the composition.

I sat peacefully painting this in August when the trees had turned their dark colours, the traffic was only a muffled roar in the distance and no cars were allowed to enter the park at this point.

The method of painting consisted of a careful pencil drawing of the lodge first and the road-line and railings, and then the iron gates and a rough outline for trees.

The background tree washes were then put in, leaving the lodge absolutely white. Then followed the big tree trunks and foliage and next some gray-brown washes on the road and then the gates and piers. Now the lodge could be painted, drawing in architectural detail with a small brush and following this with the shadows cast from the porch etc.

Finally some darks were added in the background trees and the foreground shadows were laid in.

150 Queen's Gate, Kensington Gardens.

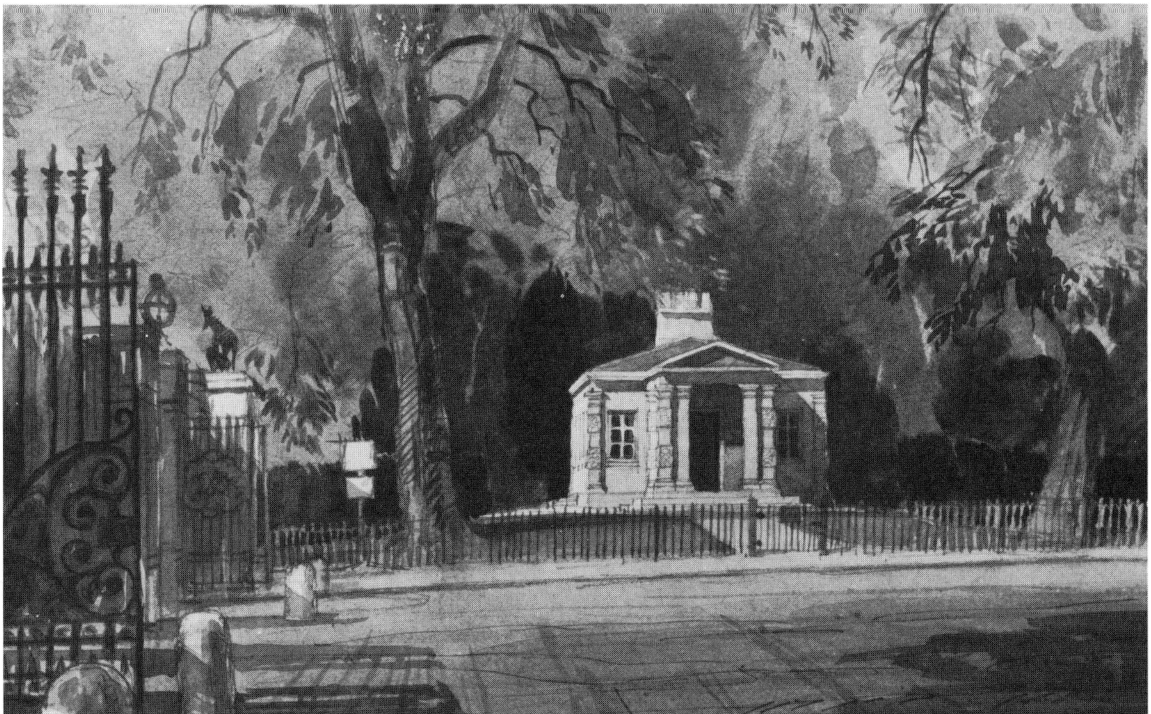

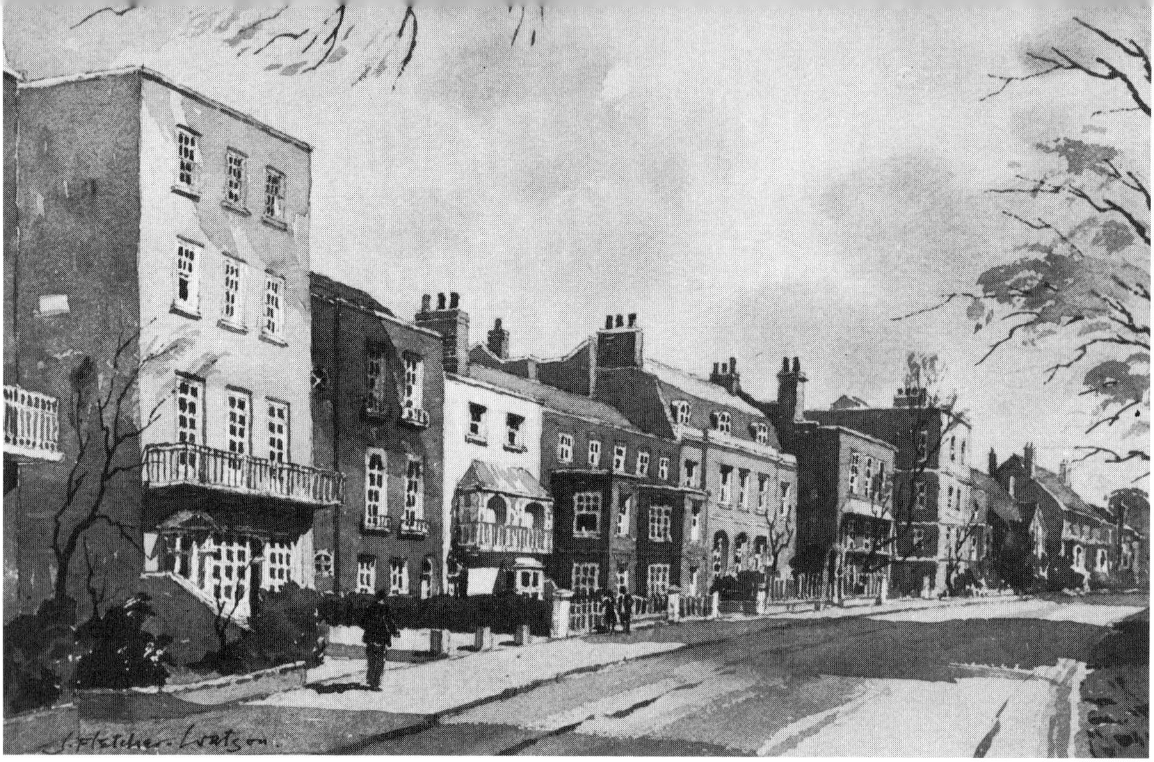

151 Kew Green.

151 KEW GREEN

Kew was originally a nice little village outside London, but now as everyone knows it is just a part of great big London town. But it retains its eighteenth-century village atmosphere as these beautiful Georgian houses face directly onto Kew Green and there is an openness and charm of character about it. It is also a very quiet spot and it seems to be cut off from London noise.

This view needed some careful drawing to get the perspective right and all the windows and chimneys and railings and so on. It really took me about an hour before I could start to paint.

Having first dealt with the sky, I washed the buildings in with light yellows, reds and browns according to the different brick colours. Roofs were all gray slate. Then came darker shades on the shadow sides of walls and chimneys and then bright red brick arches to windows and the window details showing glazing. Now the hedges and railings were painted and shadows to various balconies and verandahs and cornices.

Later the road and footpath edge and people and their shadows were painted, and the tree shadows across the road and the trees themselves. It was April and tree foliage had not appeared yet.

With these architectural subjects all you need is a good system of building up washes gradually and systematically and you will not find it difficult. Remember to simplify detail as it goes into the distance.

I was approached by two traffic wardens halfway through the painting, as I was sitting in the car to paint and I was rather badly parked. I was full of foreboding and thought I was going to be moved on or even fined. But to my great surprise all they wanted to do was to see what I was doing and have a chat about painting!

NEW END SQUARE, HAMPSTEAD

(colour plate 16, between pages 120 and 121)
23.5cm × 35.5cm ($9\frac{1}{4}$in. × 14in.)

Now let us move a little north of the centre of London to Hampstead which again was a separate village in its early days. It is a most attractive part of London with its eighteenth- and nineteenth-century squares and narrow streets. It is built on a steep hill and there are many big trees growing in its streets and gardens which are a great help to the painter when composing a subject.

Colour plate 16 shows a delightful group of old houses, a mixture of Regency and Victorian buildings and a fascinating mixture of different building materials and colours.

These houses form part of New End Square right in the heart of Hampstead, but amazingly there are areas of rough grass and big forest trees all over the place which give a unique character to the scene.

I will give you details of how this unusual little London view was painted.

I chose white Whatman paper 'Not' surface and 200lb weight, and a firm pencil drawing was first made with a B pencil. Strong pencil-work does not matter when you are going to use quite strong watercolour as the pencil becomes obscured and disappears. The

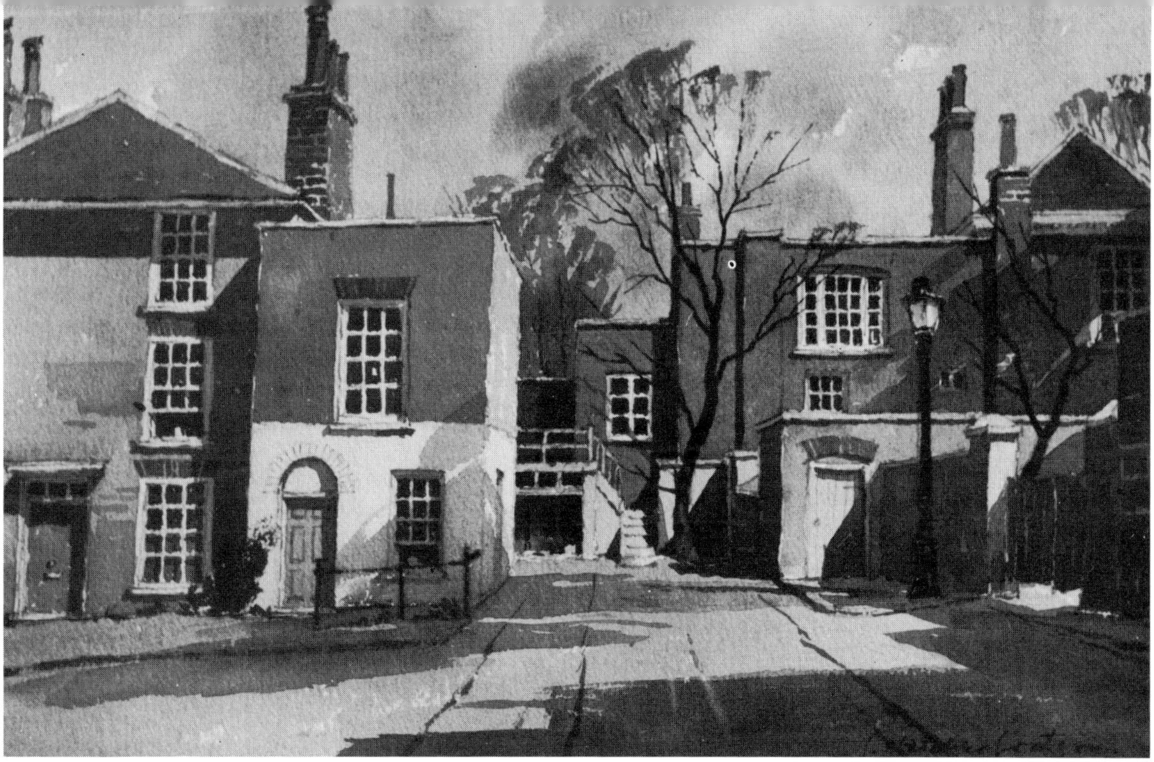

152 Mount Square, Hampstead.

composition was important; the large tree was in a happy position to the left and the block of houses kept to the right of centre which made for a good balance.

Having drawn in the ground-line and houses and big tree I could now get to work with painting.

Stage 1

We had a pleasant sky with light gray clouds and areas of blue. I wetted the paper and ran in some Cobalt Blue and Light Red for the gray and then let in some pure Cobalt in the central area, allowing this to run into the gray. I touched in a little Raw Sienna to the lower white clouds. Then I continued the gray wash down over all the paper but leaving out items of white on buildings.

This process did not take long; remember it was a smaller picture than my usual size. I waited for it all to dry out before starting the next stage.

Stage 2

The first item was *background trees*. I used Burnt Sienna and Cobalt, varying the mixture from gray-brown at the tops of trees to strong blue-brown at the bottom.

Allowing this to dry I then gave some washes to houses: Burnt Sienna and Cobalt again for the brown roof of the far house on the left, and the same colour for the gable wall and chimney of the left-hand house of the three in a group.

Then very pale gray for the upper part of the right-hand house, using Cobalt and Light Red. Now the rather strong orange for the centre house using Burnt Sienna and Raw Sienna and carefully painting round the windows. I was using a No. 7 brush for all this house work.

The far-back little house on the right had a pink wall so I used a touch of Rose Madder with Raw Sienna and the roof was a diluted Burnt Sienna and Cobalt.

The roofs of the centre and right-hand house were a strong mixture of Burnt Umber and Ultramarine. The red chimney consisted of Light Red and a touch of Cobalt, using a No. 3 brush so that brickwork could be indicated. My *old* brush was used with a blunted point.

Gray garden walls were put in the same colour as the left-hand house gray, but a touch of Light Red added. I carefully painted round the light stem of the lamp-post against the garden wall.

I wanted to have the windows painted now before going on to the next stage. Using my small stumpy brush I mixed Burnt Sienna and Ultramarine and completed the middle and right-hand house windows. It always helps to make one window open, even if it is not open at the time; it makes a house seem occupied. The extreme left-hand and extreme right-hand houses had their windows painted also with a lighter tone of the same colour. You will note the technique of indicating curtains in the right-hand bay-window house. Glazing bars are kept white over the dark central space and dark over the light curtains at the side. The green door was painted at this time with Cadmium Lemon and Winsor Blue to give a nice bright colour.

I could have a pause now to think about the next stage.

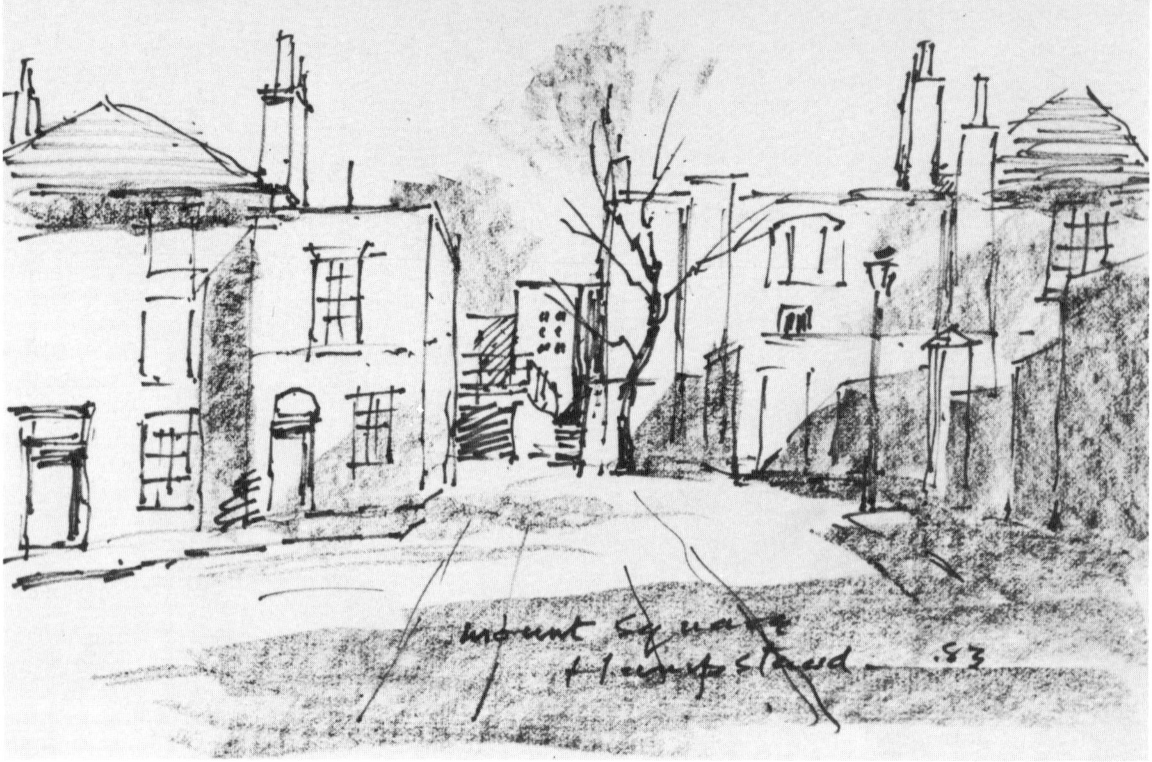

153 Mount Square, preliminary sketch.

Stage 3

The first item was to establish the foreground tone and the strength of the big tree before assessing the shadows on houses and ground. I mixed a good grass colour which was a brownish-green; being early April there was no new growth yet. I used mostly strong Raw Sienna and a little Winsor Blue and less still of Burnt Sienna. This wash went all over the ground and while it was still wet I put in the dark shrubs on the extreme right and extreme left. These were mixtures of Burnt Umber and Winsor Blue.

Next the big tree whose lower trunk was a light colour and this had been left light by carefully painting round when dealing with the wall behind. I used Burnt Umber and Winsor Blue again for the upper part of the trunk and branches, mixing it a brownish colour to start with as I worked up from the bottom, changing to a very dark blue-brown as I got higher, and making the paint thick and *dragging* the brush for some of the branches. I used a No. 7 brush changing to No. 1 for the smaller branches. I now used the No. 9 brush and flicked over some light brown areas at the top of the tree indicating thick twiggy groups. I mixed Burnt Umber and Cobalt for this.

I next painted the two smaller further back trees, one each side of the big one, using similar colours and the same method but smaller brushes.

Now I could put on some shadows. Under the eaves of the right-hand white house I used Cobalt and Light Red carefully jumping the shadow up and down over the shutters and with a smaller brush shadows were painted at the window heads. The right-hand wall of the projecting bay was painted a light tone of gray.

The centre house received various thin shadows for window cornices etc., using Burnt Sienna and Cobalt, and a strong one for the porch making it dark green on the actual door.

Cobalt and Light Red worked all right for the little house shadow on the extreme right over roof and wall and also for the far left house. Some tree shadows were falling on the centre group left-hand house, and these were again Cobalt and Light Red.

The lamp-post was painted with gray lines and a very small brush, and so also was the left-hand Regency porch of the left-hand house.

All that remained now was the foreground grass shadow; this consisted of strong Raw Sienna and a little Winsor Blue and as I applied it I added clear water to the right so that the wash would merge and fade off. A few strong touches of this colour were put on with a small brush indicating grass texture here and there – but remember not too much of this so as to make it fussy – then the picture was finished.

I was working quite rapidly on this picture as I like doing whenever possible, and although the description has been fairly lengthy, the whole painting only took just over two hours.

The colours used were Cadmium Lemon, Raw Sienna, Burnt Sienna, Burnt Umber, Light Red, Rose Madder, Cobalt Blue, French Ultramarine and Winsor Blue.

152 MOUNT SQUARE, HAMPSTEAD

23.5cm × 35.5cm ($9\frac{1}{4}$in. × 14in.)

Before I leave Hampstead I would like you to look at a smaller square (152). On this morning I found a good little patch of sun to sit in and there was not a sign or sound of traffic although there was plenty of it only a few hundred yards away.

I felt the need to make a rough sketch first to see what the composition looked like and figure 153 (18cm × 25.5cm (7in. × 10in.)) shows the drawing done with felt pen and Conte crayon. It grouped rather well with the bare tree in the centre and the shadows were good, always an important consideration with architectural subjects.

There was a quaint mixture of dignified Georgian and untidy backyard feeling which appealed to me. The colouring was a nice harmony of red and brown brickwork with gray slate roof on the left and dark brown roof on the right and the odd white wall and white sash windows gave a sparkle to the subject. You will notice I have put another open window in on the left-hand house.

The presence of trees peeping over buildings was a great asset. These are some of the items you want to look for when choosing an architectural subject groupings of buildings, roofs and chimneys cutting into the sky-line, tones of darks and lights where the shadows fall, and if possible a subject with some trees to break up the hard lines.

Hampstead and Highgate are full of good subjects and I can assure you that a stay of a week in this area would be well rewarded.

154 THE ROUND POND, KENSINGTON GARDENS

28cm × 58cm (11in. × 23in.)

Now back to Kensington Gardens for my last picture of this chapter. This was a later afternoon view when the sun was going down and all the nannies and prams and the children had gone home to tea. All the kite flying had ceased and the toy sailing boats had left the Round Pond bare again. All we had was the silhouette of Kensington Palace and the church spire and the trees with some reflections in the pond – a peaceful scene which made an intriguing long thin picture. The sky had pale Winsor Blue and gray in it, and the trees and grass were fast becoming a dull gray-green in the fading light. The water seemed to be the brightest thing left, reflecting the sky.

And so we come to the end of this short selection of London views. There are so many London subjects that I want to paint and sadly there are so many views that have gone for ever due to wartime bombing and recent re-building. Views in the old City of London and views along the Thames. But there are still plenty left and it is just a question of finding a place to stand or sit and paint; with London traffic being what it is, this is not always easy.

154 The Round Pond, Kensington Gardens.

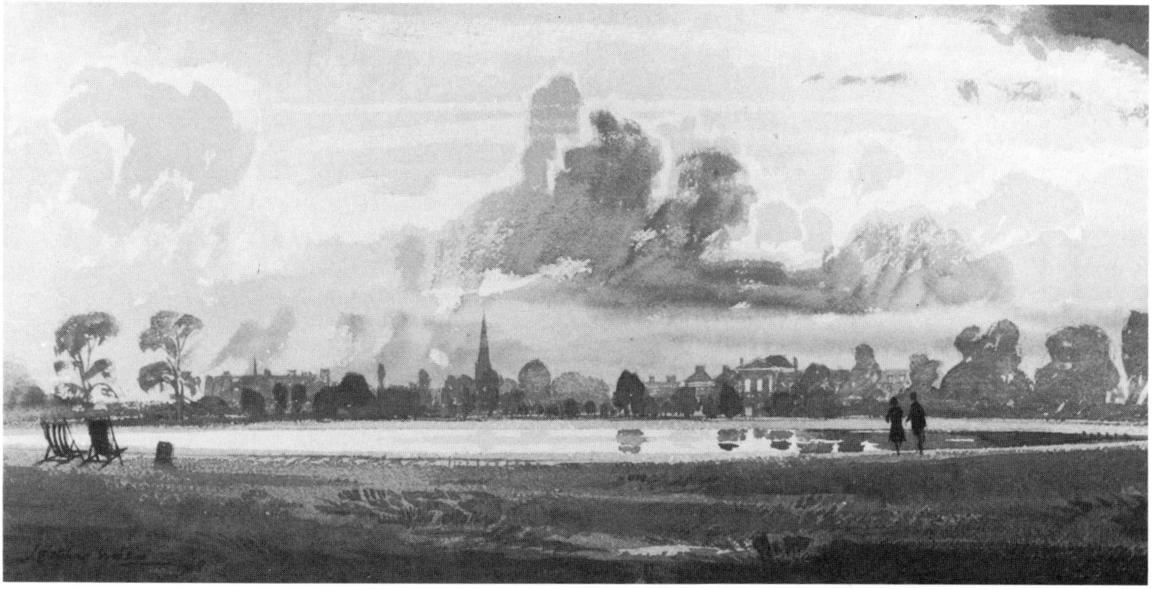

9 Painting in other places

Having come thus far in this book with you, I look back at the chapters and the places we have visited and wonder if I have fulfilled my original purpose of wanting to help watercolour painters with 'how to do it' and 'where to do it' sufficiently well. Of course one can go on endlessly finding new places and new problems to solve, but this book does not set out to give a solution for every painting problem that may arise, how could it? But I do feel that there are still one or two gaps which ought to be filled, giving perhaps just one or two more ideas on technique and method. So let us look together at the next six pictures and see if some final points emerge.

155 Lincoln Cathedral, from the south.

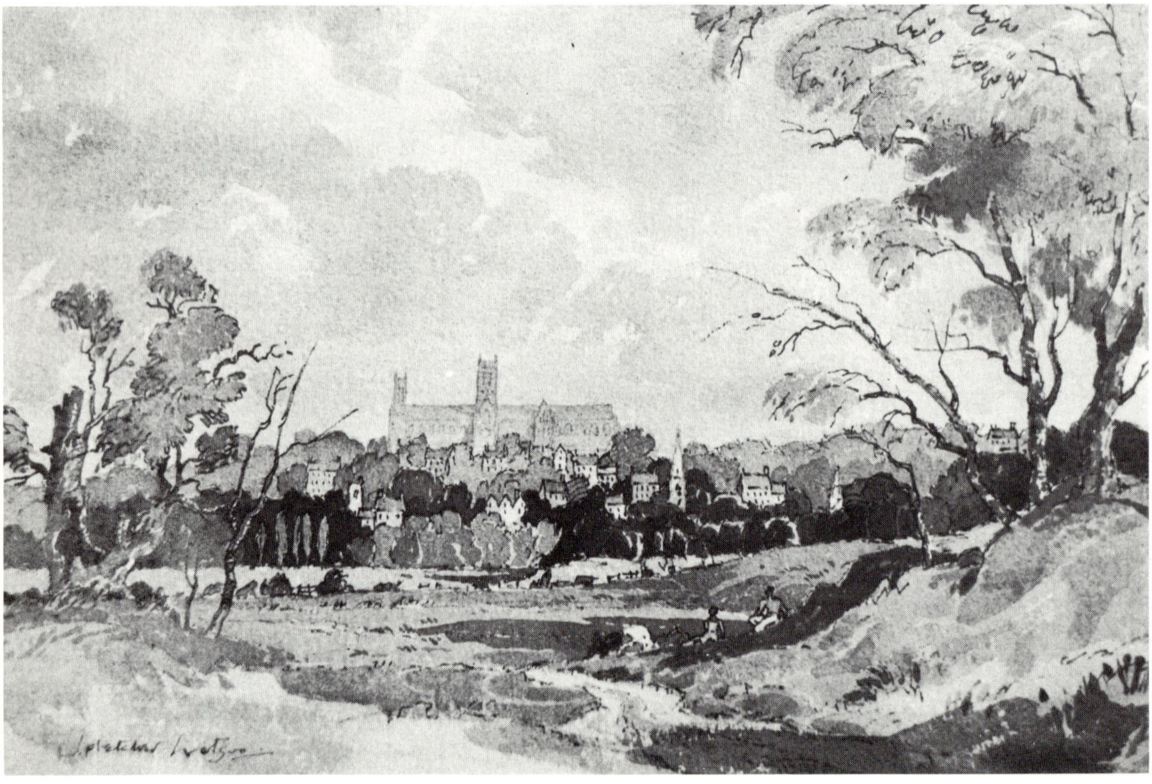

155 LINCOLN CATHEDRAL, FROM THE SOUTH

31cm × 47cm ($12\frac{1}{4}$in. × $18\frac{1}{2}$in.)

Lincoln Cathedral stands on the top of a hill with the city clustering round it inter-mixed with many trees and the whole group makes a magnificent composition, as good as any in England. This is De Wint country, and many a painting was made by Peter de Wint with a distant view of the cathedral.

When I first saw this view I had a great desire to make it in *pen* and water-colour, and what was better still I decided to use *toned* paper. I gave a piece of 300lb Arches paper a wash of light Burnt Umber and when dry this became a very nice piece of toned paper. I have mentioned toned paper before but for a rather different type of subject.

I used a brown mixture of watercolour for the pen-

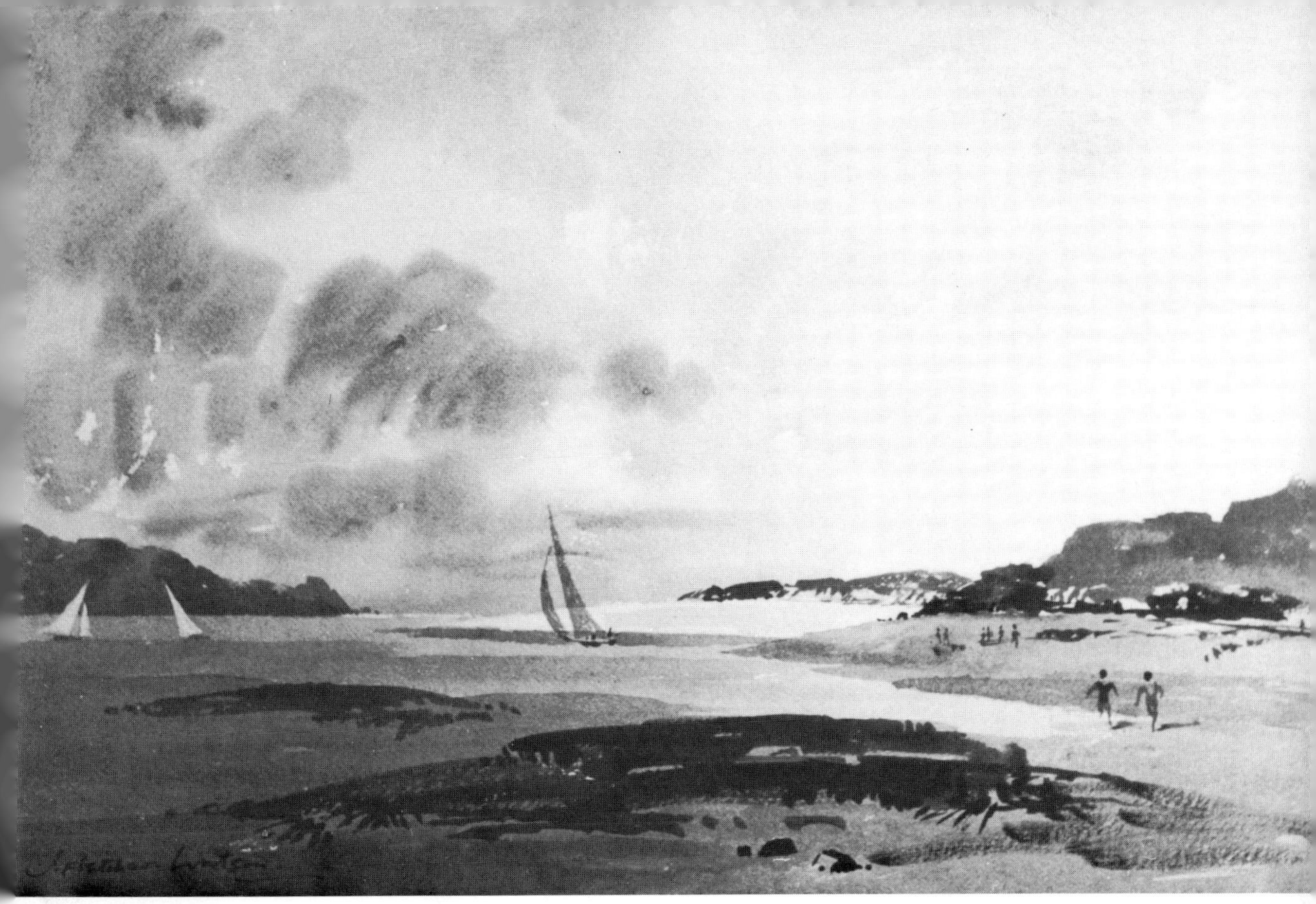

156 Rock, Cornwall.

work, Burnt Umber and French Ultramarine; this gives a good sepia colour. I prefer not to use ink out of a bottle in case it fades and I have known it do this rather badly.

I left the cathedral itself and the far trees in pencil outline and started to use pen-work on the trees and houses down the hill, gradually working towards the foreground and ending up with the old broken tree on the left and the younger trees on the right.

I could now wash in the sky using normal grays and blues on this brown coloured paper. Then light washes were put on the cathedral and surrounding trees of green-browns and yellows; the time of year was autumn. The various foreground colours were gradually handled and the middle distant trees darkened. Finally, the foreground trees were painted with strong Burnt Siennas and Raw Siennas and foreground shadows were added to complete the work.

The result on this toned paper was very mellow and pleasing and I do again recommend you try this sometime. There is something that can be very attractive about a pen and watercolour picture.

156 ROCK, CORNWALL

31.5cm × 47cm ($12\frac{1}{2}$in. × $18\frac{1}{2}$in.)

I was staying at the Cornish fishing village of Rock one August with my family and the estuary here gave many very paintable subjects. This picture caught the tide half in, revealing some lovely sandy bays and rocks. This was painted by the 'direct' method, in other words practically no pencil work. I did just touch in with a B pencil the horizon and the white spit of sand in the centre. Otherwise I painted the whole thing with brush only and painted quickly so as not to loose the shapes of the beaches with the in-coming tide.

I used Whatman paper as this would lend itself well to the glaring light-toned beaches and the white sails of boats. The two white boats on the left had in fact had their sails pencilled in first.

The far-off headlands were drawn with quick strokes of the brush well loaded with colour and changing brush sizes according to the size of the object being painted. Quite a large brush with a good point was used for the foreground rocks and seaweed. The figures were painted in at the end with a small brush, and they gave scale and distance. The larger sailing boat just to the left of centre was carefully judged as regards its position and angle to give a nice balance to the composition. A feature like this can make or mar a picture.

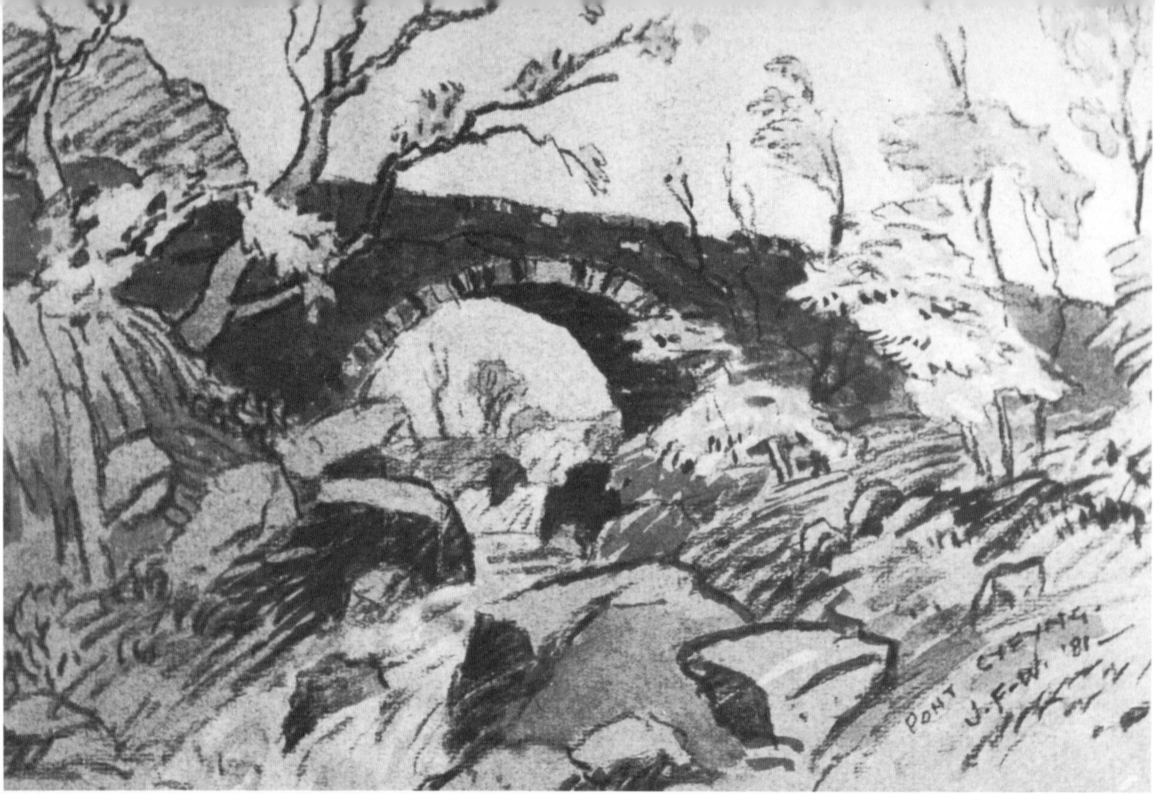

157 Pont Cyfyng, Capel Curig, North Wales.

157 PONT CYFYNG, CAPEL CURIG, NORTH WALES

21.5cm × 31cm ($8\frac{1}{2}$in. × $12\frac{1}{4}$in.)

Wales is a very big area of Britain which holds untold depths of exciting landscape for the painter, but I have not included a chapter on Wales as I already had enough mountain landscape in the chapters on Scotland and the Lake District.

Here we have a little charcoal study of a typical Welsh footbridge and a fast flowing stream developing into a waterfall in the foreground.

When time does not allow, one can have a lot of fun with a quick charcoal sketch done in this case on Ingres gray paper, and after fixing it with spray, applying a few washes of water-colour.

This whole sketch took about three-quarters of an hour and I later made a water-colour painting from it.

158 WATERFALL NEAR SNOWDON

24cm × 35.5cm ($9\frac{1}{2}$in. × 14in.)

In Wales again, here is an example of rushing water. I painted this in early November when the river was full and water tearing through the bridge openings, forming gorgeous foaming shapes as it came over rocks down the waterfall.

I painted mountains, bridge, trees and foreground and rocks first, leaving the water area all white. Then starting on the water under the bridge I began laying on faint blue-gray washes of shapes to indicate the flow direction, gradually increasing the size of these shapes as I worked downwards. At the finish one or two overall washes were applied, bonding together some of the water groups. The painting took about an hour and a half. I used Whatman 'Not' paper which gave a very brilliant effect with the strong dark bridge and rocks contrasting with the bright shining water.

159 STILL LIFE – AUTUMN ROSES

28cm × 38cm (11in. × 15in.)

I think it is a good thing sometimes to get away from landscape painting and make a watercolour still life. It is good training for one's powers of observation, one can't afford to take too many liberties with still life or your picture will not be like a jug of roses at all.

Of course 'still life' is perhaps the wrong word for flowers as in fact they are never quite 'still', and either they start reviving in the water and moving upwards or they begin to flag and droop downwards. One has to make allowances for this movement when painting I find.

The colour scheme for this picture was a delightful limited range; the jug was a yellowish apple green with a nice bright glaze which reflected well. The roses were all white except the bottom right-hand one which was an old fashioned pinky-orange colour. The background was gray-blue and the table was white. In other words it was a green, white and pink picture and the interest lay in having dark and light contrasts.

I needed a little pencil drawing first for the roses and

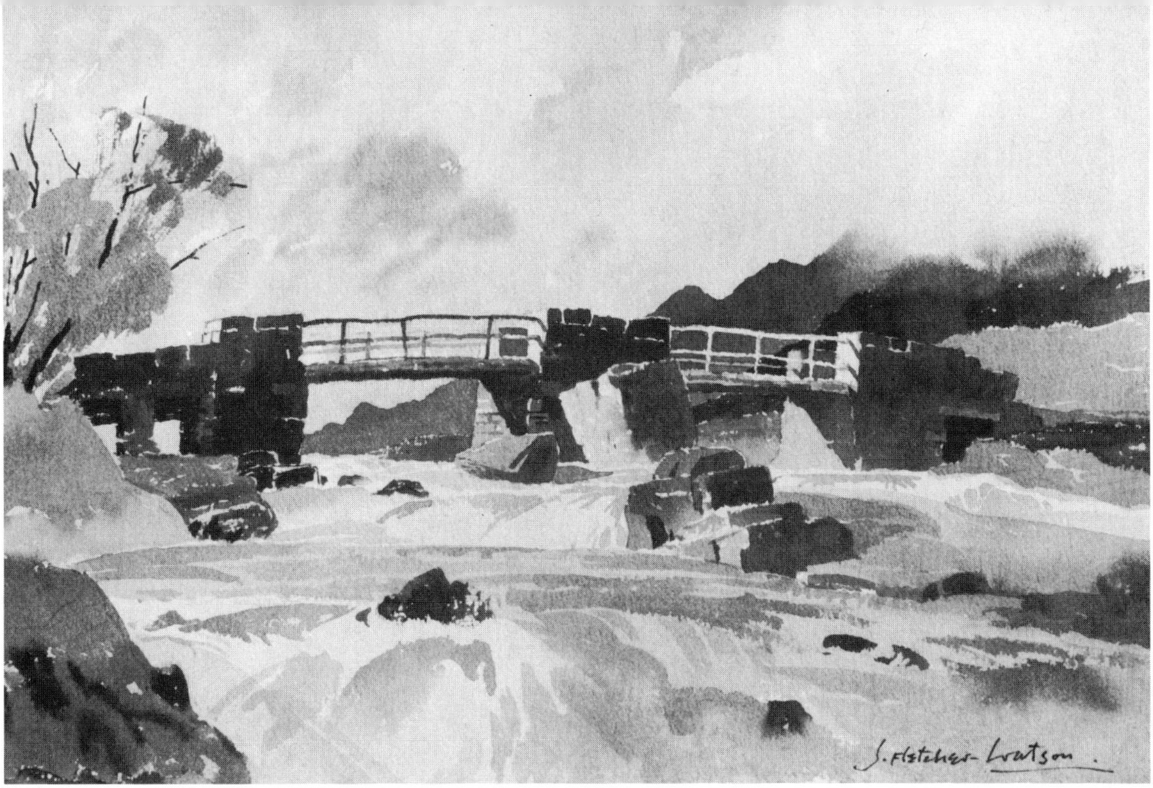

158 Waterfall near Snowdon.

159 Still life – Autumn roses.

the jug; the background colour which went on first could be worked round the roses and leave their white shape.

I think it is quite excusable to use white paint in flower paintings; sometimes a light coloured thin stalk is difficult to leave as the white of the paper, but I feel one should *aim* at not using body colour and try to use only the white of your paper as I have in this case. With landscape painting I never find body colour necessary and I enjoy the challenge of obtaining one's light passages and white areas by leaving the white of the paper. This means thinking ahead and painting skilfully and this is what watercolour is all about. Turner of course did use body colour with his watercolours on occasions but only to a limited degree. Many of his watercolours were painted, not for public exhibition, but purely as references from which he would paint a large oil landscape.

160 STILL LIFE – WILD FLOWERS
28cm × 38cm (11in. × 15in.)
If the summer is over and you are short of flowers in the garden you can often find an interesting collection of autumn leaves in the hedgerows – convolvulus and teasel and things like that. This mixed jugful gave me an excellent subject; it was mainly green but with touches of white and blue which gave it some spirit, and a lovely deep blue shiny jug.

If the weather turns unbearable with driving rain, you can always stay indoors and set up a flower subject for yourself. It helps to keep your hand in and it is a

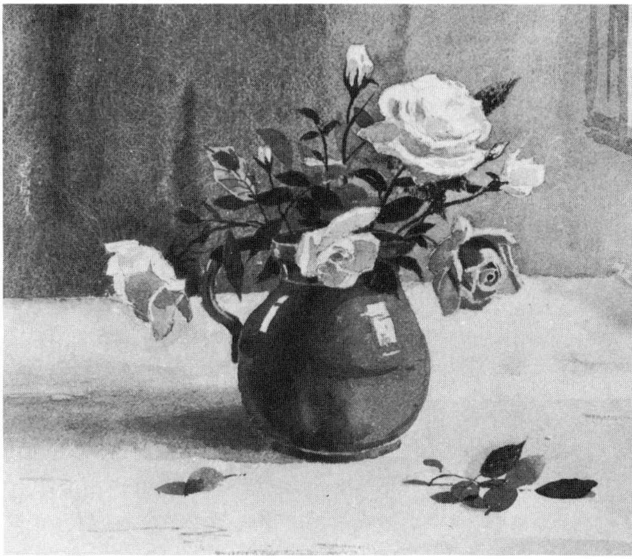

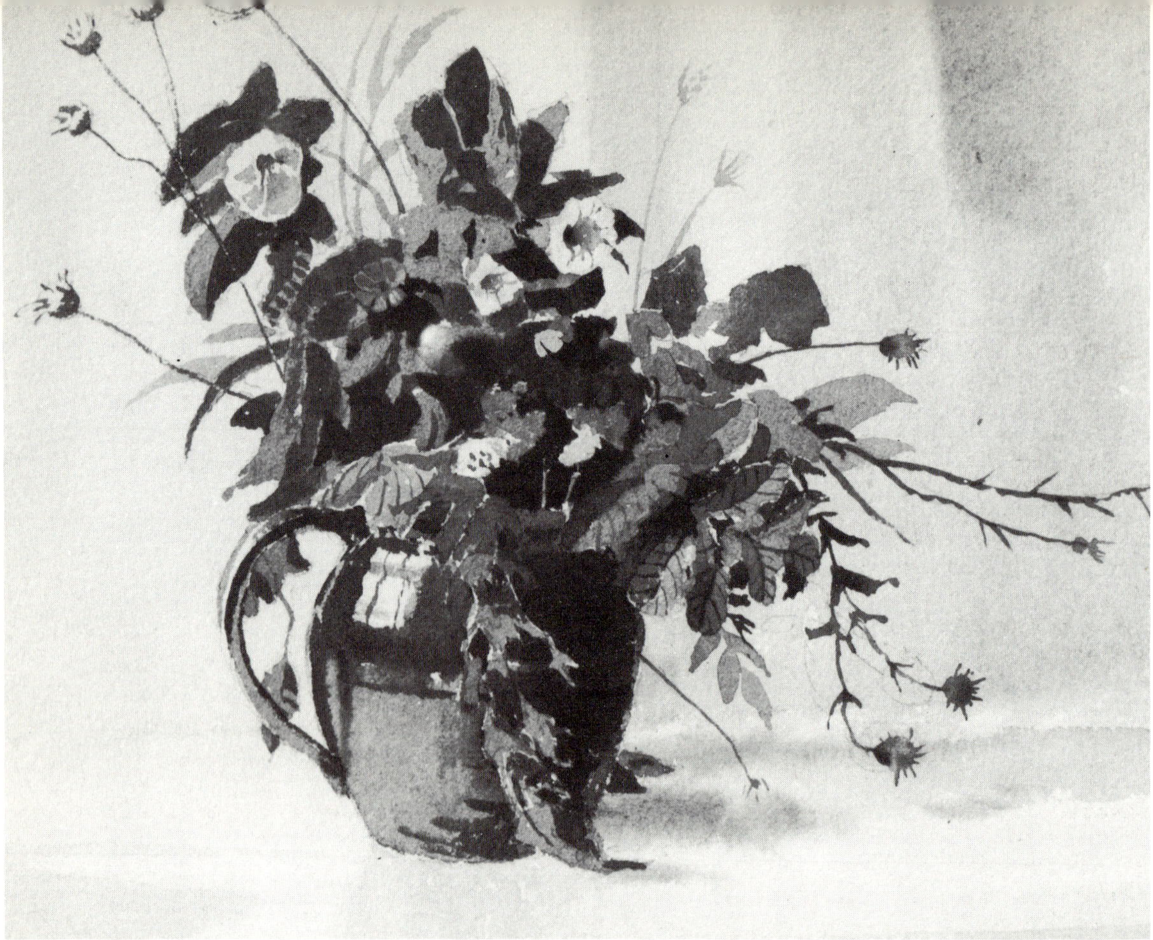

really good exercise in control of detail which will help you in doing good landscape foregrounds.

160 Still life – Wild flowers.

One final word about the actual *colours* that you use. I have given a list in Chapter 1 of twelve colours that I use, and I have arrived at this selection after many years of experimenting and painting. They seem to give me the results I like after mixing them in the various ways described in this book. But please do not regard this list as binding in any way. Try them yourself by all means and you may find they suit your own colour sense but you may find they do not. Some people like very bright colours. For example, take Winsor Green, a very intense strong colour, and mix it with Burnt Sienna and you get a *very* strong deep moss green. Or mix Scarlet Lake with Payne's Gray and you get an extremely dark rich purple. You can get a very large selection of colours these days, but whatever you choose make sure they are 'Permanent' and do not fade.

Everyone has his or her own taste for colours and different artists develop their own individual range of colours to be used. So do some experimenting with colour mixes as you progress with your painting work.

If you have persevered your way through to the end of this book, my great hope will be that you have found a few useful hints on the way and will be encouraged to carry out some experiments and venture into new subjects that you might not have tried before. There are still many places I hope to explore myself to find new painting challenges. Only recently I heard from a painting friend who lives in Melbourne, Australia, and he said 'Australia is a marvellous country for watercolours, although it must be admitted that we are rather restricted as to subject matter'. He enclosed a colour photograph of his latest picture of gum trees in strong sunlight with their wonderful silvery gray trunks and blue mountains behind. I must say it made my mouth water and one day I would like to take a painting trip in that country.

I think we all have a desire to find new subjects in new lands but we must not forget the amazing wealth and variety of subjects which we have here at home in Britain, and if this book helps you to find some of those subjects and to make good watercolours of them then I shall feel well rewarded.

Index

Alligan, 104.
Applecross, 107, 108.
Arches paper, 8.
Architectural subjects, 9, 11, 20, 21, 22, 23, 24, 25, 27, 31, 32, 55, 69, 70, 71, 72, 73, 75, 76, 77, 78, 79, 80, 86, 87, 88, 89, 110–121, 124, 128, 134, 135, 136.

Belleme, 87, 89.
Ben Nevis, 109.
Bockingford paper, 8.
Bridges, 29, 31, 47, 49, 85, 86, 99, 100, 105, 112, 114, 118, 140, 141.
Brittany, 88, 89.
Brushes, 8.
Burcombe, 125, 126.
Buttermere, 41.

Charcoal, 59, 140.
Chilson, 57.
Churches, 20, 21, 23, 72.
Cley Mill, 14, 15, 16, 17.
Cloud shadows, 13, 43, 44, 49, 50, 52, 53, 91, 93.
Clouds, 12, 18, 39, 102, 124.
Coln St. Aldwyn, 58.
Colours, 8.
Composition, 9, 33, 38, 43, 59, 71, 100, 105, 112, 120, 123, 129, 134.
Constable, 15.
Cottages, 12, 24, 27, 31, 32, 103, 128.
Crummock Water, 42.

Dampening paper, 11, 17, 18.
Dinan, 88, 89.

Eileen Donan Castle, 99, 100

Figures, 24, 69, 79, 80, 88, 113, 114, 117, 118, 121, 128, 134, 139.
Flaux, 83, 84.
Fleetwith Pike, 44, 45.
Flowers, 140, 141, 142.
Focal point, 33, 50.
Foregrounds, 14, 15, 16, 23, 91, 96, 104, 122, 123, 128, 136.

Graded Wash, 64.
Grass, 13, 60, 123, 125, 127.

Honister Pass, 46, 47.

Kerrysdale, 104, 105, 106, 107.
Kew Green, 134.
Kishorn, 98, 99, 100, 102, 103.

Langham, 16, 24.
Light on water, 40, 43, 94.
Lincoln Cathedral, 138.
Loch Long, 100, 101.
Loch Maree, 104, 105, 106.
Loch Sheildaig, 93, 96, 97.
Loch Torridon, 93, 94, 95.
Low cloud on mountains, 39, 45, 47, 91, 93, 94.
Loweswater, 43.

Malthouse Broad, 24, 26.
Materials for painting, 8, 56, 57.
Morston, 15, 17, 18, 19, 20, 21, 22.
Mount Square, Hampstead, 135, 136, 137.
Mountains, 38, 42, 43, 44, 45, 91, 92, 93, 94, 95, 96, 97, 98.
Mud, 19, 21.
Mungrisdale, 29, 30.

New End Square, Hampstead, 134, 135, 136.
Northleach, 71, 72.
Norwich School of Painters, 27.

Paper, 8.
Pencil sketches, 21, 26, 31, 33, 59, 66, 80, 98, 104, 111, 114, 128, 136, 140.
Penwork, 28, 29, 48, 57, 58, 62, 63, 138.
Perspective, 69, 81, 113.
Pont du Gard, 86.
Provence, 78–86.

Queen's Gate, Kensington, 133.

Recording shadows on preliminary sketches, 78, 80.
Reflections, 61, 86, 112, 114, 117, 121.
Rio di Bragadin, 116, 117, 118, 119.
Rio di S. Barnaba, 112, 113, 114, 115.
River Avon, 129, 130.
Road subjects, 10, 17, 24, 34, 37, 38, 42, 45, 51, 57, 62, 63, 64, 66, 68, 84, 91, 107, 126, 134.
Rock, Cornwall, 139.
Round Pond, Kensington Gardens, 137.

Sable brush, 8.
Salisbury Cathedral, 131, 132.
Salthouse, 8, 9, 10, 11.

Sauve, 85.
Seathwaite, 36, 37.
Sezincote, 76, 77.
Shadows, 12, 31, 33, 43, 44, 50, 52, 55, 68, 69, 78, 79.
Sky painting, 11, 12, 93, 106, 109, 124.
Small pictures – Cotman, Turner, Constable, 69.
Snow, 64, 65, 66, 67, 68.
St. Geremia, Venice, 119, 120.
St. Giorgio Maggiore, 118, 119.
St. Siffret, 83.
Stiffkey, 9.
Still Life, 140, 141, 142.
Stockton, 122, 128.
Stonehenge, 132.
Stonethwaite, 48, 49.
Stooks, 131.
Stubble, 15, 68, 83, 131.
Suffolk, 27.
Synthetic brush, 8.

Texture, 13.
Thatched roofs, 27.
Three colours only, for a picture, 22.
Trees, 9, 10, 13, 15, 16, 17, 18, 37, 38.
Tone value, 93, 98, 112, 123.
Twigs at top of trees – wash, 13.

Ullswater, 38, 40.
Uzes, 79, 80, 81.

Water, 19, 20, 26, 29, 41, 42, 43, 47, 49, 61, 85, 86, 92, 95, 96, 97, 99, 100, 101, 102, 103, 106, 108, 109, 112, 113, 114, 116, 117, 118, 119, 120, 121, 129, 130, 137, 139, 140, 141.
Watermillock, 33, 34, 35, 53.
Whatman paper, 8.
Windows, 12, 22, 31, 32, 69, 72, 75, 77, 80.
Windrush, 55, 62, 64, 66, 68.
Woodstock, 69.
Wylye, 123, 124, 125.